Tomás Graves is the son of Robert Graves. He lives in Deiá, on the north coast of Majorca. He is a graphic designer, printer, musician and author of the acclaimed cookbook *Bread and Oil*.

For automatic updates on Tomás Graves visit harperperennial.co.uk and register for AuthorTracker.

From the reviews of *Tuning Up at Dawn*:

'Tomás Graves has many original insights into the startling changes which have hauled Spain from being one of the most traditional European countries into one of the trendiest ... Modest and amusing, deceptively intelligent and witty, this will be a sure-fire winner ... If you liked *Driving Over Lemons*, you'll adore this'
*Daily Mail*

'[The] book's strength lies in its clear-eyed observation, and in its ranging far beyond parochial confines to characterise both the island and its outpost, Tangier. We hang out with Paul Bowles, and go deep into a Majorcan gypsy community, absorbing bags of rustic lore along the way'     *Independent*

'Graves paints a vivid portrait of the tensions involved in belonging to two cultures; of the winter almond trees in blossom; and of something he loved, that has vanished'
*Guardian*

'A big-hearted book with a beat of its own ... Foot-stomping stuff'     *Scotland on Sunday*

'... ings with authenticity ... A funny, sprawling account of life ... the island, underpinned by diversions into the musical and ... litical landscapes of Spain over the past 40 years'
*Big Issue*

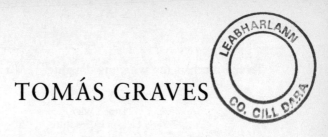

# TOMÁS GRAVES

# *Tuning Up at Dawn*

## A MEMOIR OF
## MUSIC AND MAJORCA

**HARPER PERENNIAL**

London, New York, Toronto and Sydney

To my mother, my wife, my daughter – *Mis Gracias*

Harper Perennial
An imprint of HarperCollins*Publishers*
77–85 Fulham Palace Road,
Hammersmith
London W6 8JB

www.harperperennial.co.uk

This edition published by Harper Perennial 2005
1

First published by Fourth Estate 2004

A catalogue record for this book
is available from the British Library

ISBN 0-00-712818-5

Typeset in Sabon by
Rowland Phototypesetting Ltd, Bury St Edmunds, Suffolk
Printed in Great Britain by Clays Ltd, St Ives plc

# Contents

# Acknowledgements

My thanks to all the musicians (too numerous to mention) with whom I've had the pleasure of playing over the years, especially those who've contributed to this book; to Robert C, for pointing me at HarperCollins, to Piers for seeing it through, to Lucinda, Georgina, Philip, and Jon for receiving it with enthusiasm, and to Michael for tidying up the MS without changing anything. Thank you Kevin, Batty, Simon, Frank, Lucia, Beryl, Kristen, David, Leroy 'n' Lucy and Carmen, for your helpful comments.

# Introduction

# Sound Bites

Music could be defined as organized sound. The degree of organization, variety, and volume marks each person's boundary between music and noise. Spain, where I live, is musically one of the richest countries in the world, as well as being the noisiest after Japan, according to the World Health Organization. If we distinguish social from industrial noise, Spain would probably come top of the list. Greece or perhaps Korea – 'the Spaniards of the Orient' – would come a close second.

The decibel level in the Mediterranean generally, on par with the watts of sunshine, is higher than in Northern Europe. In Latin America, the indigenous people have lent a softness and sweetness to the Spanish language, but their love of noise is also overtly Mediterranean. In the greener, lush parts of Northern Spain and Europe, the acoustics are different and although moist air carries sounds further, the damp earth and abundant vegetation absorb a lot of sound. In northern climes, light is also attenuated, refining the eye's colour sense. Only in the last generation or two have Spanish women generally begun to distinguish the subtle colour differences between 'oatmeal' and 'cream'; most Spanish men still only distinguish one stop between white and brown, which they'd rather call light brown than admit to knowing the word beige.

The Mediterranean formula *noise* + *light* = *life* implies that the lack of light can be compensated for by an increase in noise. After sunset in the hot climates, doors and windows are opened to let in the cool and families move their chairs out into the street to 'take the cool night air', to talk and sing and to argue with the family next door. With the arrival of radio and television, the set is placed on the windowsill facing outwards. This communal extended living room has all but disappeared with the advent of apartment dwelling, but the street still only comes to life after dark. Real nightlife in contemporary Mediterranean society, however, doesn't begin until after British pub closing time. At 4 a.m. on any weekend in central Madrid – the noisiest capital in the world – you can find yourself gridlocked in traffic, with drivers leaning on their horns pushing the decibel meter up to 90 dB. Any live music bar will wait until the late movie is over on TV before allowing the first band to go onstage, normally at 1.30 a.m. And if it's a town's summer fiesta, the last band will go on as the eastern sky is beginning to lighten: my band has been allotted the dawn slot more times than I care to remember.

A Frenchwoman living in Seville telephoned the Civil Guard at 4 a.m. to complain about the tremendous noise coming from the sound system of the bar downstairs. The sergeant's reply was an indignant 'We're in Spain, madam!' In Madrid, however, noise patrols were recently instated to cut down on nocturnal noise from motorbikes with sawn-off silencers. I had tuned in to a radio talk show on this subject when a group of Hell's Angels barged into the studio and grabbed the microphone. 'We demand freedom of expression!' the leader shouted. 'Why should we have to muffle the sound of our motors? Why do these poncy idiots spend a fortune on a three-litre Mercedes if they can't even hear the engine?' But Spain is becoming more civilized: the two-year prison sentence for the owner of a provincial disco bar was upheld by the Supreme Court on the grounds that it produced severe physical and emotional damage to the neighbours.

A quarter of the Spanish population is regularly exposed to doses of over 65 dB of noise, considered the maximum level by the WHO, and over two million people living near nightspots in tourist areas or city centres are kept awake on weekend nights and all through the summer by music that can register a volume of over 110 dB on the dance floor, only 20 dB below torture level. Valencia is probably the noisiest region of Spain, home of the best firework displays and the loudest discos, despite having the most detailed noise regulations and even luminous decibel meters in the streets. The Valencian *fallas* attract people from all over the country on 19 March, St Joseph's day, to witness the burning of huge satirical papier-mâché figures, accompanied by earth-shaking fireworks. But by then the noise has already been deafening for three days, beginning each morning at 8 a.m. with the traditional *despertá* (wake-up call), a volley of bangers set off to summon the faithful to the party.

The Spanish word *bullicio* (and *trui* or *rebull* in Catalan) means uproar, hubbub, or commotion, without the negative connotations. The idea of a 'madding crowd' is alien to

most Spaniards, especially those closest to the Mediterranean shores and, to a slightly lesser extent, to the Italians,
Greeks or Turks. The roar of traffic in any major Spanish
city is a good deal higher than in central London. This has
to do with Spain's narrower streets and higher buildings –
a feature introduced by the Moors in the ninth century to
maximize shade and to stimulate cool breezes – as well as
a lack of noise-absorbing vegetation. But noise is also the
Spaniard's way of asserting his identity through the use of
the horn, cut-away silencer, or car boom-box. It's no
wonder, that although the Spanish buy books, they seldom
get down to reading them.

Generating noise is a full-time occupation, as you will
notice when entering any Spanish café. The bars-to-
population ratio is even higher than in Ireland, so they're
seldom full, but just five customers is enough to assault your
ears:

- The giant TV is on at full blast, tuned to MTV, with
  nobody watching it (75 dB).
- The coffee grinder is trundling away, its blunt blades
  taking twenty minutes to get through a catering-size pack
  of coffee beans (72 dB).
- A one-armed bandit is trying to attract clients by flashing
  its lights and beeping its way through the theme from
  *The Sting* (65 dB).
- Two teenagers playing *futbolín* are gleefully insulting
  each other over the rumble and pistol-shot crack of the
  ball hitting home (70 dB): 'Gol! Golgolgolgolgooooool!'
  (75 dB). The loser lets forth a torrent of invective against
  the winner's mother, father, and deceased kin (70 dB)
  and, swearing vengeance, puts another coin in the slot

and pushes in the plunger. This releases a new set of balls, which roll slowly, thunderously (68 dB) through the sounding-board labyrinth that makes up the innards of the table and into the delivery tray. Kick off: the ball is rapped noisily against the edge of the table, with a transient peak of 72 dB, before being tossed between the two centre forwards.

- The barman meanwhile is blasting steam from the coffee machine into a jug of milk to heat it (80db) while discussing last night's match with a client at the other end of the bar (65db). Both are trying to drown out the other's argument as well as making themselves heard above the general noise. The client is slapping the open pages of *Mundo Deportivo* with the back of his hand to make his point (a meagre 60 dB). From the kitchen, where she's frying up some pork for a toasted sandwich, the barman's wife yells out her own opinion of the referee (68 dB), the referee's mother, father, and deceased kin.

Unlike British or American barmen or barbers who are trained to nod and listen, their Spanish counterparts actively participate. One Segovian barber would always ask his clients as he tucked the bib into their collars: 'With the grain or against?' This didn't refer to the haircut, but to whether the client wanted sympathy or an argument that day.

The forty years of censorship under Franco had a traumatic effect upon the Spanish, who could go to jail for unwittingly criticizing the regime in public. Any comment likely to be misconstrued would be prefaced with the words 'With the Competent Authority's leave, I would like to say . . .'. Or, my father's favourite, 'By the grace of God and of the Mayor . . .'. However, not even the paper-thin walls of most Spanish apartments would induce people to keep their voices down. In the Palma flat where I was born, my father once dared to ask our neighbours why they always spoke at the tops of their voices, to which they replied: 'Lest anybody should think us either ill or frightened.'

The mobile phone was obviously invented with the Spanish in mind; they gesticulate less and talk more than the Italians, who I'm sure will lead the world market in video phones. There is probably nothing more dangerous on the road than an Italian driver arguing via a mobile.

The twentieth century marked the triumph of the new visual culture over traditional aural culture; the amplification and reproduction of music of course made its mark but, if at all, it made our ears less rather than more sensitive and discerning. If primitive man depended almost equally upon sight, smell, and hearing to 'read' the world, in the last decades visual stimulation has far outweighed the other senses, at least in terms of information transmitted. A poor, semi-literate society – like Spain was until the mid 1950s – depends much more upon listening than reading, and has less access to processed images. Most advertising used to be aural, not only on the radio but on the street. The fish seller's conch, the knife grinder's panpipes, the street vendors' calls, the salesman's banter. Today the competition from traffic and construction noise is so strong that even the lottery sellers no longer tramp through bars and marketplaces calling 'The big prize for today's draw!' They have been provided with soundproof kiosks. Travelling fish sellers and knife grinders now blast canned versions of their traditional calls through loudspeakers. The old man who used to plough the olive grove behind our house in Majorca would sing to his mule, ending every phrase with a characteristic *ugh!* to encourage the beast forward; but today nobody would sing to their tractor, even to urge it up the steep terraced hillside.

In spite of the visual media invasion, in Spain one still uses noise to make a point, honking your horn if you drive or shouting abuse if you're a pedestrian. We share with Latin America the weapon of social protest known as the *cacerolada*, which consists of large numbers of people creating a deafening noise by hitting pots and pans in front of government buildings. During the invasion of Iraq in 2003, a regular half-hour *cacerolada* protest was held every evening in Barcelona.

Franco's dictatorship (1939–75) had always returned the support it received from the Church since the outbreak of the Civil War by imposing religious obedience. During the three days leading up to Good Friday no music was allowed to be played anywhere, except classical music on the radio. My sister's first husband, Ramón, remembers these as the only holidays that his trumpeter father had. 'As soon as noise was allowed again at 10 a.m. on Easter Saturday, all the boats in the port blasted their horns, the factories blew their sirens, everybody went out on their balconies to make a big din with pots and pans; in the street they sold little wooden mallets specially for this purpose. We'd buy them on Thursday and soak them in water so the wood swelled up and the head wouldn't fall off the handle when you beat the pans on Saturday morning.' By the early 1970s, restrictions had eased off a little; the curfew was lifted at midnight on Good Friday, when all the *discotecas* opened their doors to the hordes of impatient youths queuing up outside.

Patrick Süskind used his nose to write his novel *Perfume*,

set in the South of France. To write about India one must use one's colour sense and one's taste buds, if these haven't been burnt dry by Vindaloo curry. I've used what's left of my eardrums to describe, in this book, the culture I was born into, and to contrast it with the British culture I was educated in. My method has been simply to run up and down the waveband of Hispanic culture generally and Balearic culture more specifically, lingering for a while on any station, local or overseas, that catches my fancy. The radio is still a powerful medium in Spain: in Franco's time it was the only link with the outside world, although one could get into trouble by tuning into a foreign station. During the attempted military coup in the first years of democracy, the TV was silenced and *la radio* was the population's only way of knowing whether their fragile democracy would win out.

In the days before TV, when the cinema was reserved for Saturday nights, a generation of Spaniards was brought up on a daily diet of *radionovelas*. Some of these were so well produced that women would argue in the bus as to which of the characters was the most handsome. I myself have a cinematic memory of a Goon show – in which they cross the Channel in a replica of Dartmoor Prison – which conjured up such strong images that I now find it hard to believe they were purely aural.

We pick up a lot more information from our ears than we give them credit for – one only has to see how well the blind get around in the cacophony of a Spanish city, where guide dogs are still rarely seen. What a difference between an echoing, tiled Spanish bar and a mute, carpeted British pub! Waking up in a darkened room, we can often tell what kind of a day it is outside, heeding not just the obvious clues of sunny birdsong or tyre-hissing rain, but also the way other noises reach us. Nearby sounds may be muffled by a recent snowfall or sharpened by a wet street, the rumble of passing aircraft will be amplified by a very humid atmosphere or arrive in waves on a blustery day.

When we play back a recording of an interview or conversation, we find it hard to believe that there could have been so much background noise at the time. That's because a microphone, like the hearing aid, doesn't filter out extraneous noise the way our ears do. It's not that we're deaf; it's simply that people can zero in on what they want to hear and block out what they don't, as any parent with teenage children will confirm.

I was brought up in a household in which music was silver but silence was golden. The exception was a parlour trick played on New Year's Eve, when each person was assigned a word – art, horse, dish, rats, few – and at the count of three, everyone yelled it at the same time: the Giant's Sneeze. But normally 'That Bloody Noise' was the term used for any sound or music within earshot of my father's study. On the beach, he would warn anybody playing a transistor radio to turn it off or he would throw it into the sea, a threat I only saw him carry out once. But fighting against noise in Spain is like tilting at windmills. My mother Beryl came up with the brilliant suggestion that jukeboxes should also offer blank records, so that clients like her could buy at least three minutes of silence.

The problem with a musician's memoirs is that, as Mick Jagger says, 'if you remember it, you weren't there'. When the creative right side of the brain is on full power the analytic left side is disconnected, and vice versa. This is why road managers and sound technicians were invented, to allow musicians to give their all without having to be concerned with feedback, faulty connections, or with escorting drunks offstage. In the more modest situation of a pub band like ours, one of the musicians has to take that responsibility and as I had the 'easy' job of bass player I'd be keeping an eye on the mixing desk while freeing the cable caught on the singer's mike stand with my foot. I'd only remember the disastrous side of a concert, while my wife Carmen would come away starry-eyed with the audience's version. This led to endless arguments until she convinced me that a relaxed and happy musician does more for a band than a tense technician. Since then, the band's sound is even more chaotic than before, but we're enjoying it too much to notice. The spit and polish can be kept for the recording studio, which we've managed to avoid for over twenty years; onstage, it's the magic of the moment that counts. And it's magic because you'll never re-live it, nor probably even remember it.

This book has used popular music as a stethoscope to take Spain's pulse, but it's not a musicological study. I'm simply trying to chart the recent history of Spain (before, during, and after Franco), the relationship between its distinct regional cultures, between locals and foreigners and, to a lesser extent, the relationship with its Mediterranean neighbours and its ex-colonies.

# 1

# Deià View

Wherever the place and whatever the circumstances in which you grow up, however bizarre, tragic, or cosseted your life may seem to outsiders, these circumstances become your frame of reference. Any kind of life is perfectly normal to a child until he begins to compare it with others. Our household, half a mile from the village of Deià on the mountainous northwest coast of Majorca, was my only link to the Anglo-Saxon world; although several other foreigners lived in the village when I was a child in the 1950s, none lived a family life all year round, so I had no yardstick against which to measure ours. Anything we did differently from our Majorcan neighbours, such as making hot cross buns at Easter instead of the traditional local lamb pies with sweet pastry, smashing old crockery on Friday the Thirteenth, saying 'Rabbits!' upon waking on the first of each month, or bowing nine times to the new moon, I assumed to be standard British behaviour.

My father Robert, born in the reign of Queen Victoria, underwent a stiff Edwardian upbringing and in his maturity was considered one of the greatest love poets in the English language. Yet in spite of his Britishness he adapted much more comfortably to the Majorcan way of life than to the one he turned his back on in 1929 when he said 'Goodbye to All That'. At the age of 34, and a father of four, he left this Brave New Britain in the company of the American poet Laura Riding, after her suicide attempt and the break-up of his marriage to Nancy Nicholson. Robert and Laura considered the increasingly mechanized English countryside no longer fit for poets and decided to settle on the north coast of Spain. Had it not been for Gertrude Stein, whom they visited en route through Provence and who recommended boring but peaceful Majorca instead, my siblings and I might now be speaking fluent Basque instead of Majorcan-accented Catalan.

After a productive and eventful six years, Robert was obliged to abandon his new home at the outbreak of the Spanish Civil War, which then hawk-tailed into the Second World War. A decade passed before he was finally able to return to his house in Deià in 1946 with his new family – my mother Beryl, William, Lucia, and Juan. The paperwork for Robert's divorce proceedings with Nancy had become bogged down because, as a radical feminist, she had never taken his surname; and how could the judge divorce a Mr Graves from a Miss Nicholson? Beryl, on the contrary, had no qualms about changing her surname by deed poll to Graves, to avoid problems when entering Catholic Spain with Robert and their three children. When the divorce finally came through, they were married at the British Consulate. I was an afterthought, the eighth child of an eighth child, conceived eight years after my brother Juan's birth.

Our house was ample enough for all six of us, although

it had been built for two, Laura and Robert, each with their respective studies. The site was known as Sa Gravera, the gravel quarry – an appropriate name, since our lineage stems from the Graves region of France whose gravelly soil produces fine white wines. Laura, resentful of her partner's protagonism, especially after the success of *Goodbye to All That*, changed the name to Ca n'Alluny – literally, Faraway's House. When it was built in 1932, Robert set to work in his new study writing a 'pot-boiler' called *I, Claudius*. A room on the ground floor was assigned to the Albion handpress with which they had been printing limited editions of poetry, first in London then in Deià. Laura was so clinically tidy that it looked more like a sewing room than a print shop. When warned of an impending visit by the police – they had been accused of being foreign agents printing propaganda – it only took half an hour to transform the press room into a parlour, the old Albion now a charming antique covered in potted plants.

The press was sold upon my father's return after the war in 1946 but the room was still known as the Press Room, the place we'd go to look for scissors, paperclips or the *Times Atlas*. It later came as a surprise for me to discover that a press room wasn't a standard fixture in every British household, like pantries and airing cupboards. And although we spoke English at home, my vocabulary was limited to our family usage; growing up in a literary household, it was only natural that I should understand 'Polly put the kettle on' as 'Polly put the catalogue'.

Once, a very well brought-up child was visiting and asked me to take him to Mrs Murphy. I replied that nobody by that name lived here. Blushing, he tried another tack: 'The smallest room in the house, please.'

'The larder?'

'I have to do number two,' he said squirming uncomfortably.

I was none the wiser.

'Darling,' whispered my mother, 'show him the lavatory.'

'Oh, the *lavatory*!' I shouted as he blushed even more. 'It's upstairs, at the end of the corridor, but you can pee in the garden if you want.'

As the first beatniks began to be seen in the village in the late fifties, my classmates from the primary school reckoned these vagabonds must be worse off than the villagers because they couldn't afford to go to the barber or buy shoes. Not only did these poor devils have to roll their own cigarettes but they even had to share them. The fact that the Majorcans tolerated these foreign habits with a live-and-let-live attitude – smoking pot, walking barefoot or playing the bongos for hours – satisfied me that this was the natural order of things.

With the slow demise of the large feudal mountain estates upon which the village economy depended, many Deians had emigrated to France or Latin America in the early 1900s in search of a better life; the hard times and rationing after the Civil War had further emptied the village, so by the 1950s the population had fallen to a third, leaving dozens of houses available for a very low rent or sale. Deià was not only inspiring, peaceful, and easygoing, it was also very cheap – a perfect combination for artists and writers. It was also sufficiently cold, dark, and damp in winter for them not to feel too cushy about it.

The villagers were accustomed to accommodating extravagant outsiders. The first wave of Catalan landscape painters arrived in the late nineteenth century. Sebastià

Junyer, who had accompanied Picasso on his first trip to Paris, invited many artists and writers to visit him here. Another, Santiago Rusinyol, wrote of Deià a century ago: 'Sages, archaeologists, astrologers, painters – especially painters – herbalists and meteorologists, there is no manifestation of human wisdom that hasn't passed through Deià ... Pedro Mosso, the innkeeper ... has seen people eat in as many different ways as Noah had observed in his Ark, and he has been flummoxed by more incomprehensible languages than were ever heard in the Tower of Babel.'

Contrary to popular myth, neither Picasso nor Lord Byron ever visited Deià, but D. H. Lawrence, Arthur Rackham, and Anaïs Nin were among the extravagant characters passing through: Nin even set a couple of her erotic short stories here. Yet the foreigner who made the most lasting mark was the Habsburg Archduke Ludwig Salvatore of Austria, the ecologist and ethnologist brother of the Empress Sissi, who arrived in the 1870s and over the next forty years documented every conceivable aspect of the Balearic Islands from folk songs to agricultural land use. He collected an entourage of colourful hangers-on that was often mistaken for a circus parade when they disembarked from his yacht, the *Nixe*, in a foreign port. When he died in 1917, suffering from elephantiasis, he left a legacy of stately homes and follies (in both Arabic and classical Greek style) along this rocky coastline, linked by bridle paths and scenic walkways. He also added the Habsburg lip to the local gene pool.

By the early 1930s, while Ibiza was still 'undiscovered', the foreign colony in Deià was well established enough for a German magazine to run an article titled 'The Artists' Village' featuring the artist Ulrich Leman, who lived with a Catalan painter, 'Pep' Fontdevila. Many years after the war, Leman returned to be reunited with Pep until his death at the age of 102: the fabled Deian longevity seemed to apply to foreign residents as well, or at least those that took care of themselves. Although Leman and my father arrived in Deià in the 1920s and both died there at the end of the century, they barely exchanged a few words. There has always been very little contact between the German- and English-speaking residents, even before the Second World War. In a village of less than five hundred inhabitants, it's easy for people to meet, but in Deià there are several ways to get from A to B, so it is equally easy for people to avoid contact once they know each other's routines.

The insular Majorcans, like the insular British, are by nature discreet and, although the Deians have always known what was going on in the houses they rent out –even if they didn't know what to make of it – they'd never interfere. Whatever the outrage, problems were nearly always shrugged off or sorted out amicably before having to ask the Guardia Civil to intervene.

In the heady days of the Second Republic (1932–6) there had been a much closer contact between the foreign residents and Majorcans in the village; together they'd dance Saturday night away in 'La Sala', a garage decorated by the young Karl Goldschmit (a German art student, later Robert's secretary) and John Aldridge (later a Royal Academician). The hall had become tremendously popular with the youths from the neighbouring villages because here one could dance *agarrado* – clinging together – which was frowned upon in the neighbouring towns of Sóller or Valldemossa. My neighbour Francisca, who as a 17-year-old played violin in La Sala's trio, remembers Robert as a good dancer but large and cumbersome enough to take up the whole dance floor. 'Laura would play jazz records on a wind-up gramophone, and Louis Armstrong drove us all completely wild.' The atmosphere, in spite of the hardships that led to emigration, had been one of spontaneous fun. Franco's military uprising of 1936 changed all that.

During the three years of civil war and the decade of rationing and contraband that followed, very few foreigners were to be seen. There had been little military action on the island, yet many personal vendettas were carried out, under the guise of political executions. The libertarian breeze of the Thirties had been stifled by the Church–State oppression under which I grew up, where only the foreigners seemed to be allowed to have fun.

The Carrillo family were one of many from Murcia – the 'orchard of Spain' between Andalucía and Valencia – who had come to the island looking for work after the war. They were one of the first mainland families in many years to settle in the village, managing to pack their six children into a small, empty house in *es Clot*, the Pit, as the lush bottom of the Deià valley is known. Their two youngest daughters worked for our family, and when my parents were away, old Antonio and Encarna became my *papás del Clot*. I remember them both as being incredibly wrinkled: tiny Encarna in her spotted apron and her hair pulled tight in a bun; Antonio, tall, dark, and lean. He was a *canastero*, a basket weaver, traditionally a gypsy trade, but if he had any Romany blood he wasn't letting on. I'd share a bed with my teddy bear and the elder of the two sisters, María de la Salud. Forty years later, she keeps my teddy in a glass case and her husband Toni still teases me about my having slept with his fiancée while he had to wait for the wedding night.

The *Clot* is cool in summer but in the depths of winter, when the torrent thunders by and the sun only penetrates the gloom for an hour a day, it is damp and cold. At dawn, as the cock crows echoed from farm to farm, we would begin the steep climb to hear Mass at the church, four hundred feet above us on the crown of *es Puig*, the Hill. We'd reach the warm, dry air about a third of the way up the rough stone path as it wound past Can Pa Bó (Goodbread's House). At the same point on the way down, it was like descending into a wine cellar.

To keep warm after supper, the coals left over from cooking would be raked into a brazier and placed under a circular table, the *camilla*; the Carrillo family and I would sit around it, the long skirts of the heavy tablecloth draped over our laps to keep the heat in. If your feet are warm, the rest of the body follows; the *camilla* uses less fuel and warms you more than the fireplace, which is disparagingly known as the *escalfa-panxes* or belly-warmer. But the slow combustion of some kinds of charcoal can cause carbon monoxide poisoning, so modern *camillas* now feature electric braziers underneath.

After supper the Spanish deck of cards would come out, as we talked and listened to the old valve radio. The glowing dial promised BBC, Paris, and Hilversum but the only signals to reach the depths of the *Clot* were Spanish National Radio and the occasional Algerian station. On the other side of the mountains, the waveband offered a much greater choice of music. A story was going around about a woman in the inland town of Algaida who bought a radio and, not realizing you could change the wavelength, left it permanently tuned to the same music station, which almost drove her neighbour up the wall.

'Madò Joana, your radio . . .'

'Yes, I was very lucky, wasn't I? Just like my canary, it turned out to be a good singer – not like some other radios I've heard that only talk!'

The Carrillo children grew up speaking Majorcan and all of them married islanders. Encarna and Antonio, my *papás del Clot*, never returned to Murcia and lived for that moment of the day when they could tune in to the sound of the world they left behind. The Spanish popular music known as the *copla* – 'couplet' – synthesized the rich vocal traditions of Andalusian flamenco, the robust Valencian–Aragonese *jota*, and the Madrid light opera known as *Zarzuela*. Murcia lies in the middle of this musical triangle and has its own variant of flamenco; the Andalusian workers who in the 1850s went to work the mines at La Unión created their own style of *cante minero*, which almost died out when the mines were exhausted a century later. The *copla* singer Juanito Vallderrama, whose voice dominated the radio waves of my childhood, helped save this tradition by setting up the Festival de Las Minas, which today has grown into one of the most important flamenco festivals in the world. Other voices of that time, the singers Lola Flores and Antonio Molina and the child prodigies Marisol and Rocío Jurado, have all produced offspring who now dominate Spanish pop, TV, and cinema.

The songs that came out of that valve radio – *María de la O* and *Los Campanillero*s – still give me an *escalofrío* down my spine whenever I hear them; for all their fluttering trills, they have the passion of the blues and strike a deeper chord in my heart than almost anything I've heard since.

Our valley's natural acoustics sharpened my awareness of sound. One could compare Deià's topography with that of a sitting woman's torso: the sea reaches her slightly parted knees and the sheer cliffs of the Tramuntana mountain range is her midriff, bounded by two peaks. The village itself nests around her pubic mound.

From Ca n'Alluny, our family house on the right thigh, one could hear the piercing shriek of peacocks a mile away as the sun set over the left thigh opposite, yet closer sounds were indistinct. A sudden clap of thunder, or the rumble of a dry-stone terrace wall collapsing after the rain, would reverberate across the cliff face behind the village, the noise taking several seconds to die away. Certain frequencies travelled further: Mati the painter playing his conga drums, the rhythmic clink of the stonemason's hammer repairing a distant wall, suddenly lowering in pitch from a *clink* to a *crock* as he fractured the limestone rock and broke it open. The daily climb from the humid folds of the *Clot* to the church had shown me that sounds travelled upwards: from the top of the hill one could clearly hear the voices and barnyard noises we had left behind, yet from the valley bottom even the church bells were muffled. The white noise of sheepbells, however, was permanent and inescapable, especially at night when they seemed to – and sometimes actually did – come from the vegetable garden. Sheep voices can sound comically human, and a Majorcan voice can be equally ovine.

The weather also played with the sound, gusts of wind bringing snatches of distant conversation. When the air was heavy with rain you could hear the drone of southbound planes, laden with tourists, approaching the island long before they were visible; when it was dry, the sound lagged behind the silver specks in the sky. The level of water in the cistern could be ascertained by the amount of reverberation it returned with your voice. Majorcan children have always shown a dangerous fascination with the voice in the cistern that answers their own – Majorca's subsoil is riddled with wells and cisterns in order to last out the dry months. To discourage children from leaning too far over the well-mouth, the peasant tradition invented the bogey-woman *Na Maria Enganxa*, 'Maria Hooks-You-Down'. This ugly, wrinkled hag with a black handkerchief on her head lives in the bottom of the well and hooks any peeping children by the neck and yanks them down into the depths. Perhaps it's this fascination with the well that inspires Spanish musicians, especially gypsies, to use as much reverb as they can on their microphones. The most primitive version of reverb is the north-Indian invention of 'sympathetic strings', where a secondary set of open strings on instruments like the sitar and rabab vibrate in sympathy with certain notes, providing a depth so appreciated in arid landscapes.

I have always been fascinated with sound. As a child I discovered that any small, bare room – a toilet, a bathroom – had its own resonating wavelength. By humming up and down the scale, I could find the room's 'sympathetic' note, the point where my voice would suddenly be amplified three-fold; in some cases, the room would reverberate when I hit the octave as well, much as a trumpet or hosepipe will when you blow down it.

Like most Majorcans, we regularly whitewashed our house as part of the spring cleaning; the rooms would get a fresh coat of quicklime every two or three years, a very slapdash technique requiring the room to be emptied. It impressed me how the curtains, rugs, and furniture absorbed the high frequencies, whilst a bare room sounds sharp and echoing. The same applies, I later discovered during sound checks with the band, to empty bars: we'd have to boost the treble and reverb when the room filled with punters, especially in winter when people wear woollier clothing.

The shape of a room also affects sound, as I never tired of proving every time I went to the tower at the Cala. Every five or ten miles, all around the coast of Majorca, one can still see the conical stone lookout towers built centuries ago to warn the islanders of the approach of Barbary pirates. The tower keepers would light bonfires on the flat roof at night or send smoke signals by day to spread the news rapidly from beacon to beacon around the island. Today, any towers that are close to the coast road provide popular photo opportunities for tourists; the rest are abandoned. Most of them, like the tower on the Deià promontory, are about three storeys tall, with the door at third-storey level, accessible by a retractable wooden ladder. The one circular room is about twenty feet across, with a vaulted ceiling; like the whispering gallery at St Paul's, sound bounces around it in the most disconcerting way. When two people face the wall at opposite sides of the room, they each hear the other's disembodied voice apparently coming from the bricks in front of them.

As a child I'd spend time playing down in the cellar at Ca n'Alluny. The metallic sound effects one could achieve by pouring a jug of olive oil back into the vats fascinated both my father and me. Down in the cellar I'd also play old 78s on the gramophone that Laura had used in the Thirties. Neither of my parents listened to music on the radio but Robert had made some spoken-word recordings in the USA for Columbia, so he would occasionally receive review copies of records. This explains our weird collection: *Under Milk Wood*, *American Civil War Songs*, Annie Ross, John

Coltrane, Hank Williams. Many years later, when Bob Dylan was toying with the idea of recording an album in Spanish, he asked Columbia to send Robert his complete discography to interest him in translating the songs. Robert was in his eighties by then and not interested, but I enjoyed the luxury of playing pristine copies of the first dozen Dylan albums.

Not that Robert didn't like music: he just didn't like it canned. Perhaps that's why he insisted that all four children learned the guitar from the age of seven or eight. He had a fondness for jazz, as long as it was live. In Greenwich Village, New York, there was an active contingent of Deià regulars with whom Robert would visit jazz clubs, on one occasion embracing Cecil Taylor after a particularly impassioned gig. He became a close friend of the choreographer Jerome Robbins, who sent us the Broadway Original Cast recordings of his shows, including *West Side Story* and *The King and I*. The musicologist and blues singer Alan Lomax, who visited us in Deià, would send albums of his field recordings for the Library of Congress: *Blue Ridge Mountain Music, Negro Prison Songs* ... I would devour these and even learn the spoken parts, like the wheezing convict who says to Lomax: 'Ah's got a hackin' cough an' sometimes ah spits out blerd ... But if ah's gonna go an' you's gonna stay, woncha give me one mo' Chesterfield to help me on mah way?' That put me off smoking for the rest of my life.

It wasn't until the post-war restrictions began to ease off in the 1950s that foreigners began to be seen again in Deià. Most of them, wearing beards and sandals, were American artists who had come to Europe on the GI Bill and had found Paris too grey in winter. Discovering that their money went a lot further in Deià, a group of them formed the core of an artistic collective called Els Deu del Teix ('The Teix Ten') after the mountain that dominates the village. They were well received in the village, although the pre-war intimacy with foreigners was now replaced by tolerant respect. Their only visible (and perfectly acceptable) vice was drinking *coñac* and smoking. (A less visible one was an opium-based cough syrup available in Palma pharmacies; marijuana was still scarce.)

In the Spanish post-war culture, alcohol and cigarettes weren't considered taboo for children, at least for boys. Any wedding banquet ended with local 'champagne' for all; cigars were passed around to the gents and cigarettes to the ladies and children. They just made me feel sick. I'd once stolen some of my mother's mentholated Kools to smoke at the bottom of the garden with my village schoolmates, but for me the attraction was the mint flavour, not the emulation of adult behaviour.

The concept of 'teenager' didn't yet exist in Spain, so at eight I couldn't make much sense of my elder brothers' and my sister's behaviour. I did understand the music, though. William was crazy about American folk: Burl Ives and the Kingston Trio, talking blues and skiffle music. Calypso was all the rage in the late 50s; in Europe, the top calypso act after Harry Belafonte was Nina and Frederick, a Danish couple who had settled in Ibiza and, in spite of sell-out shows and records, lived as many Deià foreigners did, with no electricity or running water.

Juan and Lucia brought back the latest US dance crazes from their boarding school – the twist, limbo rock, the Madison – and some bland British pop, Cliff Richard's

*Summer Holiday.* By the time I was ten, rock 'n' roll had had the raunchiness ironed out of it and Juan pronounced it dead. He began buying jazz records, which were also more to father's liking. Once Juan has reached a conclusion like that, it takes a lot to change his mind, and the lot in question was a visit to Kingsley Amis's house in Sóller.

Amis was one of several British 'angry young men' to come to this area to write; Colin Wilson and Alan Sillitoe were others. Kingsley often drove over to visit us, sometimes singing blues songs till the early hours with Juan, Lucia, and her boyfriend Ramón. He was renting a beautiful house, La Soledad, 'Solitude', in the Sóller valley, where we'd occasionally return a visit. While the grown-ups were talking, Juan and I followed Martin Amis, a couple of years older than me, to a sunny bedroom overlooking the orange groves. Among the teenage debris were dozens of the latest British singles. Martin put on 'Just Like Eddie', a tribute to Eddie Cochran by Brit-rocker Heinz, which was celestial music to a ten-year-old. But then it was the Beatles' bluesy 'Love Me Do' that suddenly made sense of my endless hours of guitar practice. Juan forgot jazz and we both became Beatlemaniacs.

The two bars in Deià opened at seven in the morning to serve *carajillos* – coffee laced with *coñac* or *anís* – to the labourers, so the bar owners were ready to close well before midnight. By that hour few, if any, Majorcans were awake – TV had yet to arrive – but the foreign community was just warming up. When the bar closed, the action would move on to somebody's house. My parents didn't care for the bar or party circuit, so as a child I would only hear about it from my brothers the following morning. Once, I came downstairs for breakfast to see the wreckage of my niece Antonia's expensive guitar in the hallway and had to wait until my hungover brother staggered downstairs at midday to hear the story of how it had been smashed over an obstreperously provocative French butcher's head at a dance at the Pensión Can Quet.

Deià parties were tribal, multi-generation gatherings at which almost everybody was a foreigner or from Palma. Few houses had electricity so people danced to guitars and bongos, or at most to a battery-powered record- or tape-player. Babies would be parked in a back room, toddlers would climb over couples entwined on mattresses on the floor, and children would be playing tag or joining in dancing. I was about twelve when I first stayed up until the wee hours at one of these gatherings. Two blonde girls barely older than me were passing joints around; their father had just published a book on LSD in the States. Any drugs were of the best quality because Deià was on the hippie route –Marrakech, Essaouira, Ibiza, the Greek Islands, overland to Goa, Rishikesh and Katmandu, and on to Bali – so dope was brought in directly from Morocco or Afghanistan. The acid was also very pure because among the regular visitors was Paul A., who set up the LSD laboratory in Wales that was later busted in Operation Julie. (Paul was never caught: he changed his profile and identity and twenty years later still drops by to have a game with his old chess partners in the bar.)

For a Majorcan or foreign child growing up in this tolerant atmosphere, it seemed as conventional for a person to spend his day playing chess, painting, or meditating under a tree as to spend it ploughing a field or building a wall. To my adolescent eyes, watching my foreign elders dropping acid while freaking out to Jefferson Airplane was as unremarkable as seeing my Majorcan elders knocking back *coñac* and smoking cheap cigars over a game of dominoes in the bar as the Sunday bullfight blared from the TV. In either case, grunts and yelps were part of the soundtrack.

In spite of the profusion of illicit substances, nobody tried to 'turn me on', even as a teenager. Those who were dealing in drugs were operating on a wholesale rather than a retail basis, so they weren't trying to hook clients. It probably helped that nobody wanted to get on the wrong side of my father, who had a tremendous temper. I was unimpressed by the drug scene, nor was I a drinker. When my *papás del Clot* offered me wine with dinner I always answered: 'I want clean water, not dirty water!' I did, however, take up the typical Spanish child's habit of eating the slices of apple and orange out of the sangría. The fruit, if left to steep for a few hours *comme il faut*, absorbs a good part of the alcohol from the liquid, so I was probably a bit woozy without knowing it.

The age difference of fifty-eight years made my relationship with Robert more of a grandfatherly one and I encountered a lot less friction than my elder brothers had. William, the eldest, had a hard time coming to terms with Robert's platonic or poetic relationships with women. My mother had no problem, at least outwardly, in accepting the situation – she maintained a friendship with all but one of these 'muses' years after Robert's death – so I certainly didn't see any reason to complain.

While I was a teenager, William was managing a hotel in the village and, one miserable winter, also took on another *pensión* as a hostel for a group of Long Island students on a creative writing course. Anything that smelt of Afghan coats, patchouli, and joss sticks seemed to put William's back up, and Robert's penchant to live a second adolescence through platonic love affairs embarrassed him. I empathized with my father because I was going through my first adolescence at the same time. I was enjoying the liberty and excitement of hippiedom, whereas William had to suffer its unpleasant aspects, such as solving the students' problems with the police. Being the eldest child, it was natural that he had to define his personality by distancing himself as much as possible from his father's. It didn't help matters that Robert seemed to express more sympathy towards the dope-smoking students than towards his eldest son, while William's feelings for his parents made him all the more sensitive to village gossip. Robert's friend Spike Milligan summed it up:

> When Robert Graves
> Misbehaves
> It's the talk o'
> Majorca.

Perhaps Robert's behaviour could be attributed to presenility, but he was very much on the ball with whatever interested him. It would be true to say that, since the departure of his secretary Karl Gay, who used to keep Robert's standards of scholarship high, he was using more intuition and less detective work in his books and essays. This threatened to undermine the credibility that his controversial writings had generated over the years, thanks mainly to Karl's meticulousness. But like many artists when they reach their seventies – his friend Joan Miró for example – Robert had proved his capabilities and was now only interested in the essence, the bare-boned truth of his métier. His poems and essays became simpler, more passionate. He was writing from the right rather than the left side of the brain, which lost him some readers and critics but earned him just as many new ones. Despite being a man of another age, he could speak more directly to my generation than to the previous one. The freedom of the Sixties, with its women's movement and its interest in Eastern ways of thought, was a re-run of the Twenties, his own youth. And, as he had in the 1920s, he found a generation of women who were much more intelligent, educated, and intuitive than their

> . . . impossible men: idle, illiterate,
> Self-pitying, dirty, sly . . .
>     [ . . . ]
> Or do I always over-value woman
> At the expense of Man?
>   Do I?
>     It might be so.

I only received one man-to-man talk from Robert as a teenager, and it lasted about five minutes. Having told me that, whatever people might say, he didn't sleep with any of his 'muses', he went on to warn me against drinking any sangría or punch at a party because it could easily be laced with LSD: everyone had been reading *The Electric Kool-Aid Acid Test*. 'If you're going to drink, make sure you pull the cork out of the bottle yourself. And stay off pot and LSD if you can possibly help it. I've tried them both.' In 1960 in New York he had taken part in a magic mushroom ritual with Gordon Wasson, an authority on peyote. (Robert kept some of these dried mushrooms from Mexico, a gift from

Wasson, in his study and would show them to visitors.) On his next trip to New York he and some friends had experimented, under medical supervision, with the new synthetic version later known as LSD, which he didn't like at all.

With Wasson, Robert had undergone a true psychedelic experience, which he described to me in wonderfully vivid, sensual detail. This was a far cry from the acid-trip sagas related by the hippies in town – 'Shit, man, I mean, it was like, far out, you know?' – which I found as boring as anglers' tales at a pub. But although Robert's description fascinated me, it didn't make me want to emulate him. He believed that hallucinogenic drugs should be used as they had been in ancient times: sparingly, by the initiated, and for a specific purpose. He abhorred the idea of recreational drugs. Although as a child I had seen a lot of people dropping acid, in Deià it was pure and unadulterated: people took their trips seriously and tended to prepare themselves mentally beforehand. The first time I saw someone having a 'bad trip' was years later at a rock festival.

Frankly, I think I had as much fun as anyone else at parties, without the hangovers. As a teenager, the standing joke among my friends was that I had no need of drugs because, like Óbelix, as a child I had fallen in a cauldron of LSD. If I was later able to rave all night, it had nothing to do with cocaine or with the amphetamine tablets that my Spanish friends used when they had to swot for exams. My energy came from my raids on the host's larder – fridges weren't common yet – which fuelled me with that old Majorcan stand-by, *sobrassada* (a raw pork paste conserved in salt and paprika) and *galetes d'Inca*, a local variety of ship's biscuits. In my forays I would often come across a stash of fragrant marijuana in a tin of powdered milk, or open a tub of Tulipán margarine to find it packed with sticky cannabis resin. At any party I always found the most interesting people in the kitchen.

Marijuana was well known in the poorer parts of the country in the form of *kif*, which was brought back from the Spanish Sahara by many of the young Spaniards doing their military service there. Hashish was a luxury item and began to enter Spain in hippies' rucksacks; it was only declared illegal in 1970, probably under pressure from the US Government. But as long as a hippie was solvent and kept his habits to himself, the State didn't interfere; the local Guardia Civil were more interested in controlling the *escandalo público* of naked bathing than the consumption of narcotics, which in any case was beyond the comprehension of most lay Spaniards. Many hippies, although ragged and destitute in appearance, regularly received fat foreign currency cheques from their parents back home: essentially, they were being paid to keep their distance and so avoid embarrassing their families.

The spark-gap across which the drug habit jumped from the foreign community into the Spanish mainstream was most probably the contact between musicians. In the Sixties, as the huge demand for hotel entertainment began to attract many foreign musicians, they began fraternizing with their Spanish counterparts. Musicians in Spain had always been on the cutting edge of fashion – in the pre-war years they introduced new dance and dress styles from their tours of the Americas and later, in the 1950s, of the social clubs of Spanish migrant workers in France and Germany. A musician could get away with things that wouldn't be tolerated in others, and the tourist boom meant he no longer had to travel in order to rub shoulders with foreign colleagues, or other parts of his anatomy with foreign girls.

The most outrageous fashions have always taken off in London, Paris, or New York, places where nobody bats an eyelid at eccentricity and where it's almost impossible to shock your neighbour. In the Spain of my childhood, these fashions would be condemned publicly from the pulpits, as well as through the State TV channel and the cinema news-reels, as examples of the general depravity that was rampant north of the Pyrenees: Franco's Spain was the self-proclaimed 'Spiritual Reserve of Western Civilization'.

It was embarrassing enough for young women to suffer the wolf whistles when passing a building site dressed as Mary Poppins, let alone dressed by Mary Quant, so when the watered-down Sixties' fashions arrived in Spain, only the bravest risked running the gauntlet of invective in the neighbourhood and bringing shame upon their family. If the girl was accompanied by her mother she'd receive an indirect *piropo*: 'Madam, I'll swap your daughter for my son, who's a half-wit and doesn't finish his dinner!' or 'It's just as well your daughter doesn't lift her pretty gaze from the ground, she'd blind the oncoming traffic!' For girls to wear a miniskirt or men to grow their hair was a heroic act in traditional Spain, where nothing would go by unre-marked; even my mother would be stopped on the street: 'Señora, look, there's a loose thread on your collar.'

At sixteen and attending a progressive English boarding school, my modest George Best haircut raised no eyebrows on Petersfield High Street; but when I came home for the holidays, where my Majorcan peers had already been shav-ing for years, my pale northern complexion and smooth cheeks called my gender into question. '*¿Chico o chica?*' I was constantly challenged in the streets of Palma. Most long-haired foreigners were usually left in peace, especially if bearded; but if you spoke the local language, you were expected to act like a local and play by the rules. Spanish society today accepts the most outrageous behaviour as completely natural – even gay couples are tolerated in the Guardia Civil living quarters. What a traumatic effect the austere Fascist–Catholic morality must have had on the naturally exhibitionist Spanish personality during those dark ages!

When my brothers and sister had outgrown the Deià primary school in 1952 they moved to Palma during term time, where my parents rented the gloomy flat in which I was born. Agatha Christie, who had been my parents' neighbour in Devon during the war, wrote to congratulate them upon my birth and to announce the opening of her play, *The Mousetrap*: that dates me fairly accurately. Four years later, with my sister and brothers now studying abroad, my parents moved permanently back to Deià, where the foreign community was now buzzing. My father's annual birthday party on 24 July, a month after the village *festes* on the Solstice, heralded the arrival of the summer crowd. A satirical, one-off play would be performed by our family and friends, followed by a party with plenty of sangría, wine, and *coca de verdura*. My *papá del Clot* would let off rockets that echoed all across the valley and paper hot-air balloons that rose majestically into the night. There would be music and dancing until Robert decided to go to bed and sent everyone home.

Ava Gardner was staying at a friend's house nearby and was at the 1959 party. As our family history (and now local legend) tells it – I was five at the time – the Hollywood screen goddess took a shine to a young Guardia Civil corporal who was on duty at the gate. Ava repeatedly asked him to dance, but he timidly refused, alleging he was on duty. He was finally persuaded to dance with her 'to uphold the honour of Spain'.

Most of the birthday plays were written by Robert and Ralph Jacobs, a very funny gay high-school teacher from New York. Bits and pieces of various scripts are still kept in the archives, but, as Beryl pointed out, they bear little relation to what was actually performed. Robert would rewrite his copy of the script on the day of the performance, without warning anyone else of the changes; and Ralph never delivered his lines as he had in the rehearsals, leaving the other actors cue-less. Rehearsals were also poorly attended: who had the willpower to trudge up from the beach in the mid-afternoon heat in time for a rehearsal?

The plots usually revolved around the same sort of premise: the action occurred in Deià (past, present, or future) and the theme was drawn from the subjects Robert was working on at the time, mixed with a bit of village gossip, references to the drugs of the moment, international events, and the hit songs of the summer. The dialogue would be mainly in English but some scenes and songs would be almost entirely in Majorcan or Spanish, with a little French thrown in. A standard character was the village telegraphist, who would arrive to deliver some earth-shattering news and, as the resulting mayhem reigned, spend the rest of the action hovering around trying to get someone to sign the receipt.

The first plays were performed in the Grotto, a cool ivy-covered hollow that had once been the *gravera*, the gravel quarry below the house. It was reached through a small natural tunnel at the end of the garden. The audience sat in the shade of two walnut trees facing a raised area that formed the stage. The first play I can remember – fixed in my five-year-old mind because it featured my rusty blue pedal-car playing the part of the Deià Bus – was *Around the World in Fifteen Minutes*, a spoof on the film that had just been released. Phileas Fogg spends millions to circle the globe in a quarter of an hour and returns to Deià to collect his bet, only to discover that, by travelling eastwards, he's arrived the day before the wager was made. The 1959 play was *Solomon and Sheba* in which King Solomon – the Israeli painter Mati Klarwein – hosts a TV contest, *The Show of Shows*. I was given my first walk-on part, carrying a spade to advertise the Family Graves Funeral Home.

The news that David Lean was basing his script of *Lawrence of Arabia* on my father's *Lawrence and the Arabs* inspired the theme of the 1960 birthday play, *Lawrence and the Wetbacks*, in which the hero – Mati again – liberates the illegal Mexican workers in Texas and blows up the oil rigs. His assistant, *La Dinamitera*, was played by Margot Callas, a stunning Canadian woman who had arrived via Ibiza and whose combination of Greek and Irish blood created an explosive cocktail.

That year, Simon Gough, son of my cousin Diana Graves and the actor Michael Gough, had been expelled for trying to blow up his school in England. This was not a good recommendation for any British centre of higher education, but for a small fee he was accepted by Madrid University – our family was near enough to answer for him should he get into more trouble. He often came over to stay, spending time teaching me the rudiments of carpentry and oil painting (my older brothers didn't take much notice of me in the holidays). Unfortunately, the main trouble Simon got into was with his great-uncle Robert. Like most men in the village, Simon was smitten by the dazzling Margot – even I was, at the age of nine – but Simon unwittingly stepped into the battlefield upon which two poets, my father and Alastair Reid, were the prime contenders for her museship. The scene blew up and a thunderstorm of Robert's legendary temper banished Margot, Alastair, and Simon from the village. They took off for a hastily organized tour of the mainland until things cooled down. In the end, Margot gave all three the boot, marrying the film director Mike Nichols.

My mother, the diplomat and peacemaker, tried to patch things up between Robert and Simon, who came back to Deià at the beginning of 1962, by giving him something 'useful' to do. Under the overhang of a 30-foot cliff in our olive grove there was a lean-to sheep hut, no more than a cave with a front wall. Simon was set the task of making it habitable as a place to put up unfussy summer visitors like himself. He agreed, but asked Robert and Beryl to keep away from the site until work was finished. Before tiling the floor, he enlisted my child labour to cart centuries of dried sheep droppings in baskets up the hill to my father's compost pile. The wall was plastered and windows put in. On one side of the hut, a stray shell from a battleship during the war – probably aimed at Ca n'Alluny – had blasted away part of the rock face. But on the other side, the centuries of fallen scree from the cliff formed a small natural theatre with wonderful acoustics. Simon, being from a family of actors and aware that the grotto's stage was too small and obscured by growing trees, saw the ancient landslide as an ideal setting for a small Greek-style theatre for the birthday plays. A triangle of blue sea formed a shimmering backdrop. All that had to be done was to build a stage facing the rock wall and fifty seats into the scree slope. The theatre would be his peace offering to Robert, a surprise to be unveiled on his birthday.

Beryl was presented with the bills for cement and materials, which soon doubled the estimate. 'Don't tell me what you're doing down there and I won't have to lie to Robert.' Under the veil of secrecy, Simon did all the on-site work with help from Karl Gay's daughter, Diana, and me: we were considered discreet enough. Our work involved gathering stones to level-off and raise the ground for the stage. The musician Robert Wyatt, who was also staying with us, helped by carting the sacks of cement to within a short distance of The Secret, but wasn't allowed to look. Yet as 24 July approached, an enormous amount of work was still needed to raise and level the stage, so in the last fortnight Simon had to call in help. Robert Wyatt and his drummer friend George Niedorf were let in on The Secret and the stage was levelled off just in time for the cement to dry before the dress rehearsal. The theatre, as well as the refurbished sheep hut-cum-greenroom, was presented to my astonished father on the opening night. Beryl, however, had clandestinely visited The Secret before it was officially inaugurated, albeit at night.

Simon, Margot, and Alastair had visited a church in Toledo where they had been shown the freezing cold catacombs in which the mummified remains of Jewish victims of the Inquisition had been deposited centuries earlier. Margot was furious about the shameful fate of these mummies, which hadn't been given a proper burial; Simon, for whom Margot's every whim was a command, waited until the priest-guide had moved on and spent ten minutes trying to wrestle the head off one of the smaller mummies – probably a woman. Finally managing to tear the head off, he hid it under his overcoat; once safely past the guards, he presented it triumphantly to Margot, who was deeply touched but declined to keep it.

When, one evening back in Deià, Simon confessed the incident to Beryl and showed her the mummy's head, she was aghast but, showing her usual blend of pragmatism and superstition, insisted that it be buried somewhere immediately, before any ill should befall us and before Robert should find out and blow his top. It was too dark and the ground too hard to start digging holes so I suggested a deep narrow gully at the foot of the cliff behind the theatre that seemed to swallow as much rubble as we poured into it. So, with her Ever Ready torch and the skull wrapped in a cloth, my mother led us down to the theatre-in-progress and we rolled the skull into its final resting place. And somewhere behind the cement seats of the theatre, like the Phantom of the Opera, the spirit of a Jewish lady watches over all the plays, poetry readings, and concerts that have been put on there since.

*The Oracle* covered that year's hot topics: the interesting prehistoric finds made by the amateur archaeologist Bill Waldren and Robert's investigations into the sacred mushroom cults. Scene 1: Bill, my brother William and his Majorcan friend Po, penniless wandering minstrels, meet miles from home and wonder how to get back in time for the 24 July party. They stumble upon an oracular cave and, by eating magic mushrooms, are time-warped back to prehistoric Deià. As Neolithic Deians, Juan and I, armed with slings, smash pots and bury them for archaeologists to dig up later. Robert Wyatt plays the bongos as Lucia, in white robes, goes into a trance:

Come listen, Deians, if you please,
To what your priestess sings
Of Deià's aborigines
Who strolled about with slings.
But never underestimate
The prehistoric mind
Nor sneer at their untutored state;
They weren't so dumb, you'll find.
The rich sat gambling in the shade
The peasants tilled the soil
The tricksters ran the tourist trade
They all ate bread and oil.

The seating plan shows that the audience for *The Oracle* included the British Consul, Clare Booth and Henry Luce (owners of *Time Magazine*), the mayor of Deià, María the midwife who delivered me, the artist Jimmy Metcalfe, the Irish poet Anthony Kerrigan and his friend Camilo Jose Cela, who was later awarded the Nobel Prize. (Robert had been nominated several times without success, but, as he pointed out, 'nobody has written anything worth a damn after receiving the Nobel'. I'd agree with him in Cela's case.)

The 1964 play was *The Lighthouse*, a detective story that began with Ringo Starr being murdered during a thunderstorm. Every play had to have a storm since we now had a thunderer (a sheet of steel that hung from an olive tree and was energetically rattled) and wind machine (a wooden cylinder scraping against a roll of canvas as it turned). Scene: Merry Payson and Inspector Graymay compete to discover the assassins; the main suspects are some wandering Sufi mystics:

> I'm a Sufi, aren't we all? Goofy Sufis, on the ball
> In our mystic dreams it seems that Wisdom comes to
>     call.
> We're alarming, strong and tall, it's no wonder
>     roof-tiles fall
> We're ideal, not quite real
> Because we're Sufis, aren't we all?

This Islamic spiritual and philosophical tradition was Robert's pet subject that year, having collaborated with the Sufi scholar Idries Shah on his book *The Sufis*, the first to explain the tradition's influence on the development of Western civilization. This sending-up of Robert's 'serious' subjects was typical of the birthday plays.

In the final scene, I pick up the guitar and confess to the murder:

> In Bedales School where I'm being educated
> We think the Beatles are overrated . . .

The next year, with my squeaky 12-year-old voice, I got to sing a parody of the Spanish summer hit, *Me Lo Dijo Pérez (que estuvo en Mallorca)* –'Pérez Told Me All (about his visit to Majorca)', a paean to this paradise for both tourists and workers. The theme of the play, *Hovels in Paradise*, was a familiar one: foreigners being scammed while trying to buy cheap property in the village. The action begins in a New York bar, where Pérez, a Deian who emigrated to South America (played by the Catalan painter and set designer Esteban Francés), and his son (myself) find themselves on a stopover on their Majorca-bound flight. Pérez can't wait to get home to Majorca, but I'm fascinated by the Bronx:

For me it's Nueva Yorka, I'd much rather stay here
Fighting in a gang war, smoking pot and drinking
It's a real scream . . .

Pérez and son meet Slimy Slow (Ralph Jacobs), who has
just raided a foreign exchange bank only to find the loot is
in pesetas: he has to get to Spain to spend them. Pérez sings
the praises of Majorca, 'the terrestrial paradees'. Slow is
convinced. 'Yes, I'd buy a little Espanish house, get myself
a little Espanish wife, and grow a little Espanish sherry-tree',
but he has no passport. Enter Robert, a Professor of Magical
Sciences, who spirits us all, including the loot, off to
Majorca inside a bottle of Scotch.

Everybody but Beryl took part in the plays, singing or
acting, although I wouldn't call ours a musical or theatrical
family. My mother's father, brothers, and sister were
lawyers and I never heard her sing anything more than a
short nursery rhyme; my father's well-to-do Edwardian
childhood did include parlour games and sing-alongs
around the piano, but neither of my parents played a
note. My grandfather Alfred Perceval Graves, however,
although a school inspector, had also been a musicologist,
transcribing many Irish folksongs. He was commissioned to
write English lyrics to fifty Irish folk airs, for which he
received £80. One of these lyrics, 'Father O'Flynn', became a massive Victorian sheet-music hit, for which
Alfred received no royalties. Robert hardly ever spoke of
him; I only later discovered that the A. P. Graves who
appeared in my English school hymn book was my grandfather.

At home Robert's singing would be limited to leading the
family through the full Latin *Adeste Fideles* ('O Come All

Ye Faithful') at Christmas and a couple of ditties on New Year's Eve:

> 'Oh Jean-Baptiste, porquoi? Oh Jean-Baptiste, porquoi?
> Oh Jean-Baptiste porquoi have you greased
> Your little dog's nose with tar?'
> 'Mon chien has bad catarrh, mon chien has bad
>   catarrh,
> And zat is ze reason why I have been greasin'
> My little dog's nose wiz taaarrh!'

Or the marching song of the disbanded 88th Carnatic regiment, delivered at parade-ground volume:

> Kuchh parwah nei, good time coming
> Queen Victoria very good man.
> Rise up early in the morning
> Britain never never shall be slave.
> Hai! Hai! Kuchh parwah nei . . .

In his late seventies, however, when Robert began to relive his earlier years with as much or more intensity as his more recent ones, many of his childhood songs came back to him. When recording his poems for Claddagh Records in Dublin in 1975, he sang several that I'd never heard before and that were included on the *Green-Sailed Vessel* LP. That year I witnessed a scene that must have been a replay of many childhood squabbles, as my father, his younger brother John and elder sister Roz practised 'Widdecombe Fair' for Robert's eightieth birthday party. As I tried to accompany them on the guitar, all three began arguing over the lyrics and the rehearsal degenerated into a door-slamming shouting match. It comes as a shock to witness your elders behaving like children. A compromise was eventually reached and the song was sung by all the family members present – about twenty, Uncle Tom Cobley and all.

All four of us children were sent to music lessons to learn the classical guitar or, in Juan's case, the *bandurria*, a twelve-stringed Spanish mandolin with a neck almost as wide as it is long. We all studied with Bartolomé Calatayud, dean of Majorcan guitarists, who collected and transcribed much of the local folklore, arranging it for solo guitar or for a full *rondalla* – guitar, *llaut* and *bandurria* – much as my grandfather had done for Irish music. Calatayud was a wizened old man in thick glasses, a black beret, checked dressing gown and carpet slippers, whose use of the Spanish language was as sonorous as his name. Beryl remembered him as 'Bartolomé Catacrock' after one of his favourite onomatopoeias: 'the ladder slipped and the man fell *¡catacrock!* to the floor . . .'. This suggested the title for one of Robert's books of humorous essays, *¡Catacrock!* (Written Spanish prepares the reader for a question or exclamation by inverting the mark beforehand.)

Calatayud taught with his own particular system of fingering-by-numbers, which never caught on, although many of his compositions are still used in guitar primers all over the world. By the time I began classes with him at the age of seven, he looked about a hundred and twelve and soon gave up teaching, passing me on to the genial Juanito Coll.

At the time I took up the classical guitar, my brothers and sister had more or less abandoned it, preferring their own kind of music: Woody Guthrie, the Kingston Trio, Burl Ives, Josh White, Harry Belafonte, early rock 'n' roll. I have a distant memory of Juan, dressed in traditional Majorcan costume, playing the *bandurria* in the village *rondalla* during the annual festivities of Llucalcari, a hamlet beyond our house. The melody was *Clavelitos* – 'Little Carnations' – and whoever had to cue in the chorus forgot his part, so the rest of the *rondalla* were condemned to repeat the verse ad infinitum, to the growing hilarity of the audience every time the cue was missed.

Juanito Coll was not much taller than me and gave his classes, slippered and dressing-gowned like Calatayud, in the front room of his long, narrow flat. It was up a tight flight of stairs above a knife grinder's shop, on the edge of Palma's red-light district. The walls were covered in his own oils and watercolours and signed photographs of his ex-pupils. Juanito was always loth to end a class so I usually had to wait my turn, chatting with his wife Conchita and her mother at the kitchen table, which was covered in a flower-patterned oilcloth. The window opened on to the air shaft, through which we shared the whole building's cooking smells, clanging of aluminium pans, and the hum of the knife grinders. It was around that table that I discovered British royalty, because these two women were obsessed with *¡Hola!*, now also published in English (*Hello!*) and French (*Oh la!*). Until I was eight I only knew the Queen's face from my coronation mug; over Conchita's kitchen table I discovered who was who (and who was doing what with whom) in the British Royal Family and even which subjects Charles was taking at Gordonstoun. When I went to Bedales School, at the age of eleven, I could name more Royals – even the more obscure crowned heads of Europe and the Middle East – than most of my peers. Had the Armstrong-Joneses been at Bedales in my day, I would have had to report to Conchita every school holiday.

Spain's obsession with foreign royalty stemmed from the fact that its own royal family was in exile. Although Franco went hunting and fishing with the aristocracy, he lacked the style or bearing of a man of state; his wife and daughter were equally gauche. This craving for royal figures was filled by bullfighters like El Cordobés and Manolete and by *las folklóricas*, the singers of popular Spanish music in polka-dot flamenco dresses who fill the society pages to this day. Even the naming of the exiled King's son, Prince Juan Carlos, as Franco's successor didn't convince the millions of Spanish Conchitas; his only public appearances were at military parades, at his discreet wedding to Princess Sophia of Greece, and at the birth of the Infantas. The image of this slow-speaking, ungainly giant in drab green army uniform swearing to uphold the principles of the *Movimiento Nacional* lacked the sense of occasion that accompanied foreign royal appearances in other countries.

Conchita wore horn-rimmed glasses and a very severe expression, which only softened when she took down one of her dolls from the enormous collection that occupied most of the shelf space in the flat. Their son José María, a year younger than me, wasn't allowed to touch them or to take off his blue-and-white striped school pinafore until bedtime.

Juanito was immensely proud of his pupils, always pushing us on to greater things; and although Gabriel Estarellas was the only one to become a professional classical guitarist, many of today's Majorcan rock musicians received a good grounding from *El Duque*. He organized a classical guitar concert at the Catalan Cultural Centre in Palma for me and for another of his students, Emma Gough, Simon's half-sister, who lived just outside Palma. The concert merited a good write-up in the local papers but the only thing I remember about the recital was – typical of me – the supper afterwards at Sa Premsa, one of those cavernous Majorcan refectories known as *cellers,* full of trestle tables and huge casks of wine. José María, Emma, and I – boisterous after the tension of the recital – were shooed outside into the night to let off steam until dessert was served. José María took a banger out of his pocket and let it off in the shadows behind a bush in the square. The noise brought a pair of Civil Guards running over, brandishing their weapons and shouting '*¿Qué pasa?*' (What's up?). I froze in terror, but my weedy little friend reacted like a true Spaniard and defiantly shouted back the classic playground rejoinder '*¡Un burro por tu casa!*' (A donkey round your house!). Hearing a child's voice, the Guardias relaxed but still tried to locate us; José María pulled us through the bushes and out the other side, from where we dashed back through a side door into the safety of the restaurant. Being challenged by a trigger-happy Guardia was an adrenaline rush I have fortunately only had to endure once again, many years later, when a group of friends, swimming naked at night, were caught in a torchlight beam and made to dress at gunpoint.

Besides teaching classical music, Juanito had worked as a jazz musician and loved the Hawaiian slide guitar; until he could afford a real one he laid an electric guitar across his knees and used a huge iron key as a slide. He also played the trumpet in a big band at Tito's, Palma's most famous nightclub. During a solo he had hit a dud note and a heckler yelled out 'Call yourself a trumpeter?' Juanito, who had had a bad night, yelled back 'Not anymore!', threw his trumpet to the floor, and jumped on it until it was completely bent out of shape. He never played it again.

Some musicians are born teachers, others born performers; Juanito, when playing classical guitar, was one of the former. Even in concert he seemed to be teaching the audience: 'Now, watch my fingers . . .' He was once hired to play a classical guitar concert at a reception given by a countess, so he had to hire a proper suit, bow tie, and patent leather shoes. So elegantly dressed, sporting the white beard that earned him his nickname, he looked the most aristocratic person there. The countess presented him to her guests and he made his way to the stage, sat down, and put the mandatory footstool in position for the classical guitar posture. He then discreetly tugged at his left trouser leg, revealing sockless, hairy ankles.

Juanito always spoke and played passionately, even though he was often in the clouds. He once announced that he was writing a concerto for orchestra and guitar, dedicated to my father, which he was going to present to the great Narciso Yepes to perform, but the piece never materialized. He had two passions, fishing and bullfighting, although he was more taken with the pageantry and *pasodoble* music of the *fiesta nacional* than with the blood sport itself. After class one day he took me with him to the Palma bullring, El Coliseo Balear, to discuss a *pasodoble* he was composing with a bullfight impresario.

Once inside the perimeter of the Coliseo there are two entrances, *Sombra* for the expensive east-facing bleachers (in the shade at the classic bullfight time, five in the afternoon) and *Sol* for the cheaper west-facing ones where the audience has to endure the heat and glare. Juanito took me up to the seats reserved for the Civil Governor and other VIPs, from where the matador is awarded an ear or a tail. We then walked along gangways above the bull pens and along the corridor from where they charge into the ring. We found ourselves in the arena – the Spanish word for sand – under the glaring sun, stepping round the dark ochre-coloured patches left after the previous *corrida*. I picked up a couple of bloodstained and broken *banderillas* that were still littering the ground as souvenirs to take back to school. I had only once been to a bullfight, with my father, but how much larger the arena seemed when you stood alone in the centre! I tried to imagine how it would feel to face a bull charging in through that gateway, how long it would take to run to the safety of the *burladeros*, much further away than they looked on TV.

At that time, the Palma bullring was making a profit thanks to the tourists; the *afición* on the islands is drawn principally from the mainlanders, and has been on the downswing since its heyday in the 1950s. Only a couple of Majorcan villages include 'running with the bulls' as a part of their annual festivities; on the mainland, goading bulls is the main event in countless towns and today provides endless footage for those home video contests. What you see in the bullring is perhaps more humane than what happens in some town squares. Most of these customs are now banned unless the town council can prove that the tradition has been practised there for over a century. One town on mainland Spain has celebrated its annual patron saint's day by pushing a live 'scapegoat' off the belfry every year for a hundred and twelve years; it was allowed to continue pushing goats off the belfry but was obliged to catch them in a safety net.

I respect bullfighting insofar as it symbolizes the victory of light over darkness, probably a vestige of primitive Minoan culture. All the art and grace of the spectacle could just as easily be performed bloodlessly, although that would take away some of its morbid fascination. I agree with those who see it as a re-enactment of the battle between the ancient goddess cult, represented by the very feminine matador in his tight 'suit of lights', and the patriarchal masculine gods represented by the black bull, whose blood has to be shed in order to fertilize the earth. Juanito explained that the *banderilleros* don't stick their barbed darts into the bull's side to torture or goad the animal: it's a way of letting blood to avoid the bull suffering an apoplexy to which this special breed of *toro bravo* are prone, even in their pastureland. I've been in the back of a Land Rover as it was charged by a *toro bravo*, and can vouch for the fact that they don't need a *banderilla* to goad them. Nor a red cape: they are apparently colour blind, and in any case the cape is always pink. It's the movement of the cape, not its colour, that provokes the bull.

Years later I found myself again in the arena of the bullring. International protests against blood sports had reduced the number of tourists who attended proper bullfights, and the Hemingway mystique that drew the Deià beatniks to the Sunday afternoon *corridas* in my childhood had disappeared with the hippies ten years later. Today, tourists 'fight' their own heifers bloodlessly at collapsible beachside bullrings and the Coliseo Balear is mainly hired out for other events. In 1981 I designed the posters and tickets for the first rock concert at the Coliseo since the Kinks appeared there for a matinée performance in 1966. This concert was organized by my Basque neighbours Juanjo and Carlos, and it was one of a series of hard knocks that gave them the experience to later organize Bruce Springsteen's, Prince's, and Van Morrison's tours of Spain. This concert could have been a financial disaster, despite being headlined by the Orquesta Mondragón, the top Spanish band of the moment. Someone had run off an extra two thousand tickets on the side – perhaps not surprising since the print works formed part of a rehabilitation programme for ex-convicts. Besides that loss of revenue, more problems began once the concert had started as hundreds of fans began climbing over the perimeter wall. I was called upon to help Juanjo's security team, but it was hopeless: people were dropping over the wall like Indians in a western. You could only see their silhouettes against the skyline before they disappeared into the darkness of the grounds and mingled with the crowd. The next day I bumped into my friend Mateo walking with a limp. He and his narcotized friends from Palma are known in Deià as the *anfetamínicos*.

'What happened to you, Mateo?'

'I was gate-crashing that concert at the bullring and I twisted my ankle as I landed. Luckily I just managed to outrun those security bastards . . . but that's nothing. Jorge tried further along the wall where it was darker and there was no security, and found he'd landed in the bull pen! Luckily the bulls were asleep and he found the ladder in time . . .'

# 2

# The Road from Canterbury

Among the characters who populated my Deià childhood
there were several 'auntie' figures. One was the theatre producer Wendy Toye, another the radio journalist Honor
Wyatt, who had been part of the early Deià scene in the
1930s with her first husband and their son, the actor Julian
Glover. She later remarried and rented an enormous semi-
derelict house near Dover with her husband George and
their children Robert and Prue. To help pay the rent they
took in student lodgers, one of whom was a 21-year-old
Australian beatnik named Daevid Allen. He had very long
hair by 1950s standards, and shared the passion for jazz
that the adolescent Robert had inherited from his father and
stepbrother Mark, a sax player. Another lodger was George
Niedorf, an American jazz drummer whom Daevid had
brought over from Paris. In part exchange for the rent,
he taught Robert the rudiments of drumming. Robert had
already started a band with school friends from Canterbury,
Mike Ratledge and Hugh Hopper.

In the spring of 1962, 17-year-old Robert Ellidge (who

soon afterwards adopted his mother's surname, Wyatt) dropped out of school and headed for Deià with Niedorf, turning up at Ca n'Alluny and shyly introducing himself as Honor's son. Contrary to popular belief, my father didn't surround himself with academics and intellectuals and, to young Robert's relief, being a dropout wasn't frowned upon at Ca n'Alluny as long as you had other redeeming qualities.

To avoid confusion, he was nicknamed Batty Robert after *batería* (Spanish for a drum kit) and my father became Scatty Robert. To further clarify matters, the Québécois writer Robert Goulet, who taught me French, became Ratty (*raté*) Robert. Batty proved to be creative, easygoing, and helpful. He shared my father's taste in jazz – Cecil Taylor and John Coltrane – and ended up staying with us for six months and helping to finish the theatre. Batty remembers that summer as 'an oasis of magic'; it was also a private drum seminar. My sister's boyfriend, Ramón Farrán, had set his kit up at home and alternated with Niedorf in giving Batty drum and percussion classes.

Ramón, a Catalan whose family had moved to Palma, was only a couple of years older than Batty but he had begun working professionally as a drummer and percussionist at the age of fourteen. By sixteen he was earning more than his trumpeter father in one of the most popular Latin American big bands, with which he sailed to Venezuela. In Havana the ship took on some Cuban musicians, but on arriving in Venezuela a political coup was in progress; while the captain waited for permission to disembark, Ramón joined in the *descargas*, percussion jam sessions with which the Cubans passed away the days on deck. 'You've got too much rhythm in your blood to be Spanish – your grandmother must have misbehaved with a Cuban!'

From the moment Ramón appeared in Deià, I remember my summers as a series of long percussion sessions centred around Ramón, Batty, and the painter Mati Klarwein. Mati had built a house overlooking the cove, at the top of a 300-foot climb up the irregular stone steps; when the evening sun had set behind the promontory, leaving the beach in shade, there was still time to reach his terrace to watch the spectacular sunset. Mati, an eclectic and technically brilliant painter with a tremendous power of concentration, had first used a paintbrush as a teenager in Israel when put to work camouflaging tanks; later, to dissociate himself from his nation's political position, he adopted Abdul as his first name.

Ramón or Batty would drop in on the way up from the beach and pour themselves a glass of cool water from the well while Mati cleaned his paintbrushes, brought out his conga drums, and celebrated another good day's work by striking up a *guaguancó* rhythm; the others joined in on bongos, sheep's bells, frying pans or anything else from which a noise could be coaxed. The sound of these *descargas* would drive the fishermen down in the cove to distraction.

At this time Mati was painting a large canvas, *The Annunciation*, in which the winged, tattooed Archangel Gabriel – or Gabriella – riding a conga drum (the traditional African means of communication) over the Cala, announces the birth of the Saviour to the magnificent black nude figure of the Virgin Mary (Mati's girlfriend) on his terrace, the Holy Spirit nestling between her thighs. Mati himself appears, grinning in a straw hat and shades, as Joseph, surrounded by a trio of African nomads, the Magi. From the conga cornucopia emerges a Deià still life: pomegranates, melons, cabbage, dried apricots, salted herrings, fresh fish, a sea urchin (the eggs are a poor man's caviar), honey, aubergines, bread, tomatoes, and a bloody sheep's head, which was always the last thing to go at Magdalena the butcher's. Every ploughed furrow, every stone in the terrace walls, and every rock shimmering on the sea bed was meticulously reproduced. Carlos Santana later chose *The Annunciation* for the cover of the band's best-known album *Abraxas*, which became one of the pop icons of the 1970s.

Afro-Cuban rhythms began to form the unplugged soundtrack to the international tribe that ebbed and flowed through Deià in the 60s and 70s: the beat generation's bongo solos had given way to the communal hippie trance-dances. Juan and I ordered a pair of congas from Ramón's friend Guivernau in Barcelona, whose workshop also specialized in wooden gymnastic equipment. The smoky little loft office overlooking his workshop off the Ramblas was full of signed photographs of his clients, a curious A to Z of Latin musicians and gymnasts.

Before teaching Juan and me some basic rhythms, Ramón showed us how to soak the mule hide for two days (a stench only equalled by the tanning pits in Fez) and stretch it over the drum head, gradually tightening it and finally trimming off the excess. Congas are larger and mellower than the bongos. While the bongo is usually a solo instrument played with the fingers and thumbs, the congas – one, two, or more – lay down a solid beat made with the palms and heels of the hands.

At home, even the dogs joined in the percussion. Our pseudo-poodle had two puppies, the hyperactive Come On and the laid-back Drum On. Ramón would sit Drum On on his lap and take his forelegs between his fingers as if they were drumsticks; the puppy would relax them completely and let Ramón make him play the bongos, the paw pads on the skins making a delicious pitter-patter. The puppy loved it, always coming back for more.

At the time, Ramón was playing with Los Valldemossa, a Majorcan folk group from the town of the same name, five miles along the coast. They were the sons and nephews of Bartolomé Estarás, the musicologist and founder of a renowned folk-dance troupe, and they soon became Majorca's musical ambassadors to the world. When Franco dined in their home town, on his first and last visit to the island as head of state, they were obliged to provide the entertainment. (As the motorcade later drove through Deià, only a handful of locals came out to watch the black limousines swish past. Magdalena, the butcher, later told me she only went because she 'wanted to see the face of an assassin'.)

Besides popularizing Majorcan folk songs, Los Valldemossa included a lot of South American material in their repertoire, which is where Ramón's bongo technique came in. Their first album was recorded live at the Blue Angel club in London, where they had a residency for several months. One evening on the way to work by tube, they were stuck for ten minutes in a lift full of silent commuters. They took out their instruments and gave a spirited concert, but the commuters remained silent, re-reading their *Evening Standard*s or looking at the ceiling, at a loss as to how to react. The Majorcans, expecting the sort of applause they received at the Blue Angel, were amazed at this mute demonstration of the famous *flema inglesa*, English phlegm.

In 1964, Lucia and Ramón opened the Indigo, Palma's first jazz club, in an old stable on a steep street overlooking the port – the resident mule had to be turned out to make way for the music. This part of Palma is known as El

Terreno, where the bourgeoisie had their summer villas and the foreign community their watering holes: Mam's Bar, the Africa Bar. Palma's nightlife revolved around Plaza Gomila, a ten-minute walk from the Indigo, where centuries earlier the unrepentant Jews had been burned at the stake. In the 1960s, Gomila was neon by night and seediness by day; it still is. The main attraction was Tito's Nithg Club, as it was usually misspelled on its flyers. Here you could see Ray Charles or Tom Jones perform while enjoying a view over Palma's harbour – as long as you wore jacket and tie. Tito's is still going strong today as a no-trainers-allowed disco.

The week the Indigo opened, Britain's top sax player, Ronnie Scott, happened to be on holiday on the island. While sunning himself on the beach, he read about the new jazz club in the *Majorca Daily Bulletin*. That evening he turned up at the Indigo with his alto saxophone.

'Mind if I sit in with you lot?' he asked Ramón.

'Can you play?'

'Oh, I make do.'

'OK, then join the jam session after the next set.'

Ronnie, needless to say, raised the roof, metaphorically speaking; the already low headroom had been further reduced by egg boxes stuck to the ceiling to improve the acoustics. The tables were accordingly Lilliputian and the chairs seemed to conspire to make you slip off them.

Ronnie became a family friend and supplied the Indigo with some of the UK's best jazz musicians on a busman's holiday deal. Since the club made most of its money from tourists and American sailors, an English-speaking bouncer and *tiquetero* was needed. Batty Robert was just the man for the job, which consisted of handing out flyers to prospective customers or sticking them under car windshield wipers. At eleven I was too young to be admitted, so whenever my parents dropped by the club, I would hang out with Batty at the door. He also drummed with the fill-in band and got to jam with Ronnie Scott, Tubby Hayes – the best tenor sax player in the UK – and the Swedish trombonist Eje Thelin.

The main band was Ramón's group, which featured Errol Woisky, a lunatic mulatto jazz guitarist from Surinam whose father ran the Bar La Cubana, and Toni Obrador, a Majorcan pianist and crooner who still plays regularly in piano bars. Toni has been described by one wag as 'playing the piano like Sinatra and singing like Rubinstein'. Also in the band was Toni Morlà, with whom I would later work for ten years when he became Majorca's foremost singer-songwriter in the late 70s.

One night thieves broke into the Indigo. Finding the cash register locked, they took it with them. We've long tried to imagine their faces when they finally broke it open and only found half a Mars Bar inside – such a rare treasure in those days that Ramón had felt obliged to lock it up.

Batty had arrived at Ca n'Alluny that year with a friend from Canterbury, Kevin Ayers, having stayed with Daevid Allen on the way through Paris. Two more friends, Ted Bing and Hugh Hopper, were already in Deià. The sheep hut beside the theatre was occupied by the classical guitarist and lutenist Julian Bream, who needed peace and quiet to practise, so Batty and Kevin were given the keys of a fisherman's cottage next to Mati's house, which my father rented cheaply to put friends up in. As Kevin remembers, 'At my school I heard a lot of calypso from a Trinidadian friend and I could play three chords, but I was by no means a musician. It was Mati who turned me on to pop music by playing me the Beach Boys' "I Get Around".' The first electric guitar

Kevin ever played was a Gibson belonging to Mati's friend Didier Léon and which had once belonged to the jazz legend Grant Green. It was plugged into a little Gibson amp, which in turn was plugged into Deià's prehistoric electrical grid. 'When I turned on the amp I got a tremendous jolt from the guitar. I thought, whoa, so that's rock 'n roll . . .'

The earliest memories I have of Daevid Allen was as part of a very weird-looking duo that appeared in the village later that summer of 1964 after a busking tour of Europe. Calling themselves 'Musical Theatre of the Pacific Rim', he and the classically trained jazz musician John Howley performed at the Indigo and staged a happening at a Palma art gallery; playing kazoos, a bamboo saxophone, didgeridoo and voice percussion, the music was as free-form as you could get without stepping in it. They played with such straight faces that the audience couldn't decide whether it was heavily ethnic, very avant-garde, or a complete put-on.

When the September rains came, Daevid and his girlfriend, the poet Gilli Smyth, decided to spend the winter in Deià, writing and performing poetry, while Batty, Kevin, and Hugh Hopper returned to Canterbury to form the Wilde Flowers – the extra 'e' was Kevin's tribute to Oscar. They had become a good R & B band, drawing on much of the same repertoire as the early Stones and Kinks and gaining a strong local following in Kent. But in early 1966 Kevin returned to Deià to stay with Daevid, and they soon began working together on exciting, experimental musical ideas. It soon became obvious that this material would need a new group to perform it because the Wilde Flowers were on a different tack.

On Easter Sunday, Kevin was sitting at the bar with two American friends, the painter Tom Lipps and a bluegrass musician called Larry Nolan, when the daily bus from Palma drew up and a tall gangly Oklahoman stepped off. He introduced himself as Wes Brunson, 'a friend of June's'. June Campbell-Cramer, an English model and painter who lived in El Terreno, had met him at Mam's Bar and had promised to take him up to Deià to meet her freaky friends there, but at the last minute she'd decided against the idea because she sensed something weird about him. This is to her credit since there were a lot of weird characters around, but she noticed that 'Wes had a fanatical streak'. Having found his own way to the village he was soon being convinced by Kevin that there was a successful band waiting to materialize if finance could be found; with Tom and Larry in tow, Kevin led the way up to Daevid's house to play some of the tapes they had been working on.

In the 1960s the Easter Week processions in Deià, held on Holy Thursday and Good Friday, were still important events in village life, and were accompanied by huge bonfires at each of the large farm estates around the valley. As the little serpent of flickering candles emerged from the church that crowns the hill in the centre of the village, the caretaker of Can Borràs on the western side of the valley would light the enormous pile of brushwood and branches that had been heaped up over the pruning season; as the luminous serpent descended the hill and returned to the church up the eastern side, so the other farms would light their bonfires. These fires were all that remained of the pagan ritual that the Church celebrated as Easter. To the British side of me, the rebirth of nature was symbolized by rabbits and chocolate eggs; to the Majorcan side, by candles and bonfires.

Although our family respected and joined in with the village festivities, even welcoming the priest and his choirboys when they came to bless the house every Easter, we never directly took part in the Catholic rituals. From the sixteenth-century *finca* of Can Fusimany, we'd watch the procession wind its way around the village, the distant dirge of '*Perdona tu pueblo, Señor . . .*' wafting over the roar and crackle of the bonfire. On Holy Thursday one could just pick out the conical hats and robes of the penitents lit up by their candles. It later struck me as strange that the procession always went anti-clockwise – 'widdershins' – around the village, since in England this was always considered unlucky; perhaps it went that way to take the steepest street downhill rather than uphill.

Easter week is a movable feast, mathematically calculated from the first new moon of the year, and so is always accompanied by a full moon; however, in 1966 the full moon fell on Easter Sunday itself, a sign that seemed especially significant to Daevid, who decided that the moment was propitious for an hallucinogenic ritual. That morning, after my father had dropped by to wish him a happy Easter, Daevid climbed the mountain and swallowed a dose of some very high-quality LSD that had just arrived in the village. He had a vision of himself on stage before thousands of people, bringing a message of love and spiritual advancement through a new form of music.

Wes Brunson had experienced a similar hallucinogenic vision, in which he was told that he was to serve God and was to give his money to people who would broadcast the New Age. As soon as Daevid and Wes locked onto each other, the two visions were clearly part of the same divine plan. After three days of crazy partying around the island, Wes flew back to the USA to sell off his part of the family's optometry business and invest it in the new band. Kevin, Daevid, and Gilli, with Larry Nolan in tow, were flown to

England and set up with proper equipment and a rehearsal room in Canterbury; Batty was the obvious choice of drummer. Visions notwithstanding, Wes was a businessman at heart and expected a percentage of the profits.

The new band tried out Daevid and Kevin's new material in the Canterbury area, performing as Mr Head. The name was soon changed to the Soft Machine – a euphemism for the human being – after the novel by William Burroughs, author of *The Naked Lunch*, with whom Daevid had worked in Paris. Their first gig as the Soft Machine was at the inauguration of the new Sufi Society Headquarters at a manor house not far from Canterbury; they had been invited by Idries Shah, the Sufi scholar they had met in Deià. But their first proper London debut was at a disused engine shed in Chalk Farm, the celebrated Roundhouse: announced as the All-Night Happening, it was organized by friends of Daevid to launch the underground newspaper, *International Times*. This first concert at the Roundhouse also featured the embryonic Pink Floyd, light shows, poetry and, yes, Yoko Ono.

Robert's Canterbury schoolmate, Mike Ratledge, had by now left Oxford and joined the band on organ, replacing Larry 'easy come, easy go' Nolan. But Larry's girlfriend Janey was working for the Animals' manager Michael Jeffery (or Mike Jeffries, as he was commonly known), who agreed to promote the Soft Machine. Jeffery already ran two nightclubs in Palma and had brought the Animals to the island to play a free concert for the Palma Town Hall. They performed on the terrace of Palma's swanky Victoria Hotel, with the street below closed off to allow the people of Palma to dance. After the gig, Jeffery and the band went up to the Indigo to hang out. At that moment he was signing up an unknown American blues guitarist, James Marshall

Hendrix; he decided to launch Hendrix's career in the UK, where the blues had a much wider acceptance. It seemed that for the black blues to reach the white US audience it had to pass through England first. The Animals' bassist, Chas Chandler, left the band to join Jeffery and cover for him when he was away on business. During one of Jeffery's absences, Chas was offered a song for the Soft Machine to record. It was called 'A Whiter Shade of Pale', but Chas thought it was rubbish and turned it down – it was later a worldwide hit for Procol Harum – one of pop's biggest blunders. (Another was Los Valldemossa turning down the Beatles in early 1963 to play at the club they ran in Palma, because the fee was 'too high for an unknown group'. The following year, the Beatles' fee had quadrupled.)

In 1968 Jeffery created what became Majorca's best known club, Sergeant Pepper's. Jimi Hendrix, by then at the height of his career, came over to inaugurate it and after the set jammed with several Majorcan rock musicians. Toni Morlà was almost in tears watching Jimi destroy a brand new Fender Stratocaster, which was an unattainable dream for a Majorcan; he smashed it against the ceiling then against the amp. 'We all picked up the pieces, aghast. We then piled into the dressing room afterwards, and there was a bag of white powder on the table; Jimi said it was talcum powder to help his fingers slide better over the fretboard. We'd never even heard of cocaine in those days.'

The first Soft Machine single, released in Febuary 1967, was a very catchy upbeat pop song by Kevin called 'Love Makes Sweet Music'. It barely entered the UK charts, despite the customary underhand payments to pirate stations like Radio Caroline. It probably would have made it big if it hadn't had to compete that month with new singles from The Who, the Kinks, the Beach Boys, the Beatles, Hendrix, Tom Jones, the Bee Gees – and Procol Harum's 'A Whiter Shade of Pale'. Soft Machine weren't really a top ten act, but they were becoming the centre of the psychedelic movement in London, playing at ear-shattering volume as the resident band at the UFO Club and the Speakeasy. This didn't translate into big earnings but a weekly allowance paid out by Jeffery was generous considering the band's running expenses. However, as Robert Wyatt recalls, 'it hardly allowed me feed my wife and baby'.

The Soft Machine discovered that some of their demo tapes had been released in France as a record and had turned them into a cult band there. In July 1967 they toured the south of France, improvising music to Picasso's play *Desire Caught by the Tail* at the Cogolin Festival of Free Theatre, where they made contact with some influential Parisians holidaying in St Tropez. At the end of August they drove to Calais to catch the ferry back to Dover, where Daevid Allen was refused entry because his visa had expired. His place in the band was taken by Andy Summers for a while, and then the band carried on as a trio – Kevin, Robert, and Mike Ratledge – taking three days to record their first album in New York at the start of their first US tour with Hendrix, whom Robert remembers as being 'a really nice person'. Whenever the stream of spectacular groupies dried up for a few hours between gigs and airports, Jimi and Kevin would play chess.

The Soft Machine's relationship with Jeffery was short-lived, especially as they were becoming a highbrow, avant-garde jazz-rock band and gigs for that kind of music were scarce. Jeffery was also finding it hard to find concerts for Hendrix, who after breaking up his Experience and being abandoned by his Band of Gypsies, was turning up at concerts completely spaced out and spending his time onstage in a rambling jam session. Trixi Linnick, Jeffery's secretary at the time, recalls that 'Mike was financing a project in Plaza Gomila and flew to Palma for a September 1970 deadline on the purchase of the property. We arranged that Jimi should come over and be with us here; he was due to arrive on the actual day he died. He did try to call us the night before but a freak wind blew down the telephone lines in Bonanova where I had my house and we never spoke to him. Mike Jeffery died nearly three years later, in 1973, in a plane crash over Nantes in France when the Iberia flight to London Heathrow was touched by the wing of a French military plane during a strike of French air traffic control.'

When 'the bloody ole mum country' turned Daevid away for being an Austral Alien, he took it as a liberation and returned to Paris, where he and Gilli formed the Banana Moon with two French musicians. Finding themselves in the thick of the May 68 student riots and hunted down by the police as *agents provocateurs*, they escaped in a green-and-yellow VW bus, miraculously making it across the Spanish border and back to Deià. Safely installed once more at the Banana Moon Observatory, their house near the Deià church, they discovered that their old benefactor Wes was in town. Now he was convinced he was the reincarnation of Christ. What's more, he wanted his share of the Soft Machine's profits, of which neither Daevid nor the rest of the band had seen a penny, outside their weekly allowances.

The fact that Wes thought himself the Seventh Incarnation of Christ wasn't particularly upsetting; in that respect he was one of several who had passed through the village under a similar delusion. What was unnerving was his obsession with saving a select group of people before God destroyed the rest of humanity by dropping rocks on them. Nobody wanted to get on the wrong side of Wes. He was obviously giving God a helping hand in his task; he had thrown knives in the bar, narrowly missing a child, and was suspected of having dislodged a rock that crashed through the palm-fronded roof of the beachside café from the cliff above. Most of the time Wes seemed a harmless sunny American freak, but it was common knowledge that, apart from his magic sword with which he would prop up the moon in the sky, he also carried knives and packed a gun. So when he turned up at the Cala in his Saviour mode, dressed in a white suit and talking like Billy Graham, baptizing the children (who splashed him back), my friends and I took little notice: we were too busy jumping off rocks into the sea. However, a Spanish family that he had riled went off to call the Guardia Civil.

Bruce Wallace, one of Deià's most audible poets, called out a challenge from the beachside bar, where he was downing his tenth San Miguel: 'Wes, show us how you can walk on the water!' The Seventh Christ gamely took up the challenge but by the time the water reached the armpits of his white suit, he realized he'd have to try a new tack, so he announced that he'd prove he could breathe underwater. He waded deeper in until his head disappeared below the surface, his hat floating above him. He 'breathed underwater' for all of thirty seconds then reappeared, coughing and spluttering, to polite applause. As adolescents, my friends and I were more interested in proving our manhood by leaping from increasing heights than watching lunatics prove their divinity, so we didn't notice that Wes had commandeered our Lilo air mattress and, to save face, had begun to paddle off towards the horizon.

The Guardia were never in a hurry to show up at the best

of times, let alone when there was an armed psychopath around. The Spanish for 'better late than never' is *a buenas horas mangas verdes* – 'high time for green sleeves', referring to their paramilitary uniform. By the time the Guardia arrived, Wes had disappeared from sight around the promontory – perhaps hoping to ascend to heaven on a waterspout. But later that evening he reappeared in the village main street, jumping out in front of a lorry to demonstrate his divine protection. The lorry swerved and almost ran over a group of children, in front of many villagers at the bar who, furious, began to hurl abuse and stones at Wes, chasing him out along the road to Palma.

Early next morning, I was walking with a couple of friends to the Cala, following the narrow path alongside the deep chasm cut by the torrent, when I realized I had left my towel behind. 'Wait for me, I'll only be five minutes,' I said, and as I turned back, I heard a thunderous roar behind me and watched as a large boulder rolled down from the terrace above. It bounced across the path just where we would have been passing had we not stopped. 'Wes!' we all cried in unison, as the boulder crashed through the branches of a mulberry tree growing at the bottom of the chasm sixty feet below. We ran. Of course it could have been a sheep that dislodged the boulder, but we knew it was Wes's farewell genocide attempt. He never came back. Several rounds of ammunition and a gun were found in the house he had rented, and the last we heard was that he was selling bibles in San Francisco.

The French members of Daevid's Banana Moon Band turned up and played at Sergeant Pepper's in Palma, as well as giving a memorable concert at Mati's house that included an hour-long rock version of the Hare Krishna mantra. I had to be home at midnight, but I later heard that at dawn, as the fishing boats left to gather their nets, the partygoers had stumbled down to the beach to skinny-dip. As they got undressed, there appeared Madame Vidal, an elderly Swiss lady, out for an early-morning walk. Brandishing her walking stick, she chased them back up the hill clutching their clothes.

Deià's hippies were becoming an embarrassment to the local authorities. Gilli had given an interview to a Barcelona newspaper that only worsened matters when published – 'We're not hippies or beatniks, we're animals' ran the caption to a provocative photo – and the Guardia Civil were sent to expel Daevid and Gilli for creating a public scandal. Luckily the musicians were out of the house at the time and their neighbour, the priest, interceded on their behalf. Having seen Daevid meditate he insisted that this 'animal' was in fact a man of God and an international celebrity.

I spent a lot of time at the Banana Moon Observatory over the Christmas and Easter holidays because Daevid was helping me with my O-level Mass Media project. I had chosen the underground paper, the *International Times*, as my subject and, as a non-initiate in the use of mind-expanding drugs and the practice of tantric sex, I needed help deciphering some of the terms and understanding these concepts. The top room of the house was a haven of orderly chaos, rugs and afghan coats, incense and red lights, mandalas and manifestos, electric guitars and echo boxes, but most of all books: Rudolph Steiner and Lawrence Ferlinghetti, Bill Burroughs and the *Bhagavad Gita*. Daevid was one of that rare breed, an organized anarchist. Every tape loop was filed and catalogued; his drawing pens all had their respective caps on. He was in full creative frenzy, having recently had a vision in an olive grove on the path to

Sóller in which it was revealed to him that a mixture of absurd humour and cosmic music would prepare the world for the coming changes. He was busily working out a whole mythology centred upon a planet called Gong, populated by pothead pixies travelling by flying teapot and autobiographical characters like Captain Capricorn and Zero the Hero. There were Octave Doctors who personified the Sufi concept of a cosmic harmony based on the principle of wavelengths increasing in frequency: from years to days to minutes to heartbeats to rhythms to vibrating strings to harmonics to light waves and beyond. The whole of Daevid's project, which was to materialize over the next years in words, music, and album art, was all crystallizing at that moment.

One problem was the ghost. It had a habit of turning on the upstairs lights in the middle of the night, sending the electricity bill soaring; it had occasionally been seen disappearing up the stairs. Despite my father's interest in magic and myth, the only time I ever saw him engage in occult practices – besides ringing his African rain bell in times of drought – was one evening at the Observatory. Gilli had asked for help in setting the ghost to rest and Robert and I were among those taking part in a table-turning session in the upstairs room. The spirit – an aunt of the present owner – was contacted and, in Majorcan, told us how she had killed herself by jumping into the well. (This has traditionally been the way among Majorcan women of making a final point because of the trouble of emptying and disinfecting a cistern. According to the writer Bartomeu Mestre, 'we Majorcans are willing to die but not to kill'. So until divorce was legalized in the 1980s, the final solution to any domestic crisis was suicide, while on the mainland it was murder – 'I killed her because she was mine', in the words of the song. Mestre also points out that, while women threw themselves down wells, Majorcan men would choose to hang themselves. In the few local cases I'm familiar with, this gender division holds true.)

The Observatory ghost was forgiven by all present (I had been given the job of English–Majorcan interpreter, not the last time I had to interpret for a ghost) and was thus liberated of its ties to this world. The next electricity bill was normal. However, the house next door, also rented by musicians, continued to be haunted for a few more years by another spirit, with a striking peculiarity: since its mortal body had passed away the first floor had been raised, so it only appeared from the waist up, wading across the floor. I never discovered if its legs could be seen dangling from the downstairs ceiling.

The Soft Machine, now working with light shows and taking a more jazz-oriented direction with long instrumentals, was no longer a comfortable milieu for Kevin's introspective songs and melodies. Faced with the daunting prospect of another tour, he surrendered his bass to Hugh Hopper and fled to Formentera and then to Deià to write a whole batch of new material. I saw him emerging disconsolately from the tiny Guardia Civil post in the village.

'They just told me I have to leave, that my passport's expired. Any excuse to clean up the village of long-haired louts like me!' He returned to London to prepare his first solo album, *Joy of a Toy*. Although loth to work in another band, the album needed promotion so he formed the Whole World, which featured the veteran saxophonist Lol Coxhill, whom Kevin had spotted busking in a London tube station, and a shy young guitarist, Mike Oldfield. The band's name reflected the loose nature of the psychedelic music scene, and of the Canterbury tribe in particular, which allowed musicians to float from one group to another.

Batty was also feeling uncomfortable in the Soft Machine now that the music was getting more intellectual and his services as vocalist were no longer needed; his song 'Moon in June', which occupied one side of their third album, was virtually a solo effort and led him to record his first solo album, *End of an Ear*. He joined Kevin's Whole World for a stint before forming his own band, Matching Mole, *machine moelle* being French for Soft Machine. When the Whole World folded, Kevin joined Daevid's new band, Gong, for a year. As new members joined the various permutations of the original Canterbury/Deià musicians – Soft Machine, Gong, Matching Mole, the Whole World, Caravan, Hatfield and the North, Henry Cow, etc. – the tribe expanded until more than a score of bands were included in the broad term 'the Canterbury scene'. June Campbell-Cramer now let out rooms in her enormous flat to any Canterbury pilgrim passing through London. This earned her the title of Landlady June, which she abbreviated to Lady June as a stage name for her performances as a singer-poet on the underground circuit, and released a record, *Linguistic Leprosy*, produced by Kevin and Brian Eno.

It was at a big party at June's flat in 1973 – to celebrate her and Gilli's birthday – that Robert Wyatt fell out of the bathroom window and remained paralysed from the waist down. Rather than marking an end to a great drummer's musical career his next record, *Rock Bottom*, was the beginning of his extraordinary conversion into a keyboard player and one of the most beguiling and revered songwriters and vocalists in rock, as well as one of the most honest and self-effacing in the business. He has managed to keep true to his radical left-wing political views and even cover teeniepop songs like 'I'm a Believer' without alienating his audience.

I think that the most coherent of all the Canterbury bands, and the one with the strongest identity (although its line-up was in constant flux), was Daevid and Gilli's Gong. Perhaps the reason for this strong direction was the fact that they were simply fulfilling the blueprint vision that Daevid had had in Deià in 1969, when he wrote enough material for five or six albums, as well as creating an identifiable visual style for the album covers, combining whimsical cartoon characters with colourful Buddhist mandalas. There was a great freedom within the band to improvise over the loose but clear structure marked out from the start; Gong, which at the time was considered a French band, spearheaded the European invasion of the British music scene in the early seventies (along with Kraftwerk, Focus, etc.) and signed with the new Virgin label.

One of the pillars of Gong, right from its inception in Deià, was Didier Malherbe, a classically trained flautist who was well versed in Indian music. In 1969 he motorcycled down from Paris to visit Daevid and spent some months in our sheep hut, which, he discovered, like Julian Bream before him, was a perfect place to practise. Didier would play for hours perched like a bird on the comfortably smooth limb of a carob tree.

By 1975, Gong had fulfilled the cycle that Daevid had envisioned for it, but by now it had taken on a separate musical identity thanks to the musical brilliance and personality of Didier, the guitar hero Steve Hillage, and the excellent percussionist Pierre Moerlen. Daevid and Gilli found the music growing too technical, while the others were feeling straitjacketed by having to fit into the Planet Gong theme.

Daevid finally jumped the good ship Gong in the middle of a British gig, and thumbed a ride out of there, still dressed in his pot-head pixie stage gear. He then headed for Deià with Gilli and their two kids, having negotiated a generous contract for a solo album from Virgin, who were flushed with the success of Kevin's protégé, Mike Oldfield. The advance paid for a small studio that he set up in his new home at the bottom of the *Clot*, although he maintained the name Banana Moon Observatory from his earlier house at the top of the Puig. The Daevidless Gong continued into the realms of instrumental experimentation, just as the Soft Machine had after Kevin and Batty. Like Syd Barrett of Pink Floyd, these were all lyrical individualists unable to fit into the format of a progressive rock band.

If the Fifties had brought Deià beatniks and artists from the US East coast – intense existentialists of the jazz generation from Greenwich Village – in the late Sixties the hippies who alighted from the Palma bus were mainly mellow, laid-back Californians with no purpose other than to, like, hang out, you know, and watch what's goin' down. And on the north-west coast of Majorca, what's going down is the best sunset spectacular in Spain. While the typical American beatnik had travelled with his bongos and his battered copy of *On the Road*, his hippie successor carried a Martin guitar and *Europe on $5 a Day*, while sporting a Canadian flag on his rucksack in order to get rides when hitch-hiking.

Up until the mid Sixties, the music scene in Majorca was polarized between places like the Indigo and the Bar Bruselas, on the one hand, where Spanish and foreign jazz musicians could interact, and the tourist hotels and night-clubs on the other. There seemed to be no middle ground.

But in 1966, as Dylan was replacing cool jazz as the voice of intelligent music, a venue opened in Palma that was more in tune with these times, a godsend for a new generation of local musicians who preferred the intimacy and immediacy of acoustic music. It took up the first floor of an elegant old town house near the Bruselas in the centre of Palma, a long way from Plaza Gomila. Called *El Centro de la Guitarra* – the Guitar Centre – it soon became a meeting point for the now sizeable foreign community, for open-minded Majorcans, and for whatever musicians were 'passing through'. Although the accent was on folk, you could also hear excellent flamenco or classical guitarists there.

The Guitar Centre was run by Peter, a gentle, bearlike Californian, and his dark, stern Catalan wife Rita, who really ran the show. The atmosphere was, like the couple, a reflection of the emerging multicultural Majorca. Having rung the doorbell, one would be let into a small hallway; the aristocratic high ceilings seemed to float miles above the mellow, hip atmosphere. On the left, a bead curtain led to Peter and Rita's apartment; opposite was a small shop selling a fine range of instruments and accessories. Among the most expensive classical guitars were those handmade by the only luthier on the island, George Bowden, who had arrived as a child in 1932 and had set up his workshop in 1964. Regular flamenco, classical, or folk guitar classes were held in a back parlour with both foreign and local teachers.

Another door led to the hall where concerts were held every evening, but you had to first wait in the anteroom until clapping was heard from within; only then would Rita let you through. 'Rita the Fire Eater' laid down the rules: total respect for the musicians on stage. Only between numbers were guests admitted, drinks served, or orders taken. There was no amplification, whatever the style of music, and whoever was on stage had the total attention of the audience.

The concert room had a high ceiling and was draped in red satin curtains, which gave it the air of a New Orleans brothel; the walls were adorned with old instruments, paintings and bric-a-brac. The back half of the room was raised to allow a good view of the tiny semicircular stage that sometimes held up to a dozen musicians. The chapel, a standard fixture in any elegant Palma house, had been turned into the bar.

The Guitar Centre became my home from home as soon as I left school. Here I'd find my Spanish friends and many Deià types as well; it was also a crash-pad for the musicians who had caught the ferry over from Ibiza. While Peter's creative vision stimulated everyone involved, it was 'Lovely Rita, Peter's Maid' who made it all work. Between them they created the conditions for a lot of the musical exchanges and groups that followed. It was a place for musicians to learn from one another and for everyone else to enjoy the show. And whenever Rita took a trip to visit her family in Madrid, the apartment would fill up with musicians sleeping on the floor.

A regular folk duo at the Centre were Pepe, a young Galician musician, and Genia, an American girl who lived on the island. Pepe Milan gave guitar classes at the Centre and also played banjo and mandolin; he was a musically erudite perfectionist – the kind who will retune his instrument before every song ... 'This is an ancient Chinese melody called *Tu Ning*.' When Genia Tobin left Pepe to join Los Valldemossa, her replacement was a petite blonde, Ana Camps, with the pure, unsophisticated voice of the

Majorcan farmlands; the duo then evolved into the Driving Wheel, the Centre's resident five-piece folk band with whom I regularly played percussion – my first paid job as a musician. Although the repertoire included the inevitable 'Stairway to Heaven', they also ventured into Thirties swing ('Sweet Sue' and 'Sheikh of Araby') and traditional Spanish folk with a country-rock arrangement.

Saturday night's show always ended with all the musicians on stage with funny hats and whatever instruments came to hand: the Guitar Centre Jug and Marching Band . . .

> We play at rags and we play at drags,
> And at funerals if there's any around . . .
> Just last Sunday we made a fortune
> Playing at old Aunt Mary's abortion . . .

This being a residential building, there was a midnight curfew, even though to many Spaniards midnight falls in the middle of supper. As Cinderella-hour approached, the send-off was always 'Rita Don't Allow No Jug Band Music Here'. There was Mort Marsh, an actor who at the time was Robert Redford's stand-in, on kazoo and wearing a chicken hat, while the brilliant five-foot-tall Majorcan guitarist Joan Bibiloni clowned around in an oversize topper and huge overcoat. Joan (pronounced Joe-unn) always had the audience in fits when he spoke *bilinguish*, a hybrid of Spanish, Majorcan, and English. After the Jug Band he'd rush off to his regular nightclub gig with Majorca's top rock band, Zebra.

Among the regular folkies at the Centre were two Americans who couldn't have been more different: the tall, ephemeral 'Michael Music' and the craggy-faced handsome stomper John Fisher. There was Ronnie Martin, a chirpy Londoner, and Bob Jones, a genial Australian. Bob recalls being approached by a young, lanky-haired Spaniard in the audience: could he borrow Bob's guitar to play a number? 'It was a very expensive Spanish guitar so I said, "Well alright, but take bloody good care of it." Then he started playing flamenco and my jaw dropped. It was bloody Paco de Lucía.'

Whenever the US fleet was in port, the house was packed. Many crewcut American country boys would show up with their gleaming guitars, mandolins, dobros, and banjos to share the stage with the shaggy travelling folkies – draftees and draft dodgers – and local musicians eager to learn. One evening, with most of the officers of the USS *Santa Barbara* in the audience, the captain decided to hire the Driving Wheel for a show on board his ship. 'About fifteen of us ended up going aboard,' remembers Bob, 'along with a few beautiful Majorcan waitresses from the Centre – after all, who wants to face an audience of 3,000 men without some female backup? After two hours of fun, we were ready to leave, but the Purser stopped us, saying he knew one of us had it. Had what? His officer's cap. Even though guitar cases were searched, none of us had it, not even pranksters like John Fisher. We were finally let go and paid a generous $500 plus two crates of prime steaks, most of which we gave to the local restaurants. The Navy left a few days later, and the next weekend, during "Rita Don't Allow . . ." our very serious Argentine banjo player donned the Purser's cap.'

The Centre's musical focus reflected the times: the repertoire centred on Tim Hardin, Dylan, Leonard Cohen, Nick

Drake, Pentangle and Crosby, Stills, Nash and Young. Before Jackson Browne had even released a record I learned several of his songs from a Californian girl at the centre, Deed Abbate. The stage was open to all kinds of music and poetry, as well as frequent *espontáneos* like my father, who on one occasion got up to sing, unaccompanied, the old English folk song 'The Lambs on the Green Hills' and 'Mister McKinley', an American ballad of presidential assassination:

Mr Czolgosz went to Buffalo, and he didn't go for fun
He shot Mr McKinley with an Ivor Foster gun,
For to lay him down, boys ... for to lay him down.

Most of the regular musicians were 'just passing through' along the hippie trail from Morocco to Kathmandu, and some of them, like Teresa Tudury, had real talent. But Teresa's tremendous voice left us when she moved from Deià to the Greek Islands to live with Leonard Cohen.

John T. Fisher, however, became a fixture. You could hardly miss the only man alive capable of stuffing a whole grapefruit into his mouth. He and I formed a duo, playing regularly at the Centre and a weekly gig at the Archaeological Museum in Deià that had been set up by Michael Music's brother-in-law, Bill Waldren. The Museum, recently converted from a water mill, was the only indoor space in Deià large enough for an audience of thirty, and it soon doubled as an offshoot of the Guitar Centre.

The Museum's exhibits – implements and pottery from the Balearic beaker culture and the skeletons of an extinct local miniature gazelle, the *myotragus balearicus* – were in rectangular glass cases suspended from the ceiling. This arrangement allowed more space for people to sit on sheep-skins on the floor, although someone would inevitably crack his head on the hanging cases on getting up. The acoustics were wonderful; Bill Waldren, figure skater and sculptor before he became a Doctor in Archaeology, had applied plaster on the walls in a very organic way, applying it 'dead' – remixed after its natural setting point – which has a damp-ening effect on reflected sound, unintentionally creating a warm ambience for music. The stage was an elevated threshold that led into a smaller room with a very tall ceil-ing, the old mill itself, which gave the musicians a natural resonating chamber behind them.

John Fisher's voice was as powerful as his build, and he had a habit of keeping the beat by stamping his dusty san-dals on the floor. He was by no means a skilled instrumental-ist but he used his limitations very effectively. This, I realized, is often more important than technique in live music situations. If you have no amplifier to bring out all the subtleties in your playing, there's no point practising florid scales for hours. Over the years playing in bars and parties, I've learned a few simple tricks that are the musical equivalent of a highlighter pen – brash but effective.

John's speciality was 'hambone'. While I kept the chords rolling on the guitar, he'd stand up and use his body as a percussion instrument, slapping his thighs and chest to set up a syncopated rhythm. Playing with John, I soon realized that my vocation was that of backup musician; I felt comfortable onstage enriching the music with harmonies and occasional solos, but I froze up completely if I had to go out there on my own. John pushed me forwards by giving me a verse to sing here and there.

At one point in our set, we'd stop the raunchy country

music and I'd lead into the sultry bossa nova introduction to 'The Girl from Ipanema'. John would strike a romantic pose, and affect a nasal New York accent:

> Shoit 'n fat 'n doity 'n dumpy
> The goil from Coney Island goes walkin'
> An' when she passes
> The guys get up and go 'Yechhhh . . .'

John was also finding plenty of modelling work. The Spanish inferiority complex, after decades of being told that 'Africa begins at the Pyrenees', prompted manufacturers to search for foreign models to advertise their products. John soon became a well-known face all over the country after starring in a TV ad for a national brand of aftershave, *Varón Dandy*. John would slap this macho lotion onto his freshly shaved jowls with a wicked smile, a gesture which in Spain means 'You've got a lot of cheek' or 'Don't think you can get away with it . . .'. John never took anything too seriously: he had an infectious guffaw, and the world laughed with him. When he and a couple of Deià friends were taken into custody by the Guardia Civil for riding through Palma on the roof of a car, they were led into the grim building next to the main Post Office. The police chief recognized John: 'So what have we here? Mr *Varón Dandy* himself!' to which John replied 'Yes, that's me – remember this bit?' – and he slapped the police chief across the face. There was a second of silence, then everyone cracked up, as John slapped the policeman's other cheek. They were immediately released and drove back to Deià, still laughing.

But John's musical and occasional modelling jobs didn't quite pay for the piece of land he had his eye on, with a view over the Cala, so he took a job as deck hand on a yacht across the Atlantic. The pay was excellent because the boat was carrying five tons of high quality Lebanese hashish, but off the Canary Islands the mainstay broke and the skipper motored into Las Palmas for repairs.

The boatload of hash rode unmolested at anchor for two weeks in the harbour as the crew partied the time away in the port, phoning for funds from the trip's sponsors in the USA. The US Drug Enforcement Agency was eavesdropping at the other end and tipped off the Guardia Civil to arrest the whole crew.

When the charges were read in court, the five tons of hash had miraculously become two tons – the rest had meanwhile found its way back onto the street through the hands of the local police and customs distribution network. But even the 'meagre' two tons earned John, as an accessory to the crime, a four-year sentence and a $50,000 fine. He stood up and, with a deadpan expression, asked the judge: 'Do you accept American Express?' Again, a split second of silence before the courtroom cracked up, and the judge, in fits of laughter, yelled 'Get that man out of here!' At this time, John's ad as Spain's Marlboro Man was being aired, which made the news and probably boosted cigarette sales even more.

Never one to lose a smile, even in jail, John wangled his way into doing kitchen chores. Here he could set aside any rotten fruit to brew his own hooch in airtight catering jars hidden behind the latrines. When one of these blew up in his face, the guards rushed in to find John covered in slime and froth. Flashing his best grin, he explained: 'Nuevo shampoo'.

By this time Franco had died and the political scene outside was changing. With the democratic reforms, the 'old guard' in the local prison and police authorities was coming under scrutiny and a socialist landslide was forecast for the next elections. This probably explains why, eighteen months into their sentence, the crew members were suddenly turned out onto the street with no passports or words of explanation: what if their case were to be reviewed and the missing hash come to light? Realizing that, as a witness of the scam, he could be in danger, John took a domestic flight to Madrid, where an ex-girlfriend supplied him with a French passport. He was out of the country before the Missing Marlboro Man story hit the national press.

Meanwhile, back at the regular Saturday spot at the Museum, I paired up with another folkie-with-a-Martin-guitar, the London photographer Laurie Asprey, whose emotional, gravelly voice could bring a lump to any throat. John didn't venture back for thirty years, and only then with a doctor's degree and a new identity – but the same huge grin.

The Driving Wheel had undergone changes and had recorded Spain's first folk-rock record, adapting traditional songs from different regions of Spain, with tight harmonies, Moog synthesizer and steel-string guitars sent through a chorus pedal. The band was renamed Euterpe after the Greek muse, and in 1975 they played a memorable concert at the Ca n'Alluny theatre. After the show Daevid Allen asked them to work with him on *Good Morning*, the solo album he was preparing to record at his home studio in the village. The Majorcans' tight harmonies and ringing acoustic guitars were miles away from Gong's cosmic rock, and despite Daevid's spacey effects, Euterpe's strong Mediterranean character shone through strongly enough for Virgin Records to give them equal billing on the cover.

When Kevin Ayers settled down in Deià a few years later, he also recorded and toured with his own band of Majorcan musicians, led by Joan Bibiloni from the Guitar Centre. I'll never forget the Kevin Ayers Band headlining a festival in the mid Eighties at the quaint little bullring in Alcudia. The place was decorated like a village ball with paper lanterns and a huge crowd had packed in: the buzz had gone around the island that John Cale of the Velvet Underground had flown in to join Kevin as surprise guest. And it was true – the Welshman had appeared with Kevin on the legendary *June 1st, 1974* live album – but by showtime Kevin and John were completely and leglessly drunk backstage and were waiting for an antidote to arrive to sober them up. Joan Bibiloni (a.k.a. B. B. Lonely), by then a well-known figure in his own right, led the band onstage to confront the impatient crowd. Word came through that the supply car had broken down halfway from Palma, so the promoter had to push the woozy pair onstage just as they were. What happened next was aptly summed up in the next day's headlines: 'A Pair of Illustrious Good-for-Nothings'. After Kevin abandoned the first song in a fit of giggles, John attempted his brilliant, sombre version of 'Heartbreak Hotel'. But during his violin solo, he played an up-bow stroke with such force that the bow flew out of his fingers and disappeared backstage. They both fell about laughing and after twenty minutes, although the bow had been recovered, they staggered offstage, leaving Joan and the band to finish the gig on their own, earning them the status of local heroes.

# 3

# Honeymoon Island

Majorca the Beautiful had begun to attract foreigners well before my father's arrival in 1929. Among those who had already spread the word of the island's pastoral tranquillity and Byronesque landscapes were Georges Sand and Frédéric Chopin, the Archduke Ludwig Salvatore of Austria, Jules Verne, Albert Camus, Sara Bernhardt, Arthur Rackham, Gertrude Stein, and D. H. Lawrence. But not all spoke in favour: Sand pilloried the Majorcans as savages, Stein found the island too provincial – 'it's paradise if you can stand it' – and Lawrence, who came for his ailing health, found it just plain boring.

To bolster the more positive reputation of the island, the Majorcan Society for the Promotion of Tourism was founded in 1905 and it named Archduke Ludwig an honorary member. By 1912, Palma boasted the luxurious Grand Hotel (designed by one of Gaudí's disciples) and had become a popular port of call for steamship cruises. A line of charabancs would be waiting at the quayside to take passengers careering around the coastal mountain road, with its breathtaking views, to Deià and Sóller.

The First World War soon pulled the plug on sea cruises, yet several members of the Paris set – Europeans and Americans of independent means – decided to sit out the hostilities in the Majorcan sunshine. They converged upon El Terreno overlooking Palma Bay, where the Majorcan nobility had their summer villas. These 'northern barbarians' scandalized the churchgoing Majorcans by giving parties, mixing devilish cocktails, and allowing their women to smoke.

The Roaring Twenties sent the smart young Europeans out to discover the romantic and unspoilt Mediterranean, portrayed by Gordon West from muleback in his *Jogging Round Majorca*. But West's book made no mention of the beachside flats that were beginning to appear, nor the inauguration of luxury hotels such as the Formentor, built on its own private headland in Pollença bay and, at the time, only accessible by sea (the building costs ruined the developer). By 1932, after the Primo de Rivera dictatorship, democracy returned to Spain with the Second Republic and the island was receiving 30,000 visitors a year; the Formentor was fully booked up by the European aristocracy who could moor their yachts alongside, whilst the seaplane passenger service from Marseille to Algiers made a stopover in the bay twice a day.

The Formentor also boasted one of the few casinos in the country, which had set the scene for the downfall of the Conservative Government in Madrid. Three Dutch businessmen, Messrs Strauss, Perle, and Lowman, had invented a new kind of roulette wheel that they wanted to introduce into Spain. To smooth the way, the Conservative president Lerroux was paid off with a gold watch and within a few days the invention was working in the Hotel Formentor.

When the scandal broke it gave the left-wing Popular Front enough political ammunition to win the 1936 elections; it also gave the Spanish language a new word for illicit undertakings, *estraperlo* (from *Estra*uss, *Per*le, *Low*man), in the sense of 'bootleg' or 'moonshine'. But the reforms of the new Government, among the most progressive in Europe, led to the backlash of Franco's uprising and then to a full-blown civil war. This brought Majorcan tourism to a shuddering halt; no sooner had the war finished than the Second World War broke out. This meant leaving three thousand hotel beds empty for more than ten years; and although Majorca was by no means dependent upon tourism yet, this added more misery to a decade of hunger and rationing that was only circumvented by smuggling and bartering *estraperlo* flour, sugar, and olive oil.

My father's return after the Second World War with his new family was taken by the Deià villagers as a vote of confidence in the island's future, a sign that good times would soon be back. But it was going to take a while yet. The Allies, who had just purged themselves of Fascist states, resented the Spanish dictatorship, which mockingly sullied the landscape of a Brave New Europe. It was a resentment tinged with a little guilt among the British and French for not having defended the Spanish democracy in its time of need. This cold-shouldering obliged the Majorcan entrepreneurs to look towards domestic tourism to fill the empty hotel beds. Before the war, many of the island's visitors had been Catalan couples whose honeymoon could begin on the overnight steamer from Barcelona; so why not promote the island as a destination for the only Spaniards who travelled for pleasure, the newly-weds? The *Honeymoon in Majorca* campaign began in 1946 and within four years, thanks to domestic flights, the number of visitors had tripled its pre-war level and the island was bracing itself for its re-entry into the international market, knowing that it was going to hit the ground running.

Majorca had all the necessary romantic features to qualify as the 'Island of Love': panoramic sunset points, open-carriage rides, Moorish gardens, almond blossom in winter, and spectacular caves: one underground lake featured a string quartet floating in a boat beneath the stalactites. But in Nationalist Catholic Spain, Love meant Matrimony; right into the democratic 1980s, several years after Franco's death, it was impossible for a Spanish couple to stay at a hotel without first presenting their marriage document, the *Libro de Familia*. Many a honeymoon night had to be spent in separate rooms because the newlyweds had left this unfamiliar, oversized sex-passport behind in the rush.

The *Libro de Familia* was given to every couple upon registering their marriage. Pages 4 to 13 were reserved for details of Child 1 through to Child 10; if a couple managed to fill up every page, like a Green Shield Stamps booklet, they would qualify for the benefits and discounts of being a *Familia Numerosa*. (This prize for repopulating the Fatherland was one policy that Franco and Stalin had in common.) Halfway down each of those ten pages was a space reserved for details of the child's death – infant mortality was very high in the post-war years – or marriage. Page 15 was reserved for details of death of the parents, and page 16 for judicial sentences withdrawing parental status. Such romantic reading for a honeymoon trip! But the *Libro de Familia* is still with us: after the Socialist landslide victory in 1982, one was also given to unmarried couples upon the registry of their first child. However, there are no longer any prizes for procreation, which may explain why Spain now has one of the lowest birth rates in the world.

If any one person was responsible for turning Majorca into the Island of Love, it was the local jazz musician and composer Bonet de San Pedro. With his rakish moustache he brought swing into the gloomy musical panorama of post-war Spain; fronting his jazz band around the country and abroad, he played guitar, sax, clarinet, and the Hawaiian slide guitar. His smooth voice was made for the radio, turning Cab Calloway's 'You Rascal You' into a national hit, *Raskayú*. In the days when radio was king and travel agents hardly existed, Bonet's songs extolling the island's charms in his suave but swinging style did more to promote Majorca than a TV campaign could today.

The young had plenty of time to plan their honeymoon – courtship tended to last several years – and Majorca was close enough to be affordable, yet exotic enough to involve the adventure of catching a plane or boat. A great many mainland Spaniards of my generation were conceived on the island. In a stern Catholic society, the concept of family planning consisted of starting one right away, to make up for the time lost during courtship. Over the next twenty years – at least until foreign girls on the pill began to arrive – Majorca maintained one of the world's greatest discrepancies between conception rate and birth rate; it would be fair to guess that of every ten children conceived on the island, nine were born elsewhere. As a place to generate life, it was the mirror image of the Indian city of Varanasi, a sacred place in which to die.

I was one of the happy few actually born in Palma in 1953, just as the floodgates of international mass tourism began to inch open. Domestic visitors to the island had stabilized at about 80,000 a year, but while at that moment only one tourist in five was a foreigner, the proportion was reversed by the time I was seven. In those seven years the number of hotels had also quadrupled.

President Eisenhower had lifted the embargo on the dictatorship, now an anti-Communist ally, and allowed Franco (a full general like Ike himself and the only surviving member of Europe's Fascist trio) to slip quietly into the United Nations through the back door. Legitimating the dictatorship in this way further demoralized the few Spaniards who dared stand up to Franco and allowed him to continue torturing and garrotting his opponents while receiving a $62 million international bank loan. The Marshall Plan had helped get Europe's economy back on its feet and also began to pump money and investments into Spain in exchange for US military bases. The US satellite tracking station on the Puig Major, the highest peak in the Balearic Islands, appeared almost overnight like the giant mushrooms in Tintin's *The Shooting Star* adventure. Franco, realizing that Spain's sunshine and beaches were its biggest capital, channelled much of this foreign investment – power stations, roads, airports – towards the coastal areas and the Balearics. Majorca, where he had once served as military governor and which had supported him during the Civil War, was his darling and received 93 per cent of the tourist cake; Ibiza received a tiny slice, and the once loyally republican Minorca, the ugly sister, only got the crumbs.

The Government paid for the infrastructure, but there was no private money to invest in preparing for the coming boom; it was the foreign tour agencies that financed the building of hotels in exchange for a guaranteed number of rooms on preferential terms. Spanish hoteliers were forced to accept ever increasing numbers of tourists at rock-bottom prices and to suffer the consequences of any events that affected the agencies at home: oil crisis, devaluation, currency controls, bankruptcies. This package-tour stranglehold wasn't broken until the property boom of the 1980s and 1990s, when the real money – a lot of it in cash – began to pour directly into holiday homes and turned the island from a giant hotel into a giant money-laundering service.

In the 1950s, as cheap air travel began to allow northern Europeans access to Spanish beaches, the first to arrive in significant numbers were the *suecos* ('Swedes', as all Scandinavians are known) – the best-off at the time and the most in need of sunshine. This first wave gave rise to the term *una sueca* for any foreign girl and the expression *hacerse el sueco* – 'to pass oneself off as Swedish' – when one pretends not to understand. Close on the Swedish heels came the British and the Germans, who eventually superseded the *suecos* by far. The French, Dutch, and Belgians were less evident on the islands since they had the Costa Brava – the eastern coast of mainland Spain – within driving distance. Between the beginning and the end of the 1950s, Majorca's tourist business increased tenfold; by 1990 it had multiplied by seventy. In late 1960, the Millionth Tourist of the Year was received at the airport by all the local authorities; but every successive year the Millionth Tourist would arrive a month earlier, soon making room for the Two Millionth of the Year; thereafter nobody bothered to count anymore.

This geometric progression boosted the demand for musicians, who became as important as waiters or cooks. Package tourists had paid for their holidays at home – hotel, transport, and meals included – of which only part of the money reverted to the island. To make the exercise worthwhile for the Majorcans, the tourists had to be persuaded to spend their holiday allowances in the hotel bar or in nightclubs. The hook was music (being the food of love and what comes with it) and the demand for musicians so great that any spotty Majorcan youth knowing three chords could join a hotel band. A cocktail-lounge pianist earned twice as much in Majorca as in Barcelona ... and still does. The musical performing and reproduction rights paid by the hotels, bars, and discos of the islands generate a huge income for the music publishing business.

Spain produces some of the world's greatest wines and spirits, but also many of the worst. The real money-spinner in the holiday areas was the cheaply produced alcohol bottled locally and cunningly designed to imitate the name brands. From the client's side of a dimly lit bar they were indistinguishable. For his first drink, the client would get what he'd ordered; thereafter, too sozzled to notice the difference, he'd be given a cheap imitation – *Moreyskoff* for Smirnoff, *Cuatro* for Cointreau, *Bailen* for Bailey's – at the same price. This generated a huge profit for the bar and a dreadful hangover for the client.

Another great alcoholic money-spinner was the sangría, in which the most abominable wines and spirits could pass undetected by any European tourists except the French, who were a minority anyway. Until the French put their foot down in the 1980s and claimed exclusive use of the word *champagne*, any Catalan *Cava* felt free to describe itself as *champany* on the label, even the semi-dry, which was cheaper than a regular Rioja wine. But for many northern Europeans, *champagne* signified true luxury, an aura exploited to the full by many of the better Majorcan establishments like Gran Hotel Albatros, where once a week the guests would be invited to a Champagne Cascade Evening. Formal dress was required, and the hotel kept a cupboard full of bow ties for guests who might have forgotten to bring one on holiday. In the dining room a tower of champagne glasses would be set up, and, to a roll of drums from the group onstage, a waiter would climb a ladder to pour champagne into the top glass, from where it would overflow and cascade spectacularly down from one to another until the bottom row of glasses was full, at which point the drummer would hit the crash cymbal. The excitement was intense because occasionally the crash came not from the cymbal but from the tower keeling over. Whenever this happened, the Albatros drummer would grab the microphone and announce in a gravelly, deadpan voice, 'Mallorca Biutiful!'

If the Northern Male came to Spain for its cheap booze and cigarettes and bird-watching on the beach, the Northern Female was drawn by the Legend of the Latin Lover. All the girls' comics and magazines lying around the common room at my English boarding school – *Jackie, Bunty, Mandy, Petticoat* – seemed to be in the pay of the Spanish Tourist Office because the holiday romances that filled their pages always involved a dishy, dark, square-jawed heartthrob called Manuel or Antonio. A whiter shade of weed like myself would stand no chance of winning the heart of an English rose.

Our hairy-chested Latin lovers, known locally as *picadors*, saw themselves as macho conquerors, but I soon began to consider them unwitting victims of the flocks of Valkyries that flew south every summer to prey on them. In the hotels there were plenty of waiters and cooks to choose from, mostly mainlanders, who could procure the keys to empty rooms; however, the Northern Female wasn't looking simply for sex – there was plenty of that available back home – but romance. The Majorcan male, despite his macho image, was brought up in the old school of patient gallantry that prepared him to court a lady for years if necessary; and, since his official Majorcan fiancée had to be home by ten, he had the rest of the evening free to dance with the *suecas*. Seductive but respectful, he could make himself understood with a few words of English, sometimes scribbled phonetically in Spanish by a helpful friend on a scrap of paper. My musical companion Toni Morlà sums up the *picador*'s phrase book as follows, in phonetic *inglis*, where the j is a guttural h:

1. *Yú inglis?* (Even *cherman* or *suidis* girls spoke *inglis*, but every nationality required a different plan of attack.)
2. *Uot iss yor neim?*
3. *Uot jotel yú?* (i.e. 'Where are you staying?')
4. *Is de ferst taim in Mallorca?* ('Is this your first visit to the island?' If not, you might have to measure up to a previous romance.)
5. *Tú uiks jolideis?* ('Are you going to stay for two weeks?' Before bestowing your full attention upon a foreign girl, you'd best first ascertain how many days remained of her fortnight's holiday; if you had to rush things, it was best not to start.)
6. *Yú alón?* (If the answer was no, it was best to withdraw.)
7. *Yú dants?* (The big one: once you had her on the dance floor, you could switch to non-verbal communication, known as 'rubbing the garlic'.)
8. If things were going well, the last phrase as you led the

girl out into the street was *Camalón uiz mi* –'Come
along with me'.

8b. If the time wasn't yet ripe, *Ai ueitink for yu tumorro*,
'I'll be waiting for you tomorrow.'

Few young *picadors* had a car, let alone a bachelor pad,
in the event of striking lucky with the girl, but on the warm
summer nights anywhere under the stars would do; you just
had to avoid the Guardia Civil who patrolled the beaches
at night. All you needed was a Lambretta and a blanket;
but the more you invested in your tackle, the richer the
rewards. One Majorcan *picador* got into the *Guinness Book
of Records*, not for the number of conquests but for a jail
sentence of several hundred years: six months for every
cheque he intercepted as a sorter in the Palma Post Office.
However, it wasn't his lavish nightlife that gave the game
away but his mother, who complained to his superiors
that he 'slaved enough without having to take extra work
home'.

Majorcan mothers dote on their children, especially sons,
and participate in their questions of health even when grown
up; instead of 'he's lost his appetite' they will say 'he doesn't
eat for me'. The sexual exploits of their sons was a source
of worry to some *picadors*' mothers, not on moral grounds
but because of the locally held belief that too much indul-
gence weakened the bone marrow, stunted your growth,
and left you deaf and blind.

Toni Morlà began playing in a hotel band in 1960 at the
age of fifteen. The Fascist regime, obsessed with keeping
tabs on everybody, required professional musicians to carry
a Musicians Card, for which they had to sit a difficult exam.
However, the jobs for musicians far outweighed the con-

servatory's capacity to teach them; few of the self-taught youngsters like Toni could read a note yet they could play the Top Ten backwards, and so were issued a Theatre, Circus and Variety card instead. This could be obtained by performing a short set piece; in the interests of the national economy, everybody passed this test.

Although the money was good, the summer season wasn't long enough for a musician to provide for his family the other eight months of the year: he couldn't afford to lose his daytime job. The island's intimate geography has allowed local musicians to satisfy the demand by doing a *doblete*, playing in two or more places in the same night, sometimes in different bands: a regular evening gig at a hotel and a late-night stint at a club or a village *festa*. Often the tight schedule required having a separate set of instruments in each place, ready to plug in and play.

Many found it hard to keep awake during the final set, especially when playing soporific hotel music. Toni's drummer would get home at three only to start delivering sausages at seven. 'He'd sometimes doze off for a couple of bars without missing a beat and jolt himself upright whenever he caught himself actually nodding off. Once we noticed him lagging behind the beat and all turned around to see him, eyes closed, slowly keel over backwards and disappear behind the stage, followed by the cymbals, hi-hat and tom-toms.'

Toni maintains that the great unsung hero of the Spanish tourist boom and indirect contributor to the national economy was not the builder or hotelier but the *picador*. Unsung, that is, until the 1980s when Toni wrote a rousing paean to this endangered species:

Come on lads, summer's arrived
The island reeks of foreign girls . . .
Bring out your tight jeans
Unbutton your shirts to show your gold chains,
Tune up your lies and your Seat 600s,
The little virgins are here . . .

A musician's high profile gave him a big advantage when pulling girls, but many establishments banned musicians from having affairs with clients for fear of driving away the *picadors* who spent wads of cash inviting foreign girls to drinks. A musician had to be discreet and to count on his liaison to be waiting for him outside when he knocked off after the show. So although it was the *picador* who spent his money provoking the bull, it was often the musician who came in for the kill.

'Although we Majorcans are usually quite reserved, our band always pooled our information and gave each other tips. From the stage you could monitor the situation and play your cards accordingly; sometimes it was hard to disguise your reaction when you had a shapely blonde ogling you. Perhaps that's why guitar straps became longer, so the instrument could cover the evidence.'

Toni's band drew up a Guide to European Women. The Italian was the most difficult to pull. The French promised a lot but never delivered. The Dutch girl was very appreciative and willing, but the German *fräulein* was the surest bet of all: when she said 'I'll be waiting outside', you could bet your life she'd be there and would take you to her hotel. The British were the most attractive and the sexiest dressers, but when it came down to it they weren't as fiery as the more demure continentals. The Scandinavians were very open once they had accepted you, but they were picky.

What did the Majorcan male have that the boyfriend she'd left behind didn't? 'Nothing at all,' admits Toni. 'We probably weren't as good as lovers, but the repression of the dictatorship fired our lust. The most important factor was the atmosphere: the sunshine, the sea, the cheap booze, warm nights and light clothing. It was scary, the foreign girls absolutely devoured us. Once the pianist and I pulled two monumental Norwegian centrefolds, and the next morning we both admitted to have been so intimidated by such perfection that neither of us had been able to perform as was expected of us.'

Of course when the two-week holiday is up, tragic scenes take place at the airport. There are tears and kisses, exchanges of addresses and photographs, promises of undying love and chastity until the next August, a moment of tenderness immortalized in dozens of summer hits: 'Bye Bye Fräulein', 'Adiós Linda Candy', 'Auf Wiedersehen Mallorca'. But before the plane has left the ground, our *picador* can be spotted wandering over to the arrivals hall . . .

The Sixties was the golden age for the Latin Lover: all play and no responsibilities. In a strict Catholic country, condoms were hard to procure but this didn't matter to him as most foreign girls were on the pill. In the worst case, they could always get an abortion back home, whereas a Spanish girl would have to take a regular flight to London at three times the price of a charter and have someone in the family to pull strings to get her a passport.

Although most *picadors* took these summer romances with a pinch of salt, many affairs did bloom into marriage, producing a whole generation of *mig-i-mig* (half-and-half) offspring; people who, like myself, speak and think in

Majorcan and Spanish as well as in their mother tongue – English, Swedish, German, or Dutch. Most of these *mig-i-mig* owe their existence to the composers of smoochers like 'When a Man Loves a Woman', 'Je t'Aime (Moi Non Plus)', 'Me and Mrs Jones', and 'Feelings'.

Have I forgotten about foreign men? Their (our) aspirin-white or lobster-red bodies were at a disadvantage on the beach, but on the dance floor they had a sporting chance of a summer romance with tourist girls of their own or another nationality. Yet I doubt if one in a hundred had any luck with a Spanish girl, not even with the hotel chambermaids.

In the early 1960s, Spain's musicians began to turn their eyes and ears northwards. Until then, Italy had showed the way for a Spanish pop musician to go, as well as providing many of the tools of his trade, from electric organs to echo-boxes. Right up until the 1970s Spain's wartime trading partners still provided most of the country's technology; to buy an American Fender guitar cost three times as much as the German or Italian equivalent. And although Marcello Mastroianni on a Vespa was a more popular role model than Marlon Brando on a motorcycle, Spain – like the rest of the world – was developing a taste for Anglo-American pop culture. The Italian lyrics of *O Sole Mio* were dropped in favour of the English 'It's Now Or Never' and Ben E. King's 'Stand By Me' was soon competing with Adriano Celentano's version, *Preghero*.

Toni Morlà maintained his childhood nickname Toni Martini (earned by living above the vermouth warehouse) but as Italian became passé, stage names such as Bernardo Bernardini – pianist Bernat Bauzá – surrendered to English ones like Benny and the Benny's. The apostrophe was an important touch of class, and could easily be added to the existing name of a bar, shop, or pop group. Tito's Night Club had been the first, back in 1935, but in the 1960s everybody was using the English possessive apostrophe, whether it made sense or not. This apostrophilia soon ran wild. Los Milords (named after Edith Piaf's French hit) became Los Milord's, followed by Los Fetter's, Los Mayorica's, the Faider's and Duo Excellent's (still active today). A good example of apostrophilia *ad absurdum* was the Dinamic's Little's, one of the leading local groups of the early Sixties.

For all the new prosperity swamping the island, the Majorcans didn't lose their natural thriftiness. Although the landed gentry had been known to gamble away its estates, the peasants had, after centuries of barter, become tenaciously self-sufficient, recycling and carefully rationing their supplies. If they were unused to earning cash, they were less used to spending it. Local musicians discovered you could get an extra two weeks of life out of electric guitar strings if you boiled them up and oiled them down. Many amplifiers were home-made and dangerously prone to go up in smoke, given the island's wildly fluctuating voltage, so a current stabilizer/transformer was the most important piece of a group's equipment, since at one point four different voltages were functioning on the island; 110, 220, 360 and, in Sóller, 150 volts. (The historic Sóller railway bought its electric engines a century ago from a defunct Midwestern railway in the USA that had run on 150 volts, so the whole town operated on this voltage; the train and many houses in Sóller are today the only 150v users in Europe. A light bulb factory still caters to this tiny demand.)

In the 1960s, the average European's access to live music was quite limited, even in Britain. For a girl to have a live band playing her favourite songs every night for two weeks in her hotel was pure bliss, conducive to groupie adulation. Of course this wasn't a patch on Beatlemania, but any Majorcan band would have to print up glossy photos to sign and hand out to their fans. From there it was a small step to selling their own records to their loyal audience as souvenirs to make extra cash on the side. Your own record! Any British band had to be pretty hot to be recording artists, but in Majorca hundreds of seven-inch EPs were recorded every year for the tourist market. The quality was fairly shoddy, as the buyers would discover when they got home; but oh! it would bring back such memories . . .

Extended Plays were more popular in Spain than singles or LPs. Even 'A Hard Day's Night' was released here four songs at a time. The Souvenir EP seemed to follow a standard formula: a photo of the group in front of Palma Cathedral, Bellver Castle, an open horse-drawn carriage, a fishing boat, or their hotel if they were the resident band. The four songs would include least two dance tracks and a slow number and had to feature a version of that year's summer hit.

The concept of a summer hit was inadvertently invented by the Argentine singer Luís Aguilé. He arrived in Spain in 1963 with his song *Dile*, recently resurrected by Vonda Shepard as 'Tell Him' in *Ally McBeal*. Having received a lot of airplay, *Dile* began to take off in a big way, receiving thousands of orders just as his record company, EMI-Odeon, had closed down their pressing plant for August. They had to call part of the staff back from their holidays to press extra copies. Up until then, record sales had tailed off in the summer, there being few record shops in the holiday areas, but in the early 1960s there began to be a huge summer demand from discotheques, tourists, and the new national craze for summer *guateques*, teen dance parties. Soon records began to be stocked and sold in all the beach resorts; Philips did a roaring trade in tinny battery-powered record players, known in Spain as *pick-ups*.

From then on, all the record companies would field a candidate for the summer hit and keep their factories open in August. Luís Aguilé had twenty-three hits in a row. The formula was simple: a happy tune, a catchy chorus and a gimmicky sound effect. Some dance steps also helped, like the Dutch duo Johnny and Charlie's *La Yenka* or the odious 'The Birdie Song'– the song most requested by hotel clients and most hated by hotel bands. (The second most hated must be the 1973 summer hit, Manolo Escobar's 'Viva España', probably the most famous *pasodoble* of all time and now a standard in any brass band's repertoire. Few Spaniards realize that the music and original lyrics were written by two Belgian composers, Caerts and Rozenstraten.)

To help promote a summer hit there was nothing like a first prize in a song festival, such as the San Remo Festival in Italy (whose winner was inevitably recorded in a Spanish version), Benidorm on the Costa del Sol, and less important ones in Majorca. But nothing could beat being the winner of the Eurovision Song Contest, which was held at Easter, giving bands time to learn the winning song before it became a big summer hit like Sandy Shaw's 'Puppet On a String', Cliff Richard's 'Congratulations', Abba's 'Waterloo', or the Spanish winner for 1968 'La, La, La'. The Catalan songwriter Joan Manuel Serrat had been originally chosen to

perform 'La, La, La', with my brother-in-law Ramón con-
ducting the orchestra; but when Serrat insisted in singing in
his mother tongue, Televisión Española found a mini-skirted
replacement, Massiel, to perform it in Spanish with a non-
Catalan conductor. (Dave Davies of the Kinks later sued
the composers for plagiarizing the melody from his 'Death
of a Clown'.) Serrat's anti-Spanish stance brought him tremendous criticism, especially when he proceeded to record
the song in French, Italian, and Portuguese.

Nobody took Eurovision as seriously as Televisión
Española, who, as the Government's propaganda machine,
was desperately trying to change the popular European misconception of Spain's forming a part of Africa. The nation's
biggest confidence booster, other than a Real Madrid football victory, was a Eurovision winner. Spain did remarkably
well, thanks especially to the votes of Germany, a gesture
of goodwill to their Spanish guest-workers but also to the
many Germans working in Televisión Española.

The basic ingredient of a summer hit is a general sense
of *desenfado* – literally, 'dis-anger': spontaneity, fun. It helps
to mix in a bit of silliness, such as the *ch, ch-ch, ugh!* of
Mungo Jerry's 'In the Summertime' or the unexpected three
handclaps just before the punchline of 'Fiesta', a summer
hit written by Ramón and my sister Lucia. 'Fiesta' was a
runner-up in the race to represent Spain in the Eurovision
contest but it outsold the official entry and paid for their
house.

Another important ingredient was a simple choreography
to complement the song. The Spanish summer-hit-with-
dance-steps par excellence was the 1995 worldwide smash,
'Macarena', which even became the theme song of the US
elections and sold five million copies. This provoked a flood

of banal flamenco-pop songs, most of which would justify the diminutive '*fl-op*', until 2002's 'Aserejé'. This was an international smash hit by the unlikely girl group Ketchup, daughters of a well-known character in Córdoba known as El Tomate. The nonsense lyrics, made up by the producer and his children on a car ride, are an Andalusian phonetic rendering of the 1990s' hit, 'Rapper's Delight'; *aserejé* = 'I said hey!'

Today, beachside or airport sales are now copped by the annual Ibiza Dance/Chill-out Mix. The summer hit has evolved from a holiday memento into a hot export item. A Sony Music executive recently admitted that the world's record business carefully monitors Spain's pop production in the hope of discovering another 'Macarena' or 'Aserejé'. And they keep a very close watch on Andalucía, whose sense of rhythm, fun and silliness – the upside of the dark passion of flamenco – is at the heart of a good summer hit.

Pop in Spain was all Brylcreem and clean fingernails until 1964, when John Lennon's hoarse screams in 'Twist 'n Shout' set the alarm bells ringing. Admittedly Elvis had twitched and Little Richard had yelped, but there was some-thing more base and uncontrolled about the long hair and punk attitude of these working-class boys that worried the Spanish Government and inflamed the Spanish adolescents. When *A Hard Day's Night* reached Spanish screens it was classified 'For Viewers Over Fourteen', an age when many Spaniards were working for a living. Anybody with hair over his ears was signalled on the street as *un bitel*, an intended offence that was usually taken as a compliment. Within two years, however, the Beatles had proved to be decent lads, just as Elvis had become a clean-cut crooner, so by the time 'Help' was released, it was classified as 'Apt for All Audiences'. The new black sheep were the *Rollin Estóns*, still referred to today as *Los Rollin*.

In the early years of rock 'n' roll, Franco's protectionist laws required a song to be covered by a Spanish group before the original-language version could be issued. 'Bony Moronie' was known to the Spanish as *Popotitos* and 'Good Golly Miss Molly' was *La Pulga* ('The Flea'). Even the early Beatles or Stones hits were first released in a Spanish cover version; the 'Spanish Stones' was a band called Lone Star who covered 'Nineteenth Nervous Breakdown' fairly convincingly as *Cuidado con la Neurastenia* ('Beware of Neurasthenia'). Many rock songs are built around a catchy but untranslatable English phrase that would give the translators two options: change the lyrics completely or try to jam them into the song's metre, a tall order given the comparative verbosity of the Spanish language.

The Beatles' 'official' cover group, Los Sirex, somehow managed to get people to sing along with the awkward Spanish refrain of *Submarino Amarillo*:

> *Mi submarino amarillo es, amarillo es . . .*
> ('My submarine, yellow it is, yellow it is . . .')

But try getting your tongue around the first two lines of 'A Hard Day's Night':

> *Ha sido la noche de un dia fatigoso*
> *Y he estado trabajando como un perro . . .*

Only one Spanish band challenged British Pop on its own terms, and that was by accident. Los Bravos were all Majorcans except for their German-born lead singer, Mike

Kennedy, who had settled on the island. In the new year of 1966, as Beatlemania was at its peak, Mike Jeffery sent them to London to record an album for Decca, but the Musicians' Union demanded the backing track be performed by Union members (which happened to include Jimmy Page on guitar). Only Mike's voice was recorded; the rest of the band sat despondently around the studio watching. When the Brits went across the road for a pub lunch, the Majorcans talked the engineer into letting them lay down at least one track, 'La Moto'. But it was another song, 'Black is Black', that was chosen as the single. It was released and nothing happened. The band accepted their fate and signed a summer-long residency at a Palma nightclub. Two months later the song suddenly took off, rocketing to Number 2 and staying in the charts until the end of the summer; it also broke into the US Top Ten. But instead of international tours, Los Bravos were contractually stuck in Cala Mayor playing their own 'Black is Black' to tourists who thought they were a cover band. In pop music, once you miss the first train, you might as well walk; their autumn follow-up 'I Don't Care' barely broke into the UK Top Twenty, and the British charts had to wait thirty years for another Spanish hit.

In the last few years, the Tourism Board and the glossy magazines have been trying to drive the island's image upmarket by promoting 'the Other Mallorca', using the local spelling to underline their point. Those of us who live in the 'authentic', rural, Catalan-speaking part of the island use the term 'the Other Mallorca' to refer to the string of tourist ghettos that cling like soap bubbles to the coastline. They remind me of the Biosphere II experiment, a self-sufficient temporary community of a given nationality that has touched down on an alien planet. Apart from the main British and German life-support systems, there are smaller Dutch, French, and Italian ones; there are even small Finnish bubbles within the larger Scandinavian ones. Each offers its countrymen the illusion of being 'at home with the sun lamp on and a cheap off-licence next door'.

If a Huddersfield fishmonger on holiday in Port de Pollença can order his familiar beans on toast for breakfast then so can a Belgian engineer find a selection of his national brews in a Sóller Port bar. The larger foreign communities cater to their countrymen in seaside housing estates or apartment blocks. A foreign resident or timeshare owner can call upon one of his own nationality to fix the satellite dish, tame the plumbing, mow the lawn, give him a medical checkup, deal with the Spanish bureaucracy or massage his sunburned shoulders. Like the Latin American communities in Miami or New York, there's no need to learn the local language; there are foreign-language newspapers, websites, radio shows, religious services, Rotary Club meetings, jumble sales, AA encounter groups – any facility imaginable to avoid unnecessary contact with the inhabitants of Planet Majorca. I've always felt very uncomfortable when chance or business has taken me through the airlock into one of these bubbles, especially if it is full of Britons, with whom I have so much yet so little in common; to me it's as awkward as bumping into one's ex-wife's parents in a restaurant.

For the holidaymakers who want to venture outside their protective beachside bubble and see how the Majorcan humanoids live, there are organized excursions to an Andalusian Fiesta, the Pirate Adventure and Eldorado, a typical Wild West town.

Only once have I ventured into one of these 'theme parks', in the company of two musicians. After a concert we were introduced to the owner of one of the large Majorcan *possessions*, large estates, called Son Termens. He invited us to a free supper and show at El Comte Mal, a place I'd seen advertised for years but never dreamed of visiting. Below the beautiful old farm buildings he'd built a cavernous breeze-block edifice whose floodlit façade imitates an antique castle, complete with fluttering flags, arrow slits and battlements. El Comte Mal, 'the Evil Count', offered an unbeatable package: 'Bus from Hotel + Supper + Show + Consumation = 2,000 ptas'.

My Deux Chevaux van was the only car in the huge parking lot, cowering at the end of a row of monstrous buses, each emanating a greenish glow, indicating that their drivers were catching up on their sleep. For the drivers, often working sixteen-hour shifts punctuated by forty winks here and there, a long night's work stretches ahead. Once the gaggle of tourists have been returned – some drunk as skunks, others vomiting, many snoring – to their hotels, the drivers have to face the night-flight shuttle to the airport.

The theme of this supper + show is a jousting match, which may or may not have been a sport in medieval Majorca. My friends and I have to *exqueeze-me* our way to our seats on the Yellow section of the grandstand, beside the Green and facing the Blue and Red benches across the jousting court. Each bench has a little ledge before it that serves as a dining table. In this historical spirit, the main course is a quarter roast chicken that is pulled to pieces by the tourist, who has now been reduced by time travel to a coarse serf. The finger-food system is a good way to cut costs, the local impresarios' answer to the travel agencies cutting prices.

Our benches cheer on the Yellow Knight. At the head of the jousting strip, in the Royal Box, is an actor representing the 'Comte Mal'; at his right hand is the Comtessa. Behind me I overhear a Coronation Street accent; an old dear is telling her daughter:

'Look, luv, lookit the Count. Inne handsome? Las' year when we came, the Count was a lot older, weren't 'e? . . . the old bugger one must've died, an' 'is son's innerited. Oo, and there's a new Countess too; in't she gorgeous? P'raps the old dear died as well.'

Our Yellow Knight bites the dust convincingly; tonight it's the Red Knight's turn to receive the Count and Countess's blessing as well as cheering and footstomping from the Red Sector opposite, while we Yellows boo and hiss.

'Wot a shame. We gave up jousting a long time ago in England, din' we?'

Having seen nothing of the island but the airport, motorway, hotel and beach, there's no reason why tourists shouldn't imagine that, outside their bubbles, we island peasants live in the fifteenth century and resolve our differences by donning primary-colour outfits and knocking each other off our steeds.

Before the fake medieval castle was added, the huge old farmhouse of Son Termens was one of the pioneers of the *Mallorca Typical* industry. At first the only theme was food, wine, and Majorcan dancing. The tourists were seated at trestle tables fifty yards long; an army of waiters would first parade a few roast suckling pigs on trays past the diners, before distributing the plateloads of pork with the deftness of croupiers dealing cards. Of course the suckling pigs were for show; what was really served was the old sow. Giant vats of pugnacious red wine refilled a never-ending stream of *porrones*, glass decanters with a pointed spout. Everybody would try their hand at directing the thin jet of wine into their mouths, usually staining their clothes. At this point the photographer and his assistant would work their way along the tables. The assistant would step up behind the surprised holidaymaker, holding his jaw open with the left hand – like a vet giving a dog a worming-pill – and with the other direct the jet of wine at the back of the tourist's throat. He'd take his left hand away for a split second for the photographer to take the shot. Half an hour later, the pickled victim would be obliged to buy a portrait of his prowess with the *porrón* for a 'mere' two hundred pesetas; few were in a fit state to refuse.

Before I met my wife Carmen, she and her previous husband had a different business going at Son Termens, selling the 'typical antique *mallorquin canyet*'. This rustic instrument, hardly known on the island, was in fact typical of an Andalusian harvest festival and consisted of a ten-inch length of thick bamboo with a six-inch slit along its length. By grasping the base and rubbing the other palm across it, the two loose halves would slap together; with practice one could lay down a clackety-clack rhythm. The *cañas* were dirt cheap, produced in their thousands by an enterprising Andalusian gypsy in his Palma garage. The only local thing about it was the *Souvenir de Mallorca* decal stuck to it, featuring two Majorcan dancers. Carmen's team would intercept the tourists staggering from the dining room to the dance floor and sell hundreds of these 'antique *canyets* very cheap [despite a hundred per cent mark-up] souvenir for you friends' in an evening. An hour's work at Son Termens brought in more than their daytime jobs, and Carmen's seven-month pregnancy won her some big tips.

It is a shame that so many holidaymakers only see the island through an alcoholic haze, getting duty-free drunk on the outward flight and not sobering up until they fumble for their front-door keys two weeks later. A tipsy tourist is happy to tip and doesn't notice the shoddy rooms and bad service, but he can be a hazard to himself (every year dozens of foreigners topple to their deaths off their hotel balconies or drown in the pool) or to others on the road – especially the British who forget which side to drive on. My friend Juan Rigo foolhardily once risked cutting a blind corner on his BSA motorcycle; in the opposite direction came a hire car driven by a woozy Englishman. Luckily for both parties, the Brit was driving on the wrong side of the road, a classic case of two lefts making a right. A few yards from this corner, where the coast road between Deià and Valldemossa winds through a copse on the edge of a sharp escarpment high above the sea, a row of pine trees planted just below the road seems to act as a safety barrier. One of them has a curious kink in it that bears witness to a near-tragedy that occurred in the 1970s. As the story goes, a drunken passenger on a tour bus got out of his seat, put his hands over the driver's eyes and asked 'Guess who?' The bus swerved off the road and slammed into the pine tree, killing the driver and the drunk outright but saving the other passengers from plunging a thousand feet to the sea. Over the years, the pine tree has grown and the kink in the trunk is now about ten feet above the road level.

As a child, tourist buses were the bane of my life, belching black diesel fumes into my face on my way to school, destroying the Dinky-car roadways my friends and I traced in the dirt of the soft shoulders. The sixty-seaters had to take the sharp bends so wide that I'd be forced into the ditch on my bike. Twenty or thirty buses a day would pass the house, slowing down as the tour guide's voice could be heard over the megaphone pointing out the 'thousand-year-old' olive tree in the shape of a bird's nest and the home of the 'famous American novelist Robertson'. The guides would invent stories about landmarks to be seen out of the right-hand windows to divert the tourists' attention from the sickening sheer drops on the left.

In my own Child's Crusade against tourism I would place old tin cans or rude drawings in the bird's-nest olive tree and toss water-filled balloons over the wall at passing buses. I once climbed a tree overhanging the road to dump a basketload of gravel on a sixty-seater as it passed below me; it made as much noise as the proverbial skeletons copulating on a corrugated-iron roof. The driver slammed on the brakes and leapt out screaming blue murder, but I managed to hide behind the wall, realizing I had gone too far and vowing never again to attack a tourist.

Majorcans are well aware that their economy no longer depends on sheep, pigs, or goats but upon the travel business. Many treat it as a new kind of seasonal livestock farming; flocks of these pink bipeds are fattened in battery hotels and roasted on the beaches to improve their colour before being re-exported to their countries of origin. To keep them in shape, they are encouraged to roam freely around the countryside, sometimes alone in hired cars, sometimes in schools of cyclists or herds of jeeps. On the roads the locals treat them with the same mute tolerance with which an African villager will observe a herd of elephants or wildebeest thundering past. Yet the only evidence of xenophobic feeling I've noticed among the islanders is directed not at the holidaymakers but at those who upset the rural way of life by buying property in the farming communities and fencing off ancestral rights of way. But even this kind of hostility has never reached the levels of Corsica or Wales; no holiday homes have actually been burned down in Majorca. Foreigners are, at the worst, considered *beneits* or simpletons, and not fully responsible for their actions; the word stems from *beneït*, 'blessed'. I have a lot less patience with hired Noddy cars whose drivers think they are in Toyland, stopping on blind curves to take a photo of the breathtaking view.

A particularly dangerous time of year on the roads is the cyclist season around Easter, before the summer heat sets in and while Northern Europe is still too cold and wet to train. The teams of phosphorescent lycra suits bloom at the same time as the poppies and add an extra splash of colour to the countryside, but they try the patience of the local drivers who can't overtake a snake of thirty cyclists puffing up a winding road or a follow-the-leader safari of open jeeps who refuse to let their ranks be broken by other traffic.

The Balearic Government, aware that the local population is now beginning to weary of having to put up with this sometimes arrogant behaviour, launched a campaign with the slogan *Un Turista, un Amigo*'– A Tourist, a Friend'. My friend Román Piña paraphrased this in his hilarious novel *Un Turista, un Muerto* ('A Tourist, a Corpse') in which a local crime reporter uncovers a plot by the Majorcan Rural Liberation Front to rid the island of this neo-colonialism by hijacking a charter flight and crashing it against a hotel. (The book was written before the 11 September attacks.)

However, the only Majorcan I've heard speak openly

against tourism was a butcher from Santa Maria who thought things were made too easy for visitors. 'We are led to believe that these people are paying us a compliment by choosing our beautiful island as the place to spend their holidays. That's a lie: most of them don't even know which part of the world they're in. If anybody *really* wanted to come here, they'd be issued with a parachute and told by the stewardess: "We are now flying over Majorca. Anybody wishing to visit the island may bale out now."'

# 4

# Parrots in the Classroom

I had a two-tone primary education. In the morning my mother would teach me at home in English following the syllabus provided by the Parents' National Educational Union; in the afternoons I'd go to the Deià Boys' School to study the National Curriculum. The sing-song method was at the heart of the Spanish primary educational system. Not only the multiplication tables but also the names of the Capital Cities, the Glorious Exploits of the National Crusade, and even the Ten Commandments were learned by the class repeating the lesson in unison. The tune was always the same: the four opening notes of 'Silent Night' (G–A–G–E), the scansion of the first two notes varying to fit the lesson at hand, the final two dragged out for emphasis.

This educational model, clearly adapted from a method for teaching parrots, was as well suited to both the Fascist and the Roman Catholic doctrines, which demanded blind faith and no questions asked. Even twenty years after Franco's victory, when I began school, education was mostly in the hands of the clergy. A great number of the previous generation of schoolteachers, those with republican leanings, had fled into exile or been shot. Few of those left could be trusted to instill the National Spirit into Spain's youth or to divulge such truths as 'The Jews drink Christian blood', 'Human liberty only leads to anarchy and despotism', or 'The Enemies of Spain are seven: liberalism, democracy, Judaism, Freemasonry, Marxism, capitalism and separatism, all defeated in our Great Crusade, although not totally annihilated . . .'

The National Curriculum followed the precept 'mine not to reason why, mine just to do or die'. To know was more important than to understand. Any religious query – such as 'If Christ rose on the third day, why is Easter Sunday two days after Good Friday?' – was answered with '*Doctores tiene la Iglesia . . .*'. This was short for 'The Church has Doctors of Theology who could answer you, but this is not the time or place to go into it.'

The Deià girls were taught by the Franciscan nuns, who also attended the needy and gave injections, but we boys had a lay schoolmaster. He was no less strict; any backtalk could earn us a penitence of half an hour 'facing the wall with your arms outstretched like Jesus on the Cross', a standard punishment. If your arms dropped a few degrees below the horizontal, each upturned palm would be smacked with a ruler or a bible would be placed in each hand for added penitence. Those unlikely to move on to a higher education at least built up strong arm muscles.

This politico-theological education eventually disappeared along with the dictatorship, as did the classroom pictures of the Generalissimo and the Sacred Heart, a decade after I'd left to go to an English boarding school. Yet for adults of my generation and the previous one, the old *na-na-ni-ni-na-no* melody plays every time someone kicks our subconscious jukebox; you will hear a shopkeeper absentmindedly humming the old familiar times-table melody as he does his mental arithmetic. A facsimile of our standard elementary school textbook *El Florido Pensíl* – 'The Flowering Arbour' – recently became a bestseller (and was turned into a musical and a film) transporting us back to a world broken up into little singsong Eternal Truths.

The old school melody is especially brought to life around Christmas, but not because of its similarity with 'Silent Night'; I doubt if one in a hundred Spaniards have noticed the coincidence, as I hadn't until I tried to describe it in words. No, it's revived by *El Gordo de Navidad*, 'the Christmas Fatso'. This is the nickname of the National Lottery draw on 22 December, the biggest regular lottery in the world. Although there are a hundred lottery draws a year, as well as the football pools and the daily *cupón* of the National Institute for the Blind, *El Gordo de Navidad* has been, since 1892, everyone's dream passport to an early retirement. The dictatorship had banned any other kind of betting for money, even card games, on moral grounds, but didn't dare – and couldn't afford – to ban the lottery. Democracy brought back casinos and introduced bingo halls, which, after their initial popularity, are now patronized mainly by Spain's large number of chronic ludopaths.

The average Spanish household spends about 200 euros on *décimos* (tenth shares of a lottery number) in the Christmas draw. Many complete numbers are bought up by clubs and associations to be sold off in smaller fractions; nearly every neighbourhood bar or shop will raffle a Christmas hamper among their clients, the winning number having to coincide with the last digits of *El Gordo*. On 22 December the average Spanish wallet will contain twenty or thirty tickets of different colours and sizes: 'A two-euro share in Number 13013 of the Christmas Draw, in benefit of the end-of-year students' trip of the pupils of the Federico García Lorca Secondary School' or 'if coinciding with the last three figures of the Christmas Fatty the bearer will win the magnificent Christmas hamper provided by *La Vaca Loca* Butchers'.

From 10 a.m. onwards on 22 December business slows down as millions of people tune into the radio or turn on the TV. Everywhere you go, the air is filled with children's voices repeating that same singsong melody from primary school.

Call:   *Veinte mil setecientos diecisiete.*
Response: *Ochenta millones deee peeeeseeetaaaaaas.*

These are the children from the San Ildefonso School for Orphans in Madrid, the 'innocent hands' who have had the honour of 'singing the lottery' since 1771. The children learned to 'sing' the winning numbers and the quantity of the prize money like any other lesson; twenty years after the educational reform, the melody lives on. The lyrics and the rhythm, however, have recently changed: the four syllables of *de pesetas* have been reduced to the two of *de euros*, but the amount betted has risen to 2,300 million euros – at €20 a *décimo*.

*El Gordo* is an important part of Christmas, much more deeply ingrained than recent imports like Santa Claus, Christmas trees or Christmas cards (the last are known as *crismas*; singular, *un crisma*). Numbers for *El Gordo* are on sale from August, allowing people time to buy theirs in the 'luckiest' town or lottery stall – 'If you're going to Segovia, bring me back a *décimo*'– to give and exchange them with friends or family. All the *décimos* of a given number are usually limited to one lottery stall, which can lead obsessive punters to track down their favourite number to some distant village across the country. The Catalan village of Sort (Luck) is always the first to sell its numbers; one lottery vendor in Madrid is so popular that she has her own website to allow people to reserve their numbers. Lottery vendors, like bakers, are under the patronage of San Pancracio, whose effigy behind the counter is supplied daily with a sprig of fresh parsley. One of Palma's most popular characters was Alfons 'Es Loter', a gruff-looking man who used to hawk his numbers all over town, always following the same route, arguing over football with the fishwives in the Olivar market, where a portrait still hangs in his memory.

Favourite places to buy tickets are those that have been repeatedly lucky in the lottery or that are generally seen to be deserving luck, like Galicia after the recent oil spill. Many people buy lottery numbers as part of an informal *peña* or circle with their workmates or card-playing cronies at the bar; any winnings are shared out equally. After one *peña* took a member to court for not sharing out his winnings, a judge set a legal precedent by recognizing verbal agreements of this kind as legally binding.

Wherever *El Gordo* sheds its pounds, camera crews rush to film the scenes of wild joy, champagne flowing, incredulous faces, *peñas* arm in arm jumping up and down singing 'We are the Champions'. Within hours, the full lists are on the street in special newspaper editions and for the rest of the afternoon people will pore over them in search of one of the thousands of smaller prizes known as 'hailstones'. If you don't even get your money back – in theory half the tickets receive some prize – you have until Twelfth Night to buy another chance in the second most important draw, *El Niño*.

In Brazil, a poor child's dreams of escape from poverty traditionally depend on his football skills; in Harlem, New York, on the boxing ring; in England on a number one hit; but in Spain, you don't need to work in order to dream of being a millionaire: you just have to afford a *décimo* and pray. Spanish fatalism – or irresponsible optimism – is summed up in one of those Sixties hits, *La Vida es una Tómbola* ('Life is a Tombola'). Even the army would use a bingo wheel to choose which of the conscripts would be exempt from military service. This is a society that runs on hopes and dreams, where the Protestant work ethic is frowned upon, even though today Spaniards spend more hours at work than most other Europeans.

Many people subscribe year after year to a particularly significant lottery number: an important date or the last digits of their ID card. All numbers ending in 13 are well subscribed to. There are beautiful numbers and ugly numbers, numbers that are sought out by some because they have never won a prize and rejected by others for the same reason. A pop singer's birthdate can provoke a pilgrimage of fans to a remote village lottery stall. The Bin Laden number (11901) was the most sought after for the *Gordo* of 2001, the last draw before the euro arrived, but it won not a peseta.

Lately it has become evident that the already rich and famous win more big important prizes than would be statistically expected. It is common knowledge that a big win is a convenient way to justify ill-gotten gains and there are plenty of friendly bankers who will mediate between a millionaire who needs to keep his tax returns modest and a prizewinner who's willing to sell his lottery number for 10 per cent more than its face value in cash.

Spain has the oldest and richest gaming tradition in the world – the first numbers game was introduced in 1763. The National Lottery was established in 1812 and approved two weeks before the nation's first constitution, which shows that we've always had our priorities clear. The Spanish have always been lax paying tax, and the lottery revenue has helped to replenish the national coffers after such disasters as the Cuban War.

Although gambling and lotteries are illegal in Cuba and in many US States where Cubans have settled, their Spanish heritage has helped their secret numbers rackets to flourish. As illegal activities tend to create their own myths, the Cubans have a fully developed numerology in which any symbol, from a key to a cow, whether dreamed or witnessed, has a numerical equivalent. With the recent wave of Cuban immigrants, this system is now gaining adepts among the Spanish.

The force of luck must be counterbalanced by another force, hence the concept of *gafe* (pronounced gah-fey), 'jinxed'. Someone who is *gafe* always arrives on the platform as the metro is pulling out, is struck twice by lightning, or finds himself one digit short of the big prize. If you make a gloomy prediction, you'll be told: 'Don't be *gafe*' – you bring bad luck not only upon yourself but upon those around you. One difference between Carlos Menem (ex-president of Argentina) and King Juan Carlos is that whenever the former turns up to support his local or national team, it loses; when Juan Carlos attends, Spain usually wins. Menem has even been asked by football-club owners and the national team not to attend decisive games.

Most Spaniards are much less superstitious than Britons, excepting bullfighters, who are notoriously so. In Hispanic culture the Friday the 13th jinx applies to Tuesday 13th but only in the case of journeys and weddings. Before the cynical reader points to this inconsistency as proof that superstition is claptrap, let me explain: Tuesday (*Martes*) is the day of Mars, Roman god of war; Friday is named after Freya, the Norse goddess of war, so theologically there is no contradiction. Thirteen is the number of lunar months in the year and the number of days between the new and full moon – clearly an anti-matriarchal bias. But I have yet to discover why Spanish cats only have seven lives.

The village school offered no education beyond the age of twelve and only a couple of my schoolmates continued their studies. Most of them began to work. Three years later, while I was still a schoolboy coming home for the holidays, my classmates had become brandy-drinking, cigarrette-smoking card players who went off hunting on the weekend. There was no point of contact between our worlds. Rather than go to a school in Palma, I was sent to England, where I discovered that, for all her efforts, my mother's PNEU classes had left me unprepared for a British school. I had finally understood how to do sums with pounds, shillings, and pence but I was lost when a maths problem involved cricket scores, which neither of my parents understood; I'd never even held a cricket bat.

Luckily I wasn't thrown in at the deep end. Before being sent to boarding school, I spent two terms at a day school in London while my father travelled to Oxford to lecture as Professor of Poetry. But even this was a big shock. Runny-nosed and shivering in my itchy school cap and matching blazer, in my aertex shirt and my grey corduroy shorts held up with an elastic snake-belt, I looked like any other red-cheeked, purple-lipped, chapped-kneed ten-year-old brat. My *fraffly* British accent made it even more embarrassing to admit I had no idea of what to do with a conker, of the difference between hitting a six and getting six of the best, of why a rugby ball was squashed out of shape, or how to endure the shame of sharing a steaming shower with twenty other pink, squealing boys.

Boarding school, however, was more bearable, especially since mine was tolerant of individualists. My mother chose the liberal Bedales and Robert approved because the winter sport was rugby; also his friend Selwyn Jepson, the crime writer, lived nearby and could act as my guardian. Since Selwyn had negotiated the sale of reams of Robert's work drafts – basically the contents of the wastepaper basket – to US university libraries, there was enough money for the fees and air fares. At Bedales there were many overseas students, so I didn't feel such an impostor; but it was trau-matic for me to come face to face with the dirty British underbelly: jockstraps, cross-country runs, apple-pie beds, cold baths, athlete's foot, white sliced bread and margarine.

The Bedales Junior School had a strong musical focus so I could take refuge behind my guitar without being singled out. On the lawn stood a wooden climbing frame, known as the Jungle Gym. In Spain, the only concession to children in a public park would be a couple of swings and some sand; an artificial tree was quite new to me. That's where I'd spend most of my free time, with a couple of friends playing Kingston Trio songs – 'Tom Dooley', 'The Sloop John B' – and being continuously sneered at by the more mature girls of our class.

Although the guitar's public image had begun to change thanks to Andrés Segovia and Hank Marvin of the Shadows, the British still considered it a skiffle instrument, on a par with the washboard. But having studied classical guitar and because I could read music, I was put in the orchestra and given a violin part to play. I felt ridiculous having to pluck plodding semibreves while my fellow violinists drew them flowingly out with their bows. The only place for a guitar in an orchestra, I realized, was out front and in the hands of Segovia, Julian Bream, or John Williams.

But perched on the Jungle Gym with Perry on vocals and George thumping some cardboard boxes, we began to work out some easy pop songs: 'I Like It' and 'From Me To You'. The little credibility this repertoire afforded us was squandered on our absurd name, the Scanties. Trying to evoke the concept of uniqueness, we had no idea that *scanties* was another name for underwear.

My guitar continued to be my shield in the senior school, where I met Robin Lodge, another blond British foreigner, who had lived in Malaysia and British Guyana. We shared an outsider's perspective that made it easy to poke fun at the school institutions and together we began manipulating the lyrics to Top Ten songs and performing them at the end of term variety show. Being used to swimming in warm seas, our obvious target was that ghastly invention, the gym swim. Gym swims began in an open-air pool when the water temperature rose above 18 C – ambient temperature was of no consequence – and we used every possible ruse to get excused or sent to the sanatorium. Bob Pullen showed no mercy, addressing each purple-lipped, shivering child as 'my lad'. Paraphrasing the Beatles:

> You better swim for your life if you can, little lad
> Hide yourself in the San, little lad
> If Pullen gets the upper hand, you're a gonner, little lad

Or the Troggs' 'Wild Thing':

> Gym swim
> You make my head spin
> You make everything
> Hooomid . . .

The other object of our criticism was school food. To Country Joe McDonald's anti-Vietnam 'Feel Like I'm Fixin' to Die Rag':

> And it's one, two, three, what are we starving for?
> Don't ask me, I don't give a damn
> Next stop is veal and ham . . .

Bedales' excellent music department had fourteen sound-proofed practice rooms, each with its own piano, but no guitar teacher. My lessons with Juanito Coll had been reduced to one a week during holidays. I enjoyed getting to grips with ballsy pieces like Villa-Lobos' Prelude No.1, but as happens to so many teenagers, my classical training was losing out to other kinds of music. The steep hill of adolescence nudges many promising classical careers into the ditch. It wasn't the classical music itself that alienated me as much as the feeling that you're out there on your own when all you want is to belong. Even playing in an orchestra couldn't compare with the feeling of tribal communion brought on by the two-chord riff from the Kinks' 'You Really Got Me'. And adolescence is about belonging; the need to excel comes later, by which time many students have dropped their music studies.

Classical guitar had been a good discipline to train my fingers, but any performance seemed more like sitting an exam than sharing one's gift; the yardstick was how closely you reproduced the ideas set down on paper centuries ago. Even a priest could improvise a sermon around a chapter from the Bible, but a classical musician was condemned to repeat the same dogma for the rest of his or her life. He or she could vary the tempo and the emphasis slightly, but never change a note. That would be sacrilege, like misquoting the word of God. I found it difficult to keep practising my classical pieces; they seemed so predictable. They offered none of the musical excitement I felt upon discovering the similarity between 'The House of the Rising Sun' and 'Hey Joe', chord progressions that could have been written by Bach, but which were free to evolve. Of course many classical composers had improvised over popular tunes, but even their impromptu doodlings had been finally set in stone: 'Variations on a Folk Theme', to be reproduced note for note. Music, the most ephemeral of the arts, was a living, organic entity that had to grow, and classical music seemed comatose. A pop record was just that, a record of an event; however, the event itself was not the recording session but the context in which you first consciously heard the song, and what you did with it afterwards.

The school eventually found me a guitar teacher living close by. My heart sank on meeting this quiet, sallow-looking man in a brown tweed jacket. On the third or fourth lesson, he told me to keep practising the piece we were working on while he went to the loo, but he returned to find me playing a twelve-bar blues instead. I looked up guiltily but he said 'Keep going' and, picking up his guitar, began to play some very tasty jazz phrases over my chords. I was even more surprised when he said, 'Okay, take it away!' and we swapped roles. Soon we were spending most of each class jamming over blues chords. The day the head of the music department overheard one of our classes, my teacher was out on his ear, but by then I had learned a great deal about improvising alongside another musician, how to anticipate his moves, when to back him up and when to leave him space. During those sessions I discovered that what I most enjoyed was taking part in that wordless conversation that occurs between musicians. If I have improved very little technically since then it's because I never practise on my own; I only take the guitar down off the wall when I play with other people.

I'd begun to broaden my musical tastes as a member of the Printing Works, a semi-autonomous institution that picked two members from each new year's arrivals. I'd already learned to set type and my father had printed his own books, but the admission requirements of this select club involved other aptitudes: discretion and a streak of anarchism. Housed in a garage on the school estate, the Bedales Press financed its illicit activities by printing cards and stationery for outside customers. The spaces behind the typecases were packed with fermenting cider, nettle beer, and elderflower champagne, and packets of Drum tobacco were stashed behind the ink rollers. However, few staff ever came in to investigate.

Printing the school play programmes usually meant an all-night run in two shifts. The first shift left the dorms before midnight via the fire escape, dressed in dark clothes to avoid detection; they returned at 4 a.m. to wake up the second shift, which worked until breakfast time. A working brotherhood, cups of instant coffee, and folk-blues music on the gramophone sowed the seeds for the formation of a new rock band. We began to play at end-of-term dances where nobody demanded much of us; we were happy to ride the wave of the British blues revival and simply get people dancing. Being onstage never gained me points with the girls; in fact I'd have to watch stoically as the apple of my eye slow-danced with my rivals. When the band took a break, the staff DJ would frustrate my own chances by playing waltzes, quicksteps, and the Dashing White Sergeant. Enough to make a young man play the blues.

Juan had lent me his electric guitar, known as the *Yubagarra*, a counterfeit Stratocaster his friend Mito had built in his family's carpentry shop in Palma. Mito had copied it from a Fender catalogue but, because he didn't have the measurements, it ended up being three-quarter size, proportional to my own weedy stature. Nick, the band's singer, also built his own electric guitar in the school workshop. With Jock on bass and Nigel on drums, the band was quite competent; but I have the feeling that neither we nor the other school band ever really rocked. In the wake of *Sergeant Pepper*, that didn't seem to be important; progressive rock was aimed more at the head than the feet. Listening to Hendrix, Clapton, Jimmy Page or Alvin Lee was like eating humble pie; I preferred playing songs within my reach – Nick Drake, the Incredible String Band, Fairport Convention, or another folk-rock band, the ex-Bedalians Trees.

In Deià, our family friend Isla Cameron had already opened my ears to Bert Jansch and John Renbourne, and taught me some finger-picking technique; just grabbing up a guitar and improvising with a friend seemed to have great advantages over having to depend upon an unwieldy electric band.

Isla was a wonderful Scottish folk singer and actress who had brought many of her friends over from England to stay in the village: Maggie Smith, Julian Bream, Shirley Collins. My father loved Isla's rendition of Gordon Lightfoot's 'Early Morning Rain' and paraphrased the song on a postcard he sent me from New York:

> 'You can't jump a jet plane
> Same as you can a freight train –'
> But the B.O.A.C. food
> Is mighty far from good;
> I hope soon to mailia
> A post-card from Australia
> Or even from Hawaii
> As I go flying Baii . . .

Robert was very fit and robust for a man in his seventies, but having a father almost sixty years older than me wasn't easy, as I was going through that stage of adolescence in which one begins to consider death. I always breathed a sigh of relief when I identified his spidery writing on a letter in my pigeon-hole. Cecil Day-Lewis's daughter Tamasin was in my year and we sometimes joked about having grand-fathers for parents, although the age gap affected her younger brother Daniel more than her. I was his 'dorm boss' for a term, he was like a jack-in-the-box. Our fathers were also friends, both were descended from Anglo-Irish Protestant clergymen, and both had been Professors of Poetry at Oxford. I sometimes stayed overnight at the Day-Lewis's house in Greenwich on the way between Bedales and Deià. When Cecil and Robert were shortlisted for the post of Poet Laureate, Tamasin and I joked about the 'Battle of the Grandads'. Cecil won the appointment and later graciously accompanied Robert to Buckingham Palace to receive his Medal for Poetry from the Queen. This friendship was unusual in that Robert had always been one of the black sheep of the British literary establishment and preferred to nurture friendships that couldn't be soured by professional rivalry. Day-Lewis, e.e. cummings, and Robert Frost were the only well-known poets he got on with. He was tired of being continually pestered by writers for his opinion or endorsement and generally preferred to deal with 'real people' than with intellectuals.

One of these 'real people' was Spike Milligan, with whom he struck up a deep friendship after being interviewed by him for the BBC. In a letter to Spike, Robert quotes Woody Guthrie:

> Keep well and remember:
> 'They can't kill us
> we stick to the union . . .'
> – the union being an amorphous collection of people like us who are joined only by the knowledge that everyone else is really crazy.

This unlikely union appeared onstage to raise money for the Mermaid Theatre in London. The theatre's director, Bernard Miles, had organized an evening of poetry, song, and humour featuring himself, Robert, Spike and his wife Paddy, and Isla Cameron. Robert brought me along: he warned Spike that 'Tomás (aged 13) will appear and do a talking blues at the Mermaid; he fears nothing [ . . . ] A cool poet, and handles a guitar well.' I've always felt that 'handles a guitar well' is the greatest accolade I've ever received as a musician; I've never played the instrument brilliantly, but yes, I can handle it.

The evening could have been a disaster. Both Spike and Isla were fragile personalities who were prey to depressions; Robert's chaotic relationship with his tempestuous Mexican-American 'muse' Aemile was giving him an emotional roller-coaster ride and problems in the family; he had been on the verge of abandoning us and moving with her to Mexico. The structure of the Mermaid show was little more than a vague running order, but all participants were to be onstage throughout the evening and free to improvise or interrupt. The first half was mainly musical, with Paddy singing light opera and Isla accompanying herself on guitar to a haunting anti-war song, 'Johnny I Hardly Knew You'. Robert launched into 'Abide With Me' accompanied by the jazz pianist Alan Clare. I was due to begin the second half, but a boy of about eleven, Danny Black, found his way backstage and asked to be allowed to read a poem; he went on first and was given a chair to stand on so he could reach the microphone. Spike introduced me as 'the youngest of the Graves progeny'; then, with a sidelong glance at my white-haired father, added 'It is, I've seen the certificates! All right, man, get with it.'

I grabbed my guitar and got with it. I'd been researching my family tree for a school history project, and had set some of it to the tune of 'Bob Dylan's 115th Dream':

Well my father is an eighth child and I'm an eighth as
    well
But that is not my sole excuse for what I have to tell:
It's that Lloyd George Knew My Father and my father
    knew him too
And his father did the same, in fact these men each
    other knew.

Well my father's father saw the light in 1846
In Dublin in the famine year, a bad time for us
    Micks . . .

After the applause, Spike came up behind me and
announced: 'This is the only organized bit of the evening.
I'm supposed to say [*Ned Seagoon voice*] "Tell me, son,
what about that other song?"'

That was my cue to launch into a talking blues about
the hardships of school life, especially gym swims. (A 'talking blues', popularized by Woody Guthrie during the
Depression, is the American folk predecessor of rap.) My
teen angst had its chance to vent its rage at the absurdities
of English summer sports: 'You're all welcome to visit my
school on Parents' Day and watch me play cricket. You can
cheer me on as I float over the finishing line on my wickets.'

Bernard Miles read some amusing anecdotes in his
scholarly voice and then apologized for not being 'much of
an ad-libber', to which Spike retorted, 'I 'ad liver for lunch!'
The evening then shifted into a more serious poetical mode.
Robert introduced a poem that 'nowadays people would
call metaphysic . . . I wouldn't know, I never met a physic
myself.' He then asked Isla to read his poem 'Counting the
Beats', which held the audience spellbound. To me, this sort

of mixed and improvised performance was familiar from the Deià summers, but the Mermaid audience demanded so many curtain calls that the show was allowed to go on for another half-hour, an unprecedented occurrence there.

This kind of open-ended flexibility shown by the theatre management, by simply providing space for the magical to occur, was probably what I most missed about Spain. In England, superstition is much more ritualized than in Spain because everyday life is too ordered and mundane for magic to occur. The famous *mañana* syndrome common to most temperate climates, including India where Spike grew up, is not just a laziness imposed by the midday sun, nor is it a desire to procrastinate for the sake of it. It simply recognizes that we should live the here and now to the full; between delight and drudgery, it's better to postpone the latter.

The obsession with punctuality and delivery dates in the less temperate climates is perfectly understandable when a society has to endure hard winters and short daylight hours. As you approach the tropics, the seasonal differences diminish and time loses its urgency. This would explain to Europeans and North Americans running businesses in tropical countries why their employees don't return to work until they've spent the last cent of their first paycheque. 'Saving up for a rainy day' is a northern concept produced by a seasonal agriculture that depends on hoarding whereas much of the Third World's agriculture is hand to mouth. We tend to see hunter-gatherers as a distant stage in human history, but it still exists in much of the world. In India the castes that refused to wound Mother Earth by tilling the soil were slowly edged out of their jungle habitats and have logically turned to begging, which is the contemporary guise of hunter-gatherers.

In temperate Spain and the islands, the concept of time is as elastic as a Rolex watch-strap. The Catalans seem to have adopted the Protestant work ethic and the northern sense of cooperation but also the Germanic sense of time, even to the point of referring to 9:30 as 'two quarters of ten'. Nobody in the Balearics uses this system and in fact hours are often dispensed with altogether. Rural Majorcans have five words to classify different stages of the morning and as many for the afternoon and evening; these are usually sufficient to set an appointment. Most people arrange to meet in bars, so nobody minds much if the other is late. In Spanish, *la mañana* means the morning; without the article *la*, it means tomorrow. The word comes from the Latin *hora maneana*, early hour. The word for 'tomorrow' was the pure Latin *cras* until the fifteenth century when the phrase *cras maneana* ('tomorrow first thing in the morning') was abbreviated to *mañana*, paving the way for centuries of misunderstandings and pro*cras*tinations.

# 5

# Franco Unplugged

It was the summer of '75 in Barcelona and the bus from London, with my girlfriend Wendy aboard, was late. I had driven down through France earlier, having finished my three-year course in typographic design at the London College of Printing, and was staying with Lucia and Ramón before catching the boat over to Majorca. Also waiting for the London bus in Plaza Universidad was a Catalan girl who ambled over and struck up a conversation with me. Two hours later we had covered every topic from politics to pre-marital sex. As the bus finally drew in, we exchanged the standard kiss on both cheeks as we then each went to embrace our respective mates. What impressed me was the spontaneity and openness of people on the street like this girl, a sense of complicity generated by a common enemy, the dictatorship. It was a feeling that had probably disappeared from complacent, liberal London after the Blitz. Although it was nothing more than simple human contact, I now realize that was the moment that I consciously took the decision to make my home in Spain.

Six months later, Wendy was back at the Chelsea College of Art and I was sharing a large, heavily furnished flat near the Camp Nou, Barcelona FC's stadium, with Michael, a childhood friend from Deià who was studying medicine, and two other foreign students, Kate and Missy. We had signed the inventory itemizing in detail 'One tableau of the Last Supper; One grandfather clock; One figure of Santa Lucía, carrying her eyes on a tray; One toothpick-holder inscribed Souvenir de Benidorm; One plastic lavatory brush . . .'. The only change we had made to the rancid bourgeois flat was to castrate the clock by stuffing a rag into the bell, reducing its baleful reverberating bongs to asthmatic tonks. From then on the flat was known as Ca'n Tonk, *Ca'n* being the Catalan and Majorcan equivalent to *chez*. We were four young longhairs playing house, enjoying the incongruence of living on a shoestring in the midst of this ostentatious Spanish decor with its heavy glass-topped furniture and fake-crystal chandeliers.

The landlord was a young executive from the nearby SEAT car factory who, like anybody working in a state-run corporation, owed his position to the regime. He had warned us that he would be bringing the removal men at 7 a.m. on 20 November to take away the family safe that occupied half my bedroom. The wink he directed at Michael and me obviously meant 'Don't say I didn't warn you if I surprise you lads in the girls' beds.' It was difficult for the *macho ibérico* to conceive of cohabitation without sex.

As he let himself into the flat at daybreak, followed by two burly men in overalls, we each emerged bleary eyed but decent from our respective bedrooms only to be confronted by the news we had been expecting for weeks.

'Chaps,' announced our landlord in a faltering voice, 'I

heard it on the radio three quarters of an hour ago. Tragedy has befallen our fatherland. Our leader, the Generalissimo, died last night.' Then with a sob, he croaked, '*¡Viva Franco!*' Nobody replied, but we all put on our most sombre expressions. I caught the eye of one of the removal men who was also obviously making an effort not to crack up laughing and drop the safe on his mate's toes. As soon as it had been lowered out of the window and they had all left, we let out whoops of joy. 'Champagne for breakfast! It's been chilling in the fridge for long enough now!' We could hear similar muffled cries of joy and corks popping in neighbouring flats as people woke up and turned on the radio; down on the street passers-by were playing it cool, trying not to grin too openly, but you could see a lightness of step uncommon at that hour of the morning.

For two weeks everybody had been aware that the old man was on a life-support system, only kept ticking over by a team of twenty-four doctors, the *equipo médico habitual* of the news bulletins, in spite of his family's wish for him to die in peace. One of many jokes being whispered in all the bars told of the incombustible dictator on his deathbed. Hundreds of his diehard supporters could be heard chanting outside the hospital. Franco turns to his wife:

'What are all those people saying, Doña Carmen?'

'They're chanting *adiós, Franco, adiós.*'

'Why? Where are they all going?'

But there were still some loose ends to be tied before the Generalissimo could be freed to occupy his expected place at God's right hand; during that fortnight of agony, a dozen magazines had been taken off the newsstands by the police for having speculated about the succession.

Despite having opened the country up to tourism, the

Spanish dictatorship was ruthless to the end. The recent political execution of a young Catalan anarchist, garrotted in the Barcelona prison despite the Pope's plea for clemency, caused an international outcry, so it was not surprising that when they gave a Franco a state funeral, nobody came ... except for Augusto Pinochet, Imelda Marcos, King Hussein and Nelson Rockefeller. This international snub to the remaining Francoist Government was a great morale booster for the democratic parties waiting in the wings to be legalized, some of whose members had formed a part of the defeated Republican Government and spent forty years in exile.

Franco's death is probably the most significant single event in Spain's recent history; but the armed Nationalist uprising that brought about the downfall of the Second Republic and put him in power in 1939 caused the deepest trauma Spanish society has ever experienced, and is still the subject of dozens of books, documentaries, TV series, and films. The war inspired Orwell's *Homage to Catalonia*, Hemingway's *For Whom the Bell Tolls* and Ken Loach's *Land and Freedom*.

November 20th had been a suitable day for the dictator to be unplugged –*oonploogit*, as it's now pronounced in post-MTV Spain – from his life-support system. It was already a national day of mourning, for on 20 November 1936 the Fascist ideologue José Antonio Primo de Rivera had been executed. José Antonio's father had led, with King Alfonso XIII's blessing, the 1923 coup d'état against the First Republic, but his military dictatorship floundered seven years later precipitating local elections that the Socialists won by a landslide. The Second Republic was declared in 1931 and King Alfonso went into exile in Italy. A new constitution was passed recognizing full women's rights and denying class privileges; and a divorce law was approved that was at the time the most progressive in Europe.

Much of the Socialists' support came from the fact that they recognized the identity of the 'historical nations' of Spain, those that had their own distinct language and culture: Galicia, the Basque Country, and Catalonia. The Republic granted each its own statutes and local parliaments within the Spanish State. Catalonia soon became one of the most progressive regions in Europe, boasting mixed schools, social and cultural services, even nudist beaches, until 1933, when the Conservatives returned to power, putting a stop to many reforms. It was in this chaotic, effervescent atmosphere, when the right to strike was invoked at any opportunity, that José Antonio founded the Falangist party with which he soon won a parliamentary seat. But two years later the Popular Front, a left-wing coalition of Socialists, Communists, and Anarchists, won the elections and resumed the reforms. This galled Franco's Nationalists into 'reconquering Spain from the Reds' –the legitimate government – much as El Cid had reconquered it from the Moors.

José Antonio had been accused of illicit possession of arms, imprisoned, and later sentenced to death for military rebellion. By this time, General Franco's uprising had extended from the colonies in North Africa to mainland Spain, but his forces arrived a little too late to save José Antonio from the firing squad. Although José Antonio hadn't supported the uprising and would have been a thorn in Franco's side, he became a martyr to the cause, an example to all Spaniards. His prison writings provided the ideology that was lacking in the Nationalist Movement, since Franco was a good strategist but no intellectual. In my childhood, José Antonio's name was everywhere, even in brass letters by the main door of the church, always followed by the word *¡¡Presente!!* His stylized profile (slicked-back hair and energetic jawline looking like an ad for Brillantina) had equal status on the classroom wall with the older, chubbier Franco; only the Crucifix and the Sacred Heart stood between them.

The Popular Front government forces spent as much energy fighting among themselves as against the Nationals, to the despair of many foreign volunteers like George Orwell who had come to defend democracy. Britain and France declined to help the legitimate Spanish Government from a military insurrection and held a 'neutral position' while the Nationalist rebels had active military support from both Hitler and Mussolini, who used Spain as a warm-up for the Second World War. The only outside help to the Government came from Moscow, but Stalin would only arm the Communist militias, although the Anarchist union had eight times as many members as the Communist Party and bore the brunt of the fighting.

After Franco's victory, King Alfonso thought the throne would again be his, but the Nationalists had no need for him and he died in exile in Rome, having abdicated in favour of his son Don Juan de Borbon. Franco, now Head of State, kept Don Juan in exile but agreed to allow his son Don Juan Carlos – the dead King's grandson – to receive his military and university education in Spain.

By 1969, with no male heir to carry on the Franco dynasty, the Generalissimo named Juan Carlos his successor as Head of State and had him declared Prince of Spain. But Franco placed the real power in the hands of his trusted Admiral Carrero Blanco. The way the Admiral saw the future, 'everything's sewn up, tightly sewn up'. However, his vision came apart at the seams when he was assassinated, two years before Franco's death. The Basque separatist group (or, as it's officially referred to today, 'the terrorist band') ETA put a bomb under a manhole cover on the route the Admiral used to take after morning Mass. His bulletproof car was blown right over a high wall and into the courtyard of a Jesuit seminary. There were many whispered jokes about the Admiral who died in the Air Force, and ETA's efficiency and daring garnered a lot of grass-roots sympathy, which they subsequently squandered with indiscriminate bombings, extortion tactics and assassinating democratically elected politicians.

Shortly after the Generalissimo's death, as he had willed, Prince Juan Carlos was crowned King. There was little public enthusiasm. To the monarchists he was a traitor for accepting the title that had been denied his father; to the leftists he was a fall guy for Franco. What nobody realized was that he had already been in contact with many political exiles, asking for their patience while he prepared the ground for their return. He was working hard to avoid his grandfather's mistakes and to ensure a smooth transition from dictatorship to democracy, a re-entry that was bound to burn out many a politician and needed a Teflon-coated head of state to see it through.

Like the Emperor Claudius, I believe Juan Carlos was at heart a republican born into a royal family; he accepted his coronation out of a sense of historical duty but probably would have wished it upon somebody else. He was also destined to reign, after the death of a despot, over a people who had come to despise authority. But he and Queen Sofía, daughter of the also exiled King Constantine of Greece, soon won over their subjects with hand-shaking tours of the country, which Franco would never have dared embark upon – he wouldn't even have sent out his double. Thanks to Juan Carlos's well-chosen team of advisers, the Spanish now had a modern, apolitical monarchy as a reference point. Having had a military education and being the commander in chief of the armed forces, the King managed to keep the generals in check while promoting reforms and steering the country towards a democracy. Six feet tall, he was truly His Royal Highness. As one diplomat declared, 'Franco was so short that, at an official reception, everyone would whisper "Has the Head of State arrived yet?" Now there's no need to ask . . . the King towers over the rest of us.' And his son is even taller.

As 1976 dawned, Barcelona was throbbing with the promise of a new future, but the transitional Government, for all its liberal image, wasn't going to let the changes get out of hand. The grey-clad riot police were at the ready to quell any demonstration, and they seemed to patrol the university campuses and factory gates permanently. Before emerging from the metro at Plaça Catalunya or the Ramblas, one had to be careful not to find oneself facing a police charge or a student stampede.

Barcelona had a head start on the rest of Spain. In the dying days of the regime, it had been privileged to have a window open to the outside world: a large number of Latin American intellectuals had settled here and the bourgeois Catalan teenagers were within an easy drive of the French border. The *gauche divine*, the well-off young leftist intellectuals and liberal professionals – architects, film-makers, writers – had their own circuit of nightspots like Bocaccio, went to London to buy clothes and to Paris to listen to singers who were banned in Spain. The less conformist set up communes in the hill villages above the city, aesthetic rather than ethic hippies. Politically, things were still sewn up but culturally the knots were slipping. Books that had been suppressed by the regime over the years began to arrive all at once, often in Mexican or Argentine editions: *Animal Farm*, Mao's 'Little Red Book', García Lorca's *A Poet in New York*, Jack Kerouac's *On the Road*, Carlos Castaneda's *Teachings of Don Juan*, and of course *The Hite Report*, Fritz the Cat, and the Furry Freak Brothers. Music, theatre, cinema – it all arrived in a rush of chronological disorder. Two of the most popular 'new' films, which had been banned since the 1940s for ridiculing Fascism, were Chaplin's *The Great Dictator* and Lubitsch's *To Be or Not to Be*.

In 1976, thousands of Spaniards had been driving over the border to Perpignan every weekend to watch *Emmanuelle* and *Last Tango in Paris*; two years later, Walerian Borowycz's sexually explicit *La Bête* could be seen in a corner cinema in downtown Barcelona. Adult cinemas were authorized shortly after. This was the time of the *destape*, or uncovering, during which any Spanish actress under fifty would do her duty in the name of democracy by consenting to at least one topless scene per film. The critical news magazine that had chronicled the transition, *Cambio 16* (fifteen proposed names had been rejected by Franco's censor until the exasperated editor proposed a 'sixteenth change' of name), was eclipsed by a new glossy weekly, *Interviu*, that hit upon an unbeatable formula of politics, investigative journalism, gore, and celebrity nudity.

My first job in Barcelona had been at a design studio in the chic but characterless Calle Tuset, which was being touted as

Barcelona's Carnaby Street. The studio was run by a Swiss graphic artist and a French-Catalan industrial designer, who spent most of the day at business meetings while the rest of the team did the donkey work. The pair founded the Barcelona Design Centre, which years later would set the city at the cutting edge of international design and advertising. I was in Barcelona too early for the design boom, just as I had been too early for punk and new wave in London.

My only claim to fame in the design world, apart from designing a logo for the Miró Foundation in Palma, is to have hand-drawn the first bar code in Spain. The Catalan manufacturer of Avecrem soup (satirized in the 1962 Birthday Play as Grave-crem) wanted to export his stock cubes to the USA, 'for which the Americans insist I print some stripes on the box'. The studio was known for doing the impossible, and I was given the job of studying the fifty-page US manual detailing the bar-code system, including laser-beam tolerances in thousandths of an inch. After weeks of calculations I drew it out by hand to poster size, reduced it photographically to a thumbnail and sent it off to the USA, where it was successfully read by a computer.

A couple of doors up the street was Barcelona's best jazz club, La Cova del Drac ('the Dragon's Cave'), a basement where Ramón often played drums with the blind jazz pianist Tete Montoliu, one of Europe's best. 'Lucky he's blind,' ran the gag, 'he doesn't realize he's not black.' Ramón was one of the first Spaniards to wear his glasses on a thong round his neck; many people assumed it to be the wire of a hearing aid. They found it logical that a blind pianist should be backed by a deaf drummer.

La Cova had been set up by a group of musicians including Guillem d'Efak, whose family was from Spanish Guinea.

'I'm black, Majorcan, and a poet,' he once said disparagingly. 'All I need is for somebody to break the news that I'm also a *xueta* [a Majorcan Jew].' La Cova was famous for its live jazz sessions, but was also one of the few clubs willing to risk allowing singers to perform in Catalan during the dictatorship.

I was lured away from Tuset Street by two friends who had been given the plum job of designing an in-flight magazine for AeroMexico. But the Spanish photographers and writers hired to provide the content had obviously spent their fortnight's assignment in Mexico sunbathing and getting drunk, so there was nothing fit to print besides the ads. The magazine folded before it even left the ground; Mexico's change of president (whose family businesses had provided most of the advertising) left us all on the runway, paying rent on a studio, and picking up any job that came along. Then Ramón, who had often recommended me to take promo shots of the flamenco artists he was producing, offered me the kind of job I'd always wanted: designing record covers for his new independent label.

Besides producing all kinds of popular music for important record labels –electronic, symphonic, moronic, even Julio Iglesias – he had started a publishing business to collect the royalties from the hit song 'Fiesta', which he'd written with Lucia. His only employee was Antoni, a military bandleader who came by in the afternoons to do the paperwork and correct the sheet music. Until meeting Antoni, I thought that anybody with a military career must be a Falangist; it hadn't occurred to me that the army could even harbour Catalan nationalists. The armed forces, like the Church, were beyond suspicion, but it was in the hothouse darkness of the seminaries more than the windy university campuses that the seeds of both Catalan and Basque nationalism had been germinating during the dictatorship.

In 1975, Ramón had recorded *Olive Tree* (*El Olivo*), an LP of Robert's poems that he had set to music. It featured some of the best jazz musicians in Barcelona and the light, breathy voice of Lucia – reminiscent of Astrud Gilberto's – who had never before sung professionally. After failing to interest any record label, Ramón had decided to release the album himself, setting up his own company, Drums, in the same premises as the publishing business. This was a garage in one of the new outlying barrios of Barcelona that had begun to spring up in the 1960s on any free stretch of land, including dry river beds. The street was still unpaved and yet full of car bodywork shops with their radios blasting out all day.

The only way for Drums to finance its serious projects was to produce cover versions of current hits or artists (*A Tribute to . . .*) to be sold in revolving cassette racks at petrol stations and workers' cafés. I spent most of my time churning out awful cassette covers; the budget couldn't afford good photos or illustrations – even the recording engineers were moonlighting from other studios. To reach the darkroom I had to cross the recording studio, so my work was governed by the red recording light. Occasionally I was roped in to fill out a chorus and once even to sing the lead vocal on the cover version of Manhattan Transfer's 'Speak Up Mambo', and then only because nobody else could convincingly imitate their US-accented Spanish.

*El Olivo* had received excellent reviews, but sales were slow: Ramón was respected in musical circles, but his name meant nothing to the general public. Nor did Robert's: *I, Claudius* had yet to become one of the most popular series to be shown on Televisión Española. If the characters rang especially true to the Spanish audience it was because Robert had been inspired by his neighbours when writing the novel.

The first artist to sign up with Drums was Toni Morlà, a member of Ramón's group from the Indigo Jazz Club. After years working in hotel bands, he had turned out to be an excellent singer-songwriter and the first to convincingly use vernacular Majorcan outside traditional music. But although musically and vocally he was a cut above the rest of those singing in Catalan, his songs lacked any of the requisites to join the *nova cançó* movement: to broadcast a political message, to rescue a pure folk tradition, or to set classic Catalan poets to music. However, his songs struck a much deeper chord with me than even María del Mar Bonet, whose spectacular voice represented the islands in the big metropolis of Barcelona. It took a long time for the rest of *nova cançó* to follow Toni's example: the best way for a singer to revive a minority culture is to give it a repertoire of good songs. But in the reawakening of the Catalan culture in the Seventies, the first priority was to stand up for your rights and the second to take stock of your cultural heritage: folk songs, work songs, lullabies, poetry. Unfortunately, very little of the political *nova cançó* could stand the musical test of time.

The flat above the studio where I worked for AeroMexico belonged to the Valencian protest singer Raimón, whose 1963 song *Al Vent* ('Facing the Wind') had become a hymn of protest. Although there was nothing in the lyrics that could be censored at face value, everybody recognized it as a challenge to the Fascist anthem *Cara al Sol* ('Facing the Sun'). His flat was a meeting place for many of the best-known figures of Catalan culture, with whom I'd often find myself sharing the cramped lift: Miró's grandson negotiating a record cover deal or Colita, Barcelona's Annie Liebowitz. Our design team was almost driven mad by Raimón's voice booming down the airshaft as he tried to come up with ideas for new songs now that there was no dictatorship to protest against. It would take him ten minutes to set down a few simple minor chords, but the lyrics would be honed down in a monotonous drone over the following weeks. Although his voice was strong it lacked musicality, nor had his guitar ever done more than provide a discreet backing to his harangues; yet he had mobilized the student protests on campuses all over the country during the last years of the dictatorship, especially with *Diguem No* ('Let Us Say No'). This was a response to Franco's mid-Sixties campaign for the 'yes vote' in a referendum to support some new law, which nobody would have dared to vote against even if they had been told what it was about.

During the dictatorship, most protest singers worth their salt had spent some time in jail, not on political charges – the lyrics were carefully tailored to pass the censorship – but for 'disturbing the peace'. Any writer, singer, or cartoonist the least bit critical of the regime became an expert in the use of symbolism and double entendre, and the audience adept at reading between the lines – a talent that, luckily, few other Europeans on this side of the former Iron Curtain have needed to practise. One of the most effective anti-Franco anthems was *L'Estaca* by Lluís Llach, who used the simple image of a rotten stake to which we were all chained; 'If you pull a little from your side and I pull a little from my side, the whole thing will come crashing down . . .'

The Spanish censorship wasn't the only one operating

in southern Europe. In 1967 the Greek Military Junta proclaimed Army Order No. 13, in which 'we order that throughout the country it is forbidden to reproduce or play the music and songs of the [communist] composer Mikis Theodorakis [ . . . ] Citizens who contravene this Order will be brought immediately before the military tribunal . . .' A Greek friend told me how a policeman in his home town of Larissa was absent-mindedly whistling a Theodorakis melody on the street when a conscientious citizen approached him: 'Excuse me, officer, I thought I should inform you that you're whistling a tune by Theodorakis.' To which the policeman replied, 'Oh, really? Then I'm afraid you are under arrest for listening to it.'

Outsmarting the censor has always been a very serious game played by opponents to totalitarian regimes, whether Left or Right, religious or monarchical. In a famous incident, the seventeenth-century Spanish poet Quevedo accepted the wager that he'd dare allude to Queen Isabel's lameness to her face. Presenting Doña Isabel with two flowers, he pronounced the couplet:

*Entre este clavel blanco y esta rosa roja,*
*Su Majestad escoja.*
('Between this white carnation and this red rose, may
Your Majesty choose')

But *Su Majestad es coja* means 'Your Majesty is lame'. Quevedo's cheek won him the wager, but also a long prison sentence. In the 1960s Violeta Parra, the brilliant Chilean songwriter, defended the right to free speech in her *Mazúrquica Modérnica*; but to get the lyrics past the censors, she added nonsense suffixes to every word, like the secret languages used by schoolchildren. When sung out loud, the message came across with comical clarity.

In 1969 my eldest sister Catherine, who was involved in exposing political corruption in Australia, said something that later helped me understand the strength of humour as a political weapon. 'A sense of humour is the ability to switch quickly from one viewpoint to another; when you recognize the pattern common to both points of view, it sparks off a laugh. It's like the moiré effect you see when you lay one mosquito netting over another. But a fanatic or a bureaucrat lacks this faculty because he can only deal with one point of view, so the only way to beat a religious or political dictatorship, other than by force, is through humour: you become a human banana skin. There is nothing more debilitating for a bully than to be laughed at without understanding why.' And nothing more immediately binding, especially between thousands of people, than sharing a joke at the expense of a powerful enemy.

Barcelona has never lacked places with character, like the Bar Marsella off the Ramblas, known as La Absenta because of the absinthe it served; many of its more colourful regular customers were retired prostitutes. Another seedy establishment nearby was home to music-hall artists whose names no longer flashed in lights on El Paralelo Avenue. Here they'd put on a sorry parody of their old stage acts for their ageing fans, but the place also attracted the young and jaded set, the kind who got a buzz out of the more grotesque scenes in Fellini movies. But my favourite bar, although in the newer part of town, had dozens of guitars hanging on the walls for the use of customers, and even provided songbooks of Spanish and Latin American standards. When the rivalry between tables became untenable, they would inevitably join up for a communal sing-along.

On a grubby street parallel to the Barcelona seafront, where I once got mugged only twenty yards from the armed guards of a military building, my flatmate Michael and I had often noticed an unmarked doorway leading up five steps to a cheap-looking restaurant. From the pavement, through the frosted-glass balcony windows, you could make out the clients' feet at eye level; we decided to try it out. As we entered the large, noisy L-shaped room, nobody looked up, but one of the regulars, wearing dark glasses, called out to the kitchen: 'Pepe, some new clients!' The food smelled good and there was a cheerful atmosphere; the diners were shoddily dressed but some of their faces looked very familiar. There was no menu, not even a blackboard; the cook, a large Aragonese with a thick black moustache, came over and rattled off the day's specials, including a highly recommended *morcilla de cebolla* (minced-onion black pudding) 'from my village, just arrived this morning'. Pepe was on first-name terms with all his clients, none of whom, we suddenly realized, could see: we had walked into the canteen of the National Organization for the Blind. Of course the faces looked familiar; they all sold *cupones* for the Lottery of the Blind in different metro stations and on street corners all over the city. 'The food here is subsidized,' Pepe explained, 'but we don't refuse people like you coming up off the street if there's a spare table.' I was amazed at the sensory powers of Pepe's clients; not only did they recognize whose footsteps were coming up the stairs, but we heard two of them describing a beautiful woman who had been standing beside them at the zebra crossing. One of the older clients, having paid for his meal, would always toss a five-peseta coin from his table in the far corner, over the bar and into a tin can about six yards away. 'Pepe, get out of the way; if I miss, you get no tip.'

Michael, a medical student, had lived in Spain long enough to know that, although the medical and social services were way behind the rest of Europe, this was offset by the fact that anybody with a physical or mental handicap was treated as a normal member of society, not bundled off to some special centre. I remembered the callous jokes about spastics and invalids that everybody told at Bedales, which I now realize was not cruelty towards the handicapped but a reaction to the common dread of ending up as one of them, cut off from the world.

Pepe had a mischievous sense of humour and his clients loved him for it. As he passed by a table of two, he would engage them in conversation while deftly swapping over their plates of food; by the time they took their next bite, Pepe was safely back in the kitchen.

He soon discovered we lived on the north coast of Majorca. 'Oh, I used to work in Sóller port as a cook.'

'In a hotel or in a restaurant?'

'Neither. In a submarine at the naval base. You need to have a certain temperament to be a member of a submarine crew, and even more so to work in the galley. That's why they offered me this job when I left the navy.'

The submarine base was legendary in Sóller. Hidden beneath the rocky promontory and accessible only through a tunnel leading from the regular naval base, few locals had actually been inside; access from the sea was reportedly through an enormous underwater cave. German submarines had refuelled there during the war, and it has been speculated that some of the escaped Nazi war criminals disembarked here to spend time lying low in the nearby monastery at Lluc, learning Spanish until things quietened down, before continuing their journey to South America.

I remember as a child seeing a periscope gliding by the Cala. A paediatrician who lived in Deià and loved fishing from his boat just off the coast almost choked on his *sobrassada* sandwich when a submarine surfaced a few metres away, the hatch opened, and a naval officer popped his head out to ask if he was on the right course for Sóller port.

Pepe was very taciturn about his time at the Sóller base, and many years later I discovered the probable reason. A short time earlier, a submarine was sunk by error a few miles offshore while on manoeuvres; the incident was hushed up, but it caused a great commotion among the local families. Only recently, after the Kursk disaster, has the incident come to light.

At this time, the Spanish blind were soon to be smiled upon by their patron, Santa Lucía, the martyr whose eyes had been gouged out and whose figure, carrying her eyes on a tray, featured in our flat's inventory. In the early 1980s a new, young president of the organization, by playing his cards very shrewdly with the new Socialist Government, managed to turn this rancid Francoist institution into one of the richest and most dynamic organizations in the new economy, holding controlling interests in banks and TV stations. This was thanks to clever promotion of the cheap daily *cupón*, which was soon competing with the weekly National Lottery and financed a social programme that today provides the Spanish blind with probably the best facilities and education anywhere.

\*    \*    \*

All kinds of musicians trooped though Drums during the two years I worked there: jazz pianists, anarchist folk singers, classical and flamenco guitarists, Catalan gypsies who always brought their elders along to check the contracts, erstwhile pop stars looking for a second chance. One of the most memorable characters who ducked her head under the roller-blind door was Teresa Rebull. She was already fifty when she decided, after hearing Raimón sing in the Olympia theatre in Paris, that 'if he could do it, so could I'. The *nova cançó* movement had one thing in common with punk: 'Just get out and do it – you can learn to play later.'

New wave, nouvelle vague, bossa nova, *nueva trova*, *nova cançó* . . . when a musical or artistic style evolves from within a social context, a label is inevitable. *Nova cançó* had its roots in the post-war generation of Catalan singers who had grown up listening to Georges Brassens and Jacques Brel. Several of them formed a group called Els Setze Jutges after a Catalan tongue twister, *Setze jutges d'un jutjat mengen el fetge d'un penjat*: 'Sixteen judges of a court of law dine on a hanged man's liver'. The phrase had became a password used at secret meetings to unmask any outsider trying to pass himself off as Catalan. Els Setze Jutges decided that singing in their own language was the best way to liberate it from its political isolation. Although Catalan, like Basque, Galician, or the gypsy *caló*, was still forbidden in public places – schools or offices – the Government could hardly justify censuring traditional songs or lullabies, so folk music became the fingerhold by which this downtrodden language managed to haul itself back on deck. In 1963 a small independent record label, Edigsa, was formed to record and distribute this traditional music; it later branched out into pop and progressive rock without losing its strong regional identity.

Els Setze Jutges was to Catalan music what John Mayall's Bluesbreakers were to the British Blues scene: a musical Who's Who. Three of the original Jutges remain today the most popular singers in the Catalan language and are recognized internationally: María del Mar Bonet, Joan Manuel Serrat, and Lluís Llach. In the student atmosphere where the *nova cançó* began to flourish, one's right to freedom of speech and of language was more important than what was actually said. (Even today, on any Spanish TV or radio chat show, it is more important to be heard than understood.) In the last days of the dictatorship, professors at the new Autonomous University of Barcelona began to give classes in Catalan; Castillian Spanish, the language of repression, was only applauded when accompanied by a guitar. Students in Madrid would cheer a Catalan or Basque protest singer as rapturously as any of their own; in the struggle against Fascism, incomprehensible words wouldn't hold back the message.

The dictatorship kept close tabs on the musical scene. A professional musician's 'variety act' licence could be revoked if he overstepped the mark, and to be able to register a song he had first to pass an exam as composer and then another as lyricist. Perhaps this second hurdle obliged many singers to draw upon the verses of the 'damned' poets of the Republic – García Lorca, Miguel Hernández, Antonio Machado – whose names were venerated but whose work was only available in pirate editions.

In the late 1960s the Spanish began to discover a wealth of libertarian songs from across the Atlantic, born out of the Latin Americans' fight for workers' rights and against military dictatorships. The Chileans Quillapayun and Victor Jarra (assassinated by Pinochet's forces), the Argentinians

Jorge Cafrune (also mysteriously killed) and Mercedes Sosa, and the Cubans Silvio Rodriguez and Pablo Milanés, brought over a rich repertoire of songs that were every bit as powerful as their counterparts in Spain, and frequently much richer musically. A lot of this subversive music had found its way into Franco's Spain over the French radio airwaves, thanks to the community of Latin American and Spanish exiles in Paris – people like Teresa Rebull.

Teresa was a well-built, dark-haired, energetic woman with a hearty laugh and, like many of her age, she was a lot more liberal than our 'love generation' and, as the Spanish say, had no hairs on her tongue: she didn't mince words. In this respect, she reminded me of another outspoken revolutionary, Ivy Litvinoff, whom I had first met with my mother and Margot Callas on a trip we made to Moscow. Ivy had married a Russian émigré in London and when the revolution beckoned in 1917 she followed him to Moscow, where he became a high-ranking official. Fifty years later she returned to England as a widow. Once, while staying overnight in her Brighton flat as a teenager, I was embarrassed to find her poring over the copy of *Penthouse* I had picked up at the station. 'I was looking at this magazine of yours and I think it's marvellous how men and women are now able to show everything. But there's one thing I object to – your generation seems to think it discovered the clitoris! I mean to say, really!'

Teresa was just as frank and disarming as Ivy. She was competent on the guitar but, like many self-taught musicians used to playing on their own, had no sense of rhythm or metre. A small French company had released her first record on which she had set the sensual love poems of Joan Salvat-Papasseit to music. It had won the Grand Prix du Disque

Charles Cross, perhaps the most prestigious prize in France, also awarded to Robert Wyatt's 'Rock Bottom'. But now that Spain was a democracy, she wanted to come home to record her own songs in her native Catalonia. Her material was still in a primitive state and after a couple of sessions Ramón gave up in despair and passed on to me the job of knocking her repertoire into shape. It was a delicate situation; as a prize-winning, mature artist, Teresa didn't believe she had anything to learn, so all I could do was build up arrangements to each song around her peculiar sense of time.

The daughter of militant Catalan anarchists and an activist herself, Teresa Soler i Pi was only nineteen in the freezing January of 1939 when she and her boyfriend Pep Rebull, member of the Central Committee of the anarchist POUM and director of the party newspaper, escaped Franco's advancing Nationalist forces and sought refuge over the French border. 'This exile was our honeymoon; we managed to find some relatives of Pep on the outskirts of Paris', and so they escaped the fate of so many other Republican refugees in the concentration camp of Argelés-Sur-Mer.

But there seemed to be no escaping Fascism, because two years later France fell under Nazi control. This, and the pull of her homeland, prompted Teresa to risk secretly visiting her family in Barcelona, but she returned safely to Pep's side in Marseilles. The city was seething with refugees from all over Nazi Europe, and there the couple soon came into contact with the CAS (*Centre Americain de Secours*, American Aid Centre), which paid the rent on a villa where many artists and intellectuals from all over the Continent awaited evacuation to the USA.

When the CAS went underground in 1942 the couple acted as its liaison with the French Resistance. Pep and his contact were arrested by the Nazis but liberated soon after by the Allies. Little has been said about the tremendous contribution of the defeated Spanish anarchists to the Resistance: they were the most experienced combatants and explosives experts. When Paris was liberated, one of the columns that entered triumphantly was entirely made up of Spanish Republicans.

The war over, Pep's contact summoned him to Paris to edit *Franc-Tireur*, the Resistance journal subsidized by the USA. Teresa, now a mother, devoted her spare time to the Casal de Catalunya, an intellectual and artistic centre for the large Spanish and Latin American exile community and also edited two US-financed cultural magazines in Spanish.

In the late 1960s, with their child now grown up and Pep retired, they moved back to Roussillon, the Catalan-speaking area around Perpignan. But the May 1968 riots had brought Teresa's old anarchist militancy to the surface again, and after listening to many of the new Spanish and Catalan protest singers, who could only perform north of the border, she picked up her guitar and went out to sing 'in order to defend the language that had been trampled upon by Franco'. Pep stayed home writing the occasional article and pottering around the garden. There was close contact between the Catalan activists inside Spain and the exiles, but while the French Catalans (like the French Basques) lent polite support to the cause, they lacked the yearning for liberty that fuelled the movement inside Spain. The French enjoyed full linguistic and democratic rights, so there wasn't much to fight for – unlike Corsica, Rousillon harboured no separatists. But it did offer the Catalans south of the border an important focal point, the Catalan Summer University in Prades, set up in 1969 and still active today.

Prades, a small town in the northern foothills of the Pyrenees, near the Catalans' venerated mountain of El Canigó, was the home in the ninth century of Guilfred le Poilu (Wilfred the Hairy), later celebrated in an epic *gesta* as the founder of Catalonia. It was also the home of Pompeu Fabra, who compiled the first authoritative dictionary of the language. Each summer during the last years of Franco's regime, the town would see a tent-city spring up and fill with all the Catalan intellectuals and university students lucky enough to obtain a passport; here, between concerts and recitals, the Summer University laid the foundations for the future of their language and culture, out of reach of the Spanish police.

It was King Juan Carlos who, contrary to expectations, pushed to legalize all political parties and granted an amnesty to prisoners of conscience, many of whom had spent forty years behind bars. The Communist Party was legalized in April 1977; amnesty was granted in May, opening the way for the exiles to return in time for the first elections in June. The Spaniards could now see the faces of the mythical figures from the past; the poet Rafael Alberti, friend of García Lorca, now sporting a mane of white hair, gained a seat in Parliament. So did Dolores Ibárruri, *La Pasionaria*, now in her seventies but no less stirring in her speeches; and of course the chain-smoking Communist leader Santiago Carrillo, who had been invoked by post-war parents as a child-eating bogeyman when their toddlers misbehaved. The only politician to have governed before and after Franco's forty-year rule was Josep Taradellas, who had been a Minister of the Generalitat of Catalonia in 1936 and returned in 1977 as its president, with the famous phrase: *Ja sóc aquí!* – 'Here I am at last!'

Many more anonymous exiles returned; there also surfaced a small number of maquis who had been active in the remotest Spanish mountains and some Republicans who had been hiding in cellars or attics since before Anne Frank began her diary. Teresa didn't want to miss out on this atmosphere of liberation and rented a small pied-à-terre in Barcelona where she renewed old contacts and threw herself again into the re-emerging intellectual mêlée, as she had in Paris.

Teresa and I got along very well in spite of our musical differences. Although the songs were as yet in no fit state to record, I began to understand the method to her madness, such as stealing half a bar from one line and adding it to the next. She was so pleased to find a musician who could follow her that she asked me to accompany her at her first important appearance in the city at the Ateneu Barcelonès. This imposing, gloomily bourgeois building had seen better days before the war, when it was the most influential cultural and scientific centre in Catalonia and the scene of literary and political debates. A secret meeting of the factions of the Republican Left held here in 1931 had resulted in their electoral victory, the declaration of the Republic of Catalonia, an autonomous government, and the drawing up of its own statutes. Since the war, however, the Ateneu had been reduced to functioning as a library and now, like so many other entities and institutions, was slowly beginning to react to Life After Franco, although without the dynamism of the libertarian (anarchist) ateneus that were springing up around Barcelona. The Ateneu Barcelonès had the air of a rather dilapidated gentleman's club in London, but besides a few elegant doyens of the Good Catalan Families, whose capital and hard work had made the region Spain's richest and most productive, our audience was made up of students, factory workers, and intellectuals. Many of these bearded longhairs, fifteen years later, would be wearing jackets and ties, chauffeured in official cars of the Generalitat and negotiating power-sharing deals with the Government in Madrid.

The new Generalitat's educational programme, designed to right Franco's wrongs, has imposed a Catalan nationalism almost as obsessive as the dictator's National Unity. If my generation's textbooks defined the Ebro as 'a Great Spanish River that flows through Aragon and Catalonia to the sea', a textbook approved by the Generalitat recently described it as 'a Catalan river that is born in a foreign land'.

The political weight of a language is reflected in the number of voters who speak it, which in Catalonia was by no means the majority; although Barcelona had the industrial clout to ensure its voice was heard, much of that wealth had come from the workers who had flocked from other parts of Spain, especially Andalusia. The new Generalitat needed the support and energy of the radical Catalan youth who had grown up speaking their language at home – the only place they'd been allowed to use it – but, surprisingly, the most fervent *catalanistas* seemed to be the children of the Andalusian immigrants, youngsters who had found in this language a sense of identity that their uprooted parents had lost.

To strengthen its political position, the Generalitat defined the linguistic area as the *Països Catalans*, the word *Països* signifying nations in the human as well as political sense. This was a neat way of drawing in Valencia and the Balearics – each of which had their own autonomous governments – as well as French Roussillon (now known as Catalunya Nord) and even parts of Sardinia, areas which, although sharing the same language, wouldn't naturally consider themselves Catalans. This pan-Catalanism made it important for any festival or concert to feature artists or singers from each of the *països*, a situation that certainly favoured Teresa, who was one of only two representatives of Catalunya Nord on the circuit.

Twenty years later, it is evident that the concept of the *Països Catalans* never gelled at a grass-roots level outside of Catalonia proper; perhaps if the language had another name – say *languedoc* or *limousine*, for instance – all the regions speaking it would consider themselves on an even footing. But today few Majorcans or Valencians will identify themselves as being from the *Països Catalans*, a concept they interpret as Barcelona's attempt to impose itself in the same way Madrid had done forty years earlier. A popular joke has Jordi Pujol, President of the Generalitat, visiting Beijing to promote Catalan business interests.

'So you represent Catalonia, Mr Pujol. Where's that exactly?' asks the Chinese Premier.

'On the north-eastern coast of the Iberian Peninsula. There are six million of us!'

'Really?' asks the Premier, nonplussed. 'And in which hotel are you all staying?'

When I left Barcelona in 1979, Teresa wrote me a letter saying she was now being accompanied by two excellent musicians from Catalunya Nord, but she missed playing with me. 'I need to feel energy from the people I work with, and these two, for all their musical knowledge, have no joy inside. With you I feel much more relaxed, you lift me up with your chords and rhythms, I feel happy and full of energy because you give me security and understanding. Maybe it's because you always seem to be happy when you're playing, the rhythm seems to come out of your pores, and that really gets me going. To feel the happiness of your musical partner is to feel happy yourself.' This was something I had been increasingly aware of in the world of the *nova cançó* but hadn't been able to articulate until then: an increasing earnestness, a lack of spontaneity. Music is emotion, it has to have feeling – *el filin*, as they say in Spain and Latin America – and that *filin* can be love, joy, sadness, or outrage. It can create the conditions for political change, and even help the new order to cross the street, but then, as the Spanish say, *con la musica a otra parte* . . . 'Take the music on down the road'. Evolve.

Teresa and I represented Catalunya Nord in several festivals – the same stages on which a couple of years later, with Toni Morlà, I'd be representing the Balearics. Although Teresa never gained the musical or political importance required to play at the Palau de la Musica de Barcelona, a gem of Art Deco, we were invited to play at one of the most magical of venues, the cloisters of Saint Michel de Cuxà, near Prades. This monastery was founded in 833 in a cool valley that descends from the Canigò. One of the most beautiful of popular Catalan airs goes:

*Muntanyes del Canigò, fresques són i regalades*
*Sobretot en l'estiu quan les aigues són gelades . . .*
(Mountains of the Canigò, cool are they with flowing
   springs
Above all in the summer, when their waters are still
   icy . . .)

The cloisters of St Michel de Cuxà still host the Pau Casals classical music festival, named after the exiled genius of the cello, the 'most universal Catalan' alongside the painters Miró and Dalí. The abbey is considered the spiritual home of Catalan culture, just as the monastery of Montserrat near Barcelona is considered the cradle of its resurgence during the dictatorship. For although the Catholic hierarchy had supported the dictatorship and taught its propaganda in schools, erasing all traces of the cultural and linguistic diversity that made up Spain, the post-war generation of 'progressive' seminarists and priests was working in the opposite direction, laying the groundwork for Catalan and Basque (and, to a lesser extent, Galician) nationalism to flower. In the late 1960s, the dictatorship decided to improve its international image, crucial for attracting more tourists, with some lukewarm concessions towards freedom of language, if not of speech. So while the Franco Youth Scouts sang *Cara al Sol*, the summer camps organized by *progre* priests would sing spirituals in Catalan around the camp fire –*Kumbaya, Senyor, Kumbaya* – along with *Paff, el drac màgic*.

The Falangist bovver boys, furious at these 'traitors to the Fatherland in the bosom of the Holy Mother Church', sprayed the graffiti 'Red Priests, up against the wall!' on youth clubs, seminaries, and churches. But thanks to these 'red priests', Spain today probably supplies more missionaries to the Third World than any other country, and is one of the most generous donors of aid. Many missionaries, like the Catalans Vicente Ferrer in India and Pere Casaldáliga in Brazil, have practised what they preached. Casaldáliga has been instrumental in the spread of the Liberation Theology movement that has done so much to help the world's poor to uphold their rights instead of simply accepting their fate.

One of the most popular films of 1979 was *El Desencanto* ('The Disenchantment'), a documentary about the family of a poet who had supported the regime. The title seemed to summarize the mood at the time in Spain. The four years since the death of Franco had provided many moments of joy – the political amnesty, the new constitution, the Generalitat reinstated, the first elections and granting of civil liberties – but moments of joy that seemed to leave an empty feeling. It was as if the slate hadn't been wiped clean, only dusted. This sentiment was especially poignant for those who, like Teresa, had lived and fought for the Republic: as far as the more pragmatic young politicians were concerned, the ideals she had risked her life for were fine for motivating the electorate, but too radical actually to put into practice. Teresa saw the Sandinista revolution in Nicaragua as being much closer to her heart than the tepid Spanish transition. 'Here in Barcelona we are breathing the anguish of this poor democracy, so young and yet already wrinkled and toothless,' she wrote me in a letter to Managua later that year, where I was spending six months documenting the revolution in field recordings and photos while playing music with the Teatro Popular Sandinista. Compared to the hands-on revolutionary fervour in Nicaragua, she found Spain 'sad, so sad . . . all these people with their false joy. Franco has left a very deep wound that affects the behaviour and way of thinking of two generations. This apprenticeship in liberty is being done with shoddy tools; this isn't true liberty . . .'

Now that there was little left to fight for politically, the moment of musical truth had arrived for many protest singers. The next battle in the autonomies – the Basque country, Catalonia, and Galicia – was to rebuild their own culture. No longer did they have to fight against the national Government: they had their own government to subsidize them and their own radio and TV channels at their disposal. This was the kiss of death for all those who had no music beneath their message. In the words of a rumba by Gato Pérez, 'after years of politics and pondering, it's about time we had a little fun'. Barcelona was a melting pot of musical influences. In the old quarter near the port, close to the Via Laietana police station where so many musicians had spent sleepless nights, a popular club called Zeleste had been giving birth to a fusion of funk, rock, flamenco, and salsa known as the *ona laietana*. A popular postcard by Mariscal (who later designed the Olympic postmodern mascot, Cobi) broke Barcelona's Catalan identity into its constituent parts: *Bar*, *Cel* (sky), and *Ona* (wave): a beachside bar. Catalan was now being used in a less self-conscious way in all kinds of musical formats, from intergalactic whimsy of the Daevid Allen kind – Pau Riba and Sisa – to the new *rock català*. One of the most interesting bands, whom I convinced to sign up with Ramón's record label, was Pernil Latino. A *pernil* (leg of ham) is musicians' slang for instruments descended from the Arab *oud*: the mandolin, laud, and bandurria, all ham-shaped and played with a plectrum. Pernil Latino managed to combine the sounds of the traditional Spanish village music – *rondallas* and oompah brass bands – with Latin percussion, ecological lyrics, and good vibes.

Although playing with Teresa had been fun and brought in some pocket money, musically it was an uphill slog. Being in the thick of the *nova cançó* had been stimulating, but I felt I was fighting somebody else's battle. Had I made any money at it, I might have even felt mercenary. This feeling became more evident when I began to accompany Toni Morlà on his visits to Barcelona. Toni's songs not only had rich melodies and harmonic possibilities, but his Majorcan lyricism struck a deeper, more emotional chord. Up until then I had thought of the island as simply my geographical home. In England I had often felt homesick for its landscapes, aromas, and sounds, but Toni showed me that *sa roqueta*, the little rock in the middle of the sea, meant more to me than I had imagined.

# 6

# Little Rocks in the Sea

Toni Morlà is an atypical Majorcan. It's not his freckles and red beard that set him apart; the redheaded gene was probably brought to the Balearics by the Berber settlers in the tenth century, although in Toni's case it could be traced back through his grandfather to the British occupation of Minorca almost three hundred years ago. No, what distinguishes Toni from other laidback Balearics is the fact that he's a chain-smoking, motor-mouthed insomniac. This is probably a vestige of his years as a musician on the Palma nightclub circuit. When I picture him, the first phrase that comes to mind is *els nirvis me mengen* ('my nerves are devouring me') – a line from one of his love songs, 'Seven Days Without You'. However, once he has a guitar in his hands his tautness relaxes and he radiates a warm serenity. I had added some guitar and harmonica to Toni's first solo album, produced by Ramón in his Barcelona studio, so I was the obvious choice to accompany him for his first paid solo gig in Majorca as a singer-songwriter in 1978.

The mountain village of Puigpunyent, the 'Hill in the West', had once been the summering place of the Palma court, and it is said that the best Majorcan is still spoken here. It has no access to the sea, so the few foreigners living there at that time had chosen it as a quiet place to work: the painter John Ulbricht, the botanist Anthony Bonner, and the writer Ruthven Todd. The people of Puigpunyent have managed to combine a respect for their own culture with a broader outlook than most inland villages. It was the first on the island to hire Toni for their *festes patronals*, and later the first in Spain to declare itself a nuclear-free zone.

Like every Majorcan or Spanish town during their summer *festes* – a three-day celebration in honour of their patron saint – Puigpunyent was decked out in paper streamers that stretched from balcony to balcony across the main streets. Although spaced at least a yard apart, the perspective gives one the impression of passing through a fluttering white-ceilinged tunnel to the heart of the festivities in the village square, where the streamers converge upon a pole in the centre, forming a big top. The slightest breeze rustling through the fringes of tissue paper creates a discreet susurration that is as refreshing as the sound of a fountain playing in a courtyard; it's one of those summer background sounds, like the buzz of cicadas, that you only notice when it ceases.

When arriving to play in an unfamiliar village in Toni's car, loaded up with his primitive PA system, there's no need to ask directions; any streamer-trimmed street leads to the stage. After our first concert in Puigpunyent, this became a ritual: at every corner I'd get out to remove a traffic barrier, and if challenged by a policeman the magic words were '*som els mùsics!*'

'Ah, so you're the musicians! Take that side street, it will take you directly backstage.'

The street plan of a village provides a strong clue to its history. The centres of towns whose names identify them with the Muslim colonization – Sóller, Inca, Muro, Banyalbufar, Alaró, Binissalem – remain true to the original Arabic street plan, although it's impossible to identify a single building as dating from that period: the mosques were rebuilt as churches and in any case vernacular architecture in the Balearics hasn't changed significantly since Roman times. The streets follow the original water courses, from the spring through the village to the public laundry troughs, from where the water flows to the orchards. When King James II induced Aragonese and Catalan settlers to repopulate the island after the Muslims were expelled in the thirteenth century, the towns he founded on the dry plain – Campos, Llucmajor, and others – followed a Northern European street grid. The settlers would only receive building subsidies if they built terraced houses with narrow façades and an open kitchen and patio out back. The result, a front door every four instead of every seven metres, gives these towns more social bustle. Nevertheless, at siesta time in summer, any Majorcan village is as shuttered up as Dodge City at high noon.

With the exception of Palma, which celebrates the patronage of Sant Sebastià on 19 January, all the parishes in the Balearics seem to have sought the protection of a saint whose name day falls between June and September, allowing them to celebrate their main *festes patronals* in good weather – an obvious relic of the pre-Christian harvest festivals. The festivities usually last three days, but if the *Sant* falls on a Wednesday the *festes* are often stretched out to include the weekend – five days in all. The religious ceremonies in honour of the *Patró* take place in the morning with a brass band leading the procession through the streets to church; the festive activities, however, begin in the cool of the evening as families in their Sunday best emerge from behind closed doors to take a stroll past the stalls set up on the main streets.

Over the years playing at different villages *festes* with Toni we coincided so often with these stallholders, many of them gypsies from the mainland, that we would greet each other like neighbours. The fat man selling slices of coconut, tiger nuts and almonds coated in burnt sugar became fatter every summer until he had to be carried. The biggest stall, as long as a bus, is always packed with noisy cap pistols, battery-powered police cars, dolls that cry when they wet their knickers, plastic tambourines and trumpets . . . anything that makes a racket and falls to pieces the day after the stallholders have left town.

I became friendly with a melancholy couple of Portuguese gypsies whose stall consisted of a row of empty Fanta cans on a shelf, to be knocked off with a tennis ball; the only prize they could afford to give out was a full can. Every year some mishap befell them – the wind blew their stall over an embankment, their old van caught fire – but they struggled miserably on, improving their stall year by year until they moved up into the lucrative trade of *bombetes*. This is what village children talk about most as the summer approaches, the item most likely to empty their piggy banks; for adults it is the bane of all *festes*. The small cardboard box of fifty *bombetes* appears to only contain sawdust, but shake it and little twists of coloured tissue paper rise to the surface, like the twists of salt that Britons of my generation will remember finding in bags of crisps. About the size and weight of a pea, the *bombetes* contain fine gravel and gun-powder that explodes with a loud crack when thrown on the floor, usually at somebody's feet. They are harmless enough even for six-year-olds; when thrown against the body they don't explode and the only damage they do is to parents' nerves. More dangerous, also available without parental supervision, are the little green bangers the size of undernourished cigarettes. A favourite trick of the pre-teens was to crawl under the stage, find a gap in the planks, place a banger right under a musician's shoe, light the fuse, and crawl to safety. When the bangers had run out, the village terrors would poke sticks into musicians' soles from below. I would have tipped my bottle of water over them had it not been for the ever-present peril of electric shocks. The gaps between planks held other dangers: once, while launching into a mandolin solo, I edged my chair closer to the microphone and the rear legs slipped into a crack, tipping me on my back.

During my first few years with Toni, any village stage drew its electrical supply from an unearthed cable connected to the nearest street light. A background buzzing through the speakers was inevitable, and any band who didn't provide its own current stabilizer risked burning out their amplifiers. The municipal electrician was a breed we got to know quite well, usually an elderly man who had received so many shocks during his lifetime that he probably wouldn't flinch in an electric chair, and who assumed that musicians were as juice-proof as he was. I'd once seen one of this breed open a junction box and test the terminals with two fingers: 'Let's see . . . mmm . . . this one's 110 volts . . . this other one's 220 . . .'. Although three-pin plugs began to appear around this time, most people seemed to think that the third was a spare in case one of the other two snapped off. The new law required electricians to install three-pin sockets, but did not oblige anybody to connect the earth.

As the one-upmanship game between villages turned into a battle for more dazzling stage lighting, not only did the municipal fuses frequently blow during the performance, but an unfamiliar species of giant flying insect, attracted by the glare, would bat around the spotlights and dive bomb us when the varnish of our instruments flashed a reflection at them. Although we never had to dodge rotten eggs, tomatoes, or other flying objects, I was once hit on the back of the head by an airgun pellet ricocheting from the shooting stall behind the stage.

Until Toni came along and created his own audience among the rural population, there was no slot within the typical three-day structure of the village *festes* for a singer-songwriter, or indeed any other manifestation of contemporary local culture. The highlight of the *festes* was the *verbena*, a ball featuring two dance bands; the entertainment of the other two evenings consisted of a stale folk-dance routine and a hackneyed Majorcan bedroom farce. All the comedies invariably featured a pretty girl, a stupid suitor, a crafty aunt and an emigrant cousin returning from Venezuela, whom all believed to be rich but who was really after the deeds to the family farm.

Catalonia, with no natural borders, was far more aware of and protective towards its own language and culture than were the islanders, who took theirs for granted. The Majorcan singer-songwriters Guillem d'Efak and María del Mar Bonet were well known in the Balearics mainly because they had made their names in Barcelona. This kind of 'committed' music, which demanded the attention of the audience, was usually performed in a club or theatre, not in a village square. But thanks to Toni's tenacity and the complicity of a few young left-wingers and nationalists who had been voted onto the village councils in those first elections, a door was opened for other Majorcan singers and folk groups to reach the rural audience that still made up half the Majorcan population.

The sun was going down over the western hill behind Puigpunyent as the showbands were doing a sound check in the main square for that night's ball, the *verbena*. Not far away, a small stage had been set up for us in the school playground. We helped the mayor's wife set out the folding chairs while the town crier, an amiable dwarf perched at the top of an extra-long ladder, finished hooking up a string of coloured lights. We connected the speakers to Toni's Spanish-made valve amplifier and reverb unit, which occupied two metal boxes that weighed twelve kilos yet only produced eighty watts of sound, as much as a domestic stereo. We set them up on a folding chair beside us so we could control the volume; whenever someone stepped on a loose plank anywhere on the stage, the primitive spring reverb made a tremendous crashing sound, like a Steinway Grand falling down a flight of stairs.

As the whole village turned up to take their seats, the dwarf warmed them up with a cocktail-lounge version of 'Brazil' on the priest's Farfisa organ. At that time, people only knew Toni from his song 'Coses d'es Camp' ('Countryside Things'), which was the first song in Majorcan to make a national hit record – admittedly it was the B-side – by a handsome rock singer from the centre of the island, Lorenzo Santamaría.

As I sang the harmonies over Toni's rich, deep voice I could feel the audience's emotion, the same emotion I'd felt the first time I'd heard the song: it's the voice of a city-bred Majorcan who instead of playing down his peasant background proclaims it openly. The repetition of phrases echoes the cycle of the soil and the rhythm of the waterwheel, of the plough breaking open the dry earth.

Many of Toni's songs contributed greatly to the self-esteem of those rural Majorcans who had decided (or were obliged) to resist the call of the tourist trade; few of them ever bought records, but they became a wonderful and loyal audience. 'I was in very close contact with my record-buying public,' he recalled, 'because I distributed the records myself, walking around record shops with a straw basket full of LPs ... Someone would stop me and say "Toni, I bought your record!" and I'd reply "Oh, so it was *you*!"'

'In the Seventies it wasn't done to put your photo on the album cover and we had no access to TV, only to the radio; the music was much more important than the image. Once a friend was playing in a swanky piano bar and called me onstage to sing "Coses d'es Camp". Afterwards an elegant Palma lady came over and said, "I really enjoyed listening to your performance, you sing just like Toni Morlà."

'"Thank you, *senyora*, Toni Morlà at your service."

'"Oh,' she exclaimed, disconcerted. "I expected you to be younger and taller."'

There were few record shops in the small towns, which is where most of Toni's audience was. 'The first 500 copies would sell within a fortnight to the buyers in Palma, but the next 500 would take a year, because villagers only went to the capital if they had to; "Next time I'm in town I'll buy Toni's new record ..." It's like the peasant who goes to Palma on business and drops into an optician's for some new glasses.

'"Long-distance?" asks the optician.

'"And why would I need long-distance glasses?" replies the peasant. "I hardly ever leave the village!"'

Toni's songs were neither political nor did they try to update the local folk tradition, but they addressed issues that were much more pertinent to village life and helped me understand the true character of the people I had grown up amongst. I had always considered the Majorcans to be as dry as the British, but Toni's songs spoke openly of emotions in the earthiest vernacular. 'Our character is naturally a bit wary; we always want to know who's at the door. If we're slow to open, it's because we've been looted so often throughout history, but once the door is open, you'll always be welcome.' I'd be watching the expressions of the old peasants, the shopkeepers, and bank tellers in the audience. Heads began almost imperceptibly nodding in recognition as he sang of seeing his sweetheart betrothed to a rich man and covering up the pain of it with a 'what do I care' bravado; of discovering that the best fishing holes on the seafront have been paved over by the coastal motorway; of a workmate turning his back on his friends after inheriting money from a maiden aunt; of a girlfriend confessing to not being a virgin and his replying that he'll marry her anyway. One of the most popular was 'Oh, Catalina' about his cousin whose mother was so fussy about choosing suitors that she ended up a spinster, 'making clothes for the saints in Church', instead of for her own children, and becoming as wrinkled as the sheets in the laundry basket. Or Mestre Pep, the old man who passes the time of day on the bench outside Cort (the Palma Town Hall still known as the Court six hundred years after Majorca lost its own Crown). When *En Figuera*, the clock, chimes the hour Mestre Pep checks his pocket watch and winds it up – 'We'll see which of us runs down first'. (The worn stone bench is still known as *el banc de si no fos* – 'if it weren't'– because the dirty old men would gather there to catch a glimpse of petticoat when the country ladies alighted from the carriages that arrived from the villages: 'If weren't for my game leg/arthritis/gout/ weak heart, I'd walk up to that one and . . .'.)

My own musical contribution to the evening's entertainment consisted of simply adding a few splashes of musical colour, with harmonies and guitar; Toni's years of stage-work in the most adverse conditions gave him a relaxed authority in his new role as solo artist.

After the show, the Puigpunyent council laid on some food. Any official activity remotely associated with the local culture in a village *festa* will offer free wine and baking trays of *coca de trempó* – a cheese-less vegetable pizza introduced by the Romans – cut up into squares. The generosity of the authorities can be measured in the size of the slices of *coca*: the dimensions of a CD jewel case in the smaller villages, cassette-box size in the larger towns. The council also provided bread with *sobrassada* and even a tray of *cocarrois* (a savoury turnover stuffed with spinach, cauliflower, and raisins). As the mayor pointed out, there wasn't much time for people to go home for supper before the *verbena* began.

The villagers, having seen me onstage playing and singing harmonies to Toni's lyrics, treated me as one of their own and I soon found myself conversing in *mallorquí* as I never had in my own village. Context is all-important: as a musician accompanying a Majorcan singer, I *was* Majorcan. In spite of speaking the language passably well, I had never before been treated as such; even in the Deià school, I was considered at the most a half-breed. I had missed out on the adolescent bonding rituals that my elder brothers and sister had gone through at secondary school in Palma; I had been sent abroad at an earlier age and had become more British.

I never really considered myself Majorcan until living in Barcelona, when I began to feel homesick for *sa roqueta,* that little rock in the sea only eighty miles away. These pangs were brought on by listening to demo tapes of Toni's songs and by sharing a student flat much frequented by other homesick islanders, who survived mainly on the *sobrassada* and ship's biscuits sent over by their mothers.

My brother Juan has always been much more *mallorquí* than I'll ever be. Before he left for boarding school abroad, his Majorcan pace, stance, and attitude to life had been well established and over the years have only consolidated. A very amusing book, *Beloved Majorcans* by Guy de Forestier (pseudonym of a Catalan architect), explains the local character from the historical perspective. I had great fun translating the book into English – it was Bill Clinton's bedtime reading during his visit to the island – because it dedicates whole chapters to explaining such topics as the paradoxical and roundabout use of language, the elastic sense of time and commitment, manifestations of discretion and distrust, the fatalist attitude to life, the social obsession with funerals and the distaste towards any kind of protagonism: 'Who the hell does he think he is?' But one of the most succinct definitions of the insular character was Toni's: 'We love to do the C-C-Claudius bit, pretending we're stupid. But try and make a property deal with a Majorcan farmer and he'll run circles around a Wall Street broker.'

You can buy your way into the American Way of Life, whereas the Majorcan Way of Life costs little money but a great sacrifice, at least to northerners. It has obliged me to take things with philosophical calm and to rein in my speedy genes, and over the years of playing with Toni I must have absorbed many of the islander's mannerisms and attitudes. For despite my Anglo-Saxon appearance – a Majorcan friend likened me to a sheep thief bound for Botany Bay – I'm now usually addressed in the local dialect by islanders who don't know me from Adam, whereas the normal reaction to a stranger is to speak Spanish.

Although I still see myself externally as an Englishman, I must project some sort of Mediterraneanty. On a visit to London, a Greek waitress in a doner kebab café in Tottenham Court Road immediately challenged me: 'You're not English, are you?' In Madrid, my origin is similarly called into question:

'You're not Spanish, are you?'

'You're right,' I reply, 'I'm not. I just happen to have Spanish nationality. To tell the truth, I'm Majorcan born and bred.' That's a good conversation stopper: *Madrileños* prefer not to get into a discussions with crazy regional nationalists. In Nicaragua, however, my Spanish accent with its lisped 'c's and 'z's immediately earned me the epithet *padre*: the only Spaniards most Nicaraguan peasants had come across were Catholic missionaries, some of whom had taken up arms and fought alongside them against the Somoza dictatorship.

Over the ten years I accompanied Toni regularly – first as a duo, at times with my Catalan-speaking Dutch girlfriend on the violin, and finally with Salvador López – we performed in almost every town and village on the island, well over fifty different places, many of which we returned to several times. We also represented the Balearics in many Catalan song festivals in both Spanish and French Catalonia, yet we were never invited to Ibiza and the three concerts we gave in Minorca were thanks to Toni's family connections there, but we never played in the capital, Mahón (Maó in Catalan).

Morlà is a Minorcan surname, probably a corruption of Morley, one of the many remnants of the British domination of the island between 1712 and 1802. During this period the island briefly fell into the hands of the French, commanded by the Duke of Richelieu (who is credited with having introduced the local *all i oli* sauce to the royal chefs in Paris, who omitted the garlic and called it *Sauce Mahonnaise*). The British recovered Minorca and then lost it for a few years to the Spanish before George III was obliged by the Treaty of Amiens to return it definitively to Spain. The seventy years of British domination is still evident in the local language and agriculture; even April Fool's Day is celebrated on 1 April, not on 28 December, *Los Santos Inocentes*, as in the rest of Spain.

If Majorca is shaped like the head of a goat, Minorca is shaped like a kidney bean. At its western end is the port of Ciutadella, once capital of the island until this title was usurped by the larger port of Maó at the eastern tip. It was a British governor, Richard Kane, who built a road to link the two ports. It is still known as Kane's Road, and the Governor's genes are well represented in the halfway towns of Mercadal and Ferreries, where he would break each journey, claiming his *dret de pernada* (or 'legover rights' as the *droit de seigneur* is aptly called) with a fresh *menorquina* each time.

Most of the scant interchange between the three main Balearic islands is for administrative reasons; otherwise each entity ignores the existence of the others, for the distances between them are almost equal to their distance from the mainland. Although the name 'Balearic Islands' now refers to the whole archipelago, it reflects an administrative or geographic concept rather than a common history. 'There is no such thing as a Balearic people,' claim Clement Picornell and J. M. Seguí, though '. . . tourism has honed down the differences between the islands, acting as a leveller.' On an international level, Ibiza, Majorca, and Minorca still have a much higher 'recognition factor' or 'brand identity' individually than collectively.

The Catalan spoken in the Balearics since the thirteenth century reflects the idiosyncrasies of each island through their local dialects, but these still have more in common with each other than with mainland Catalan. 'Few islanders would declare themselves to be *balears* to the outside world,' writes Pere Fullana. 'There is relatively little sense of collective belonging and the word *Balear* arouses little popular sentiment compared with *mallorquí, menorquí* or *eivissenc.*'

We share the same regional government but each island has its own council; Formentera and Ibiza together comprise *les Pitiüses*, a name that dates back to the Carthaginian colonization in 654 BC. The Balearics had been inhabited since Neolithic times and, despite trading with the Greeks and Phoenicians, the *talaiotic* beaker culture remained intact in the two larger islands until the Romans made their appearance. The *Pityoussiae* became federated to Rome but Majorca and Minorca, the *Gymnesiae,* defended by fierce local slingers who had worked as mercenaries in the Punic Wars, resisted colonization for another five centuries until 123 BC.

The slingers didn't like anybody to land on their territory and most trading exchanges took place on small offshore islands. The Roman General Quintus Cecilius Metellus was sent by the Senate to subdue the *Insulae Baliares* as they were now known, a name stemming from the Greek *ballein,* to throw – also the origin of the words *bullet* and *ballistics*. Other theories suggest the Punic *ba' lé yara* – 'masters of throwing', the Phoenician *baal yaron* 'skilled thrower', and the myth that Hercules gave the islands to his shipmate Baleo.

After having many of his ships sunk by stones skilfully aimed at the waterline, the Roman General returned with armour-clad vessels and managed to make a beachhead. Roman culture was imposed on the locals by the garrisons in Palma, Sinium (Sineu), and Pollentia on Balearis Major and in Mago (Maó) on Balearis Minor, and was consolidated by settlers brought over from the Roman provinces of Hispania. The *Pitiüses*, on the other hand, maintained their Punic identity; for the next four centuries the Romans still considered them a separate entity from the rest of the Balearics. Today, two thousand years later, they still build their flat-roofed North African style houses while the other islands maintain tiled roofs and a Roman floor plan. A recent study has proved the genetic difference between the inhabitants of the *Pitiüses* and the rest of the islanders.

Traces of the British occupation are similarly present in Minorcan homes with their sash windows (known as *boinders*, from bow-windows), door latches, and two-up two-down terrace houses. Mulled wine, known as *calent*, is still drunk here over Christmas, and the British sweet tooth is evident. The Minorcan dialect of Catalan has a lighter, more birdlike lilt than the gruff cawing of the Majorcans.

Minorca's traditional system of inheritance has saved its countryside from suffering the same fate as Majorca's. While on the larger island properties were divided up equally among heirs to the point where a smallholding was unable to support a family, Minorcan farms passed on intact to the eldest son, maintaining their productivity; the younger siblings would work on the farm or learn a trade. In hard times, the net result was the same: emigration of the less favoured. But whereas in Majorca these subdivided small-holdings were abandoned as unprofitable, Minorcan agriculture and trade carried on in a good state of health, in which it still finds itself, without the need to depend exclusively upon mass tourism.

The fact that these islands live back to back is evidenced by the fact that you can't buy a latch in a Majorcan ironmonger's nor a map of Palma in a Minorcan stationer's. In fact there is probably more inter-island networking among the resident foreign population than among the islanders themselves. The only true cultural exchange between islands is gastronomic. Minorcan gin is still made to the original British recipe and has a strong taste of the juniper berries that grow profusely on this windswept island. *Un gin* is not to be confused with a standard *ginebra* like Gordon's.

Minorca turns to its southern sisters for olive oil because its colder, windier climate only produced wild olives. However, its rolling hills made good pastureland for the dairy farming introduced by the British, although butter is rarely used for cooking. The island's best-known export is its crumbly, mature cheese, while the local ice cream manufacturers are credited with having invented the frozen, ice cream-stuffed lemon.

I've visited Minorca seven times, about six more than the average Majorcan of my age, and despite everything it has in common with its Balearic neighbours I still feel I'm visiting a foreign country. For me it's a curious mixture of my two upbringings, British and Majorcan; there are details that echo the images of nineteenth-century rural England from

Randolph Caldecott's picture books, details like the traditional costume of the Minorcan horsemen and the tobacco pipes that Toni's grandfather made to pass the time.

We had come to play in Mercadal, where his old *pai* still lived, making the pipe stems from *vima*, a local reed, and turning the bowls with a lath powered by a washing-machine motor. (*Washing-machine*, incidentally, is an English word all Spaniards find hilariously funny; another is *cauliflower*.) Toni also introduced me to the village blacksmith, who looked every inch a Scottish Highlander – he only needed a kilt to be given a part in *Braveheart*. He was, however, as laid-back as a Minorcan could be, only working when he had to. Toni confided: 'My brother-in-law asked him to make a gate for his new house and by the time he delivered it, the house had changed owners twice. If someone told him "You should go in for the Laziest Man Contest!" he'd answer "No, better if you go in for me." The Minorcans are even more laid-back than us Majorcans – too much *gin*. Although there's plenty of work in Minorca, nobody would suffer an emotional crisis like a Catalan might if he had to go on the dole. In the 1950s my grandfather came over to Majorca for the first time to live with us in Dog Orchard, a very quiet neighbourhood on the outskirts of Palma with only eighteen houses. But after a few months he returned to Menorca: "Kaaaa! I can't take this craziness. Too many people, the noise of bicycles rushing by is driving me crazy . . . I'm going back to Mercadal to die in peace at the old folk's home."' At the time of writing, the oldest man in the world is the Minorcan Joan Riudavets, born the same year as Chaplin and Hitler, who's never had a headache in his life.

\* \* \*

Mercadal was in the middle of its *festes*, which, like most
on the island, has a strong equestrian element. On the morning of the concert, we joined Toni's cousins on Monte Toro,
a modest hill that is the highest point on this flat, windswept
island. The name is etymologically related to the English
word *tor* and not, as most people suppose, 'Bull Mountain'.
A long procession of riders on thoroughbred horses,
elegantly dressed in their traditional black breeches, jacket,
and riding hat, wound their way up to the esplanade in
front of the Sanctuary of Our Lady of Monte Toro, where
a brass band awaited them. From where I stood, I noticed
the tuba player filling up his companions' shot-glasses from
a bottle of Nelson's Gin – made to the Admiral's own recipe
– out of sight of the conductor behind the huge bell of his
instrument.

There was a brilliant display of rearing horsemanship, a
strong sign of Minorcan identity. In the big summer solstice
festivals in Maó and Ciutadella in honour of Sant Joan,
hundreds of riders and thousands of revellers crowd the
streets, and it's considered good luck to pat the belly of a
rearing horse. Toni led us down to the Bar Romaní (Rosemary) in Mercadal for a bite to eat before going on stage;
he introduced me to the owner, Jaume, and ordered a round
of *pomada* – an 'ointment' made of gin and lemonade that
everybody downs like cups of tea.

'Jaume, Tomás here is very interested in the local culinary
culture.'

'Have you ever eaten *arròs de xiribil.lí* [rice with stone
curlew – pronounced cheery-beal-lee]? No? Well, now pay
attention. First, you take a new earthenware *tià* . . . it has
to be new . . . and rub it with garlic. You pluck the bird . . .'
and he launched into a step-by-step description of the

preparation of the dish. My mouth began to water as he described at length the complicated use of condiments, the slow cooking in the *tià*, adding a splash of cold water at crucial moments to 'scare' the rice ... everybody in the bar was solemnly nodding their heads in agreement as he continually refilled my glass with *pomada*.

'But the real secret of an authentic *arròs de xiribil.lí* comes at the very end. This is very important. You must take the *tià* off the stove and carry it out into the street.'

'To cool it down suddenly?' I asked

Everybody in the bar turned to watch my reaction.

'No, to smash the whole dish against the opposite wall, because there's nobody on earth who can eat that damned bird! Not even the worms!' Another British legacy to the Minorcans is an Edward Lear-like sense of humour.

I hadn't realized the potency of the 'ointment' I'd been downing for the last half-hour and had to be frogmarched five times around the block by Toni and his new backup musician Dorín before I was rid of my idiot grin and in a fit enough state to go onstage.

*Dorín* is a diminutive of Salvador, arrived at by that round-about Spanish route – reminiscent of Cockney rhyming slang – whereby a name is affectionately augmented to Edu-ardito, Tomasita, Vicentete, or Salvadorín, only to have its root sawn off, leaving Dito, Sita, Tete, or Dorín. For all his Majorcan manner, Dorín is really a *mig-i-mig*, a half-and-half like me, with a very good ear for music He began taking master guitar classes with Toni and ended up standing in for me on stage while I was away for half a year in Nicaragua.

Technically speaking, neither Dorín nor I are authentic *mig-i-mitjos* because neither of our parents is an islander; his are both *forasters* (outsiders, the name given to mainlanders) while mine are *estrangers* (foreigners, which are often more readily accepted than the *forasters*). However, having been born and schooled on the island and speaking the local language goes a fair way towards compensating for the lack of Majorcan blood. Dorín's family is in the construction business in the Port d'Andratx, which doesn't stop him from singing out against the blocks of apartments that now cling to every rockface in the bay where he grew up.

Upon my return from Managua, we hit it off musically and so, with Toni, decided to carry on as a trio, which allowed us to develop some much richer musical textures and harmonies and to experiment with different instruments. But living in distant parts of the island (a half-hour drive is long-distance to a Majorcan) meant that splitting Toni's meagre fee three ways hardly covered the petrol and sandwiches, so we referred to ourselves privately as *Fam, Fam i Gana* – Hungry, Hungry, and Starving.

In the 1980s in Spain, before the term 'world music' was coined, only the more inquisitive folk musicians from the Països Catalans and Andalusia seemed to be conscious of the common heritage of the Mediterranean cultures. All the countries bathed by this sea share the same raw musical material, but we each approach it in a different way, much as our diets shared the same ingredients but combined them into different recipes. Flamenco and other kinds of Spanish folk music seemed to be divided, as in the British and American folk scene, between the purists and fusionists. The new wave of flamenco musicians had made contact with their Moroccan, Algerian, and Egyptian counterparts and had even recorded with them. Like Maria del Mar Bonet, Toni had always turned his ears eastwards towards Italy and

Greece. 'Catalonia backs on to the whole of Spain, so Catalan musicians don't bother to investigate much musically; we islanders only have our arses behind us, so we're free to look towards other shores, whether Portugal or Turkey. Working as a hotel musician I've been immersed in the *chanson Française*, in the classic Neapolitan melodies. I could re-record any of my albums in Portuguese or Italian and get away with it. I've never been a folklorist or a purist; we Majorcans are a mongrel breed anyway.' Toni's more nostalgic, intimate songs seemed to beg a swell of rippling mandolins, which Dorín and I added with great gusto, spending hours working out soaring harmonies. 'I can't finish a song unless I start with a musically rich melody,' explains Toni. 'I can't stay in the three-chord rut that most Catalan protest singers fall into. Serrat and Lluís Llach have a strong musical basis, but most protest singers are like Raimón. Although I appreciate his message, his songs drive me up the wall, every chord is predictable.' That's how I felt about playing with Teresa Rebull in Barcelona. For me, Toni was composing music which, though often simple, gave a musician something to get his teeth into.

The Neapolitans insist *napolitano* is a language, not a dialect of Italian. The first time I heard it spoken in the streets of Naples it sounded just like Majorcan. I later discovered that for part of the fifteenth and sixteenth centuries the Balearics, Sardinia, Sicily, and Naples were united under the crown of Aragon; many other similarities are still apparent today. One of the most popular and beautiful folk songs in the Catalan language tells of the Baron's daughter who falls in love with the voice of a prisoner singing in his cell. She asks her father for the key, but he refuses because the gallows rope is already paid for. 'In that case,' she replies, 'let me share the rope with my beloved.' Most Catalan variants of this popular lullaby set the story in Lerida or Toledo, but the Majorcan version, as Toni's mother used to sing it, is called 'The City of Naples'.

In the Balearics, the east wind is called *gregal*, the Greek wind. Although there has been little contact with Greece since the medieval trade routes fell into disuse, there are certain Majorcan folk tunes that sound as if they were composed on the bouzouki. The traditional Majorcan *bolero*, *El Parado de Valldemossa*, begins almost note for note with the same tune as Manos Hadjidakis's Oscar-winning theme song for the film *Never on a Sunday*. Toni had been lent a bouzouki and the warm, rich, nutty sound so captivated us that we bought a second one. A bouzouki could be described as a cross between a mandolin and a giraffe: the same boat-shaped sound box and a tremendously long neck, a tenor to the mandolin's soprano. The two bouzoukis brought a breath of fresh *gregal* into our sound.

When we found ourselves playing before the Spanish Royal Family at a charity concert, Toni addressed our Greek-born Queen Sophia: 'Majesty, you'll probably find these two instruments familiar.' After the show she came up to thank us: 'This is the first time I've heard the bouzouki played in Spain.'

The similarity between Balearic and Aegean landscapes led the producers of *Ari*, a bio-pic about Onassis, to shoot some sequences in Majorca. One scene needed a couple of bouzoukis, for which the producer was willing to pay generously. 'If you don't have anybody to play them, Dorín and I are professionals,' offered Toni. They were hired. 'We got paid the same rate as our instruments. In that scene

Onassis tosses plates over his shoulder, and it took two days to get the 22-second sequence right. With a couple more days like that Dorín and I could have bought ourselves a Vespa each.'

Although we never considered ourselves part of the folk revival, we often found ourselves sharing the bill with new groups like Musica Nostra who also felt that freeing Majorcan music of its formal constraints could bring it closer to its real roots. Twenty years later they are still going strong and explain their musical philosophy thus: 'Folk music is the soil's way of expressing itself musically. We are a link with a way of life that has all but disappeared. We've kept the essence but have given it a new energy with arrangements for voices, flute and violin, things that didn't exist before. Ours doesn't have the prestige of Celtic music because it hasn't been allowed to evolve. It's been used as a tool by politicians, always kept in check, without risking any development, whether in the words or the music. The town councils think it's just something to put on for the old folk in the village square. We believe in a revival of folk music, a tribe in which folk musicians can live and work together. We're ecologists. Things have to evolve, but on the islands the change has been so great that it could break the human harmony between one generation and the next.'

When I first met Dorín, he was even speedier than Toni or me. He ran a shop selling ceramics and garden furniture in the tourist resort of Paguera, and would arrive at a gig at the last minute, having had to close the shop, go home for a shower, and then drive halfway across the island. Once we were sharing the bill with María del Mar in the Manacor Theatre. The concert had been widely advertised and the theatre was full. Dorín, as usual, arrived just as we were going onstage. Toni was in such a state of nerves by then that he couldn't calm down enough to start singing, so he played a chord and began talking about his socks. The audience was wetting itself laughing, and María del Mar realized she'd have a hard act to follow.

We never followed a script and that always helps break the ice, especially with a rural audience. The first time we played in the village of Consell, the Town Hall assured Toni that there was no need to bring any equipment – 'We have everything you'll need.' Toni was living in a fourth-floor flat with no lift and didn't need to be told twice – anything to avoid carting his PA, 'the corpse', around. But that was the last time he'd trust to luck because when we arrived, there was one mike between the three of us, one of those 1950s carbon-microphones sellotaped to a fishing rod that was jammed between the stage planks. The priest had plugged it into his Tannoy system, the tiny speakers hanging from the church door. There was a great expectation and at one minute to ten the audience had already taken their seats, and we were on stage. In those days electronic tuners were unaffordable, so we checked our tuning by ear – over eighty strings between us – before the first number, which that night was in the key of D. Suddenly the church clock began to strike ten, also in perfect D, so we began to improvise around the chimes, and from there slipped into the song. Other performers would have probably waited until the bells had stopped, but we've always gone with the flow instead of against it, and this usually puts the audience in our pocket. I've also noticed that the lower the volume you play at, the more attentive an audience is.

The closest we came to playing traditional folk music was the half-dozen humorous *jotas* that we included as light relief in the village fiestas. These were what today would be called bonus tracks – excluded from the albums because they weren't the sort of thing you want to listen to repeatedly, but they were great fun to play live, to get the audience laughing at themselves. Majorcans love a bit of a laugh, the fruitier the better, and the songs described the characters and situations familiar to all. There are knowing looks and nudges among the older members of the audience during *Madò María* when she's asked not to be too hard on her unmarried daughter for 'celebrating Easter before Palm Sunday' by losing her virginity under a tree to a fair-haired lad from Manacor. 'Don't scold her,' sings Toni, 'it's the fault of the discothèques, the rum-and-coke, the ton-up motorbikes and Virginia tobacco; things have changed, there's no long courtship like when you were young. And if your husband has a fit when you break the news, remind him that he would have done the same thing, given half a chance.'

*Els Picadors* is a tribute to the village lads, mentioned in Chapter 3, who would practise their English while heading for the coast after work to pick up foreign girls:

> 'Is you first time in Mallorca?'
> Top her up with cut-price rum
> As you gently take her hand . . .

Here we break into tight barbershop harmony:

> 'I waitink forr you to-morr-ohhhhh . . . ohhḥhhh . . .'

Over the years that my wife Carmen and sister-in-law Frances went to the regular Majorcan dancing sessions in the village, I got the hang of playing the castanets. The local variety are made of pomegranate wood and are very different from the larger, flatter flamenco ones made of ebony. The technique is also different. Flamenco castanets are played with the fingers, whereas the Majorcan dancers use their arm- and hand-movements to create a flapping effect that does most of the work. There is a male and a female castanet – one 'tuned' a third above the other – and I found that I could play them fairly convincingly on Toni's comic songs, most of which are in *jota* time, giving them an even more festive air. As the Spanish say, it's a sound that makes you 'happier than a pair of castanets'.

As a trio, Toni, Dorín, and I have performed in some beautiful settings, from the Abbey of Saint Michel de Cuixà in France to the Roman Theatre in Alcudia; we've played under the stars in the nave of the huge unfinished church at Biniamar, once the dream of the ambitious village priest. 'A week after playing to a faceless crowd of 50,000 people at the Canet Festival in Catalonia, we were playing to fifty people in the candlelit theatre at Ca n'Alluny, where the faces of the audience also shone like candles,' remembers Toni. One of our most memorable concerts took place on the steps of the cathedral in Gerona under autumn stars. A cold night, and a complete silence that was hard to believe in the centre of such a large town. A professional sound engineer was manning the PA, and the audience was as absorbed in our music as we were – the front row was only a few feet away. As the last, dominant chord of *Quatre Estacions* was left hanging in the air, a man in the front row let out a sonorous tenor fart that was picked up by all six microphones and broadcast over the loudspeakers.

There have also been some gigs we'd prefer to forget, like the huge Mediterranean Festival held on a football ground in Manacor. We islanders took second place to the big names from the mainland, who had the primetime midnight to four a.m. slot. The mood in the dressing rooms was great, with the Argentine rumba-rocker Gato Perez rolling joints with the new wave gypsies Lole y Manuel. In Gato's band was my friend from Pernil Latino, a mandolin player who is the spitting image of Robert Crumb. Although due on at eleven, we had to make way for the bigger names who wanted to catch the last plane to Madrid, so we ended up playing to a snoring audience of thousands at 5 a.m. But perhaps our most tiresome engagement was providing the live instrumental accompaniment for a two-week run of *Les Alegres Casades de Windsor*, the first Catalan adaptation of Shakespeare, at the plush Teatre Principal in Palma.

Soon afterwards, we headlined our own week-long run at the Principal. No longer were Dorín and I just adding a few rippling washes to Toni's music; we had been working out some spare but sophisticated arrangements as a trio, taking care not to swamp his voice. It was especially exhilarating to be able to synchronize intricate runs up and down the fretboard in close harmony, in different instrumental combinations: warm Spanish guitar, jangling Cuban *tres*, ukelele-like Minorcan *guitarró*, tremulous Italian mandolin, quavering Portuguese *fado*, and the resonant bite of the Greek bouzouki. The arrangement for two bouzoukis of *Lo Cant del Mariner* always made my heart leap every time Dorín and I pulled together like two oars through the swell of Toni's guitar. He had set this wonderfully lyrical poem by the classic Majorcan poet Monsignor Miquel Costa i Llobera to a melody that seemed to have drifted from port to port around the Mediterranean. Although written a century earlier, the description of a fisherman setting out in his *llaüt* at dusk brought to my mind a childhood image of Sebastià and his brother pulling out of the inky shadows of Cala Deià and into the rays of the setting sun to lay their nets, while the Mediterranean lies as still as a millpond:

> The mariner sings as he rows his craft alone
> While the deepening blue sky awaits the evening star
> The sweet offshore breeze flitters across the sea
> Setting the swell a-tremble with its lightness of
>     breath . . .

Nowhere in the Balearics is more than twenty miles from the coastline, yet it's an inward-facing society, much more dependent upon the soil than the sea. The tourist-friendly, shark-free Med is a concept that has now been accepted by most islanders, although many of the older villagers still eye the coast with misgivings as a barren, dangerous place. There are parts of the Deià coastline that, even today, give me the willies, even though I've swum, paddled, or rowed every inch of it. Only a generation ago, one could still come across the occasional old Majorcan who had never seen the Mediterranean, and many of those who emigrated in the nineteenth and twentieth centuries saw it up close for the first time as they boarded ship. Even coastal towns in Majorca were built at least two miles inland from their fishing ports as a safety measure against attacks by pirates and corsairs: the only two actually fronting onto the sea were the walled cities of Palma and Alcudia. Inland transport used to be so slow that fresh fish hardly found its way to the centre of the island, and even in these refrigerated days the housewives from Inca or Sineu always look a little lost in the fish section of the supermarket.

The Balearic islanders learned to be self-sufficient and not to count on outside help, even from neighbouring islands. The unpredictable Mediterranean storms and the threat of pirates from as near as North Africa or as far as Turkey made maritime transport unreliable. The islands had always had a measure of autonomy from the mainland, and from each other, both under the Moors and then under the Crown of Aragon. Then Philip V's centralist *Décreto de Nueva Planta* of 1715 pulled the political, cultural, and linguistic rug from under the feet of all the outlying regions of Spain. It wasn't until 1983 that these rights were permanently returned to the islanders with the approval of the Statutes of Autonomy. During the preceding years of transition, while Galicia, Catalonia, and the Basque Country – the *historic nations* – were pressing for home rule, Toni was one of the few singers to avoid jumping on the political bandwagon: had he done so, we might have all made some real money. As it was, we only once played at a political rally, sharing the bill with María del Mar in the beautiful Plaça del Rei in the Gothic quarter of Barcelona. The Catalan Republican Left Party could only pay our hopover air fare – they saved on hotel rooms because Toni and Dorín, like true Majorcans, insisted on catching the last plane back to *sa roqueta* to sleep in their own beds. (After any mainland trade fair or convention, when the rest of the delegates are out painting the town red, the Majorcan contingent invariably heads for the airport.)

Separatist and nationalist movements tend to feed on the need to erect barriers to protect their cultural identity when political borders have been eliminated by the engulfing state. An islander doesn't need to draw these lines: his identity is clearly marked by a physical frontier, the sea. Nor does he need to partake in mass rallies to make his point. It was the 'historic nations' who fought the hardest to gain their autonomy after the Fascist state was dismantled. The Balearics and the Canary Islands received theirs by default when Madrid decided upon the Solomonic decision of dividing the whole country into autonomies, including Castille and Leon, which had never even asked to be one.

There is, of course, a Day of the Balearic Islands, a puffed-up institutional affair with a big bash celebrated on a different island each year, an event that nobody but the politicians would attend if it weren't for free food and music. The only mass public display of grass-roots Majorcanhood is the annual pilgrimage from Palma to the monastery of Lluc, high in the Serra de Tramuntana, known as the *Marxa d'Es Güell a Lluc a Peu* – the 'March from the Güell to Lluc on Foot'.

It all began on a hot summer evening in 1973 in the Bar Güell, one of those cavernous cafés on the outskirts of Palma, on a shadeless asphalt junction of three wide streets. Bartolomé Barceló, the rubicund owner – Tolo *Güell* to all who knew him – had closed the bar and invited a dozen of his card-playing cronies to supper in the back room. At midnight, someone suggested going out for a stroll in the cool of the evening. 'The only cool place on the island right now is Lluc – it's almost a thousand metres above sea level,' someone pointed out. 'Well, let's walk to Lluc then.' Nine hours and almost fifty kilometres later – half of them uphill – as the sun rose, the group of friends stumbled into the cool valley of the monastery.

Lluc (pronounced 'yook') is famous for its boys' choir known as the *blauets* after their blue cassocks and is the spiritual heart of the island, much as Montserrat is to the

Catalans. Not only do its rocky outcrops remind one of Montserrat, but it is also the sanctuary of a Black Madonna, *la Moreneta*. The Latin word *lucus* referred to a hallowed forest, which suggests that the sacred nature of the place is probably pre-Christian. Miraculous apparitions of the Virgin, like the one in Lluc, tend to occur close to an ancient place of worship – a cave, forest, or mountain peak – once dedicated to the Mother Goddess.

The weird rock formations surrounding the monastery set the scene for many *rondallas*, folk tales of the Majorcan oral tradition, full of bandits and giants, of kings and their beautiful daughters. One tells the tale of *El Salt de la Bella Dona*, 'the Leap of the Beautiful Lady', which gives its name to a chasm beside the road to Lluc. An unjustly jealous husband convinced his beautiful wife to accompany him on a pilgrimage to the monastery, which has always been a popular way for Majorcans to express gratitude to the Madonna for favours bestowed or prayers answered. A few miles before arriving, on the pretext of showing his wife the spectacular view, the cad pushed her into the chasm. When he entered the monastery an hour later, jauntily unrepentant, he found his wife prostrated before the altar in prayer: the Madonna had caught her in her fall and carried her bodily to the monastery. Needless to say, the villain saw the error of his ways, and so on and so forth.

The only serious bloodshed the island has witnessed in the last five hundred years was a medieval peasants' revolt against city taxes. When it was finally crushed, many rebels fled to the hills and for several generations the Majorcan mountains were full of bandits. The most famous of these was Mateu Reus of Alaró, alias *En Rotget* ('Little Red'), who lived with his men in these woods, robbing from the rich pilgrims and giving to the poor. The authorities found no way of capturing him, his invincibility being guaranteed by a tiny silver box hanging from his neck. But in the summer of 1728, while the annual dance was under way on the large esplanade before the monastery, all the men's eyes were fixed upon an unknown beauty who politely refused all offers to dance; she seemed to be waiting for someone. Soon, in a cloud of dust, three horsemen approached. The tallest of them, unarmed, dismounted and went directly towards the beautiful girl. She again declined to dance but, giving in to his insistence, she finally accepted on condition that she could wear his little silver box around her neck while they danced. The temptation was great and the risk small, but no sooner had Rotget untied the thong than he was suddenly overpowered by four armed agents. He fought like a man possessed, but he had lost his talisman and nobody lifted a finger to help him. He was imprisoned and hanged the following January.

Word of Tolo *Güell*'s after-supper pilgrimage to Lluc soon got around the neighbourhood and when, the following August, he decided to repeat it, many more of his regular clients joined in. After a few years, the *Marxa d'Es Güell a Lluc a Peu* had become an annual event attracting hundreds of people from all over the neighbourhood, which centres on the popular marketplace of Pere Garau. ('Wherever did you get that beautiful dress? Is it Pierre Cardin?' 'No, dahling, it's *Pierre Gareau*.')

In the towns that lie along the route, the people sitting outside their front doors enjoying the cool night air would offer slices of melon and cool water to the *marxaires* as they trooped through. By the late Eighties, the event attracted walkers from all over Palma and had become institutionalized: just the logistics of registering 20,000 people and getting them home again demanded the collaboration of police, Red Cross, and six hundred volunteers. The *Güell a Lluc a Peu* was heading for the *Guinness Book of Records* as the largest nocturnal march in the world. It is not just a show of brotherhood: for many, both young and old, it's also a personal rite of passage. From 9 p.m. on the first Saturday of August, the junction outside the Bar Güell is closed to traffic and becomes a huge square, with every possible manifestation of Majorcan music and culture taking the stage. There's a rapid turnover: folk groups, Catalan rock, and traditional music. At the start of the 1993 *Lluc a Peu*, King Juan Carlos bestowed on Tolo *Güell* an honorary award before setting off the fireworks to mark the beginning of the march. To hear hundreds of radical separatists cheering as a centralist monarch lit the fuse was in itself a wonderful display of the famous Majorcan tolerance.

Toni, Dorín, and I played at these send-offs several years running, probably the largest and most enthusiastic audience we'd ever had. Once, backstage, I bumped into my old guitar teacher Juanito Coll. I hadn't seen him in twenty years and with his long mane of white hair he looked every inch *El Viejo Duque*, the Old Duke. Although he had become a fervent Majorcan nationalist in his old age, he still spoke to me in Spanish, as he had felt obliged to do during our classes back in the days of Franco. 'Tomasito! My Tomasito, look at you! Whoever saw you and who can see you now! Let me embrace you . . . listen, I'm writing a concerto for guitar and orchestra dedicated to your dear father . . .' Juanito died a couple of years later, probably no closer to finishing the concerto than when he first announced it two decades earlier.

At the word go, the twenty thousand with their banners and scarves – almost 10 per cent of the city – move off into the night. This is not a race, and it doesn't raise any money for charity; it's simply a huge mobile party. Many don't make it to the top of the mountain and are picked up, exhausted and blistered, by a shuttle service of volunteers with cars. Some of those that do reach Lluc still find the energy to dance a *bolero* with the welcoming committee of folk dancers. A hearty breakfast is provided in the huge monastery grounds before the Sunday service in which even atheists take part and during which nobody nudges you if you doze off.

The big march inevitably sparked off a reply from the *part forana*, the Majorcan hinterland. The historical rift between the city folk and the country folk after the peasant revolt still lingers; and although Palma lost its power to Madrid in the seventeenth century, its relationship with the rest of the island is often tainted by mutual distrust. Thus, a month after the *Güell a Lluc a Peu*, the pilgrimage from the *Part Forana a Lluc a Peu* is held.

Groups of pilgrims from all the villages on the island set off at different times to arrive at the monastery at dawn – almost twenty-four hours for those that have crossed the plain from the southern tip of the island, Santanyi, or who have followed the mountain range from Andratx. Most pilgrims have arrived from the plain and converge upon the town of Selva at about 4 a.m. There begins the uphill climb, through the village of Caimari, and up the winding road past the Salt de la Bella Dona to the crest of the hill overlooking Lluc.

While my rock and roll commitments often carried on until dawn, Toni's concerts tended to end at a reasonable hour, say one in the morning. This one, however *began* at 4.30 a.m. We were hired to play to the walkers from the *part forana* as they staggered up the final leg of the march. The organizers had arranged for us to perform in a cave in the cliff face across the valley from the road that zig-zagged up the opposite slope. A state-of-the-art sound system had been set up, using dozens of small Bose speakers strapped to the trees and rocks; the natural acoustics of the valley were magical. It took us half an hour to scramble up through the stone terraces in the moon's shadow, carrying our guitar cases and dodging the long power cables. The cave was discreetly illuminated; from the road we must have looked like the Holy Family in the stable.

We are used to intimate contact with our audience. Sometimes in large concerts the spotlights don't let you see the crowd, but at least you know they're just in front of you. Perched in our cave, we could hear sparse, distant cheers from the pale figures in the moonlight across the valley on finishing a song. We'd never played to a moving audience before, and although our 'theatre' covered almost a kilometre of zig-zagging road, at this point the walkers were so strung out (in the geographical sense) that our audience never reached a hundred at any given moment.

The big visual event to accompany our music featured several rock climbers abseiling down from the top of the cliff, across the mouth of the cave, each pulling after him alternating bolts of red or yellow cotton, to make up the *senyera*, the banner of pan-Catalan culture. The whole show was supposed to last half an hour but technical hitches delayed the descent for so long that, although we played for time – well over an hour extra – in the end it was abandoned.

The spectacle was intended as an allusion to the origin of the *senyera*. In the medieval legend, when Charles the Bald battled against the Normans one of his bravest men on the field was the Count of Guifré. As Guifré lay wounded by his gilded yellow shield, the grateful Emperor dipped his fingers in the Count's open wound and smeared four bloody fingermarks down the shield, announcing: 'This will now be your coat of arms.' *Senyera* simply means a flag but the root word, *seny*, signifies direction, purpose, and common sense and is fundamental to the Catalan identity. The official flag of the Balearic Islands, however, sets the four red bars horizontally on a yellow background, the top left-hand quarter showing a white castle with five towers on a purple background. Of course during the dictatorship the only flag allowed to be displayed in public was the Spanish, a horizontal red-yellow-red.

Both the *Part Forana a Lluc* and the *Güell a Lluc* still continue to attract tens of thousands every summer, even though the Bar Güell itself was torn down to make way for a bank. (There is now also an annual pilgrimage to Lluc *amb Bistia*, with pack animals.) Tolo *Güell* stood for Mayor of Palma and would have had a good chance of being elected had anybody recognized his real name, Bartolomé Barceló, on the ballot papers.

# 7

# The Second Most Famous Unknown Band in the World

Daevid and Gilli had returned to the village in the mid Seventies to live and work, to 'touch base' after the insanity of touring, and Kevin followed their example a few years later. These musical cult figures were drawing creative characters (as well as some loonies and hangers-on) to the village much as my father had in the previous decades. After recording *Good Morning* with Euterpe at his Banana Moon Observatory, Daevid began touring with them and came into contact with the progressive Spanish music scene. He began to produce records at the Observatory for Pau Riba – 'the Catalan Daevid Allen' – and the Valencian Pep Laguardia. Up until then, the only Spanish-speaking bohemians to be seen in the village had been discreet Catalan painters, or Latin American writers who would come to visit or stay with our close friend Claribel Alegría, the Salvadoran poet. Her son Erik and I played music together and we knew all the words of 'Alice's Restaurant' off by heart – all twenty-five minutes of it. Claribel and her husband Bud shared my mother's left-wing views: in Paris they had formed part of the émigré circle with Gabriel García Márquez, Julio Cortázar, and Mario Vargas Llosa.

The father of modern Latin American poetry, the Nicaraguan Rubén Darío, had lived in Valldemossa in the early part of the century, as had Jorge Luís Borges a few decades later. Borges returned in 1981 to visit my father but the chauffeured car provided by a local publisher had broken down in the centre of the village. A couple of poets at the bar recognized the great man and escorted him and his secretary Maria Kodama to Ca n'Alluny. At this time Robert had begun inhabiting a different dimension and was beyond recognizing even some of his own family. Since my father was being uncooperative and the Argentinian writer was blind, I had to help them find each other's hand, a handshake described by Borges as 'mystical'. Beryl kept the conversation going while I went out to make tea. After a cup or two Borges needed to relieve himself before the return trip, but in Ca n'Alluny there is no toilet on the ground floor. Rather than risk the stairs, Beryl led him outside behind the woodshed, where Robert would also occasionally water the flowers.

Borges's chauffeured car was still out of action so I drove him back to his hotel. During the half-hour ride he recited long passages of the epic poem *Beowulf* to me in fluent Anglo-Saxon – his passion – which was one of the most memorable moments of my life. Had I experienced it a few years earlier, I would probably not have ended up failing my English Literature O level.

By the end of the 1970s many Spanish longhairs, not only musicians, began to blend in unobtrusively with the Deià freaks. The only ones to really stand out were three conspicuous members of the fledgling Spanish Drug Squad. Wearing wigs, squeaky-clean jeans and shiny shoes, the undercover trio could be spotted a mile off; the genial touch was their rather ineffectual dope-sniffing Alsatian decked out in a garland of plastic flowers. They had learned all the hip talk in order to infiltrate the North Coast Drug Scene, but after a week they headed off for Ibiza without so much as having been passed a joint at the bar.

Although the new political climate allowed a Spaniard complete freedom of speech, dress, and hairstyle, he would still have to face the dirty looks of a reactionary part of society. He could only really let his hair down in places like Ibiza, Formentera, or Deià, where the locals never batted an eyelid at transgressional behaviour. At the turn of the century Deià had attracted the Catalan bohemians – the black sheep of the best families – and the pattern was repeated in the 1970s. Spain's new rock impresario Gay Mercader, the fashion designer Toni Miró and other pioneers of Barcelona designer chic merged into the Deià landscape to chill out with the rest of the straw basket and espadrille set.

Now that the common enemy had evaporated, the protest song movement had begun to regroup into different political factions: libertarians, leftists, nationalists, separatists. The annual folk festival at Canet de Mar, an hour's drive up the coast from Barcelona, had been increasingly open to more experimental, hedonistic tendencies until these had taken on a life of their own in 1975 as Canet Rock, the gathering point of the most progressive musical trends in the country. The 1978 event was organized by the floating anarchist Pau Riba himself, who designed a poster featuring the Virgin Mary praying inside a Glastonbury-style transparent pyramid. This was considered sacrilege by the Catholic Church, which pressured the authorities to cancel the festival. The event finally took place, but the Church had nailed the coffin lid on future Canet Rocks.

I've never much enjoyed festivals, but that September I motorcycled down with a backstage pass to see Daevid perform and take some photos for a rock magazine, a job I got on the strength of the promo shots I'd done for Daevid and Euterpe's tour. Pau Riba had proclaimed this Canet as the beginning of the Age of Aquarius, but in retrospect one can see it as marking the end of a utopia. The previous August, a week-long libertarian festival had attracted half a million freethinkers and anti-authoritarian radicals from all over the country to party on the empty streets of Barcelona while most of the city's population was on holiday. But none of the mainstream political parties, least of all the Catalan nationalists, could allow this anti-establishment movement to get too strong: the anarchists, they reasoned, had already put Spain's stability on the line during the Republic. The second Libertarian Festival, due for August 1978, was aborted by the authorities and its potent street-level energy diverted into 'safer' areas.

The dream was over, and that September Canet Rock, for all its big names – Blondie, Ultravox, Gong, Nico – seemed to lack any direction or warmth. There was Catalan psychedelic whimsy from the bespectacled, galactic Sisa, whose hippie anthem, 'One of These Nights the Sun Will Shine', rang hollow that night. Madrid had provided home-grown punk with Los Masturbadores Mongólicos and teenage rock and roll from Tequila. Nico had been lured out of hiding in Ibiza to perform solo with her harmonium. In spite of her legendary reputation as part of the Velvet Underground, the crowd soon expressed its boredom and Nico left the stage in tears. The only band to rekindle some of the magic onstage was Daevid's. As always, his visuals were striking; the Catalan audience had never seen such dazzling theatrics. His costume was part Aztec priest, part Bill and Ben the Flowerpot Men, and he was buzzing with hard-edged energy having recently toured the UK with the punk band Here and Now.

This ad hoc incarnation of Gong shimmered and rocked very tightly considering it was a fourteen-piece ensemble made up largely of travelling musicians that Daevid had recruited and beaten into shape over the summer. Rehearsals had taken place in the Observatory in the midst of a domestic crisis brought on by excessive drunken partying – this spurred Gilli on to form her own band, Mother Gong. Among Daevid's new recruits – some of whom also formed Mother Gong – were Hamish Macdonald, who could come across as a full-on London punk, and Jerry Hart, a laid-back barefoot Woodstocker from Wigan. Jerry had shaved the left side of his skull and the right side of his jaw, so that by facing one side or other of the stage he metamorphosed from a bearded baldie into a clean-shaven longhair. Another newcomer was Jordi, a teenage Deian, on congas.

That night also inspired someone to shine a light pointing a way out of the doldrums for Spanish rock music, which was still slavishly dependent on foreign archetypes. Two brothers from Madrid, Santiago and Luís Auserón, wrote in *Disco Express* magazine: 'Canet 78 could have initiated a change . . . That dark night we had the suffocating feeling of being surrounded by people locked within their consciences, we felt their clumsily flailing hands cutting off our wings . . . but there's nothing to be done until we create our own myths. Spanish Pop is craving to exist . . . we have to break out of our provincial way of thinking. The essence of pop is its universality. Its real strength, all that makes it "foreign" to us, is also what is closest at hand.' These two musicians, true to their manifesto, were instrumental in helping Spanish pop outgrow its Anglo-Saxon straitjacket and find its own idiom; together they founded one of country's most successful and articulate rock bands, Radio Futura.

Pau Riba also realized that something had been lost; the pure energy that powered the underground movement had been hijacked by the new political parties for their own ends. 'Those who had been fighting against Franco's politics didn't realize that Fascism was only circumstantial, that we really should have been fighting against the system.' Today, Lluís Llach agrees: 'We thought that democracy was an end in itself, and that was a big mistake, because it is a means, not an end.' With the approval of the new constitution that year, many activists sat back and let the politicians get on with things. But, as Llach points out, 'If you don't treat democracy as an instrument to be perfected it becomes perverted, and that can be very dangerous.'

Back in Deià after playing at Canet, Hamish had decided that mellow Majorca needed the kick-start of its own punk/new wave band, and he was going to be the front man. He roped in two of his bandmates from the Canet show, Jerry Hart and Jordi 'Ramone' Rullan, to form the core of the Offbeats.

Jordi was from a family of fishermen that had settled in the village in the fifteenth century. He had spent his childhood in a cottage above the bay, adjoining the one my parents rented to put up their friends and family. He grew up to the throbbing *tuf tuf tuf* of the Perkins Marine engine that powered the fishing boat, and this beat got into his blood.

In the early Seventies I spent a couple of summers in the cottage with my friends from school. On the communal terrace Sebastián and his brother mended and tarred their nets while little Jordi ran about looking like one of the tar babies from my bedtime books. His grandmother would walk up to the village every morning with a wicker basket full of fish, which she sold from a wooden slab on the parapet by the schoolroom. This wasn't enough to support a family of seven, so Jordi's father took over the lease on the Bar Las Palmeras and left his bachelor brother to do the fishing.

Jordi was barely sixteen but had an air of a young Marlon Brando in *The Wild One*, moving with ease between the foreigners at the tables and playing Clash and Ramones tapes behind the bar. The Offbeats materialized in my basement, where Hamish plugged his microphone and Jordi and Jerry their guitars into my old amplifier from school. The essence of punk is its immediacy, and Hamish picked up on that aspect in looking for gigs. Having no bass player, drummer, or equipment didn't stop him.

The Offbeats' first public appearance was at a free concert in Palma's Plaça Major. It was a protest against a housing project on the virgin island of Dragonera, off the western-most tip of Majorca (the campaign was finally successful). The Deià representation onstage included a song from Lady June and an Irish jig from Ronnie Wathen on Ulleian pipes, both accompanied by Jerry. I was the Offbeats' bassist that stifling evening; I had never played the bass before, which qualified me as a punk musician. Hanging from my shoulder, besides the bass, were two large straw baskets, for no reason that I can remember. That night was also a premiere for Jordi, who played drums for the first time. Punk seemed like a lot of fun with (to use the current phrase) no future. I escaped the evening unscathed and unspat upon, and the band naturally dissolved with the first autumn rains.

In the spring of 1979 Hamish decided to relaunch the Offbeats. Jerry had been living an ascetic existence in a tepee in Ibiza, where he had followed a Basque-Scottish couple from Deià, Juan and Leslie, with whom he had worked on the record/portfolio *The Book of Am* (after Amerghin). Jerry was participating in the follow-up (soon to be released) when he was tracked down and abducted by Hamish, Jordi, and an Afro-haired bass player from Sóller, Pere 'Jimi Santana' Colom. The Offbeats' Ibizan adventure could be described as High Noon meets the Monkees. Getting arrested and hitch-hiking to gigs tempered the first Anglo-Majorcan punk band, and led to a gig at the 1979 Glastonbury festival and a contract with Charley Records in the UK.

As the Offbeats were surfing the new wave, my brother Juan had tripped over his rock and roll roots while playing at a party with David Templeton, a portrait painter from Worksop who had recently settled in the village with his wife and child. Juan was so struck by Dave's ability to impersonate rock legends from Elvis to Buddy Holly, as well as mimicking Dylan or anybody within earshot, that he decided that this could be the nucleus of the rock band he had always wanted to form. Although never in a hurry, when Juan has a vision he carries it through. The dream of playing in a rock and roll band had been simmering on the back burner ever since his best friends Dito and Mito had formed the Four Winds in the early 1960s. Juan already had a name for his dream band, Pa Amb Oli ('Bread and Olive Oil'). It had cropped up years earlier as a humorous translation of 'jam session' – bread, oil, and sugar being the local equivalent of the Liverpudlian jam buttie. A '*pa amb oli* session' soon became the byword whenever people got together to play. The first time it appeared on a poster was in 1972 for the *Miss Turismo* fiesta organized by the Deià Town Hall, who couldn't afford to hire a professional band and asked us to play. My girlfriend Wendy, Claribel's niece, won the title; her earthy Latin American beauty, although the antithesis of the typical blonde *turista*, won the judges over.

This Pa Amb Oli was a 'whoever's-in-town' line-up; Mito on bass, Juan and I on guitars, Ramón on keyboards, his sister Marta on drums. A Cuban-American sat in on congas and a black adolescent New Yorker, Mark 'Maceo' McDowell, played tenor sax. We had a shot at 'I Feel Good' and a few Latin and bossa nova standards, all driven along by Marta, a solid powerhouse of rhythm who led her own pop band in Barcelona.

Six years passed before the name Pa Amb Oli rode again, this time as a rock and roll band, on the polished cement dance floor under a pergola in the garden of the Pensión Can Quet. Jordi's drum kit drowned out the rest of the band, who all played through my 20-watt Baldwin guitar amp: Juan, two French musicians, Dave Templeton on vocals and Daevid Allen guesting on space guitar. The set was straight rock and roll, and all eyes were on the singer. Dave, a Richard Burton lookalike, had never sung in public before, let alone with a band, but the audience reaction convinced my brother that Dave was his man.

When I arrived home from Nicaragua on April Fool's day 1980, Lady June was in hospital with a broken arm, having driven her SEAT 600 into a sandstone parapet. The spot was now known as Lady's Leap since a few months earlier she had fallen asleep on the same parapet returning from a party and had woken up with a broken leg ten feet below, at the foot of a carob tree. In the days before street lighting, it was usual for foreigners to fall off terraces or into the torrent as they staggered home from a party, but since most were drunk and relaxed, few were seriously injured.

To help pay for June's hospital bill, a benefit concert was organized by a plump, smiling Australian hippie entrepreneur known as Buda (short for Buda Madre, a play on *de puta madre*, the Spanish equivalent of 'fuckin' brilliant'). Buda managed the Offbeats and the Kevin Ayers Band in Spain but neither were available for the gig: the Offbeats, now renamed the Sex Beatles, were in the UK promoting their single. Buda convinced Juan that this was the opportunity to put Pa Amb Oli on the map and printed up some flyers announcing the 'Pa Amb Oli Band' on 11 April 1980 at the Club St Germain in Sóller Port, 'their first performance in Majorca'. Buda added the word 'Band' in case anybody thought Pa Amb Oli was a Majorcan folk group. Dave was polishing up all his rock and roll lyrics, Juan was practising his Chuck Berry riffs, and Jordi was aching to play drums – he'd lost his place as the Sex Beatles' drummer when, after visiting his family for Christmas in Deià, he'd been refused re-entry into the UK.

Ten days before the gig, the band was still without a bass player, but that problem would be solved 'when Tomás gets back'. But if I had been cool about rock music before my trip to Nicaragua, on my return I was radically opposed to this blunt instrument of cultural imperialism, and told Juan as much. He mentioned the problem to Carmen, a beautiful Segovian girl who had come to live and work in the village while I was abroad. She had taken the lease on the local bookshop and stationers, and she loved rock and roll; 'Let me try and convince him,' she said. To my everlasting gratitude she succeeded in talking me into performing, easily overcoming any resistance on my part. I had just met her and was so bowled over that when she argued that music was way above politics, she could have convinced me to play the bagpipes strapped to a kite. I borrowed Toni Morlà's amplifiers, my friend Jeremy lent me his £15 bass with a bungee strap, and we were away.

Sóller Port caters mainly to Belgian and French tourists, which explains the Club's name, although in the off-season the clients are all from the surrounding villages. The heavy, padded wooden doors attempt to convey a sense of Parisian luxury, but the raised metal shutter betrays the fact that the St Germain was originally a garage. Like any small club on the Mediterranean seafront, the first thing that hits you in the narrow entrance way is the combined smell of last night's spilt San Miguel lager, Nivea suncream and stale cigarette smoke, all being pumped back through the rattling, dripping air-conditioner. The narrow entrance opens out between velveteen-covered columns supporting a ceiling so low that you could balance the mirror ball on your nose. The décor features the standard 1960s posters of a naked couple outlined against a sunset; semi-circular booths wrap around little Formica tables punctured by holes in which to set your Cuba libre, Lumumba (rum and chocolate), or gin-tonic.

An 80-watt PA system is ample for a band within kissing

distance of the audience. Ten seconds after opening with 'Long Tall Sally', all that separated us from the sweaty crowd on a stainless-steel dance floor six inches below us was the flimsy knee-high balustrade that penned us in on the tiny stage. With only one rehearsal, the repertoire was limited to the most basic rock and roll songs of all time: 'Be Bop a Lula', 'Johnny B. Goode', 'Heartbreak Hotel'. It was a tribal gathering with kids in pyjamas playing with bows and arrows and scuttling among the legs of the dancers. Emma Gough was in town with her boyfriend Charlie Ainley, a well-known pub rocker who led us through the Stones' 'Miss You'. I was, as the Spanish say, having as much fun as a midget, and from the ecstatic grins a few inches from my own, I realized that rock and roll, far from being an imperialist plot, was the folk music of the Global Village.

A few hours later, having loaded the equipment into the car, I was just setting off home when Carmen ran out in front of my headlights. I slammed on the brakes, she jumped in. Twenty-five years later we're still together; so are Juan, Jordi, Dave and me, the Pa Amb Oli Band.

The age of 27 supposedly marks the start of a new astrological cycle. In my case it marked the beginning of my life with Carmen, of my profession as a craftsman printer, and my newfound vocation as a rock and roller; it was also the year I acquired a social conscience in revolutionary Nicaragua. But 1980 also brought the first stirrings of confrontation in Deià that would strain the placid relationship between the established Majorcan families and the *artistas* whose bohemian lifestyle had been cheerfully tolerated for almost a century.

The dictatorship had always appointed or vetoed any candidate for a position of authority; even the essentially decorous position of village mayor, the kind of job the Spanish call 'a flower vase', could only be trusted to Franco loyalists. Any important municipal decision was taken by the Civil Governor in Palma and implemented by the Guardia Civil; day-to-day decisions were taken by the Secretary and carried out by the town crier. But even with so little to do, it was hard to find someone willing to accept the job of mayor. Majorcans have a natural aversion to sticking their necks out unless there is some benefit to be gained, but a village mayor's salary was low and in a rural community, opportunities for lining one's pockets were few. After our stone-mason-mayor retired in 1973, his position was filled for a short spell by the pious village taxi driver, whose sole contribution to the municipality was to give names to the streets and put up traffic signs. But even mule carts found it hard to respect his new 3 mph limit on Clot Street.

The last Deià mayor to be appointed directly by the central Government was a young Basque whose father, a Civil Guard, had been killed while on duty. His brother, also a Guardia, had married a Deià girl, and he had followed suit, marrying the granddaughter of a previous mayor. He was an unlikely choice for the post, the youngest mayor in Spain at the time, but there were no other contenders and it allowed the moribund regime to make reparation for his family's sacrifice to the Fatherland. This ambitious young *foraster*, who hardly spoke any Majorcan, immersed himself in the job, realizing the potential benefits open to him if he could hold onto it when democracy returned. In small Majorcan villages, party politics don't exist; since the return of democracy, it's the clan system that swings the votes, and the Basque found he had married into a powerful clan. Especially in the mountain communities where everybody had always worked for the big landlords, nobody dared challenge the status quo. In their first opportunity to vote, the Deians confirmed the mayor in his post.

In those first local elections the newly legalized opposition parties all over the country made their timid advances, learning the workings of democracy on the job. The different regions had not yet been granted their own autonomous governments, but these new Socialist, Communist, and Regionalist town councils managed to wrestle back a lot of the power that had been denied to the local authorities during the dictatorship. Many took the opportunity to demonstrate what their party could do if it ran the country, by setting up town libraries, day-care centres, parks and bicycle lanes. But the new decision-making powers and increased budgets also fell equally into the hands of reactionary mayors like ours.

The first sign of change was seen during the village *festes* in June 1980. When the Corporation walked up to the church to pay homage to the patron saint, it was escorted by two municipal policemen in full regalia. Policemen in Deià! Since the Guardia Civil post had been closed down ten years earlier, this was a peaceful yet lawless town; the only figure of authority to be seen was the carpenter, who doubled as Justice of the Peace, and the occasional Guardia patrols who'd stop for a *coñac* in the bar. In the Seventies, the telegraph office had also closed down, as had the village butcher and baker, making the whole village dependent upon the 7.30 a.m. bus to Palma. But things were moving under the new mayor: we now had a pharmacy, a new butcher and bakery, a bank – and policemen! They were at first dismissed as a bit of a joke; if no villager wanted to be mayor, even less would anybody take on the job of policeman. The only candidates were Roberto, a loud-voiced Aragonese barfly, and Toni, a sour-faced man from Sóller.

These *Agentes de la Autoridad Municipal* were the outward signs of change, but a lot more was cooking behind the scenes, much of it fuelled by the ambition of a person who had been elected by a community who nevertheless still considered him an outsider. And in rural Majorca, a *foraster* from the mainland receives even less consideration than a foreigner. He had the votes but not the hearts of the locals; he'd learned to play *petanca* and *truc*, but that wasn't enough. He decided to take on the foreigners instead – they couldn't vote anyway and were all bent on preserving the village as they had found it, which was an obstacle to Deià's progress. Bohemians were fine for attracting the wealthy tourists, but they should stick to painting instead of politics or partying.

Roberto, the Aragonese, soon realized his mistake in taking on the job of *policia municipal*; he couldn't have a cool beer while on duty and the only respite from standing in the sun in full uniform was to get the cold shoulder from his old drinking buddies. He and the sour Solleric were known as 'Pro y Bido' after writing *prohibido* as three separate words on a parking ticket. Fate offered them one chance for glory but they blew it. A pair of thieves had broken into a weekend home and were busy making a paella when the owners walked in. The thieves, *forasters*, hadn't realized that it was a red-letter holiday in Majorca. They fled, followed by the owner, who spotted them mingling with the crowd on the bar terrace. Pro y Bido were alerted and managed to grab one. The other dashed towards an open car, hot-wired it and gunned the motor shouting 'Run for it, mate!'

'I can't, these two are too strong for me! Get away while you can!' answered his crony in front of the packed bar.

Pro y Bido flushed with pride and relaxed their grip, the thief wrestled free, ran for the car and the two thieves escaped to the cheers of the crowd. After this public humiliation, we could expect the worst from Pro y Bido. In Spain, the strumming of a guitar can provoke a policeman just as the twitching of the matador's cape provokes the bull. Historically speaking, the guitar performed at the Court, but it lived in the tavern. It was only natural, then, that the mayor's 'Clean Up Deià' campaign should begin with a ban on music after dark.

One evening after supper, Carmen's teenage brother was sitting in the garden quietly playing 'Moonshadow' to the cat. Pro y Bido marched in, snatched the guitar from his hands, and threatened to put him in the town hall cell – now a broom cupboard – for 'disturbing the peace'. The mayor magnanimously offered permission for 'one party per household per season, if previously solicited in writing'; any unofficial gathering would get a visit from the Guardia Civil, even though Franco's law against public gatherings had been revoked. As parties were essentially spontaneous, this obliged all the village youths, both locals and foreigners, to head for the Sóller discos instead. The catchphrase as midnight approached was 'Got a car? Going to Sóller?' Many parents, worried about the safety of their kids after several pre-dawn accidents on the hairpin bends, pressured for the village bars to stay open later. Soon there were two late-night bars operating in the village, causing more annoyance than the sporadic parties had ever done, but at least they were paying their taxes to the Town Hall.

A delegation of uncontroversial Spanish-speaking residents – myself, a marine biologist, and a home-appliance salesman – went to speak to the mayor about Pro y Bido's heavy-handed tactics. He listened politely, then took out his blacklist, accused each of us of petty infractions of the law, and threatened to make life difficult for us if we 'again criticized his agents'.

Spanish village politics work like this: the mayor will 'overlook' a missing document to speed up a building permit or 'forget' to send an inspector round to check that your business complies with the regulations; without realizing it, you now owe him a favour. This explains why so many people donate useful bits of property or water rights to the Town Hall. However, the foreigners were slow to understand this mutual backscratching, making it hard for the mayor to get any leverage on them. He then tried another tack, holding the foreign community responsible, in hysterical missives to the local newsletter, for holding up the village's progress. When an olive grove was reclassified as an 'industrial zone' and razed to make way for a water-bottling plant, the justification was 'to give work to the village'. Despite the foreigners' protests, the noisy eyesore was built but only offered three jobs, which were taken by Sollerics. The bank for whom the mayor worked had opened a branch in the village, and the foreign community began to close down their accounts in protest. When obliged by his superiors to choose between the bank or the mayorship, he wisely chose the former. It has taken a decade for the social wounds to heal.

In an interview in *El País*, the Moroccan poet Mohamed

Chukri observed that the American writer Paul Bowles 'would have liked the country to stay as it was in the 1930's. He didn't love the Moroccans, he loved his own Morocco.' The same could be said about many of the 'lotus eaters' who settled in the Mediterranean. 'Nearly all the foreigners during Tangier's golden years came here looking for exoticism and pleasure, hash, kif, girls, boys . . .', continued Chukri. 'I'm not against these people, but they never gave me the opportunity to live the good life like they did. The worst part was the humiliation of living on the other side.' All the world's beauty spots have seen friction between the outsiders who want to preserve its quaintness or exoticism and the locals who want to capitalize on its attraction and be able to live the good life themselves. Both options signify the end of a way of life: if you preserve it, it becomes a sterile St Tropez, beautified and prohibitively expensive; if not, it degenerates into a seedy Magaluf.

The live music scene in Deià until the 1980s had consisted of low-key folkie gatherings, psychedelic noodlings, and tribal percussion at parties. Formal, electric line-ups like Daevid's or the Kevin Ayers Band, the Offbeats or Pa Amb Oli, only played in the village on special occasions. The shift in the nightlife from spontaneous parties to late-night bars opened the way for a more structured approach to music: rehearsals, song lists, equipment. At first, the musicians were paid in drinks, a system that had its obvious drawbacks as far as the music was concerned. But it soon became clear that business went wherever the live music was being performed, so we musicians began to be paid token wages.

The Offbeats, on changing their name to the Sex Beatles, had won the *NME*'s Best Name award and sold a respectable number of singles in the UK. Since it was legally easier for the English musicians to work in Spain than the other way round, the band moved to Madrid. Jordi joined them there as rhythm guitarist: not only had he lost his job as drummer to another Spaniard, but his drum kit had been kept as back rent on a rehearsal room in Camden Town. The Sex Beatles' stage act had benefited from the strong sexual presence of Hamish's beautiful American girlfriend Lisa, whose contortions and vocals went down a storm.

In Madrid, the *movida* was just beginning to put the city back on the cultural map after the demise of the Barcelona scene. Pedro Almodovar, working for the national phone company and filming his first movies on Super-8 while fronting a punk band, was at the forefront of this initially small but tremendously influential movement. *Movida*: a to-do, hustle and bustle, a whirl . . . it was more of a cultural explosion than a movement. It was the first since the generation of Dalí, Lorca, Alberti, and Buñuel to draw upon the Spanish creative spirit while ignoring foreign points of reference.

On 20 November 1980, the fifth anniversary of Franco's death, the Sex Beatles were in a Madrid club playing one of their strongest live numbers, 'No. 9', a send-up of Nazism to the tune of Beethoven's Ninth Symphony. Some young neo-Fascists in the audience took the message at face value; they enthusiastically joined the band onstage and began giving the Fascist salute, to a hail of bottles from the rest of the audience. The democratic process was constantly being threatened by these *Fuerza Nueva* bullies, the equivalent of the British National Front, an amalgam of young skinheads and rancid old Francoist diehards in dark glasses and trim moustaches. But if the Fascist rallies could rule the streets it was only because they were echoed by the rattle of swords in the barracks. Three months later, on 23 February 1981, the country underwent the longest night in its recent history, seventeen long hours of tug-of-war between the old and new Spain.

The whole parliament was in session for the investiture of the new centrist Prime Minister Leopoldo Calvo Sotelo; the debonair Suarez, who had led the transition, had been forced to resign. Most of the country was watching the live broadcast on TV when suddenly a group of Civil Guards stormed in, led by Colonel Tejero, looking like a character from a comic opera in his patent-leather *tricornio* and bushy moustache. Spain watched amazed as he fired several shots at the ceiling, yelling '*Al suelo, ¡coño!*' – 'Hit the floor, dammit!' (Spain's favourite four-letter word literally means 'cunt'.) All the MPs hit the deck except Suarez and the retired general Gutierrez Mellado, now Minister of Defence and a convinced constitutionalist, who stood up to the Guardias. After a tussle, he was pushed into his seat. A few minutes later, the TV cameras were disconnected, but the radio microphones carried on broadcasting, unnoticed as the whole parliament was held hostage by Tejero's *guardias*, awaiting instructions from the Army generals who had planned the coup. The country spent the night with its ear to the tranny like in the old days. Video may have killed the radio star, but in Spain, that night, the radio received a new lease of life. The night of the coup, Deià had been cut off by snow for the first time in twenty years; many foreigners and any Spaniard to the left of Tejero were wondering how to escape the impending bloodbath. Four previous right-wing plots had been foiled since Franco's death, but none had got this far.

The seventeen hours of uncertainty ended when King Juan Carlos appeared on TV in full uniform, announcing his commitment to the constitution. Juan Carlos hadn't reacted as the Generals had anticipated, and as head of the armed forces was able to order them to withdraw and to negotiate their surrender without any loss of life. The military came out of the incident with little loss of face – only in Valencia had the tanks actually taken to the streets – but they lost their grip on the country's short and curlies. The 'rancid right', without the army behind them, could no longer play the bully. But although the coup failed, it jolted the Spanish into toning down their demands for a more libertarian and plural nation, for fear of reawakening the dozing dragon.

The Sex Beatles, who were still working in Madrid, commemorated the events of 23 February with a dance number that took the radio waves by storm. It was a funk groove with a catchy refrain:

> Try to get funky when you can't say what you want
> Try to get funky when they say no . . .
> *Al suelo, ¡coño!*

Shortly afterwards, the band broke up, although Hamish continued to use the name with a new all-girl line-up in the UK. Jordi turned his back on rock and roll when the Sex Beatles disintegrated. His family had sold the Deià bar and invested in a large fishing boat docked in Sóller, for which Jordi had obtained his captain's licence.

The Pa Amb Oli Band was now becoming the North Coast's house band, playing in the villages around Deià. We had no drummer but many guitarists had been willing to sit in with us on drums, whenever we could borrow a kit. Not only Pere Colom and Jerry of the Offbeats/Sex Beatles, but for several gigs our drummer was Joan Bibiloni, then beginning a successful solo career as one of Spain's top progressive guitarists and producers.

I had known Joan from the Guitar Centre. He and Pepe Milan – Milan & Bibiloni as they were known professionally – were the Spanish Bert Jansch and John Renbourn. From their base in Deià they had toured the country warming up for Supertramp and for a while ran a live music club overlooking Palma bay called Yesterday (pronounced *Jess Too Day*). After Pepe had toured Spain with Daevid Allen as part of Euterpe, he and Joan went to Paris to back Daevid for a week-long residency at a jazz club there. Daevid dressed Pepe as Maurice Chevalier with a canary on his shoulder and Joan as a Majorcan peasant. 'Pepe and I saved Daevid's life. He had been "clean" for a long time and hadn't allowed any drugs or alcohol on the Euterpe tour. But the first night in Paris was a special occasion, with many previous members of Gong present, and he allowed himself a toke from the improvised hash-pipe that someone had prepared in a glass. Daevid took such a hit that he inhaled not only the burning hash but the thumb-tack it was speared on. He was speechless and turning purple, but we gave him a big thump on the back and he coughed it out.'

On the drum stool Joan appeared to be the same height as when standing up. 'I willed myself to stop growing when I could reach all the frets on the guitar', he claimed. Joan and I shared the same sense of musical humour; by then we'd played together in many folkie gatherings and had worked on Ramón's Mediterranean-salsa-fusion album, *Tabaco*, with Pepe and one of Daevid's musicians, the tabla player Sam Gopal. We could communicate a change in rhythm by raising both eyebrows or a syncopated beat with the drop of a jaw. Eye contact is fundamental for the rhythm section of a band, especially if the band never rehearses song endings. Joan's bubbly enthusiasm, my brother's Mr Dangerous stance, Dave's complete possession of and by the microphone, and my born-again rocker zeal combined to give the band a contagious energy. Although in the first two years we only played a proper gig every couple of months and rehearsed half as often, word got around the island that there was 'a rock and roll goldmine in them thaar hills'. Deià bars were beginning to attract people from all over the island, eager to soak up some of the magic. By the spring of 1982 we were on to guitarist-cum-drummer number four. Ollie Halsall had come to Deià a couple of years earlier to work with Kevin Ayers and over the next four years, between his touring and recording commitments, beat the band into shape.

In 1978, Kevin had bought a large house in the *Clot*, sweet revenge for one who ten years earlier had been run out of town by the Guardia Civil. He arrived with the tall, willowy blonde Kristen Tomassi and their baby daughter Galen: the three of them appeared to have walked out of a celebrity magazine. They had previously bought Daevid's house in the South of France, but found it too isolated to bring up a child. As Kevin's family settled down in Deià, Daevid's was preparing to leave for Australia. Perhaps the town wasn't big enough for two rock stars. But while Daevid and Gilli had been tapping into Deià's creative energy and were ready to move on, Kevin was soon to be dragged under by its excesses and wouldn't escape the village until it nearly destroyed him.

Kristen was still married to Richard Branson. They'd lived and worked together in a damp, cramped houseboat/office on Regent's Park Canal as the Virgin empire began to take shape. The boat was sold and the Bransons bought a spacious house from Peter Cook not far away. But the house soon became just as crowded, doubling as an office; Kristen would single-handedly organize press parties for three hundred guests there, and craved a little more privacy. When Richard assigned her the job of convincing Kevin Ayers to sign to the new Virgin label, she and Kevin fell in love. Together they bought another houseboat, the purple-painted *Duende*, and moved in. Kevin never signed with Virgin but he did recommend his guitarist Mike Oldfield to Richard, who was setting up the Manor, Britain's first live-in recording studio. Kevin also gave Mike his old tape recorder, on which he began the instrumental experiments that later emerged as *Tubular Bells*, Virgin's first LP, which ended up selling over five million copies. At this point Kristen and Kevin sold the *Duende* to Richard and headed south to the Mediterranean.

Kevin had worked with Nico and John Cale of the Velvet Underground but also with Brian Eno, Terry Riley, David Bedford, Lol Coxhill, and Elton John. All this gave him Decadent Superstar status without losing him his street credibility and bohemian image. Among Kevin's former guitarists was Andy Summers, who had toured with Soft Machine and later formed The Police. But his favourite musician and collaborator was Peter 'Ollie the Owl' Halsall.

Ollie had been described in the British music press as looking 'like a seedy stand-up comedian'. Born in Southport, he began thrashing the drums with local bands but then switched to vibraphone, playing jazz in Butlins holiday camps. He finally took up the guitar, which he played left-handed. He soon became the 1970s guitar hero's guitar hero, having played with Timebox, Patto, and John Hiseman's Tempest. His trademark was a jazz musician's sense of harmony and dissonance, executed with the blistering speed and pyrotechnics of heavy rock. In the late 1960s he developed a style using a four-finger 'hammer on' style, producing those fluid but staccato runs later copied by every rock virtuoso. If he hit a wrong note during a solo it only set him banking off into a whole new improvisation in a dissonant key, to be resolved when least expected with a humorous crash landing back on deck. Neil Innes invited him to join him and Eric Idle in the Rutles, the Beatles parody band, and Ollie became 'Leppo, the Fifth Rutle'. As Innes declares on the Rutles' website: 'he's got to be the most underrated guitarist that there ever was. He was daring. He was an acrobat musically, you know. He'd try anything and fiddle about. If everything went wrong, he turned it right. It was uncanny . . .' Ollie also formed part of Grimms, with Innes, Viv Stanshall, Mike McCartney, and the Liverpudlian poets Adrian Henri, Brian Patten, and Roger McGough, combining virtuosity and deadpan humour.

Ollie first accompanied Kevin on the classic *June 1st 1974* live album and for the next eighteen years became his guitarist, arranger, drinking companion, and confidant, pulling Kevin – 'shouting in a bucket' – out of the well of despair several times until he finally fell into the well himself.

Unlike Daevid, Kevin was no well-organized workaholic. His recording and touring schedule was too irregular to fully occupy such a sought-after session man as Ollie, who had worked with rockers from Joe Cocker to Gary Glitter. I first met Ollie in Ramón's studio in Barcelona in 1979, where he and Kevin had come to record five new songs with Ramón on drums. The atmosphere reflected Kevin's return to warm, live musicianship after a string of 'produced' albums. The feeling was Afro-Caribbean, from the calypso 'Fisherman's Song' – Kevin's main passion is underwater fishing – to a momentous Soweto-style number called 'Africa' (predating Paul Simon's 'Graceland' by a few years) in which the three musicians cooked up a storm that didn't abate until the 16-track tape ran out. The recording never saw the light of day because Ramon's equipment was repossessed shortly afterwards and the master tape was on the machine at the time. The only evidence of this brilliant session was a cassette copy that had been knock, knock, knockin' round Kevin's floor for a year until someone stepped on it.

Kevin didn't seem to care. While he had been in Barcelona, Kristen, left alone in Deià and fed up with his sudden vanishing acts, was wooed away by the property developer Axel Ball, with whom she later set up, decorated, and managed the Hotel La Residencia, one of the best-known luxury hotels in the Mediterranean. Although Kevin had probably brought it upon himself, he took years to recover from the blow. He once slipped Dave a note: 'Next time you see Kristen at one of your gigs, please dedicate Dylan's "Positively 4th Street" to her'.

One of the finest guitarists of his generation, Ollie was still a percussionist at heart. When he heard the Pa Amb Oli Band were short of a drummer for the 1982 Deià Carnival party, he offered us his services. He immediately put us through our paces with a couple of intense rehearsals, something completely new to us. 'Come on, Pambs, you half-arsed pop band, let's ROCK!' As a guitarist, Juan was the antithesis of Ollie; he played chunky Chuck Berry licks, as primitive as my bass playing, but thick and tasty. Ollie loved it. 'Go for it, Juan!' he'd cackle, 'you absolute *bustard*!!' Ollie was overjoyed at being able to play the music he loved the best, on the instrument he most enjoyed bashing, in the familiar atmosphere of a village bar, so far removed from the big concerts he was used to.

Over the next few years we played whenever Ollie wasn't touring, which was increasingly often since his money went a lot further here, his main expense being Mahou beer. His interest in painting, poetry, and people was satisfied with just hanging around the village and working when he had to. Like many gifted musicians, he wasn't particularly ambitious; professionally, he had all the doors open to him in England, but he felt more at home in Spain. While Kevin rested, went fishing, and fell in and out of love between tours, Ollie had found plenty of session work in Madrid. With his Swedish girlfriend Zanna on keyboards, he began writing and performing film music, which developed into a successful commercial adventure called Cinemaspop. This was in the early years of the New Spanish Cinema, when the Oscar-winners Almodovar and Trueba were directing their first features. Ollie and Zanna also toured with the Barcelona gypsy Manzanita and his slick rumba-pop band whose 'look' emulated John Travolta's character in *Saturday Night Fever*. 'We got on fine with Manzanita's band,' Ollie confessed, 'but back in the hotel after a gig, they would douse themselves in cheap cologne and lay on some call girls, leaving Zanna and me waiting in the lobby for our room to be free.'

Ollie had just begun to play with us when our Basque friends Juanjo and Carlos got us our first gig in Palma.

Known locally as Los Vascos, they had organized the macro-concert in the Palma Bullring and Kevin and John Cale's ill-fated gig in Alcudia; they were the only promoters willing to run the risk of bringing the new bands of the Madrid *movida* to the island. On this occasion we were opening for Los Elegantes at the 'coming out' of the Gay and Lesbian Front of the Balearics at the famous Barbarella's Disco, aptly renamed 'Colapso'.

'Now lads,' said Ollie, the voice of experience after playing with headlining Spanish bands like Ramoncín, 'this is going to be a tough gig. We're really going to have to be together, so let's all stay sober. We'll probably have a lot of stuff thrown at us, so keep your wits about you; duck and make a run for it if things get rough.' Perhaps he was expecting the *Fuerza Nueva* thugs to break up the show, but in the event the audience was impeccably civilized. When we came onstage, we were all stone-cold sober but for Ollie, who had downed a dozen Cointreaus and was completely legless, cackling with laughter all the way through the gig, to the consternation of the gay and lesbian couples who were probably dancing in public for the first time in their lives. He managed to keep a straight face however while taking lead vocal for 'It's my Party, and I'll Cry if I Want To' in falsetto.

Dave was evolving from pop impersonator to rock singer, although his passionate screams would sometimes drive the more sensitive members of the public out of the hall. He'd also change song lyrics around – 'Now I'll never dance with my mother' instead of 'with another'– which would go by unnoticed by the Majorcan audience but had Juan and I turning our backs to the audience to dissimulate our laughter. Ollie's experience in the Rutles and Grimms allowed him to keep a straight face while feeding Dave new lines.

Most of the band's repertoire was drawn from a period I had missed out on but that the rest of the band, all born in the 1940s, had lived to the full. This gave Pa Amb Oli a feeling of authenticity that no other band on the island could deliver. The audiences had to take the good with the bad: the opening riff taken too fast, the disjointed endings, the out of tune solos, Dave singing in a different key to the rest of the band. On one occasion, Juan's dog Syrup trotted onstage and peed on Dave's leg while he was singing 'Bird Dog'. On a couple of gigs, Dave's ten-year-old son Joe guested on trumpet: he couldn't play a tune, but managed to produce a wildly effective cascade of notes. This what-next anarchy was an attraction in the glossy, polished, smoke-machine electronic Eighties. When the poetic Ollie and the artistic Dave got together, they reverted to the sort of cheery beer-and-football yobs you'd cross the street to avoid. Both were by now completely at home in Spain; Ollie was only homesick for Newcastle Brown Ale and pickled onions. When he discovered I pickled my own, he devoured my supply. I offered him a deal: he'd peel the onions in exchange for half the next batch. I have an image of him in front of a huge tub of onions, wearing only his swimming trunks and his glasses, sweating in the sun, crying his eyes out while singing 'It's my Party . . .'

As a guitarist Ollie was a wild man, his old red Gibson holding up to a tremendous punishment; but behind a drum kit, he became a barbarian. 'A drum will only give up its soul if you really lay into it. Anything less than that isn't the true sound of a drum kit.' During the years Ollie played with us, I would never go to bed after a gig without a ringing in my ears. Juan remembers feeling the breeze generated by the cymbals. Ollie would kick the bass-drum pedal so hard that the drum would walk away from him; he'd have to tie it to his stool with a rope. It was getting impossible to find someone willing to lend the band a set of drums, so we eventually bought a second-hand kit between us. Miraculously, we're still using it after twenty years.

Ollie was used to having a roadie to see to his equipment, so he expected someone to replace sticks and drumskins for him. That someone was always me. I'm a sucker for offering to solve other people's problems and then complaining when they get too dependent on me. One Saturday night we arrived for a gig at Can Costa, a roadside farm turned into a restaurant-bar, and Ollie set up the kit with the drumstool in the bay window, the only place it would fit. 'Oi, you didn't think to buy some sticks, did you? No worry . . .' and he began to dismantle a rickety wooden chair. In the middle of the second number, we heard muffled yells and turned round to see that Ollie had drawn the red velvet curtains in front of him, his two arms poking out from behind them, laying into the drums with a couple of varnished chair legs.

We were still on the pub circuit – you needed a record or a management contract to make the grade to the well-paid summer *verbenas*. For some strange reason we became very popular in the large town of Esporles, the next but one along the mountain range. The shoe factories in this town had been hotbeds of union politics before the Civil War, and the burned-out shells of these factories stood for years as mute reminders to workers to keep their mouths shut. We played regularly at the Central Park, a seedy bar that serviced the Esporles basketball courts. Ollie usually managed to sweat out most of the beer he consumed, but in the intermission he asked the stout *madona* where he could go and pee. 'The loo's on the other side of the court, next to the woodshed; just look out for the rats.' Ollie came back with two stout sticks of olive wood.

'Kill any rats, Ollie?'

'No, but I found myself a couple of spare drumsticks for the next set.'

If Juan and I usually take things in moderation, Ollie, like Dave, preferred to 'really steam in there, y'know'. The day Kevin returned from London with an expensive new Anniversary Model Stratocaster guitar and a Fender Twin amplifier to go with it, the amp's European-standard plug wouldn't fit the smaller Spanish socket. 'Gi's that guitar and lemme have a go,' said Ollie, grabbing the silver Strat and taking a swing at the stubborn plug, hammering it permanently into the socket. 'See that? It works.'

Our standard fee of free drinks plus a token wage suited the rest of the band but I felt short-changed because I could never get through more than a small beer. Any cash went into the kitty to buy strings, picks, and cables, but most of it was spent in keeping Ollie supplied with new sticks for every gig and a new drumskin every three or four. Only after he left the band did we discover his attrition rate quadrupled the average drummer's, and that a bass-drum pedal is not usually considered an expendable item, as he had claimed.

Although Ollie was closest to Dave in temperament, there is always a special complicity between drummer and bass player as the backbone or 'rhythm section' of a band. I've never bothered to study bass or improve my technique, but I've always managed to lock on to the drummer to create a unit stronger than its constituent parts. With due respect for the virtuosos like Jaco Pastorius who have turned it into a solo instrument, I still consider the electric bass as simply one half of the rhythm section, like the front legs of a pantomime horse: only when playing with the percussionist or drummer does it form the complete animal. Whether locked in sync or bucking off each other, bassist and drummer together form the steed upon which the rest of the band can ride. Bass or drum solos are fine within a jazz framework, but their only justification in rock music, as far as I can see, is to give these musicians-in-the-shade a chance to show off.

The treble control on a Spanish amplifier is marked *Agudos* and the bass control, *Graves*: this was a presage that at least one of the family was cut out to play bass. I had by now discovered that this was something other than a guitar with two strings missing; it has a different role to play, and I realized that very few people are aware of what a bass player actually does in a band. Like air-conditioning, you only notice when he stops playing. So let me briefly digress for once and introduce you to the least understood member of the band.

The first electric basses were played vertically, having been adapted from the stand-up or double bass used in jazz bands. (I have yet to see a single bass.) These big, booming instruments have always been difficult to amplify. I borrowed Toni Morlà's electric stand-up bass to play with the Deià jazz band and on the early Elvis numbers with the Pambs, but it's a very different instrument from the bass guitar. Sometimes known as a 'stick bass', it's essentially just a vertical fingerboard with a pick-up at the bottom.

In the 1950s, after the success of his first solid-body electric guitar, Leo Fender adapted the four-stringed acoustic *guitarrón* used by the Mexican mariachi bands: there's no reason, other than the resonance produced by the double bass's huge body, to play it vertically. And if the function of the sound box is replaced by a speaker cabinet, you can get a nice full sound without having to play an unwieldy contraption. Fender simply adapted his Telecaster to accommodate heavier strings. Unlike a stand-up bass, which has a smooth fingerboard and requires precise fingering to play in tune, Fender's invention had frets – hence the name Precision Bass – allowing anybody who could play a guitar to become a bass player overnight.

For every vocational bass guitarist for whom this was his first instrument there are a hundred guitarists like Kevin or myself who ended up playing it by default, simply because they were the last to join the band. Most footballers aim at being forwards or goalkeepers; few set their sights on being half-backs. One of the few vocational bass players I've met is Daniel Lagarde, a brilliant Uruguayan jazz and salsa musician who played with Bibiloni in the Kevin Ayers Band. Not only are his father and three brothers all bass players, but I've met at least four more Uruguayans in the same profession, a statistical improbability.

You can't do much with an electric or even an acoustic bass except play in a band. Luckily, it's the instrument on which mistakes are least noticed, especially if you stick to the lowest notes. Take for instance the Sóller dance band with whom we often shared the bill. It was led by a middle-aged trumpet player whose daytime job was driving the butane gas delivery lorry; the band's name is irrelevant since everyone knows them as *los butaneros*. The leader was set upon having his son in the band despite the lad's total lack of musicianship; the obvious solution was to give him a bass so he could learn on the job and contribute his share of the family income. For a couple of years he plonked away on the deepest notes, completely out of key but tolerated by the indulgent local audience, until it was obvious he'd never learn. Eventually unplugged, he continued 'playing' the bass, while the keyboard player filled in his part on the bass pedals of the organ.

Toni Morlà and I witnessed a similar case of bass incompetence in Inca: the tuba player of the municipal brass band that opened for our show. We cracked up as he bluffed the lowest possible notes while pretending to read the sheet music. (I was laughing because I recognized myself in him: when playing the stand-up bass with the Deià Jazz Band, I'd often find myself lost and I'd back-pedal awhile on the bottom string until I regained my bearings.) As a child, Toni and his friends would walk alongside the tuba player during the Palma *festes*, provocatively chewing lemons; it's almost impossible to play a wind instrument when your salivary glands are in action. 'And once I was in a band whose bass player was tone deaf and believed that when all four tuning pegs were horizontal, the instrument was in tune.'

Jugbands got their name from the gallon jars that provide the bass notes when the player blows across the mouth of the vessel, an instrument also used in Northwest India. Then the 1950s skiffle boom produced the washtub bass. Skiffle was a precursor of punk inasmuch as you didn't need to be a proper musician to play the washboard, kazoo, or washtub. This primitive stand-up bass consists of a string attached to an upturned washtub – the soundbox – and the end of a broom handle. By standing the broom handle on the tub and pulling it towards vertical, the string tightens and the note rises. It's not exactly a clear note, but you can encompass the complete range from *thump* to *thomp*. It's hard to imagine anybody inventing a more primitive bass than this, but the Cuban peasants did. Here, the string is attached to the broomstick and to the middle of a square wooden board. Wherever the band sets up, the bassist digs a hole in the ground, lays the board over it and stands on it to play, the pit acting as a soundbox.

Cuban musicians have always realized the importance of the bass notes to get people to dance; they also carry a great distance, attracting more dancers. Cubans use another rural bass, the *marimbula* – a large version of the African *mbira* or thumb-piano. I was lucky enough to watch Carlos Puebla's octogenarian *marimbula* player in action in Managua. He sits on this box and twangs the large steel prongs with his fingers; beside him on the floor is the lid of a tin of shoe polish that he occasionally picks up and hits against the side of the *marimbula* to underline the rhythm.

There's always plenty of work for versatile bass players. They tend to be good musical arrangers and composers, perhaps because they are in a privileged position midway between melody and rhythm. Of all the band members, the bass player has greatest dominion over people's feet. The standard rock and roll bass pattern is called the 'walking bass line' or stride. But when the bass deliberately omits the beat that the dancer has been led to expect, his body feels it has been left floating in mid air. By leaving out a few beats and dropping them back in elsewhere, the bassist can turn the song around. The best rhythm section of all time, the Jamaicans Sly and Robbie, can make people move their feet in a different time to the rest of their body, to float, to suddenly hit an air pocket.

The only bass playing tips I ever got were from a huge, square-jawed Glaswegian called Archibald Leggett. Archie was built like a rock and he played with total economy, dismissing the slap-bass technique as a passing fad. 'Any fahkin idiot can play a million notes, but that's not the point. You have to know which are the important ones an' then leave the rest out. Jest keep it simple and keep your eyes on the drummer.' He and his wife Jenny began to spend summers in Deià visiting his old mates – as a lodger in Lady June's flat, Archie had fallen in with the Canterbury scene, playing with Daevid and Robert Wyatt and forming the duo Kevin Ayers and Archibald.

Dave, Juan, and I would sit open-mouthed when Ollie and Archie began to swap stories, each harder to believe than the last. Some of the more improbable ones were actually true. Archie had accompanied American rock and rollers and soul singers when they were obliged to use English backup musicians to tour the UK. 'I've been on the road with Brenda Lee, Jerry Lee Lewis, Lee Dorsey, Wilson Pickett an' even Smokey Robinson an' tha' fahkin' Miracles.' He had backed Tony Sheridan in Hamburg, Charles Aznavour and Françoise Hardy in Paris, and was hired for a while by France's top rocker, Johnny Halliday. At the time, Hendrix was hanging out in Paris waiting for his British work permit to come through. 'Jimi came round the Olympia Theatre and we'd be jamming in the dressing room between sets. He asked me to play bass in the new band he was putting together, the Experience, but I was under contract to Johnny fahkin' Halliday.' Back in London, during a recording session, 'Paul McCartney was in the next studio an' he says "Listen, Archie, I'm having some trouble with this fahkin' bass riff to Paperback Writer", so to give him an idea I sat in with the band for one take, and that's the take they used on the record.'

The last time I saw Archie, he had just returned from a tour with one of my musical heroes, Dr John, whose New Orleans funk depends on a sparse, almost absentee style of bass playing with just enough well-placed notes to hold it together. I'd been hooked on swamp-rock since hearing Lee Dorsey's funky, laid-back 'Working in the Coalmine' as a teenager. This record was the first to wake me up to the chemistry between bass and drums. Although Lee Dorsey's band was from New Orleans, I've been assured that the bass player on the record was none other than Archie Leggett.

As Ollie pointed out, a football team is as good as its goalie and a band is only as good as its drummer, which is probably why drummers tend to have the highest turnover rate in the business and are usually the scapegoats when things go wrong. Many band leaders, from John Mayall or Daevid Allen to Nick Cave, have tried to solve the problem by eliminating the drums altogether, but they usually come round to the fact that it's a necessary evil. (In my opinion, a drum machine is an unnecessary evil.)

Ollie was now renting Ca Sa Salerosa with his Spanish girlfriend Eva, the same cottage my father and Laura Riding had rented upon their arrival in 1929; it still had no running water or bathroom. Behind the house was the plot of land the Californian folkie John Fisher had tried to buy with his ill-fated drug run; now Ollie set his sights on it, but decided to raise the money legally, working as a producer in Madrid. One Saturday evening we were setting up in Las Palmeras, expecting him back in time for the gig, when he phoned up the bar to say he had been hired to stand in for Radio

Futura's hospitalized guitarist on a big tour starting the next day. Jordi happened to be on the terrace having a beer.

'Jordi, we need a drummer for tonight . . .'

'Forget it, I don't want to know about rock and roll or groups or drums. Anyway, I haven't played in six years, I'm a fisherman.'

Jordi is a barker, not a biter; of course he was dying for a chance to sit behind a kit again, and although he hadn't touched one since 1981, he always played along in his imagination with the Ramones, the Clash, or the Stones blasting out of his boom-box on deck. Sitting astride a drumstool after a seven-year sabbatical was like jumping on a bicycle for the first time in decades. That night, Jordi became once again the Pa Amb Oli drummer. Ollie's Spanish career, meanwhile, was taking off as a producer and session musician in the highly competitive Madrid scene. He'd often come over for a weekend, and once, after singing a few songs with the band, he wistfully said, 'You don't know how lucky you are to play for larks and get a bit of cash for it. If you want my advice, keep it that way, stay out of the music business. It can kill you.' We took his advice; unfortunately, the music business did kill him. On the Radio Futura tour, one of the band was on hard drugs; Ollie, having been Kevin's chaperone and doctor on so many occasions, volunteered to keep the man clean. Ollie, although a drinker, had emerged from a career during the heaviest years of rock unscathed by drugs, so it came as a complete shock to us all when he died of an overdose in 1992, having spent all his considerable earnings on heroin. He had been hooked on it by the very musician he was trying to protect, who had insisted that there was no danger if you smoked instead of injected heroin. It may have been a safer method, but it was much more expensive, leaving Ollie virtually broke. One night, desperate, he tried the cheap way, misjudged the quantity, and was found dead in the flat he shared at 13, Calle de la Amargura ('Bitterness Street'), Madrid. The Musicians' Union paid the expenses and his Argentine girlfriend Claudia, a rock singer, brought his ashes back to be buried in the Deià cemetery, where Ronnie Wathen played a farewell Irish air on the bagpipes. The artist Michael Kane used our workshop to engrave Ollie's name on a tombstone that featured a jack socket, volume and tone controls. When it was finished, Michael propped it up against the door to get a good look; a gust of wind slammed the door shut, and the stone split in half. 'That was typical of Ollie,' he said. 'There's no point in trying to hide the crack, let's make a feature of it. I'll stick the two halves together with some bright blue resin.' The tombstone can be seen next to Mati's in the Deià cemetery.

One of Ollie's precepts stuck with the band: never mind the spit and polish, go for the feeling. In twenty years we've had a lot of cassette recordings of Pa Amb Oli gigs, but there's not a single song without some mistake in it – a bum note, a harmony vocal out of tune, a bumbled lyric, the drums too loud. How come nobody noticed it at the time? Because everybody was having such a good time.

The new mayor of Deià, the grandson of the stonemason who built Ca n'Alluny, had been a schoolmate of Jordi's and was a real party animal, so we were immediately hired for the 1987 Deià *verbena*, at the standard showband rate – about three times more than we'd ever earned with Ollie. All our slogging around the bar circuit began to pay off as kids from the mountain towns along the Serra de Tramuntana – Esporles, Puigpunyent, Sóller and Valldemossa – began to pressure their own mayors into hiring us for their annual *festes*. The band's catchment area was more or less limited by the range of a *mobylette*, the ubiquitous rural moped, our audience's most common form of transport. Today's adolescents drive natty Yamaha Jogs, but the range is still about twenty kilometres.

The *verbena* season along the Serra begins in late June with the *festa de Sant Joan* – Midsummer Eve, the shortest night – in Deià, and ends in Fornalutx in mid September, each event attracting swarms of motorized youths from neighbouring villages. The exception to the rule is the *verbena* of the Sóller May Fair, *Es Firó*. The *Firó* commemorates a historical event – the town's patron saint, Sant Bartomeu, has his own *festa* in August – and it gives a foretaste of the impending avalanche of summer celebrations that begin as soon as school's out.

I had first experienced terror at the age of six, in broad daylight in the back of our Land Rover. We were driving from Sóller to the Port to have lunch and watch the *moros i cristians*, the annual re-enactment of the May Eleventh Victory of 1561, in which the Christian defenders of Sóller defeated the Moorish (in fact Turkish) pirates who were sacking the town. Along the hot, dusty road we were flagged down by a group of six Moors, who climbed into the back of the Land Rover with me. There I sat quaking in the corner, a little blond boy alone among this rowdy crowd of blackened faces, smelling of alcohol, gunpowder, and boot polish, their scimitars flashing and shotguns broken open, being loaded with blank cartridges. These were the longest five minutes of my life.

The battle begins at three o'clock. The Moors sail into the bay but the local Christians have been warned of the attack by a smoke signal from the lookout tower: commending their fate to the Virgin Mary at the church of Santa Catalina, they are ready to repel the Saracen pirates who try to gain the northern beach. Grappling and throwing each other into the sea, which at the beginning of May still maintains the winter chill, the Sóller folk drive the Saracens back. Volleys of gunshot echo around the bay as they sail across to the southern side, where they are again repelled with a tremendous roar of blank cartridges. The Moors sail away only to quietly disembark further up the coast and head for the town, two miles inland, while the Christian forces regroup. Captain Angelats organizes the resistance, sending for help to the villages of Alaró and Bunyola on the other side of the mountain. On the way up the valley, the Moors spot a group of peasant women who rush back to their farmhouse, barring the door; from an upstairs window they pour boiling water over the invaders and drive them off. This brave act is commemorated every year by awarding the title of *Valentes Dones* to the two most deserving or eligible girls in Sóller.

When the Saracens arrive at the Pont d'En Barona, a strategic bridge affording entrance to the main town, Captain Angelats and his troops are ready and waiting to defend their post. Outnumbered, they are again forced to retreat by the invaders, who head for the main square, raping and pillaging as they go. (This explains why more Sóllerics volunteer to be Moors than Christians, even knowing they will be defeated.) Reinforcements arrive, the Saracens are forced to surrender and hand over their prisoners; Captain Angelats is the hero of the day and a huge *traca*, a string of deafening bangers, hung from tree to tree around the square, goes off to signal the end of the *Firó*.

This whole festival is a good way to let off steam, make a lot of noise, get completely inebriated, and have a great time. Similar heroic acts of the Christians against the infidel invaders – *moros i cristians* – are celebrated in Pollença and in several coastal towns on the mainland, the noisiest of which, of course, are in the Valencia area.

In Sóller, the battle is celebrated on a Monday, which is declared a fiesta; Tuesday is officially a working day but in fact is reserved for curing hangovers; the whole town is on half-throttle. The week before, secondary students are handed out slips of paper for their parents to sign, excusing them from Tuesday's classes.

The *Firó* doesn't affect neighbouring Deià, but my primary-school teacher would always contrive to organize a two-hour botanical walk over the rocky headland to the Port that Monday. In 1960 the Sóller council, taking the lead from the richer and more tourist-oriented Pollença, had invested a fortune in new costumes and had forbidden both forces from throwing one another in the sea, wrestling each other to the ground, or smearing their costumes with shoe polish. This prissiness lasted 'as long as cake at the school gates', and reason almost immediately lost out to passion.

Without counting the women and children who wear traditional peasant dress for the event, at least a thousand Sóllerics participate in the battle, most of them falling naturally into one or either group. Jordi is an obvious Moor, with little need of boot polish: a scimitar, robe, and turban are all he needs to become a fearsome Turk. Now that the tourist season is no longer limited to the hot summer months, the festivities attract a large number of foreigners, despite the danger of having their faces blackened or their sun hats snatched away and a hole blasted through the crown with a shotgun (blank cartridges can do a fair bit of damage). Most of the visitors are alerted about what they are letting themselves in for, but there is usually some tourist who doesn't share the joke of being tossed fully clothed into the water, or parents who watch aghast as their child's sandcastle is assaulted by fifty drunken Saracens.

The *moros* play out their parts to the full, only overlooking one small detail: the consumption of alcohol is supposedly against their religion. But it has always been a part of the festivities for both sides, to the point where beachside stalls were handing out free shots of *herbes*, a potent aniseed liqueur. Miraculously, there have been no mortal accidents, but to be on the safe side, in 2002 the town council forbade the free alcohol and reminded the bars and shops that it is an offence to sell spirits to those under sixteen. Many of the bars decided to close down for the day to avoid problems. A group of Christians, interpreting this as a dry law and furiously protesting, locked the mayor (dressed as a Christian), the councillors, the Valentes Dones and Capitan Angelats himself in the church as they were paying their respects to the Virgin before the battle. They had to be liberated by the municipal police, whose offices were pelted with oranges and lemons; the Guardia Civil had to be called in. During the mêlée several people were injured; and despite the prohibition, various youngsters passed out under the combined effects of alcohol, sunstroke, and sleeplessness accumulated over four days of *Firó*, which had begun with the *verbena* the previous Friday night.

Jordi, now a married man and father of two, no longer plays the Moor. 'It's become too commercialized, it's getting out of hand because people from all over the island turn up in costume and go ape-shit. I live in the Port, but now I take my family up the mountain to my hut in the olive grove until the *Firó* is over.'

The increase in Pa Amb Oli activity coincided with Toni Morlà's gradual retirement, so I seldom faced any conflict of interests. With Jordi on drums, the band soon began to get into the *verbena* rhythm. A few days after the Deià *festes* comes Sant Pere, the patron of Esporles; 16 July is the Verge del Carme (Stella Maris), patron of the fishermen and celebrated in all the ports of the islands with a procession of boats decked out with coloured lights. Ten days later, Sant Jaume – also known as Santiago, patron of Spain – is a national holiday. Of these holy patrons, only one is Majorcan: the *beata* (Blessed) Santa Catalina Thomàs, popularly known as Sor Tomasseta. Born into a Valldemossa family in the sixteenth century and orphaned as a child, she went to work on her aunt's farm at Son Gallard, which is just inside the Deià parish boundary and overlooking Miramar, where the other holy Majorcan, the Blessed Raymond Llully, lived and meditated. An attractive girl, Sor Tomasseta's sanctity is attributed principally to her stoic withstanding of the great torments and temptations afforded her by the devil, who, according to my father, rose out of the plughole of her aunt's sink in the form of a phallus, only to be beaten down again by Tomasseta brandishing a scrubbing brush. (Robert later bought the stone sink and installed it in the Ca n'Alluny kitchen, where the devil can still be heard slurping lasciviously from the depths of the plumbing as the water runs out.) Lucifer also tormented her in other ways, like kicking over the food she was carrying up to the charcoal burners in the woods or pushing her off a cliff while picking olives near Son Gallard. Her fall was broken when she was caught by angels and, as my father told the story, 'she carried on picking olives at the bottom as if nothing had happened'. These and other devilish misdeeds are recounted in the song that every Majorcan child knows and is sung by hundreds of people who accompany her carriage through the streets of Valldemossa every July 28th. Every year a little Valldemossan girl is chosen to play the part of the *Beata* while the secondary roles of angels and peasants go to her classmates, and all throw sweets from tiny olive-pickers' baskets at the crowds they pass.

All over the world, adjacent villages have always squabbled. In the past, Majorcan youths from one village would sometimes pelt their geographical neighbours with stones, but this historical antagonism is now more discreet. From the stage, we've often seen tussles break out when outsiders get too friendly with local girls, but it was at the Valldemossa *verbena* in honour of Sor Tomasseta that we had our only bit of 'bovver' onstage. A group of teenagers from neighbouring Esporles had motorcycled over to hear us. By now we knew these kids well, especially the red-headed son of the grave digger who was always at the front of the crowd yelling for us to play the Stones' 'Out of Time' and Chuck Berry's 'Yonnibigoot!' In Esporles and Puigpunyent, the redhead and his gang would always come up on stage with Carmen and Frances, Juan's wife, to join in the ascending chorus of our closing number, 'Twist and Shout'. When they attempted this on Valldemossa territory, we didn't stop them, but the locals didn't take kindly to this occupation of sacred ground and began to pull them offstage. We finished the show with four members of the Guardia Civil standing between us, arms akimbo.

Most *verbenes* are free, subsidized by the Town Hall, which takes a cut of any proceeds from the bar. It's in everybody's interests, not least the punter's, to keep the bar open as long as possible. The Pa Amb Oli Band soon became a guarantee of alcohol sales, because of all possible combinations – rum and coke, gin and tonic, Scotch and soda – the most popular is rock and alcohol. Of all the rock bands on the *verbena* circuit, Pa Amb Oli have always been the most ragged and unpredictable, but they've also provoked the biggest sense of tribal communion, which is the whole point of the *festes*: a sense of communal belonging, especially with a full moon overhead. Even 'Out of Time' becomes an anthem; there's nothing like a chorus of hundreds of drunken voices yelling *'Beibi, beibi, beibi, ¡choo rau roff taaaaim!'*

The longer we could keep the punters singing and drinking, the more money the Town Hall recouped on its outlay. We began to be scheduled as the closing act, which, given the inevitable backlog of bands, meant tuning up to go onstage as the eastern sky was beginning to lighten. Often Jordi would have to drive straight from the gig to his fishing boat where the crew was waiting to set out to gather nets. Perhaps the latest we ever played was at the Colonia de Sant Pere, a two-hour drive from home, where the sun was shining pitilessly across the debris in the square while we finished our last encore. As we stumbled offstage, an enthusiastic girl asked me, 'Who's on now?'

The *verbena* has always been the high point of the *festes*, where the whole village, from toddlers to the elderly, can enjoy dancing, drinking, gossiping, courting, and generally letting their hair down. Over the last twenty-five years, having played in more than sixty towns, villages, and hamlets all over the island, I've seen how one-upmanship has caused the stages to grow in size and in height, from a few planks balanced on bricks to a steel platform the size of a tennis court. The strings of coloured light bulbs have disappeared in favour of lighting rigs. Where once the village electrician was on call in case a fuse blew, now a team of technicians with intercoms is needed to handle the show. In the 1970s, each band brought their own PA in the car boot; today the Turbosound system deployed at any self-respecting *verbena* is loud enough to knock you backwards. At one sound check I saw how an amplified *oomph* from Jordi's bass-drum lifted his little rat-catcher dog off the ground.

Having all this technology at your disposal is very comfortable for a musician; you can hear every note through the monitors, and there's an expert out there adjusting the levels. Yet the distance between musicians on stage, and between the band and the audience, creates a gap that is harder to bridge: the height, the power, and the smoke machine makes us feel as detached as Olympian gods. We play a lot tighter in a small space when we're on top of each other and can smell the beer on the audience's breath. (It also helps to be able to see what chord my brother is playing if I get lost.)

At first this technology impressed the rural Majorcans, until they realized they were no longer the protagonists or even participants in their celebrations: they had simply become an audience. Nobody used really to care what was going on onstage as long as the village was enjoying itself, but now the spotlights turn all heads away from their dance partner and towards the stage. When the volume drowns out conversation, a street party becomes a sterile outdoor disco. This led many towns to hold two different *verbenes*:

a rock night (midnight to dawn) for the teens-to-thirties and a traditional *verbena* (ending at 3 a.m.) for everyone else.

This is probably a repeat of what happened fifty years ago when the modern music of the time – foxtrots and *pasodobles* – became incompatible with the traditional *ball de bot*. The new dance bands ended up having their own space, the *verbena*, while the old *rondallas* were relegated to backing choreographed *bailes mallorquines*.

Pa Amb Oli has played (or at least attempted) well over a thousand classic rock and pop songs in public. Ollie's description of us as a 'half-arsed pop band' is still apt, but we've also been described as 'the Most Famous Unknown Band in the World'. However, we'd much prefer to be known as the Second Most Famous Unknown Band in the World. Although our repertoire includes such hot new numbers as Dylan's 'Hurricane' or Springsteen's 'Hungry Heart', it's firmly based on the early rock and roll standards that Juan, Dave, and Ollie had grown up with and that Jordi knew by heart. We also cover a lot of the raw British rhythm and blues from my early teens – the Kinks, Stones, Animals, and Small Faces. Most of our audience heard these songs for the first time in our version: 'Hey, have you heard? The new Julia Roberts film is based on a Pa Amb Oli song, "Pretty Woman"!' Every season one or two new TV ads would feature a number that the Esporles kids had chorused at our concerts: 'Hey Baby' announcing a Spanish beer, 'Dock of the Bay' for a perfume. Many new Majorcan bands in our area are now drawing from 'our' repertoire, but the confirmation that the Pa Amb Oli Band has now become an institution in the Serra came from my sister Lucia. When she went to cash a check at a Sóller bank, the teller recognized her surname.

'Graves? Oh, you must be related to . . . to . . .'

Since *I, Claudius* made ours a well-known name locally, we're all used to this kind of situation, especially when they confuse Robert with the actor Peter Graves from *Misión Imposible*. To avoid unnecessary embarrassment, Lucia took up the slack: 'Yes, I'm his daughter.'

The teller looked perplexed. 'Whose daughter? The guitarist's or the bass player's?'

# 8

# Saint Anthony and the Devil

Whether playing in hotels or at the village fiestas, a semi-professional musician's year in Majorca is almost always void between September and June. November is the time of the year when top Spanish acts embark on their South American tours as summer arrives in Argentina and Chile. The modest hotel bands have to find work in warmer tourist destinations such as Tunisia or the Canary Islands, where the hotels are open all year round, or on Caribbean cruise ships. The Majorcans like Toni who stay at home over the winter only have three dates circled in red: New Year's Eve, St Anthony's Eve (16 January) in the farming villages, and the Eve of St Sebastián, patron saint of Palma, a couple of days later.

Sant Sebastià is Palma's big annual bash. Only the most popular local groups and top names from the mainland and abroad are hired – maybe forty acts all told – and all on one night. Stages are set up in each of the main squares in the old town centre, a different venue for each type of music: pop, jazz, flamenco, nostalgia, progressive, Catalan rock, *ball de bot,* singer-songwriters. With Toni we played once on a huge stage blocking the end of the Borne, Palma's main boulevard, obliging the icy January air to pass over the musicians on its way down to the port. Between numbers Dorín and I had to warm our hands on the spotlights. Our fingering with the left hand was severely limited but at least we got a good tremolo going with the right.

During the *revetlla* or revelry of Sant Sebastià, rivers of people elbow their way through the narrow streets checking out the different performances, buying or bringing their own bread and *sobrassada* to grill over the communal barbecues. Thousands of people are rocking in the Plaza Major, bopping to jazz in Plaza Coll, dancing the *jota* in Plaza Santa Eulàlia, or strutting to the rumba in Plaça Sant Francesc.

The Palma revelry would attract a lot more people from outside the city if it weren't for the *Festes de Sant Antoni* two days earlier, which leave much of the rural population exhausted. Sant Antoni is especially venerated in the east of the island – Son Servera, Manacor, Pollença – and the farming towns of Muro and Sa Pobla, which are important suppliers of early potatoes to the United Kingdom.

Every town has its own Sant Antoni tradition. In Pollença, an enormous pine tree from the mountain estate of Ternelles is felled and carried down to the village on the shoulders of the villagers, most of whom are fuelled with *mesclat*, a high-octane cocktail. In the Port of Pollença, a rival ceremony fells a pine in Cape Formentor and carries it to the shore, where it is towed by sea into the port. A couple of years ago, the floating tree 'hooked' the corpse of a man who had gone missing a week earlier while fishing. In Sa Pobla, the village youths, accompanied by a brass band, all head for the commons of Sa Llebre to gather timber for the bonfires.

As the sun goes down on 16 January these towns are invaded by dozens of horned demons roaming the streets, goat bells tied to their heels, accompanied by the traditional duo of *xeremiers*, one with the bagpipe and the other playing the fife and drum. The demons are out looking for Saint Anthony the Abbot, carrying brooms with which to swipe at the children, who in turn try to pull at their tails. Sant Antoni then appears in his white beard and brown hooded cassock, putting the demons to flight with a shake of his staff. But after dark, when the bonfires are lit to symbolize Sant Antoni's victory over the Devil, the music is provided by the *ximbomba*, an instrument that sounds like Lucifer himself muttering vengeance.

In most of Europe, Christmas carols are sung unaccompanied by solemn, rosy-cheeked choirs. Spanish carols may be less spiritual but they're spirited enough to make 'Jingle Bells' sound twee. They are sung at rowdy, red-nosed family gatherings where anything that makes a noise is bashed, scraped, or shaken to a *jota* rhythm: a ribbed bottle of *anís*, a brass mortar and pestle, a tambourine, and of course a *zambomba* (pronounced thambomba) to give some foundation to the rhythm. This rustic instrument, which the islanders call a *ximbomba* (pronounced chimbomba), resembles a flowerpot with a stick growing out of it. It's simply a clay drum with a reed or cane fastened to the centre of the drumskin. Instead of hitting it, you tuck it under your left arm, wet the palm of your right hand, grab the cane and rub it up and down rhythmically in an obscene manner, producing an equally obscene grunting noise.

The *ximbomba* is technically a friction drum, which amplifies the vibrations caused by wet (not oily) skin on a hard surface. Following this principle, you can also run a wet finger over the taut skin of a tambourine to make a staccato rattle, or around the edge of a crystal goblet to make it sing. (I've even applied the principle to the nylon strings of a guitar, producing a scale of squeaks that rival fingernails on a blackboard.) The Brazilian *cuica* is a more sophisticated friction drum. The stick is attached to the underside of the drumskin, and the left hand presses on the skin to alter the pitch, producing those familiar syncopated whining and yelping noises heard on so many samba and bossa nova tunes.

The question of how to keep the hand moist without stopping to wet it was traditionally solved in Majorca either by spitting into your palm every few bars or wrapping a cabbage leaf around the stick so that its juices would be slowly squeezed out, keeping the stick moist. Today, *ximbomba* players keep a plastic squirt-bottle of water at the ready in the left hand.

By squeezing harder on the downstroke or upstroke, you can vary the intensity and even the pitch of the grunts and turn them into a recognizable rhythm – GRUNT-a grunta GRUNT-a grunta GRUN' GRUN' GRUNT-a grunta – over which a solo voice, male or female, sings an Arabic melody:

| | |
|---|---|
| *Sa ximbomba ja no sona,* | The ximbomba no longer sings out, |
| *Ni sonà ni sonará* | It never did and it never would |
| *Perquè té sa pell de ca,* | For the skin is made of dog-hide, |
| *I sa canya que no és bona.* | And the stick is just no good. |

The chorus picks up the last two lines. Then the assembled company takes turns in singing humorous, critical, obscene, or lascivious lyrics. A book called *A Thousand Songs to Play on your Ximbomba* appeared recently; since you can barely get two notes out of the instrument, I took the title to be the Majorcan equivalent of *A Thousand Words of Wisdom by George W. Bush*. But no, the book actually does contains a thousand different popular verses to sing over the basic *ximbomba* rhythm. And although there are *ximbomba* schools in several villages, few people seem to experiment beyond the classic grunt-o-matic beat. I'm sure there's room for development there; with a bit of spit and a good *ximbomba* I myself can lay down a convincing Bo Diddley beat or a cha-cha-cha.

This rudely rudimentary instrument really comes to the fore in the winter months. Cheap versions in all sizes are sold alongside equally shoddy tambourines in the Christmas markets; but a proper *ximbomba* with a rich, mellow grunt has to be made to order, preferably with goat skin and a reed from the marshes of s'Albufera near Sa Pobla.

The Eve of Sant Antoni is a magical night in which the Majorcans find their most ancient roots as they gather around the bonfire. Whereas Catalans light their fires on midsummer eve (Sant Joan) and in Valencia celebrate the *fallas* on the night of Sant Josep (the eve of the spring equinox), in Majorca this ancient fire ritual is held on the date of the Roman *sementines*, during which the fields and animals were blessed. This pre-Christian tradition is celebrated on the following morning, the Day of Sant Antoni, patron saint of animals. Pets, livestock, traction animals and beasts of burden are led before the church to be blessed by the village priest. Wouldn't Saint Francis of Assisi be a better candidate as protector of animals, since he could speak their language? What leads a holy figure to be assigned a particular protectorate? My guess is that, if the saint or Virgin in question fulfils a role in the community previously assigned to an earlier divinity (after all, agricultural and human cycles have changed little in the countryside since Christianity arrived) then that particular function was also linked to a time and a season. In other words, the saint assumed the duties associated with his saint day, or to put it another way, was assigned a saint's day consistent with his duties. The *Parenostic*, the Majorcan farmer's almanac, is based on the lunar calendar and the *santoral*, the saints' days, because these were the points of reference for illiterate peasants who couldn't read a calendar. The curious name of this annual almanac, sold in all stationers, is a cross between *pronòstic* (a forecast or prediction) and *pare nostro* (the Lord's Prayer).

Most of the large mountain estates were run as serfdoms by absentee landlords, many of whom were descended from James the Conqueror's barons. The Majorcan plain, however, was repopulated after the conquest by homesteaders brought over from Catalonia and Aragon. These small-scale farmers have always been at daggers drawn with the civil and religious authorities in the City of Palma. The council demanded a tax for them to sell their wares inside the city walls, and the powerful Order of St Anthony's Hospitallers collected all alms given to any image of Sant Antoni in any village church, under threat of the image being confiscated. Because Sant Antoni was so popular, receiving alms in gratitude for having saved or cured animals or people, this represented big money. But in 1643, the people of Sa Pobla, supported by their town council and the priest, refused to give in to this spiritual extortion; the litigation lasted six years and was finally resolved in favour of the *poblers*, who celebrated by yelling '*Visca* [Long live] *Sant Antoni!*' This became a cry of independence for the farming villages all over the island until it was censored in 1918, yet it took another ten years to eradicate the rebel yell completely, even when backed by a hefty ten-peseta fine. It wasn't heard again in Sa Pobla until January 2002 when the town historian proposed its resurrection. Right after Mass, the whole congregation stood up to yell '*Visca Sant Antoni!*' Nothing political, just a healthy bit of primal scream therapy.

The historical St Anthony the Abbot, a.k.a. St Anthony of Viana (or 'of the Asses', as he's commonly known in the countryside), was a well-to-do young man who lived in Egypt in the third century. One day, upon hearing verse 19: 21 of Matthew's gospel in church, he gave all his wealth to the poor and went off to the desert to pray, where he was continually assailed by demons who tempted and mortified him. He was the first non-martyr to be sanctified, thanks not only to his fight against evil but also to his curative powers. His role as the protector of animals came later, and the only vestige of the original story resides in his ongoing duels with the Devil, recounted in many popular songs. St Anthony became very important in farming areas, not only as the protector of livestock but, more importantly, of working animals. The figure of the pig that always appears at his side is linked to the wild boar who accompanied the Celtic deities associated with this festivity.

Although Spain has been devoutly and even obsessively Catholic since Isabel and Fernando's reign, the ancient pagan rituals were never far beneath the surface, especially in the farming communities. Catholicism has been able to redirect pagan beliefs by providing a substitute that doesn't contradict the message of Christ. The ancient Mother Goddess, Ceres, assumed the form of the Virgin Mary in her appearances at places like Lluc and the hilltop monastery of the Puig de María overlooking Pollença. Perhaps the largest cult in Catholic Spain is devoted to Our Lady of the Morning Dew, *La Virgen del Rocío*, also known as the White Dove, probably originally a White Goddess figure, who appeared in a marshland in Huelva. Every year, seven weeks after Easter Monday, over a million people arrive at her sanctuary in Almonte near the Portuguese border, having spent days walking, on horseback or travelling by caravan from Cádiz, Sevilla, or Córdoba. Every night along the route, the pilgrims stop not so much to rest as to party, dancing *sevillanas* around the campfires.

The different Virgins in Spain (and Latin America) have an important role to play as protectors of a district or region. Compare the birth registers of different regions: María de Lluc is a common name in Majorca, as is María de la Macarena in Seville or María de la Fuencisla in Segovia. More often than not, the *María de* ... is now dispensed with, leaving plain Montserrat in Catalonia, Aranzazu (Arantxa) in the Basque country, Covadonga in Asturias, Pilar in Aragon. While these Virgins' constituencies are mainly geographic, the ancient role of minor deity in charge of a specific trade or area of life was usually assigned to different saints. Saint Anthony would protect the mule while St Christopher would protect the cart and cargo. Every social group, from prisoners to policemen, from taxi drivers to students, have their own saint or Virgin keeping a watchful eye on them. Not to mention everybody's personal *angel de la guardia*.

However formidable these safety features of the Catholic faith may be, they don't fully foil the forces of evil. The mischievous demons that in Northern Europe are portrayed as trolls or goblins are represented in Majorca by the *dimonis* who come out to play on 16 January before being put to flight by Sant Antoni. But these represent the forces of nature that are necessary to the farmer as long as they are well behaved: wind, water, and heat are necessary to agriculture, but when they run out of control they become dangerous. This, rather than the Christian concept of malignant beings, is how the demons are portrayed in the peasant culture: mischievous forces to be tamed symbolically, like the dark bull being tamed by the feminine figure of the bullfighter in his suit of lights. Lucifer or Satan, the force of evil rather than mischief, is represented by the ominous character of the *Dimoni Gran*, a skeletal figure dressed in black, wearing a huge and terrifying papier-mâché head with bulging eyes, sharp horns, and even sharper teeth.

On the evening of 16 January, Sa Pobla could compete with any Chinese New Year celebration for sheer firepower. There are thousands of visitors in the main square, which is the size of a football pitch. Last year's billboards advertised the event in the style of an old boxing poster, with Sant Antoni in one corner and the Devil in the other. Although this scandalized some of the more devout Catholics, the folk tradition has always portrayed the face-off between them in popular terms, even sitting the Saint and the Devil at a game of cards. The 2003 T-shirts were printed with the e-message:

*Sant Antoni*
+<:-)
*i El Dimoni*
=>:-(

The demons, having scared the kids through the streets of the town, proceed to light the bowls of kerosene that are bracketed to the tree trunks lining the square, turning it into one of the halls of hell. Then all kinds of fireworks go off as devils run around with Catherine wheels, pushing fire-spitting contraptions. The town hall becomes an exploding arsenal with flames pouring out of the upstairs windows while rocket launchers send great canopies of fireworks exploding overhead from behind a wall of sandbags by the main door. All the while, a 10,000-watt sound system blasts out a Wagnerian soundtrack over which the spine-chillingly piercing peasant voice of the 80-year-old Madò Buades sings a traditional Majorcan folk air.

Although I've been onstage several times in previous editions of this festival, this year I've just come to watch. I spot Alexandre Ballester the playwright and town chronicler – hunched and pallid in his dark glasses – and his sidekick Toni Torrens, the pharmacist, a curly-haired leprechaun. This incombustible pair of agitators have done more for Majorcan popular culture than any government department. I first met them when they organized a bread and oil ceremony for hundreds of people outside the Sa Pobla Town Hall to celebrate the publication of my book *Volem Pa amb Oli*, a treatise in Catalan on the world of bread and olive oil. I was invited to 'officiate' while the hundreds of *poblers* tucked into the free grub and excellent local wine.

When the pharmacist's son began to attend Barcelona

University, he realized he'd miss the next few Sant Antoni celebrations. 'Well, we'll take Sant Antoni to Barcelona then,' said Toni Torrens. Letters were written, strings pulled and the *Festa de Sant Antoni* is now a regular fixture every year in Barcelona, the only full-scale manifestation of authentic Majorcan culture outside the island, complete with bonfires, bagpipes, bangers, barbecued *botifarrons* (blood sausages) and hundreds of *dimonis* running around the streets of the Gràcia district scaring the hell out of the Catalan children.

Alexandre was now organizing a bagpipe festival for later that year and had already got in touch with over a hundred Majorcan *xeremiers*. There's always a *xeremier* or two at the head of any Majorcan street march, whether in honour of a saint or against the war in Iraq. 'Just imagine the racket of a hundred bagpipes playing in unison!' he cried in glee. The mayor wandered over: 'Aren't you the chap who wrote the book about bread and oil? Then you must join us for the official supper after the fireworks.' (I later discovered that forty years earlier my father had also been recognized by the then mayor of Sa Pobla during the Sant Antoni celebrations and invited to the official supper.)

The *politicos* were driven to the restaurant while the rest of us walked through the streets lined with stalls selling food, toys, and *ximbombes*, and across a large fairground. We passed half a dozen Senegalese and Nigerians selling pirate CDs, a huge business known as *Top Manta* – a *manta* being the blanket on which the records are laid out for a quick escape. If the police arrive, you just grab the four corners of the *manta* and make a run for it. I was walking alongside a friend of Ramón's, the Balearic Delegate of the Society of Authors. 'The *top manta* robs our composers and musicians of millions every year, and I should really denounce these guys to the police, but they are just as much victims; they only earn ten cents on each sale. The blank disc costs another ten cents and the Mafiosi make a clean profit of 90 per cent.' Spain and Greece have the biggest turnover in pirate CDs in Europe, probably because their Internet connections are still too slow to make downloading MP3s worthwhile.

The restaurant was laid for about two hundred local VIPs. I felt uncomfortably incongruous sitting next to the Secretary of Industry and Commerce and opposite the editor of the *Ultima Hora* ('Stop Press'), the biggest circulation tabloid in the islands, known to the English residents as the *Ultimate Horror*. Next to the mayor at the main table sat María Antònia Munar (President of the Majorcan Island Council) and various other bigwigs. After serving the traditional *espinagada de Sant Antoni*, a spinach and eel pie (eels are plentiful in the marshlands), it was time for the *gloses*, a popular form of improvised verse. A group of the best-known *glosadors* took their stand before the top table and laid down a heavy grunting rhythm on their *ximbombes*.

There are two kinds of *glosadors*. There is the armchair or reflexive variety, who works on an idea with pen and paper, and then there is the *glosador de picat*, who makes up the verse on the spot, often in a duel with an opponent – a forerunner of a modern poetry slam. When a *glosador de picat* sings instead of reciting, wit is more important than musicality. After the required references to Sant Antoni and his ongoing battle with the Devil, the fun began with sexual-political innuendoes suggesting that the mayor's Conservative Party might be wooing Ms Munar's Nationalist Party away from its coalition with the Socialists and the Green Party. The mayor was obliged to reply in verse, continuing the joke with many references to devils and horns – to 'put horns on someone's head' is to cuckold them. The prim Ms Munar kept quiet and smiled demurely, knowing that in the next elections she would be hopping out of one bed and into another. The whole restaurant was cheering as each *glosador* took a verse, especially a very sharp-tongued woman in a heavy duffelcoat who would have looked more at home in a Wiltshire village fête than in Sa Pobla.

After coffee and almond cake, we were each presented with a keepsake, a glazed honey jar with a *dimoni* sitting astride the lid. Some of the VIPs were chauffeured back to Palma, but for most of those present the night was young. On every other street corner there was a bonfire blazing as the neighbours held their own party around the flames, and the mayor and the councillors would do the rounds, dropping by each one to join in the fun.

> In the sky we see the moon
> And twinkling stars of every hue;
> Saint Anthony, please keep me safe
> From falling off my mule.

There was a time when futures were read in the flames of the bonfires, and predictions for the following week's weather were made according to the flow of the sparks. Every so often the embers are shovelled into a split oil drum a few yards away, to allow people to grill their *botifarrons* and *sobrassada* on skewers without getting their faces roasted by the flames. With wine and spirits flowing freely, singers' tongues get looser and, by the wee hours, downright obscene, especially when the men are goaded by the old *madonas* who take the opportunity to turn away from the flames and lift the hems of their skirts to allow the glow to warm their frozen behinds. Most of the *gloses* would merit an 'explicit language' sticker in the USA, but of course this is what Jaume Aiats calls the *erotisme fertilitzador*, appropriate to this point in the agricultural cycle, and explains the curious mixture of the religious and the profane. 'Why', he asks, 'do we honour this Saint in these times of mad cows and genetic manipulation? Because now we need him more than ever, to re-invent our links with mother nature and her demons, which our contemporary society has yet to understand and to come to terms with. Because we need an alternative to the institutionalized Catalan culture which has excluded the wild partying, the powerful voices, the body itself and its eroticism.'

The veneration of Sant Antoni is by no means unique to Majorca:

> Saint Anthony is protector
> Of Mahón and Ciutadella.
> Since we can't afford a glass
> We toast him straight from *la botella*.

Festivities and bonfires in his honour are also celebrated in at least three hundred Valencian towns and villages, in Catalonia and Aragon, as well as in Sardinia and central Italy. You can be sure that wherever Sant Antoni is fêted, the Devil is the required gatecrasher.

One mustn't confuse Anthony, the Abbot of Viana, with St Anthony of Padua, whom at home my parents always called upon to help find lost objects – especially keys and passports – and who never failed in his task. One of my father's favourite irreverent stories told of the fresco painter who was working on the ceiling of the main nave of Palma Cathedral, a hundred feet up. Suddenly one of the ropes supporting his platform snapped, but the artist managed to grab the other. Dangling in mid air, while the paint-mixers below looked up in horror, he cried out.

'Saint Anthony! Saint Anthony!' he cried, 'save me!'

A deep voice echoed through the cathedral:

'*Which* Saint Anthony?'

'Er . . . Saint Anthony . . . of Padua?'

The other rope snapped.

Antoni Calafell was a thickset Majorcan patriarch with a deep, slow, nicotine-stained voice and the sort of earthy vitality portrayed by Anthony Quinn in *Zorba the Greek*. Toni Morlà and I met him through his son Ramón, who had often sung with Dorín, but the old man soon became our guru. Like most rural Majorcans, he was known by his *malnom*, Antoni 'Viler' – pronounced *veelay* – which means 'townsman'.

Since the repertoire of Christian and surnames on the islands is rather limited – few have been added in the seven centuries since the Christian conquest – every Majorcan household or family inherits a *malnom* or sobriquet to distinguish, say, this Antoni Calafell or that Joan Pons from several others in the same town. Some *malnoms* derive from an ancestor's profession, others from his physical peculiarity; thus we'd be able to distinguish John *Seamstress* Smith from John *Bowlegged* Smith. (Wales has a similar system, as in the joke about the German who parachutes into a Welsh town during the war looking for his contact, with only a surname scrawled on a piece of paper: 'Oh, it's Evans *the Spy* you'd be wanting.') In Catalonia and the Balearics, the *malnom* preceded by Ca'n or Ca Na (like the French *chez*) is used to identify the family house or business premises. 'Let's meet for a beer at Ca Na Velleta [The Old Lady's]' or 'Go and ask Bel of Ca'n Blau for a cup of flour.'

Curiously, the *malnom* of this branch of the Calafell family made no reference to the fact that it had produced eight generations of church builders. Antoni's father Joan had built the church in the Port d'Andratx, but after Franco's victory, ecclesiastical construction went into a decline, despite the power of the Church under the new regime. In the late 1950s, however, good stonemasons like the young Antoni Viler began to be sought after to build luxury villas for the foreigners who were beginning to settle in the port of Andratx, people like the Duke of Somerset or the Viscount de la Rochefoucault. While the small mountain villages like Deià and Galilea attracted the goat-footed bohemians, the gin-and-tonic set preferred the more civilized areas of Andratx, Pollença or El Terreno in Palma, all within easy reach of their yacht moorings.

The construction boom of the Sixties was a different matter, based on a penny-pinching, deadline-rushing shoddiness that made Antoni turn his back on the family tradition and instead open a fish restaurant in the Port with his wife Margarita. She had a head for business and was well known to the foreign community. Her father had turned to painting late in life – if these foreigners can do it, why can't I? – and was soon selling his *art naïf* canvases as fast as he could paint them.

Following the Spanish custom, Antoni's second son Ramón had been named after his maternal grandfather, the painter. Old Ramón Vera had assimilated a vast store of colourful imagery after years as skipper of a fishing boat in Andratx and then in Batabanó, Cuba, where the Andritxols ran the sponge-fishing business. Few artists could boast the skipper's familiarity with the Mediterranean and Caribbean tropical seabeds, which, in the days before scuba goggles, fishermen would view through a glass-bottomed barrel hung over the side of the boat. Everything in his canvases is movement, from sharks and waving sea anemones to boat builders or Majorcan kitchen scenes, depicted not with the detachment of an observer but with the authority of the participant. Although he was heavily built and with bulldog jowls, Ramón Vera's pictures are light and playful; in one, a barrow boy carting tuna along the quay is being shadowed by a pair of sardines walking on their fins. Another canvas portrays a guitar propped up against a stone parapet, behind which a sheep is strung up by the neck from an almond tree, eyes bulging and tongue hanging out in a strangled bleating.

'What does that painting represent, Ramón?'

'What I think of Flamenco music.'

Ramón's enthusiastic foreign buyers arranged exhibitions in Madrid and New York, but his favourite paintings still hang on the walls of Antoni Viler's restaurant.

Despite his peasant appearance, Viler was very well read and could be described as an illustrated man, a personal friend of foreign and local intellectuals and artists including Joan Miró. Yet this intellectual luggage only seemed to root him all the more firmly to his own Majorcan peasant culture, one whose identity and values he saw fast disappearing beneath the tarmac and concrete of tourism and the uniformity of institutionalized Catalan culture. Not content simply to pontificate, he practised what he preached. With the restaurant's profits he bought and restored an abandoned farm in neighbouring Estellenchs to its full productivity, and saw Toni, Dorín, and myself as a mouthpiece for his message. We would spend many summer evenings in the back room of the restaurant with our guitars, eating organically grown peaches and melons from the farm and listening to Antoni's deep, paused voice philosophizing until the early hours. Viler had been a zombie for a decade. That, at least, is what he claimed a year after I met him: he had been saved from death thanks to a shot of penicillin, but rather than be thankful for a new lease of life, he seemed to feel that the doctors who cheated death did nobody a favour. 'Modern medicine has saved lives, but created a legion of living dead.' Perhaps he was feeling guilty and despondent after the sudden death of his son. Ramón, with his rakish moustache and wonderful baritone voice, had always been the life and soul of the party. Like his father and brothers, he was a natural-born builder, but was killed when a part of their farmhouse collapsed during renovations. This loss brought us all closer together.

The conversation – when anybody managed to get a word in edgeways – centred around the paradox of the way the information culture has impoverished rather than enriched local culture; how every trade had its own vocabulary; how staying in one place and respecting family traditions gives a much deeper understanding of one's world than gallivanting all over it. Believing in the idea that one lives on through the work one has accomplished, Antoni would always refer to his forefathers not as *avantpassats* (passed-befores) but as *avantpassants* (passing-befores). However, he was very wary of the local nationalists, especially those who tried to get political mileage out of the local culture. He loved to put his money (or his time) where his mouth was, the more provocatively the better, financing and organizing one-off cultural acts, or showing up the folly of so-called progress.

Meanwhile his wife Margarita did the accounting and his numerous sons and daughters worked in the kitchen or served the tourists on the seafront tables outside, a few yards from the quay where regular visitors like Peter Ustinov moor their yachts. The wages stayed in the family: the farm supplied much of the produce and the family boat supplied the fish, reflecting the Majorcan tendency towards self-sufficiency. Although Antoni Viler was a typically Majorcan patriarchal figure with a strong misogynistic streak, his daughters were strong-willed and independent. The eldest, while travelling alone overland to India, managed to foil an attempted gang rape in a women-only train carriage in Pakistan; 'I'd lived long enough under my father's thumb to know how to deal with the Moorish mentality.' On the journey she met a young Indian hippie whom she later married, only to discover he was the eldest son of a Maharajah; her sister married a country-blues singer, Eric Bibb, who had been playing in the Guitar Centre. (Eric, the nephew of John Lewis of the Modern Jazz Quartet, is now a major figure on the international blues scene.) A third sister paired up with a Colombian ex-guerrilla and a brother married a Dutch girl, so the family farm soon began to look like a Benetton ad, overrun by black, blond, Indian, and Mediterranean kids.

The *glosa* or *glosat*, whether written, spoken or sung, is probably the most genuine characteristic of the folk culture of the islands, an expression of the Mediterranean rural wit that can be just as lethal as Oscar Wilde's or Dorothy Parker's. Although he was more of a *glosador reflexiu*, Antoni Viler could improvise a devastating verse on the spot, yet not even the most scatological rhyme failed to make some philosophical point. One night when Toni, his mother, Dorín, Carmen and I were at the restaurant, Viler sent one of his sons to fetch another *glosador* who lived in the port. Teixidora, who was in his late sixties like Viler, signed his published *gloses* with the pseudonym *Ja Està Dit* ('Enough Said'), but his wife had the last word and wouldn't let him go out so late at night. So Antoni sent him a *glosa* referring to his manhood:

Were it not for the full bladder
That provokes our dawn salute
Most of us would not dispute
That we've been sliding down the ladder
We grab the handle of the mop
And sweep from coast to coast
Just so we can later boast
That in this game we're still on top . . .

The sun rises in the east and in the west it lays its head
The same befalls all of mankind, no matter how we
    pray
Only when our song's complete can we truthfully say
That in the world enough's been said . . .

And so Teixidora came, and so did Baltasar Espern, and we all got caught up in the dynamics of the *glosadors*. It was fascinating to listen to the mental agility of these elderly men, who not only had to give a clever riposte to their antagonist, but also had to do it in the correct rhyme and metre. They were able to answer anybody in any situation. Antoni recalled how his father had been caught short on the road to the Port and squatted behind a wall. A passing neighbour spotted him and said, '*Mestre Joan, que anau de merda?*' ('So, Master Joan, you like a good shit, do you?')

Without missing a beat or getting up, Antoni's father turned the question into a four-line *glosa*:

> *No l'haugessis endivinat,*
> *Perque si fossis escarabat*
> *Ja t'hauria convidat*
> *Que tanmateix s'ha de perdre!*
> (I thought you'd never guess;
> Had you been a dung beetle
> I'd already have offered you some
> Because in any case it'll go to waste!)

By no means are all *gloses* thorny roses; they can be a posy to celebrate a friend's birthday, conquer a woman's heart or ask a friend a favour, or to simply entertain company with a display of wit and ingenuity. The advent of radio and TV almost did away with this form of entertainment, but a renewed interest in the last few years means that an evening of *glosadors* can pack out a theatre, some of them arriving from other islands, even from the Canaries, Valencia, and Tarragona.

Conversation at Antoni's restaurant often revolved around the Andratx–Cuba connection. This subject fascinated me. I'd been hooked on Afro-Cuban music since I was a child. I had begun to play the *tres*, a small Cuban guitar with three pairs of steel strings, which I'd been lent by a neighbour who had emigrated from Cuba after the revolution. He had also lent me some 1950s records of Cuban *son montuno*, which Toni and I were crazy about. Most *sones* began with an apparently very simple riff on the *tres*, but what appeared to be the onbeat turned out to be the offbeat when the rest of the band came in. This was a typically Cuban teaser, the musical equivalent of Escher's visual conundrums, designed to throw dancers off balance. In one of the scant breaks in the conversation I launched into the offbeat intro to *Papá Montero* on my *tres*, knowing that Toni would follow. He loves imitating the distinctive voice of the *sonero* and savouring the contrast between the jaunty tune and the turgid lyrics:

Gentlemen, the family of the corpse has commended
  me
To sing the praises of the deceased who, while alive,
Went under the name of Papá Montero . . .

The essential Cuban *joie de vivre* comes through in this song from the 1940s. It was originally improvised at the wake of an old black man from the village of Isabel de Sagua. Papá Montero just lived to dance with the prettiest girls and died with a smile on his lips asking for a party instead of a funeral. He got one, with all his friends laying down the beat on the sides of the coffin. His widow broke her silent grief to yell at the corpse 'You rumba-dancing swine, you!' This was picked up by the assembled company:

*A velar a Papá Montero, zumba ¡canalla rumbero!*
(Let's all mourn Papá Montero, and razz that
  rumba-dancing swine!)

Many of the lyrics we learned from these old records were built around the traditional form of *glosa* used in the Canaries, the *décima,* whose ten-line rhyming structure (a-b-b-a-a-b-b-a-a-b) is the basis of a great number of Cuban and Mexican songs. Teixidora immediately picked up this verse form and improvised his own *décima* in Majorcan:

| | |
|---|---|
| *Andratx ja no té glosadors* | Andratx no longer has glosadors |
| *Com un altre temps tenia* | As it used to in the old days |
| *Ni feim betlems de María* | Nor offers flowers to the Virgin |
| *Per maig un temps tan formós* | In the pretty month of May |
| *Aquest poble era ditxós,* | Fortune smiled on this town |
| *Una vall de pau i harmonia* | A valley of peace and harmony |
| *El poble se divertia* | The townspeople all had fun |
| *I els pobres eren senyors* | And even the poor were gentry |
| *Perque amb un bitllet o dos* | Because with a peseta or two |
| *Tothom menjava i bevia* | Everybody ate and drank their fill. |
| *Ja no veuen mariners* | We no longer see mariners return |
| *Venir de Cuba com antes* | From Cuba like they used to |
| *Ni gastar-se en bullangues* | Nor spend on wild partying |

273

| | |
|---|---|
| *Tot lo que guanyaven i més.* | All they'd earned and more. |
| *Te dic que no és lo mateix,* | I tell you, it's not the same |
| *Ses coses han canviades* | So many things have changed |
| *He vist confits a grapades* | I've seen sweets by the fist-full |
| *Estirar-les p'es carrers* | Scattered all over the streets |
| *I per sis cèntims es forners* | And bakers hawking ensaïmades |
| *Passetjar ses ensaïmades . . .* | For only six centimes each . . . |

– thirty lines that Toni later set to music as one of the strongest numbers in our set.

All this activity brought out the best in Viler. He'd be talking about three or four subjects at once, weaving them in and out of his philosophizing: Spanish and European history, country lore, local characters. It was always difficult to leave the restaurant because you'd be wondering how he'd eventually bring these separate threads to a common conclusion – which he always did, and like a good novelist he'd keep you hanging on. One evening, while talking about the superficiality of contemporary society, he'd occasionally look out of the window and say: 'Look, there goes Tutankhamun' or 'That was Cleopatra'. After an hour of these asides we were wondering what it was leading to, then he suddenly called out to one of his neighbours passing by, 'Stop, but don't look at me, keep looking straight ahead as you were . . .'. Then, turning to us, he said, 'See? We've returned to Egyptian times. Today's world isn't made up of people; it's just made up of two-dimensional profiles!'

Viler spoke the old Majorcan of his generation, his rich vocabulary full of stonemason's and fisherman's terms, each of which had a wide panoply of connotations no youngster would ever pick up. If one in a hundred of my generation recognized *alabern* as the name of the variety of reed used to make lobster traps, even fewer would recognize it as a symbol of flexibility and longevity because it can last for years underwater without rotting.

Antoni patiently explained all this to his disciples, since his own children had other interests. I think he saw us as a means of leaving his cultural legacy. Not only did I learn of the existence of *llet de figuera,* a buttermilk curdled with fig-tree sap, I also learned that only a certain variety of fig tree produced the right kind of sap. I've always regretted not having recorded these seminars in Mediterranean peasantship.

Any Majorcan village's identity is defined by its human and physical geography; mountain people or plainsmen, charcoal-burners or fishermen, bat-fowlers or rabbit hunters, homesteaders or estate workers, dry-crop farmers or irrigators. But a deep part of the village's identity has a more distant geographical influence, subtly marked by the country to which its inhabitants emigrated in the lean years. Each had an overseas community that would receive and place new arrivals in the sector they controlled. Sóller had a foot in the fruit business in Marseilles, hence the predominance of their guttural *r*; Valldemossa controlled the bakeries in Montevideo, where, it is said, they weren't the only ones working at night because some upstairs rooms were used as bordellos.

Emigration was nearly always a question of networking. Majorcans, being bilingual, could fit in anywhere in Latin America while also having access to a more exclusive network thanks to their own 'secret' language.

The young men of Andratx who went to Cuba could count on their own colony in the sponge-fishing village of Batabanó to the south of Havana. This wasn't strictly speaking a case of emigration: the Andritxols commuted on an annual basis. After the sponge harvest, they would sail to Holland to sell their crop and then down to Andratx to spend a couple of months with the family before returning. It was generally accepted that many of these fishermen had a second family waiting for them when they returned to Batabanó. Viler told us the story of a young Cuban sponge-diver who visited Andratx for the first time. Having grown up listening to endless stories from the homesick Majorcans, he not only spoke the language perfectly but also knew his way around the town and could identify any of the local characters as soon as they entered the bar, all on the basis of the exhaustive descriptions he had heard back in Batabanó.

The sponge trade collapsed with the arrival of synthetics, and regular contact with Batabanó was further interrupted by the Cuban revolution. All this notwithstanding, several old Andritxols could still remember Cuban songs, some dating back to the war of independence. Not only did the *son cubano* make its way from the lush farmlands of Cuba to the dry, austere mother country; the transatlantic voyage itself bred a new music. The sea shanties known as *havaneras* formed a whole subculture, especially in Catalonia, where every coastal village has a vocal group in sailor stripes.

Madò Boneta, a 90-year-old neighbour of Dorín whose husband had been to Cuba, began to sing us *havaneras* and *sones* from the Cuban war in a quavering voice but with such a strong sense of rhythm and musicality that we were able to restore them to their original musical setting. We later discovered an early recording of a song we'd learned from Madò Boneta sung by the Trio Matamoros; our 'reconstructed' version was almost identical, so we knew we were on the right track. But to perform these songs and others we'd learned from our old Cuban records, we needed to expand the trio and form a separate group.

Batabanó, as it was called, consisted of Dorín, Toni and me – guitar, stand-up bass, and *tres* – and Cati, whose piercing Majorcan voice was perfectly suited to the *son cubano*. A 13-year-old accordionist, Manolito, gave an authentic touch to the *havaneras*. For well-paying gigs we added a Dutch percussionist and an Argentine bongo player who left the band soon after to go to jail. The trouble with Batabanó was that we were thirty years too late – nobody remembered the stars of the 1940s, such as Beny Moré or Compay Segundo. Or perhaps we were twenty years too early – the Buenavista Social Club wasn't yet a twinkle in Ry Cooder's eye. Buenavista's 1998 success in the USA, where the embargo against the Castro regime had denied the American public access to this music for forty years, opened the floodgates and traditional Cuban musicians began to play all over the world. Even in Majorca there are now two or three Cuban groups playing much of Batabanó's old repertoire. The music that seduced us twenty years ago, the world's richest mixture of melody, lyricism, and rhythm, finally 'exists' because it has triumphed in the USA.

The country singer Ned Sublette points out, 'the musical legacy of Cuba is also the secret ingredient in American music. . . . The *son montuno* fascinated me. First comes the

verse, which sets up the *coro*, the repeated hook over which
the fun really begins. It's the most marvellous combination
of structure and freedom. The songwriter tells his story,
then the singer gets to kick it.'

In 1982, when we began Batabanó, you either played
salsa or you didn't. Salsa has an urban electricity to it but
our rural *son montuno*, though danceable, was more laid-
back. Our point was to make the Majorcans aware of the
broadness of their heritage; it was a cultural show, but our
manager would place us anywhere that paid. He once sent
us to provide the music for a street party in Portals Nous,
where the Palma bourgeoisie spend the summer, but we
weren't told it was to be a Roman Fiesta. Halfway through
the second number, the stage was seized by a cohort of
drunken Roman legionaries who snatched away Toni's
microphone and began to harangue the crowd. Toni
snatched it back and quoted the Graves family motto in
sonorous Latin: '*Aquila non captat muscas!*' ('The eagle
doesn't bother catching flies') and led us offstage.

Having two groups in one allowed us to offer a full
evening's entertainment for village *festes*. We opened as a
trio featuring Toni's repertoire, and while a mime artist did
his set we changed into white cotton outfits and straw hats
to perform as Batabanó. Matthew Scudamore, who had
been visiting the island since we were both children, had
studied mime with the legendary Étienne Decroux. Miming
was new to the village *festa* scene, and Matthew was rapturously applauded, especially in Sa Casa Blanca, a mile from
the airport runway. Here, gestures were the only viable
means of communication: not only does a busy trunk road
form one side of the village square, but every seventy
seconds an incoming planeload of tourists scrapes the roof-

tops. I don't know if the village church ever had a steeple, but today it's the lowest one on the island.

Our show also featured as guest artists Marita Haalse, a Dutch jazz singer living on the island who had recorded an album with Dorín, and Toniet (Little Toni) Fuster. Toniet was a perky 11-year-old who had knocked on Toni's door one day: 'Are you Toni Morlà, the singer? Well, I've written a song, and it goes like this:

> As I was walking down the old road to Sóller,
> Through the meadow of the Devil Cucarell
> I saw a young girl sitting on a stone . . .'

Toni immediately saw the song's catchy potential and wrote out an arrangement for guitar and bouzouki. We all went into the studio to record, where I added the playful sound of the *guitarró* (a ukelele-like instrument from Minorca) and Dorín added the gruff voice of the Devil Cucarell. He and Toni wrote some more songs to round out the LP, which became a local hit among the pre-teens and parents. Although Toniet only sang a few numbers in the middle of the set he held the village kids' attention long enough to stop them poking sticks up between the floorboards. But Toniet's voice soon broke and, now considering himself too old for 'that kid's stuff', he moved on. The last time I saw him he was selling jeans in a boutique.

Cati, Batabanó's vocalist, stood us up one night in favour of a romp with her boyfriend and was replaced by Carmeta, a Catalan girl with an excellent voice who had forsaken her doctor's licence to live an alternative lifestyle with her crazy Irish boyfriend in Sóller. Manolito, meanwhile, was going through a growth spurt and would wolf down huge quantities of food before a performance. This nearly had tragic consequences during a performance in Can Picafort where, in the middle of a solo, he had to rush offstage, still strapped to his accordion, to be violently and sonorously sick.

One of the most popular numbers in the set was a series of *Cubanas* (Cuban *gloses*) dating back to the Cuban war that we had learned from Madò Boneta. Some referred to the politics of the time; some were politically incorrect –

| | |
|---|---|
| *Estaba bañando un negro* | I was washing a black man |
| *Pa' ver si emblanquecía* | To see if he'd get whiter |
| *Y cuanto más lo bañaba* | It seemed the more I washed him |
| *Mas negro me parecía.* | The blacker he got, the blighter. |

– and others bawdy:

| | |
|---|---|
| *No hay nada como la Habana* | There's no place like Havana |
| *Que ahí se baila la rumba* | Dancing rumba all over town |
| *Y la mulata se tumba* | While the mulatto girl lies down |
| *Para gozar de la banana . . .* | To enjoy the big banana . . . |

In many of our concerts Batabanó's indirect tribute to the Majorcan emigrants certainly touched a large part of the audience, for every family in the Balearics has some distant relative abroad. Perhaps the first islanders to emigrate to the

Americas were the 110 Minorcan families recruited by a Scottish doctor in 1768 to work on his plantations in Florida, where some of their Minorcan surnames, words, and customs still survive among their descendants.

Spain's most valuable export has been its people. This of course has been true of much of the Mediterranean: Italy, Greece, Portugal, and Turkey have also cast a good deal of their seed to the wind, as have the North Africans. Yet the Spanish, as an ex-colonial power upon whose empire the sun never set, had less qualms about crossing the ocean because their own culture was there to welcome them on the other side. Especially in the fifty years before Franco's uprising, the object of nearly four million Spaniards was to 'do the Americas': not to escape persecution or famine as many other Europeans had before them, but to get rich and come home in style. The greater part of them did; the most ostentatious houses in the Canary Islands or Galicia were built with fortunes made overseas. The Galicians (like their fellow Celts, the Irish) are notorious for suffering a nostalgic homesickness they call *morriña*. In fact, in much of Latin America, any Spaniard is referred to as a *gallego*. Having a safety net on the other side of the puddle made things easier; not having to invest heavily in adapting to a different culture like the Greeks or Italians also made it easier to weigh anchor and come home when your pockets were bulging. Only a quarter of this wave of emigrants settled permanently in the Americas.

The *americanos* or *indianos* only came back if they had something to show for it, and not everybody made it big. A much quoted gag went 'See that man over there? He left the country with only enough money for the boat fare, and now he hasn't a penny to his name!'

Another gag tells of a Majorcan returning from the Argentine to see how life has treated his brother back home.

'Well, while you were away in the Americas, I bought this bit of farmland to grow melons . . . it stretches from the well over there to that almond tree.'

'Call that a farm? In Argentina I can get on my steed and ride flat out for two hours in a straight line without so much as leaving my property!'

'Yes,' commiserated the stay-at-home, 'I have a donkey like that.'

Curiously, there were many more Spaniards in Latin America *after* Spain it lost its colonies than before, and they probably did more to develop the continent than the Spanish Crown ever had. News, music, words and fashions travelled in both directions, enriching popular culture on either side of the Atlantic. Castilian Spanish was enriched by the languages of the indigenous Americans and the African slaves; our own florid *lírica* or light opera, when adapted to the Afro-Cuban rhythms, bred a rich new music that took the world by storm. It took the form of *son montuno*, bolero, mambo, *bugalú* and eventually salsa, in the same way that English and Irish folk music crossed with the West African-rooted blues tradition to form rock and roll.

The Spanish Civil War provoked another wave of emigration, but the forty thousand political exiles – many of them intellectuals who escaped mainly to France or Mexico – were outnumbered twenty to one by those escaping the hunger and scarcity of the post-war years. These Spaniards weren't looking to get rich quick, but simply to survive; since Europe was now at war, the only hope was the Americas. The human side of this economic migration was brought home to me by the first song I ever heard Toni sing, about his uncle and namesake who emigrated to Argentina. The melody is worthy of a classic tango and its deadpan lyrics, though understated, still provoke a shiver down my spine:

> Uncle Toni emigrated with his wife and babies to live in the Argentine, as did many Majorcans who wanted to ensure their daily bread for the rest of their lives. Working from dawn to dusk so he could one day return to the street where he was born, he saw his children quickly grow up and himself slowly grow old. And then poor Uncle Toni finally realized that he was one of those who were going to be stuck there for ever, one of those who'd ask any acquaintance who was going to Majorca: 'Bring me back a tender olive shoot, a sprig of almond blossom; that way I'll always think of the island, God only knows how deeply . . . oh, and should you run into any of my neighbours give them my regards, I'd be so grateful . . .'
>
> Uncle Toni, the little house in Dog Orchard still stands exactly as you left it: the well in the middle of the court-yard, the gutter that fills it with rainwater; the larder and the hearth, the bed in which your two sisters used to sleep . . . we all look after it in case you should return one day . . .

In the 1950s, as Europe got back on its feet, the line to Latin America went dead. Enormous numbers of Spanish workers were bussed north to play their part in the German economic miracle. These, however, were temporary émigrés that Franco wanted to recover, along with their new skills, once they had sent home plenty of Deutschmarks. To make sure they didn't lose contact with their roots, the Government sent the top Spanish popular stars, comedians, and flamenco groups, as well as plenty of romantic musical films, to keep up Spanish morale in that totally un-Mediterranean society and climate.

Ten years later the Spanish economy also began to boom, so there was no longer such a need to emigrate abroad. Whole villages emptied as peasants headed for jobs in the industrial belts or in the coastal resorts. Many Spanish *gästarbeiter* came home from Germany to put their experience to work in the new industrial plants building cars, TVs, and refrigerators; others put their German-language skills to good use in the tourist trade. The transatlantic ebb and flow of émigrés dried up, as did family links; the subsequent generations grew up apart. In a gesture of solidarity with these 'Tio Tonis', the national airline Iberia subsidized *Operación Retorno* to reunite long-separated relatives. After democracy returned to Spain the regional governments, with money to spend, began to sponsor their own 'embassies' in the Americas; 'Balearic Centres' began to appear in Cuba, Santo Domingo, and Argentina. The Spanish Government recognized the émigrés' right to vote in the municipal and autonomic elections of their native province, even if they hadn't been back in fifty years. President Aznar's conservative Popular Party, in its democratic zeal, managed to convince many of these émigrés to vote for them in the Balearic elections. It later transpired that on the island of Formentera, 10 per cent of these absentee Argentine voters had cast their ballots from beyond the grave, and all for the Popular Party.

As a result of the 2001 economic crisis in Argentina, the grandchildren of those who emigrated to the breadbasket of the Americas in search of their daily loaf began to return

to Majorca for that same reason. The island's massive
investment in public works also attracted thousands of African workers, many of whom had risked their lives crossing
the Straits of Gibraltar illegally, to handle pneumatic drills
and mix concrete. If we add to this sum the hundred thousand or more northern Europeans who have settled here, we
can say that the island has begun to recover its population.

Batabanó petered out after a couple of years, without leaving any legacy on vinyl, because the management companies
insisted on selling us as a dance band. There was no way
around this, because the five big Majorcan impresarios have
always monopolized the village *festes* and hotel circuits and
parcelled them out between themselves. This state of affairs
also finally led Toni to retire as a singer-songwriter.

Toni had produced an excellent fourth album and we had
embarked on a series of gigs in which the trio was joined
by some of the best classical and jazz musicians on the island
for the summer *festes*. Jesús Palazón, a lanky young surgeon
at the Son Dureta Hospital, had recorded a cascading
Parisian accordion solo on *Alfons es Loter*, a vignette about
Palma's best-loved lottery seller. Jesús himself is quite a
character, with a rare musical sensitivity that was, unfortunately, offset by a shaky sense of time. (Jesús, incidentally, is
a very common Spanish name. Imagine one of our English
guest's consternation to find a note by the phone: 'Jesus called
this morning. Please call him back.') In his spare time, Jesús
invents exotic instruments like a slide-whistle made out of
a Tampax applicator tube, a trombone whose bell is a toilet
bowl, and a violin whose sound box is a sardine tin.

He also added chromatic harmonica to another musical
vignette on the album, dedicated to *l'Amo en Macià*, an

amiable miser who sold comics and marbles from his run-down shop in Carrer del Socors, where Toni grew up. *En Macià* died alone in his dark, cat-infested storeroom although he owned a whole city block of the most expensive real estate in Palma.

El Carrer dels Socors was a seedy thoroughfare known, thanks to its popularity with the visiting US Navy, as 'Help Estreet'. Palma had always been one of the favourite Mediter-ranean ports of call for the US fleet, whose regular visits were as important to the city's 'submerged' economy as conven-tional tourism was to the official economy. The fleet's impending arrival, like the arrival of summer, was announced by the sudden appearance of the *golondrinas*, swallows. This was the name given in the 1950s to the prostitutes from the mainland who somehow had access to the Navy's schedules and would turn up in any Spanish port of call a few days beforehand to prepare lodgings or temporary employment.

A line of taxis at the dock would offer two main desti-nations within the city: El Terreno for restaurants, night-clubs like Tito's, and music bars like the Indigo Jazz Club, or Carrer dels Socors for *verigoud foqui foqui*. 'Help Estreet' was at the centre of the red-light district or *barrio chino*, 'Chinese quarter', of Palma, where I went to guitar class. It was full of seedy bars with American names in neon lights – the Kansas, the Kentucky – which, when the fleet was away doing whatever fleets do, were frequented by many of the city's more liberal citizens. They came not so much to use the services offered as to talk freely about social issues over a game of cards without being spied upon. In the 1980s, thanks to new-found freedom of speech and of assembly, this kind of conversation could take place in more agreeable surroundings. Unfortunately this street began to go even further to seed with the added problem of hard drugs. Other parts of the *barrio chino* have now been subjected to Covent Gardening, making way for the new law courts and a crafts centre; most of the gypsies who used to live there have been rehoused. El Carrer dels Socors is still its sleazy self, but now has some real Chinese living there. One recently knifed his brother during an argument over the volume of the hi-fi, at – you guessed it – 13, Help Estreet.

Every year, as a greater part of the municipal budgets went to increasingly spectacular stage effects for the annual *festes*, there were leaner pickings for musicians from September onwards. Toni would look for any work as long as it didn't offend his dignity. The local government began to sponsor *A Winter in Majorca*, a programme of cultural events to promote off-season tourism, named after George Sand's unkind book about the Majorcans. Under dark November skies we'd drive to the ghost-town resorts and play to a handful of receptive and respectful OAPs at the Anglican Church in Santa Ponsa or to a group of bird-watchers staying at a hotel in Paguera, whose manager knew my father: he turned out to be the main character from the short story 'A Toast to Ava Gardner', an anglophile who appears as 'Wilfredo Las Rocas'.

We quite enjoyed it when, as frequently occurred, our trio almost outnumbered the crowd. In intimate situations like that we would step offstage, form a circle with the chairs and play unplugged amongst the audience, which was much more enjoyable for all. Toni depended on every possible gig to survive the winter, but the drop that made his glass of patience run over was to arrive at a hotel in Magaluf only to discover we'd been hired to play for a first communion.

When the indignant parents, who had paid the impresario in advance, demanded we play the 'The Birdie Song' and 'Hola Don Pepito', Toni said, 'That's it, lads, I'm going to get a proper job. I can't pull my trousers any further down without taking them off altogether.' (Shortly afterwards he was given his own daily radio programme, to which I'd contribute once a week via phone-link in the role of 'Mr Paddington', an ex-pat Briton giving his views on local affairs in Belgravian Catalan.)

'Why did I stop playing? Because there were no longer any listeners, there were just hearers. There was a time when even in the main square during the *festes*, the audience respected the person on stage to the point of smacking their child if it made a noise. When we played in a village, the mayor would come and introduce himself, and the neighbours living nearest the square would offer their homes for us to get changed and tune up, and even invite us to join them for supper.'

When I began playing with Toni, we'd walk offstage and the municipal treasurer would be waiting with our cheque, even though sometimes this would be simply a note from the mayor to the local bank manager, scrawled on a paper serviette. By 1990 many of the larger town councils had begun to sub-contract the whole three days of celebrations to one impresario who would provide a full service, from the inflatable castles for kids to the sound system, from the bands to the porta-loos. Nowadays musicians often have to get changed and tune up in the public toilets before going on stage, and then have to wait six months to get paid. The villagers, meanwhile, have become paying spectators rather than participants in their own *festes*.

Toni has returned to his beginnings, playing numbers like

'Alone Again, Naturally' and 'Song Sung Blue' in hotels and piano-bars, a repertoire whose clock stopped in the 1970s. 'I've stopped singing my own songs, I only sing *Coses des Camp* as a request. My audience is mainly in their late thirties or forties, younger than me, but they grew up with these songs. I'm completely out of the music scene. I know that many of my contemporaries from the *nova cançó* are now singing or writing books in Spanish; that's understandable; they were once flag-bearers of Catalan culture, but they have every right to reach for a wider audience to make a living. María del Mar once said that she'd never sing in Spanish, and she seems to be sticking to that promise, but she tours all over the world.

'I could never sing my own songs in Spanish, but I enjoy singing Spanish standards, just as I enjoy singing in Italian, English or French when the songs aren't mine. I love imitating Charles Aznavour, Edith Piaf, Tony Bennett, Marino Marini, Louis Armstrong. Now I'm no longer *making* music, I'm *performing* music. I'm like a good lover; instead of walking out leaving my woman naked in bed, I've been easing out bit by bit, so it's not so painful.'

The last time I played with Toni was during Antoni Viler's golden wedding service at the church his father had built. It was really his going-away party, and he knew it. One of his poems, which we had set to music, recorded a conversation he once had with his father on the Pont de s'Aluet, a rickety bridge near the port. I've always felt that the lyrics reflected the Majorcan's ambiguous nature.

A no is as good as a yes, a silence or a 'we shall see'
In the end we'll each tell our story resting by the
    wayside . . .

When we played his favourite song, Toni's tear-jerker *Tornar Enrera*, Viler put his hat in front of his eyes:

> If I could turn back the clock,
> Let all my headaches fly away
> Find myself sitting on that kerb
> Playing marbles in the dust . . .
> If I could only be like the almond tree
> Whose leaves slowly wither, content to know
> It will fruit again next year . . .

'I had to rush back to Palma to do my radio show,' remembers Toni, 'but Viler took me aside. "*Toni, anem malament* . . . Things aren't going too well." And I said, "Wherever it is you're going, put in a good word for me." And he liked that; he knew he only had a month to go. He could be possessive. Both his tongue and his pen could be deadly weapons. But he had absorbed so much from life that he could handle the dark side of his character. Both Sant Antoni and El Dimoni. One of his *gloses* ended like this:

| | |
|---|---|
| *Res és bo, res és dolent,* | Nothing's evil, nothing good, |
| *a tot hem de posar mida,* | To every thing we must give due measure |
| *si sabem viure la vida* | Every moment lived is a treasure |
| *la viurem cada moment . . .* | When the act of living is understood . . . |

'Everybody has some clear memories. I can remember the smell of Cala Major the first time I played in a discotheque

there, the smell of the guitar case, of the Massot amplifier when it overheated; we can all remember the smell of
school, the leather satchel when it got wet, the cedarwood
pencils, the Milan eraser. But Antoni seemed to live every
moment of his life with that kind of clarity, living the
here and now profoundly instead of gadding around like
most people do. He was a man who didn't have to look
anything up in the dictionary; he kept all the videos of his
life, not just the best scenes, in his mental archives. This
meant you'd often have to sit through the good and the
bad, which was sometimes hard to take. Once I sat listening
to him for eight hours without even getting up to pee. When
he was inspired, you could have set his whole monologue
to music.'

After the golden-wedding ceremony, the esplanade in
front of the church was full of well-wishers as Viler and his
wife Margarita, their eyes still tearful, came out of the cool
darkness into the bright spring sunshine. People grouped
into carloads to drive the ten miles to the family farm in
Estellenchs for the party.

I've likened the island of Majorca to a goat's head facing
west; the Port of Andratx would be its mouth. In front of
its nose lies the uninhabited island of Dragonera, its arched
back rising like a dragon's out of the sea. But the caravan
of cars doesn't follow this coastline; it leaves the port behind
and cuts due northwards through a mountain pass to the
sheer cliffs facing the Gulf of Lyon. Guarding this pass is a
majestic pinnacle of rock that looks just like a bearded friar
in his robe, very similar to the popular image of Sant Antoni.
The figure of *El Frare*, which Antoni Viler passed by so
many times in his lifetime, had become his alter ego, the
ancient voice of the island, its underlying soul. I once

recorded him reciting his *glosa* on the origin of the name Andratx, from the viewpoint of *El Frare*:

> From where I stand I've seen approach
> The Argonauts from Grecian lands
> Three banks of oars on either bow ...
> 'An Drach!' I hear them shout.
> 'Beyond the Dragon, there's a safe haven ...'

For the recording, I placed Viler at the mouth of the pear-shaped cistern that is gouged out of the bedrock beneath the farmhouse. I hung the microphone down the well and recorded his deep voice reverberating like a roll of thunder across the valley. It gave me the willies: it was the voice of *El Frare* himself.

Viler's sons by now ran three restaurants, so the organization and catering at the farm was impeccable. The multi-racial tumble of kids had grown into a stunning collection of black, blond, and Indian teenage grandchildren all speaking broad Majorcan. One boy, whose other grandfather was the Maharajah of Gabhana, had just returned from his father's funeral in India, where he had undergone a three-day ceremony naming him the heir to the title. But the future Maharajah of Gabhana was serving the tables with all his cousins.

A local showband had set up on the cobblestone terrace as the late afternoon sun illuminated the long table under the enormous porch. A slice of Mediterranean sparkled beyond the acerola trees in flower. After the marathon meal for fifty, Viler beckoned me over and, with a mischievous twinkle in his eye, asked me to accompany him on the guitar while he sang the classic love song 'Margarita' to his wife.

'But Antoni, I've never played it, I don't really know it, I didn't bring my guitar . . .'

'The band's guitarist knows it. He'll show you the chords and lend you his instrument. But it's you who has to accompany me.'

Luckily it was such an emotional moment for all those present, that nobody noticed me fumbling my way through the chord chart while Viler's thundering, soaring, out-of-tune voice drowned out my dud notes. He put everything he had into that final plea for forgiveness, that public declaration of love.

A month later, after Viler's funeral, Toni was adamant. 'A philosopher is almost always an anti-feminist: he can't be in love with womankind. That's not to say Antoni didn't love Margarita; he proved that at their golden-wedding celebration. But it was "one minute for my woman and the rest for me". Although that one minute was pure gold.'

# 9

# Teruel Also Exists

It's strange how the eye recognizes details in even the bleakest landscape; a tumbledown stone shed, a line of trees in the distance indicating the Jiloca river. Five years after my first visit, I was back in the Aragonese province of Teruel, where my wife Carmen was brought up. For her, twenty-five years had passed since, at the age of seven, her family moved to a Barcelona apartment and banished her from her Garden of Eden. Her father had been the manager of the sugar-beet processing plant in the village of Santa Eulalia, and she still remembered the way through the wide, dusty streets – 'now turn left past the primary school' – to her childhood home, the biggest in a row of company houses. In those days, the house came with a gardener, a cowherd, a cook, a seamstress, a nanny, and a man to stoke the boiler. By the 1980s anybody not involved in farming or the factory had gone to look for work in Saragossa, the regional capital, or one of the three big cities that border on Aragon: Madrid, Barcelona, and Valencia. But other than the lack of domestic bustle and the arrival of street lighting, nothing had changed in the village.

Teruel, the nearest town, is best known for the love story between Diego de Marcilla and Isabel de Segura, *Los Amantes de Teruel*, which came to a tragic end in the year 1217 and which supposedly served Shakespeare as an inspiration for his play *Romeo and Juliet*. In this case, the two families weren't enemies but Diego was refused Isabel's hand because, although the Marcillas were well off, his elder brother was first in line to inherit their wealth. Diego was given five years to present a dowry and left to seek his own fortune. Isabel, determined to wait, rejected all other candidates presented by her father, but when the five years were up she had to accept marriage to another. Diego returned just after the wedding and, on hearing the news, visited Isabel in her chambers to ask for a last kiss, which, as a married woman, she refused; broken-hearted, Diego died at the foot of her bed. Isabel's cry awoke her husband who, wishing to avoid a scandal, carried the lifeless Diego and laid him at the Marcillas' door, where his father discovered him at dawn. Among the throng at the funeral in the church of San Pedro was Isabel, unrecognized behind a cloak and veil. Kneeling before the lifeless Diego, she granted him the kiss she had denied him earlier. The kiss took so long that eventually Diego's father, wishing to proceed with the service, went over to pull the unknown woman away, only to discover it was Isabel, as cold and lifeless as Diego. Her husband blurted out the story and it was decided there and then that the unlucky lovers should be buried together. Their tombs can still be seen in a mausoleum close to where the events occurred. As a child Carmen was taken to see the tombs, laid side by side; the lovers' effigies repose upon them, holding hands. She was so struck by this romantic story that she bridled every time someone repeated the popular ditty,

*Los amantes de Teruel:*
*Tonta ella y tonto él.*
The lovers of Teruel:
She was a fool, and so was he.

Today, Teruel is the part of Spain that missed the train. No important resources, no tourism, industry, or mining to strike it rich, nor enough unemployment to justify being bailed out by Brussels like the poorer parts of the country. 'Teruel Also Exists' is the name of a political lobby dedicated to persuading the Government to share some of its wealth with a province that hasn't a single kilometre of motorway, only livestock, cereals, sugar beet and, in this part of Teruel, saffron.

I've been commissioned to write an article for a glossy US magazine, *Connoisseur*, on the subject of saffron. Although other parts of the country produce greater quantities, this windswept landscape has been cultivating the saffron crocus since Moorish times. But the main reason we're here and not in bigger centres of saffron production like La Mancha or Novelda is a musical one. Five years earlier, when making some field recordings of *jota* singers for Ramón's record company, I made friends among the saffron farmers in the village of Monreal del Campo, just downriver from Santa Eulalia and which has produced more champion *jota* singers than anywhere else.

Flamenco music has such a strong identity, one that has served the Spanish tourist industry so overwhelmingly, that few foreigners realize it is only a small part of Spain's wealth of traditional music. Everybody knows that flamenco is the music of Spain, just as most Spaniards know that all traditional British music is played by men in kilts. A new generation of Spanish folk musicians is finally breaking down this misconception, spearheaded by the Galician pipers Carlos Nuñez (who has recorded with the Chieftains) and Hevia, who has sold millions of records of his Celtic-rock fusion outside Spain. If these and other Galician musicians have been able to break free of the 'Spain = flamenco' cliché it is thanks to the tremendous popularity of Celtic music, a tradition to which Galicia belongs as much as Ireland or Brittany. (Galicia, incidentally, is in the northwest corner of Spain and shouldn't be confused, as *The Times* recently did, with the central European Galitzia.) But there is a lot more to Spanish traditional music than the Arabic-gypsy flamenco in the south and the Celtic movement in the northwest.

Spanish folk music and dance varies tremendously from one region to another, reflecting the character of the people. Take the *sardana*, a symbol of Catalan identity. Whereas most Spanish dancing is centred on the individual or the couple, the *sardana* is danced in a ring. This symbolizes the Catalan focus on cooperation and mutual support (more characteristic of the Baltic than the Mediterranean), the same organizational spirit that made the Barcelona Olympics an example of teamwork for the rest of the world. The steps are restrained, precise; the rhythm a medium-tempo *pom-pom-POM, pom-pom-POM*. The visual element is not the dancers but the ring itself, hands joined and arms lifted, shifting back and forth with little drama but total participation. This inward-looking circle opens to admit anybody who wishes to join; the *sardana* isn't danced for any audience but the dancers themselves. The music is provided by the *cobla*, a group of ten wind instruments that provide a backing and counterpoint for the poignant melodies played on the *tenora*, a very expressive oboe-like instrument. A cousin of the double-reeded *tenora* is the *dulzaina*, which provides the music of the Castilian plain along with the fife and drum and noisy percussion – tambourines, brass pestles and mortars, frying pans struck with iron front-door keys, ribbed *anís* bottles scraped with cutlery.

Voltaire once defined the Basques as 'a people who dance at the foot of the Pyrenees'. The clergy would be the first to join in the street dances, until a royal decree prohibited them from doing so. Not that the Basque clergy were of loose morals, quite the contrary. The Basques are a noble, industrious, freedom-loving people who love to celebrate when work is over with a spontaneity that is contagious. But the traditional *gizon-dantza* is a solemn and highly ritualized solo dance performed by a man, in traditional white costume and espadrilles laced up the calves, to the music of the whistle: this is the dance performed before a visiting dignitary and on ceremonial occasions. Traditionally, the political pecking order would be reflected by the sequence in which the different men of the village, or mayors of the villages, performed the dance.

If the Catalan express their group mentality with the *sardana*, the Basque concept of collaboration is reflected in the *txalaparta*, a rudimentary xylophone made of logs or planks and played by two people. One of the *txalapartis* sets up a rhythm and melody, while the other 'breaks' this established order; the rhythm appears and disappears, reaching unbelievable levels of complexity and speed. It was also the Basque equivalent of a talking drum: a friend from Álava told me that the *txalapartis* spread the news of his grandmother's death from village to village. When something has to be celebrated on the spur of the moment a *txalaparta* can be improvised with whatever's to hand. The *quintos* (army recruits) of Lasarte, after the ritual farewell supper before getting their hair shorn, dismantled a signal box on the Bilbao–San Sebastian line and used the planks to make a *txalaparta*. This certainly fits the identikit of the Basque character.

Spain is a musicologist's paradise, and flamenco itself is the subject of hundreds of studies and theories. But on a less academic level, I'd say that the most popular folk music in Spain after flamenco is the *jota*. The name refers to both the style of music and the energetic, rapid folk dance in waltz time. It forms part of the folk tradition of the Balearics, Valencia, Navarre, and Castille regions where the Crown of Aragon held sway – a version also exists in the Canary Islands – but it is always associated with the Aragonese, *baturros* or *maños* as they are fondly known. The image of the noble *baturro* with his waistcoat and breeches, sash and *cachirulo* (a checked handkerchief knotted around the head) is well known all over Spain, and very popular with humorists who love to imitate the *maño* accent. But to imitate them singing is impossible, because the Aragonese have probably the most potent voices in the Mediterranean.

The word *jota* – also meaning the letter J – is pronounced like the British 'hotter', with a slightly guttural 'h'. (This sound doesn't exist in Catalan, where *jota* is pronounced like the English 'jotter'.) Although the name seems to come from the vulgar Arabic word for dance, a more popular theory traces it to the twelfth-century Moorish poet and musician Aben Jot (probably Ibn Ben Jot), born in what is now Valencia and banished from that city. Jot sought refuge in Qal'at Ayyub (today the Aragonese town of Calatayud) bringing with him a music that over the centuries developed into the *jota*.

Like many folk dances, the arm movements of the *jota* reflect the agricultural cycles: arms over the head symbolizes picking fruit, a sweeping movement as you stoop represents sowing or scything, hands on hips mimic the form of a pitcher of water or wine. In the Balearics, when dancing the *jota*, it's the woman who leads the man, teasing and challenging him to follow her steps; he symbolically tries to steal a kiss or lift the hem of her dress, while she ducks out of his way.

November 1978 had been freezing cold when I first came to Monreal del Campo. For the recording session, Martínez the shoemaker had offered us the workshop where he produced *albarcas* using old tyres for soles. He had a wood stove going full blast at each end of the long room. 'The last time I saw a foreigner interested in the *jota* was in the 1950s; it was an American, Alan Lomax, who came to record the older *joteros* for the US Library of Congress folk music archives.' Martínez admitted that he's not a *jotero* himself, but showed us press cuttings of his son, a child prodigy known as the Nightingale of Aragon. 'He even appeared on TV.'

The workshop, full of bundles of leather and rubber, had good acoustics: the test is to walk around clapping your hands and listening for any echoes. Our recording set-up was a little more sophisticated than Lomax's; we had a four-track mixer feeding a Revox reel-to-reel, set up in the tiny fishbowl accountant's office. The *rondalla* from the next village, Torrija del Campo – a guitar, two *lauds*, and three *bandurrias* – set up in the middle of the room. At the far end stood Marcelino Plumed, sugar beet and saffron farmer as well as reigning champion singer of Teruel, hands on his hips and almost imperceptibly swivelling his body left and right in time with the music.

An Aragonese *jota* will begin with a short, spirited instrumental introduction from the *rondalla* – *diddly diddly DIDdly diddly diddly dum* – which suddenly drops to half-speed, cueing the voice to come in:

What is it about the Jota, Mother
Oh Mother, what does the jota have
That makes the youngsters happy and the old folk cry?

Usually, a vocalist accompanied by half a dozen acoustic instruments needs a microphone if he wants to be heard. In Aragon, it's the band that needs miking up. As Marcelino hit the high note, the needles on all four VU meters beat their pointy heads against the red end as if trying to escape from the mixer; my cranium seemed to resonate at the same frequency as Marcelino's voice, which surged through a wave of phase, completely numbing me to the final furious instrumental burst from the *rondalla*. To avoid saturating the whole recording, we had to place the vocal microphone at a distance of ten paces from Marcelino and hang several blankets between him and the instrumental microphones at the other end of the room.

As in the blues, *jota* lyrics are all about love and death, lyrics to be belted out at full volume. I remember the scene I witnessed as a child at Ca n'Alluny: a burly Alan Lomax in a lumberjack shirt, sitting at the head of the dining room table singing a Leadbelly song at tremendous volume while playing a steel-string guitar – the first I had seen in my life. Opposite him, their eyes locked together, was Shirley Collins, the British folk singer who was accompanying him on his field trip through Spain. I have a feeling he learned to project his voice like that from these *joteros*.

So, what is it about the *jota*, mother, apart from sheer power? Whatever it is cannot be pinned down because, as the musicologist Carlos Cava explains, it isn't so much a style of music or dance as a feeling that affects everyone, whether performer or listener, in a different way. 'For the Aragonese and the Spanish in general, it is something which, upon hearing it, makes the fibres of our very being vibrate; it fires up our emotions, it both presses upon and broadens our hearts, opening us up to love, to heroism, to faith.' It's not surprising, then, that the *jota* should follow the Cross and Crown to the ends of the empire. Its influence can still be felt from Cuba to Argentina, but the only ex-colony where it survives intact is the Philippines, although the instruments of the *rondallas filipinas* have a markedly oriental accent.

Aragon is Spain's agricultural and spiritual heartland, a land of baking summers and freezing winters, producing a hardy, noble, hard-working people with a strong sense of country humour. The regional capital, Saragossa, is the home of Our Lady of the Pillar, known affectionately as *La Pilarica* and one of the patrons of Spain, whose saint's day is a national holiday. Aragon also produces a hardy wine from the sunburned grapes and an excellent *serrano* ham cured in the freezing dry winter winds – a winter so cold that in January the water of the Jiloca steams as it comes out of the spring and is still steaming as it flows by Monreal del Campo, a few miles downstream.

\* \* \*

Rattling into Monreal del Campo with Carmen in our 2 CV van on a sunny October afternoon in 1993, there's nobody in sight, nothing to suggest that this is the heart of saffron country at the height of the saffron season. Nothing except for a few piles of withered purple petals in the corner of an apparently bare field. Yet once the short saffron harvest has begun, everything else takes a back seat: the whole family is involved, including the dog. No housework is done, christenings are postponed, the dying are asked to try and hold out for a couple of weeks.

It's evening when Carmen and I meet up with Marcelino and his friend Vladimiro at the village *peña* or social club, El Cachirulo, over a glass of wine. From there we all drop in on Martínez in his workshop; he remembers me well and takes us downstairs to his tiny cellar. 'Twenty years ago I caught a wild boar in the mountains, cured a couple of his hams and then dropped them in this barrel,' says the shoemaker as we knock down glasses of robust *tinto*. 'Six months later, I fished out the bones: they were white as ivory. Every year I top up the *barrica*, but the taste is as good as the first time; it has impregnated the wood.'

'Somewhere in France,' chips in Vladimiro, the village communist, 'an English deserter from the Battle of Waterloo tried to hide in a vat in a winery and drowned. The wine from that vat became famous for its taste, and later they discovered his skeleton and sword inside. Since then it was known as *le vin de l'anglais*.'

'When I was in the Caribbean part of Nicaragua,' I chip in, 'they gave me some Red Monkey rum, the strongest I've ever tasted. You can guess how it gets its name.'

'There you are. *En todas partes cuecen habas*, as they say – wherever you go, people cook beans.'

Carmen asks after the characters she remembers from her childhood in the next village. 'Don't tell me, you're the daughter of Don Luís,' enthuses Marcelino. 'He ran the factory when I was a young 'un.' The conversation turns to the mysteries of saffron. Although sugar beet is important, saffron is the sacred cash crop in this area and nothing is allowed to interfere with the October harvest, when far-flung relatives and student offspring arrive to help out. Saffron is simply the dried stigma of the saffron crocus, which has to be picked before it opens with the sun's first rays; this means the working day begins before the break of dawn. Once open, the *crocus sativus* is unable to close up again and the stigma withers, so the same field must be picked over four or five times to gather the flowers in time.

The next morning Dennis Stock, the North American photographer, arrives from Paris where he works for *Magnum*. Thanks to Marcelino's regular bulletins over the last weeks, we've been keeping Dennis informed by phone about the progress of the crocuses so he can time his shoot to coincide with the height of the season. He has been hired at great expense by the magazine because he is one of the top flower photographers in the world, although he's also known for his shots of James Dean and Marilyn Monroe on film shoots. But that kind of status means nothing to the members of La Peña El Cachirulo; Aragonese farmers aren't as impressionable as the people of Madrid. Here you are treated with respect but you have to prove your worth in terms of sentiment, honour, and respect for wine. As Dennis is a teetotaller, that's already one point against him.

We all assemble at four a.m. in Marcelino's kitchen for a few shots of *coñac* and *anís* to keep out the cold; breakfast must wait because one can't bend over to pick crocuses on a full stomach. We all pack into the vans for the three-mile drive out to the crocus fields, all except for Mister Deneess, who last night said he would follow us out at seven, 'when the light is a little better'. His standoffish attitude has already earned him the epithet 'Mister', the word used in Spain for a football coach. It doesn't help his standing in the village when the news of the US invasion of the Caribbean island of Grenada reaches us that evening: the anti-US imperialist feeling in grass-roots Spain is still strong almost a century after the Cuban and Philippine wars, in spite of the Marshall Plan, which bailed out the national economy. Nobody seems to swallow the official line about the Marines 'protecting the lives of the US students on the island'.

I had felt a lot of sympathy for the Grenadian premier Bishop after hearing him speak at a rally in Managua; Mister Deneess voices the opposite opinion: 'All communist regimes are boring, and the sooner they're gotten rid of, the better,' he declares. Vladimiro seethes when I translate this comment.

Marcelino's team move in a line across the field in the dawn light, stooping to pick the purple flowers and tossing them into a basket. Candida the dog sniffs out field mice so that Marcelino can smoke them out of their holes; they are considered vermin because they eat the bulbs. Last night Vladimiro sang us the *Jota del Azafrán*:

> Young maid, so early in the morning
> You set off to pick the saffron rose
> And the icy winds freeze your fingers . . .

One doesn't expect such a delicate crop to thrive in such a harsh climate. Mister Deneess turns up at sunrise, when the team is finishing picking. 'Let's see, I need a valley or hollow full of saffron flowers, so I can get a good perspective . . .'

'The saffron doesn't grow well in hollows, it needs the wind to keep the soil dry; all the saffron is planted on the ridges.' Mister Deneess refuses to accept this reasoning; but if the Americans are stubborn, the Aragonese are more so. Eventually I drive him back to the village for a ladder so he can get his overview, but of course by the time we've returned all the open crocuses have been picked, so we leave that shot for tomorrow. Meanwhile, he wants a worm's-eye view of the bearlike Marcelino picking a delicate crocus with his big paw. I have to translate his instructions: 'Lift the right leg a little . . . raise your chin . . .'. The rest of the family is in fits of laughter, but Marcelino is getting cramp and is grumbling that it's time for breakfast. 'I'm a *jotero,* not a ballet dancer. This Mister is wasting my time.'

Breakfast consists of enormous helpings of fried *morcilla* blood sausage, chorizo, and plenty of red wine. Then the baskets of crocuses are dumped onto the plastic kitchen tablecloth to have the stigmata removed by the nimble-fingered women and children.

The whole family sit around the table *esbrinando,* splitting each flower with a thumbnail, pinching the three orange stigma where they join and dropping them into an enamelled tin plate. The TV is blaring out the news about Grenada, the family all talking at once, gossiping and telling jokes; but it's not the picture that Mister Deneess wants.

'I want you all outside in the sunlight, the whole family taking out the stigmas . . .'

'We don't do this outside, it's an indoor job,' I translate.

'I don't want an interior shot. This is Spain, we have to see the sunshine . . .'

Although I argue that there's nothing more typically Spanish than a family sitting around a oilcloth-covered kitchen table watching TV, Marcelino's wife Josefina and family finally acquiesce. Two trestle tables are joined together for the shot, but everyone seems very uncomfortable outside, *esbrinando* in full view of their neighbours; it takes a lot to coax a smile out of anybody. Later that evening, speaking to one of the local saffron merchants, I understand why.

When the shot is complete, the women carry the flowers back inside to continue their work, leaving the men grudgingly at the Mister's disposal: he asks them to convince an old codger to drive his horse and cart repeatedly across the sunset skyline until Dennis gets the perfect shot, although they all have plenty of other work to do. 'I know they think I'm a helpless American idiot, but that's the way I want it to be,' he explains. 'I can get much more work done if they can shake their heads and humour me, and say to each other: "You know what the asshole wants now?" I don't care if they laugh at me as long as it gets the job done.' I had to admit it was a good strategy if you work with people you'll never see again, but neither Carmen nor I could bring ourselves to deal with the honest, direct *maños* in that way.

The only indication that this is the door to an office is the word AZAFRAN typed on a slip of paper above the doorbell. Marcelino has arranged a meeting with the saffron merchant so I can write about the next steps of the process.

'The saffron trade is perfectly legal, but it's traditionally a covert operation,' admits the merchant. 'There's no price-fixing, it's a free market. It's not so much a cash crop as a tax-free savings account. Saffron bulbs have a three-year cycle before they have to be divided and replanted elsewhere, so the farmer has to plan his crop three years ahead. The demand and supply are frequently at odds, and he'll use this in his favour. When he needs to pay for a new tractor or a daughter's wedding he'll arrange an appointment with a merchant. Business hours are after dark, because nobody wants their neighbours to see their saffron stash or know when they are selling. It's always been done this way; we still use the weights and measures introduced by the Moors.

'Most of the production is sold as natural saffron, some of it powdered, but a lot goes to the Swiss pharmaceutical industry – it's the active ingredient in teething lotion for babies – and one of our biggest clients is Fernet Branca.' I later cross-reference this information with Culpeper's *Complete Herbal* of 1652, which agrees that saffron cures a hangover and is an anti-spasmodic as well as soothing babies' gums.

It's well after suppertime that the day's picking, a heaped table of saffron flowers, has been totally *esbrinado*, producing a heaped plate of saffron stigmas. These are dried over the embers in a fine-meshed sieve, where they begin to give off their characteristically heady aroma. After about half an hour the saffron has been reduced to a fifth of its weight, and barely fills a teacup; it's wrapped in cotton and stored in a zinc-lined chest. A song-riddle:

There is a lady of the fields who sparkles in the light of
    dawn.
Five suitors take her home and lay her on the table.
Ten of them pull her apart and roast her over embers.

The lady, finally at rest, is sent off to the Indies
For the benefit of Spain.


Saffron was the only spice exported to (rather than
imported from) the Spanish colonies. It has been at the heart
of the Mediterranean culture for three thousand years. The
word *crocus* comes from the island of Corycus, off the coast
of Turkey, but *saffron* derives from *al-zafaran*, the Arabic
for 'a thread', which the dried stigma resembles. It is fundamental in festive dishes from Spain to the Far East, from
North Africa to Sweden, especially with rice: paella, risotto,
pilaff, biriani ... but it is still cultivated and processed in
the same way as the ancient Romans did, which means that
the price per gram is close to that of cocaine. Of course,
half a gram of good quality saffron goes a long way, but
the price puts it out of most people's reach, and only a
good restaurant will put real saffron in a paella; most use
tartrazine as a colouring agent.

For the last picture of the shoot, Mister Deneess orders
a paella at the truck-stop by the cross-roads – the only hotel
and restaurant within miles. Carmen suggests that he order
a nice big one and so be able to invite all the local people
who had given him their time: Hearst Newspapers could
afford it. 'No, I think a small one would look better. Besides,
I don't want to change any more dollars than I have to. The
exchange rate was down two pesetas on yesterday's.'

The Mister departs to the relief of all. We're also heading
off the next day, so we go to El Cachirulo for a farewell
drink. We decide to make up for the Mister's penny-pinching
and, with Vladimiro, we prepare a list of expenses in the
name of La Peña El Cachirulo to be presented to Hearst
Publishers: 'gasoline for four trips to the saffron fields for

the Mr Stock, hire of a stepladder for the Mr Stock, hire of two trestle tables for the Mr Stock, oats for a horse required to cross the landscape four times for the Mr Stock . . .'

'After all,' says Vladimiro, 'Hearst still owes us Cuba.' Strange words from a convinced communist, but he's referring to the sinking of the USS *Maine* in Havana harbour in 1898. Although responsibility for the incident has never been established, William Randolph Hearst, founder of the publishing empire, wrote a newspaper editorial blaming Spain, thus forcing the newly elected President McKinley to declare war on this country. Hearst reportedly sent the following telegram to his illustrator in Havana: 'You furnish the pictures and I'll furnish the war.'

The US press, led by Hearst and Pulitzer, claimed that the Spanish soldiers, like the bullfighters they were, cut off their adversaries' ears as trophies. This only fired anti-Spanish sentiment and led 200,000 volunteers to enlist, Buffalo Bill himself among them, for a war against Spain. According to Augusto Zamora, Professor of International Law at the Universidad Autonoma de Madrid, ours was 'the first foreign power to substitute the redskins as the US's mortal enemy . . . we were the Iraq of that era.'

Hearst's editorial intervention did more to drive the Spanish out of the island than forty years of armed struggle by the native Cubans, and it marked the end of four centuries of Spanish colonial rule in the Americas and the Philippines, a rule every bit as brutal as Britain's. The Spanish, under the Majorcan General Weyler, had adapted the US idea of the Indian Reservation to come up with the concept of *campos de concentración*, which they implemented in Cuba in 1896 as a tactic to cut off support to the rebels. Over the next couple of years, almost half a million peasants passed through these concentration camps, where it has been estimated that only half survived. This, and the international outcry it provoked, only gave more strength and legitimacy to the rebels and caused the camps to be closed down. Besides, Spain was now fighting the US not only in Cuba but also in the Philippines. Within a few months it had signed a treaty in Paris, recognizing the independence of both colonies. As the Spanish Empire collapsed, the US military took over many of the ex-colonies in the name of democracy, which in Cuba meant only granting the vote to white males with over $250 in the bank. Whenever a disaster occurs, a Spaniard will look on the bright side: 'Well, more was lost in Cuba.'

We get out the guitars. Martínez lends me a plectrum and teaches me the standard fiddly introduction on the *bandurria*, as Marcelino and Vladimiro take turns singing. Some *jotas* are pure poetry while others remind me of the wit and wisdom of the blues:

> Dark beauty, your breasts are two snow-capped
>    Pyrenees
> Let me slip my hand inside, although my fingers freeze.

> Neither with you nor without you, can I rid myself of
>    woe;
> If alone, I have my worries; if with you, a whole lot more.

> I'd be the golden nail on which you hang your
>    candle-light
> And see your pretty breasts when you retire at night.

Curse the little worm that brought the phylloxera disease
Since there's no wine to drink, my woman's got me on
my knees.

In the belly of these mountains, how much gold must
be concealed
And in the heads of the poor, how much talent
unrevealed!

Then Marcelino and Vladimiro dedicate the *Jota de la Despedida* – the 'Farewell *Jota*' – to Carmen and me. I have a lump in my throat, but Carmen is almost in tears: the last memory she had of her childhood home was of a big send-off, with the *rondalla* of Santa Eulalia del Campo singing this same 'Farewell *Jota*', naming each of her family in turn. Until this visit, her only link with the Aragonese life she had left behind was Martina, a girl from the next village who accompanied the family to Barcelona as domestic help. 'When I felt wistful I used to ask her to recite some of the recipes from the village,' remembers Carmen. It was this yearning to return to a village life that had brought her to Deià.

The poverty and backwardness of agricultural Spain in the 1950s was such that even working as a charlady in a city was considered a passport to wealth and security. The rural youth saw no future at home and left the past behind them in the hands of the elderly; as the old folk died or joined their urban offspring in the cities, so the villages died. Others, even prosperous ones, were abandoned when their valleys were flooded to provide hydro-electric power and water for the cities and agribusiness; the most common image in the newsreels during the Sixties was Franco inaugurating a new dam. But even if these villagers had been allowed to protest, the general exodus of young people would only have prolonged the agony. I recently read about a rural school in Teruel that had remained locked since the academic year ended one June day in the 1960s. The following September the Ministry of Education decided there were no longer enough village children to warrant reopening. When somebody finally unlocked the door forty years later in the year 2000, it was like opening a time capsule. The classroom was exactly as it had been left on the last day of term, complete with inkwells, blotting paper, yellowing maps of Europe and Francoist textbooks. It has now been turned into a museum.

Hundreds of village schools all over the country are still in permanent danger of closing down for lack of pupils. One remote village recently offered a house and a job to a Latin American family so that their two children could maintain the necessary quorum to keep the school open. There are abandoned villages all over Spain, many only accessible by mule or jeep, with no telephone, electricity, or running water and whose only visitors are those who bring flowers to the overgrown churchyards on All Saints' Day.

In the Seventies, some villages were repopulated by young couples or communes from the 'back to the country' movement, taking the lead from the hippie communes in Ibiza and Majorca. Yet few of these were actually 'going back': most were city-born urbanites opting for a new lifestyle whose rigours and isolation many discovered they couldn't handle.

In Barcelona, Carmen made a habit of striking up a conversation with taxi drivers or workmen whose accents marked them as immigrants from other regions: 'Where are you from, why did you leave?' They would always say that they had left because life was very hard there, but after living in the city they would love to return, 'but now it's impossible, my wife and kids couldn't handle living there with no running water or TV, let alone a supermarket or a school ... besides, we took my parents to a home for the elderly. So you tell me, what's there to go back for?'

# 10

# In the Shade

Majorca is unreal to most tourists, who see their beach resort as a Hollywood set with nothing but desert behind the line of hotels. To holiday here is to be in a state of grace far from your daily grind, suspending belief for ten days as you let yourself be waited upon. Few tourists get a whiff of the island's armpits or have even considered that half a million inhabitants might need a few industrial estates, a doss house, facilities for the mentally ill, or a prison. Yet more than a few lager louts on holiday have woken up with a hangover in a cell shared with five serious criminals.

The old Palma jail shared a wall with the Convent of the Jeronimos on the southern corner of the Plaza de España. It had been the scene of a 1950s black comedy, Berlanga's *El Verdugo*, one of landmarks of Spanish cinema, in which the unemployed son of a retired state executioner takes on his father's job in order to secure a bank loan, on condition that he won't have to actually execute anybody. When he's sent to Majorca to execute a prisoner, his father assures him that the pardon will come through, and that he should make the most of the trip to look for a home on the island. But the pardon doesn't arrive.

Whenever I passed the dirty ochre-coloured walls of the old jail as a child, I'd look up at the barred windows and tried to imagine the inside. The way Robin had described the inside of the place to my parents had made a deep impression on me as a child. 'The latrines were so disgusting that for the two days I was there I refused to eat or drink, to avoid having to use them.' Robin was an English juvenile delinquent at a borstal run by friends of ours. He had inherited £40,000 when he came of age, bought a Jaguar, crossed France in a day, demolished a three-wheeler on his way through Barcelona and caught the boat to Majorca, where my parents had been asked to 'keep an eye on him'. Fat chance. He was jailed for reckless driving and carrying an illegal firearm. I remembered his words whenever I had to use the filthy drop-hole at the village school, and vowed that if prison was any worse I'd keep out of trouble for the rest of my life.

In the early Sixties, a new Centro Penitenciario was built on the road to Sóller with a capacity for about three hundred prisoners. This was at least triple that of the old building, which in itself was considered out of all proportion to the needs of peaceful, honest islands like ours. But, as the locals say, 'for the same price, buy your shoes a size larger'. What nobody had foreseen was that the massive arrival of foreigners and nationals would soon boot the statistics right off the graph and that the penitentiary population would grow proportionally even higher. The new Centro was soon full and, since it's not feasible to enlarge a prison once it's built, by 1990 it had to house five hundred inmates. For not only mainlanders but also many foreigners were *amigos de lo ajeno*, 'friends of that which belongs to others' – an elegant Spanish euphemism for 'crook'. Another expression is *hacerse el agosto*, 'to make your August' by earning a lot of money in a short time. Over the summer months these *amigos* would make their particular *agosto* by diversifying; the thieves, purse-snatchers and pickpockets would follow the holidaymakers to the coast or the islands while the burglars stayed behind in the deserted cities to clean out apartments.

In the 1960s lots of money began pouring into the Balearics along with plenty of holidaymaking fools from whom to part it. Almost since the tourist boom began, each new season would bring shiploads of waiters and cooks from Andalucía looking for work, followed two months later by large gypsy families who would set up camp on the outskirts of Palma, the men ostensibly looking for a job and the women selling flowers to the tourists. Having already short-changed the unwitting foreigner, the smiling women proceed to arrange the carnation (hence the name *claveleras*) in the victim's buttonhole, while discreetly lifting a wallet or camera. This practice still goes on, and causes a lot of friction with the small local gypsy population who are often (but not always) wrongly accused of their mainland cousins' crimes.

The combination of an easy life, tanned bodies, and foreign currency has also attracted con men, shady business-men, drug dealers, rapists, and plain honest thieves from abroad. This last group, seldom caught red-handed, are mainly *descuideros* ('carelessnessers') who mingle with tourists in public places waiting for one to commit the *descuido* of leaving their luggage unattended in the airport or their hired car unlocked as they admire a breathtaking view at a popular beauty spot.

Several foreign mafias have local delegations in the islands and other tourist areas. The Latin American, West African, and Chinese clans deal mainly in illegal immigrants, forced prostitution, and drugs, their exploits highlighted by the news-hungry local tabloids, much to the chagrin of their hardworking countrymen. The North European and Slavic groups specialize in more discreet rackets such as real-estate frauds and money laundering, although the occasional settling of accounts is carried out in true *Miami Vice* style: hitmen poisoning the Rotweilers and fitting silencers before shooting a whole family in their beds, their bodies later found in the concrete foundations of apartment buildings.

Two of our internationally best-known (and much more civilized) *amigos* are Howard Marks (a.k.a 'Mr Nice', 'the Marco Polo of Marijuana') and the late Christopher Skase, the un-extraditable Australian property swindler whose case has put Majorca on the map Down Under. But the Centro Penitenciario's usual foreign clientele is a steady turnover of British or German hooligans who have beaten up a taxi driver, disco bouncer, or rival football supporters. Very few prisoners (let alone screws) are fully Majorcan; it is the gypsies, probably less than 15 per cent of the inmates, who have the highest profile. When you drive past the Centro, there is always a rabble of gypsy women – some stuffed into Day-Glo lycra, others draped in black mourning clothes – queuing up to visit their relatives on the inside, giving one the impression that these must outnumber the rest. But the gypsies simply feel no shame in visiting their kin; after all, it's not the gypsy law that put them there but the State's.

Not only do the gypsy inmates receive the most visitors (especially for the vis-à-vis sessions during which drugs often find their way into jail via condoms) but they also have the highest turnover rate. They tend to return for short spells on charges of petty theft, usually stealing to support a drug habit. In Spain the drug cartels are mainly Galician but the *camellos* – local dealers of hash or heroin – are recruited from the gypsy population. Not only are they harder to arrest – the police steer clear of many gypsy settlements – but they can only be charged for what they have in their pockets. Nor do they much mind spending a few days in the shade if caught. In fact, for some, a brief stretch in jail is not so much a punishment as a social visit, with three square meals a day provided and a chance to catch up on sleep. If a *camello* is good at his job, the *capos* will use their influence to get him out of jail quickly and back on the beat.

Like any other social or professional group, prisoners in Spain have their own patron saint. Taxi drivers have St Christopher, teachers have St Thomas, computer programmers have Santa Tecla, and prisoners have La Virgen de las Mercedes, Our Lady of Mercy, whose feast day falls on 24 September and is also celebrated in a big way in Barcelona, as *la Mercè*. At the end of August 1990 I got a call from our friend Pablo who was a monitor in the Centro, where he had set up a silkscreen workshop and a small offset press for the young offenders.

'The Director has received a subsidy for our *Festes de la Mercè*, and asked me to help organize them. Do you think the Pa Amb Oli Band would be willing to play for 40,000 pesetas?'

Who wouldn't jump at the chance to play 'Jailhouse Rock' in its natural setting! Dave and Juan immediately began to draw up a set list: the Animals' 'We've Gotta Get Out of this Place', the Beatles' version of 'Money', Del Shannon's

'Runaway', Elvis's 'I Want to be Free (Like a Bird on a Tree)'. Then we'd do a short acoustic set including 'The Midnight Special', Dylan's 'Billy the Kid', and Tracy Chapman's 'Sorry'. Other classic jail songs were rejected outright: it would have been unfair to inflict 'The Green, Green Grass of Home' on a captive audience, let alone 'Tie a Yellow Ribbon'.

When we arrived at the prison gates, the band had more than doubled in number to a nine-piece. Carmen, Frances, and Dave's Swedish girlfriend Kerstin didn't want to miss the occasion; Paul Matthews, my godfather's grandson, had four hours to kill before catching the Gatwick flight, and brought along his tenor sax. Toni Rigo, the poet and diesel mechanic, came along to sing the Spanish lyrics to 'Jailhouse Rock', a good excuse to see his heavy-metal ex-junkie brother-in-law, who was finishing a five-year spell. Frances, always dressed for the occasion, came in an extra short skirt and a low neckline. She had asked her son Brendan's opinion and he had replied, 'Oh, yes, Mum, you look great!' But when we met at the prison gates, Kerstin had dressed deliberately low-key.

'Frances, what are you going to do to those guys in there. They haven't seen a woman for ages!'

'But I wanted to give them the best of what I could give,' remembers Frances, 'so I asked the guard, "Is it OK if I go like this?" and he said "They're going to love it."'

Having passed through metal detectors and checkpoints, we drove the instruments through to the kitchens and from there hauled them onto a stage set up in the empty triangular courtyard, shimmering in the mid-afternoon heat. 'In the shade' was a misnomer in this case; there was none. The stage had been set up the day before for Sara Montiel, a cigar-smoking, husky-voiced Spanish diva who had not only starred in a Hollywood movie in the 1950s but had actually had an affair with James Dean. She had done the show for charity or PR; we were here for the money and, I suppose, a morbid curiosity.

Dozens of chain-linked windows overlooked the yard, most of them curtained with underwear hanging out to dry and to keep the sun off. The sheer number of yellowing Y-fronts and the acrid smell of stale sweat and disinfectant brought home the fact that by now the jail was stretched to over three times its official capacity.

After the sound check, the siren went off and the prisoners began listlessly to saunter in. Among them we spotted our French-Majorcan friend Jean-Claude, a gardener from Sóller in his third month awaiting trial for illegal gardening. The Guardia Civil had found thirty marijuana seedlings in his back yard, but the report only mentioned the number of plants, not their weight or THC content. Since the question of cultivation is legally fairly open to interpretation – for personal use it is generally tolerated – he was optimistic, but having no money to pay a fine he was in danger of losing his house. How was life inside? 'I shower with my shoes on and scrub myself down with bleach, to avoid catching anything.' Not only was the Aids virus rampant, the humid heat was a perfect culture medium for every known virus. To paraphrase the Godfather of Soul, 'Get down and get fungi!' The corrugated asbestos-fibre roof of the jail absorbed the sun's heat during the day and then, throughout the summer night, radiated it down on the top-floor prisoners, literally grilling them.

We waited for the patio to fill up with yardbirds eager to rock, imagining a turnout like Johnny Cash got at Folsom

Prison, but many were still lolling in their cells and the few who were jammed against the far wall, hogging its ten centimetres of shade, didn't even look our way. Most slouched sullenly, some chatted idly, each group keeping a wary eye on the others: the gypsies, the Senegalese, the Teutons, the Colombians, Algerians, and Moroccans. Some of them – we didn't know which – were Basque ETA terrorists.

Disheartened at the prospect of having to warm up this crowd, we decided simply to get it over with quickly. Juan put on his Mr Dangerous face, hit an opening Chuck Berry riff at breakneck speed, Jordi and I grinning at each other as we caught it in full flight, Dave spitting out the words as if he were feeding an ammo belt through a Gatling gun. Two minutes of dirty rock and roll, a tight finish, then silence. No reaction from the inmates. No clique was going to show a weakness to the others by so much as tapping a foot, let alone clapping.

Most audiences react emotionally or physically to rock 'n' roll; by the middle of the first set people have usually loosened up with a beer or a joint, and have begun to dance. But here was an audience with a hard exterior shell, whose emotions were buried deep within. It was tough going. Carmen was behind us, gearing herself up to come on and play the tambourine. The yard was beginning to fill up, but the hostile indifference from all but a couple of old codgers was palpable. The inmates would walk across in front of the stage to the serving hatch for a can of Coke or alcohol-free beer, without acknowledging our presence, as if to prove a point: 'The screws have organized this, and I'm damned if I'm going to give them the satisfaction of letting them see me enjoy myself.' Most couldn't help stealing a peek at the girls, who were chatting to Jean-Claude and a couple of other inmates.

We cut the first set short and went into the acoustic numbers, to see if a change of pace would improve things, opening with Dylan's 'Billy the Kid' with guitar and mandolin. I translated a couple of lines; 'The sheriff and his men are out to get you ... Billy, they just don't like you to be so free.' There was some polite interest, but this wasn't working.

Some inmates began shouting 'Let the *rockera* have a go!' So Dave took a break and handed the mike to Frances, who regularly sang a few songs at the band's gigs. She strutted up to the front, flaunting her Irish-gypsy looks, struck a Dolly Parton pose, and suddenly the mood changed. All those who had been holding up the far wall began to approach the stage. Frances's father had been Chief Constable in the Australian outback, so she and her sisters were used to dealing with rough characters in the town lock-up, but being ogled by nearly a thousand hungry convicts, on a low stage with no guards in evidence, was altogether a different billabong. Looking the audience back in the eye she launched into 'Walkin' after Midnight', and the whole crowd slowly began to drift over.

'Now I'm going to sing a sad song ...'

'No, sing us a happy song!' a jailbird yelled back.

So we went into the chug-a-chug rhythm of 'The Locomotion'. 'Come on, Carmen!' called out one of the gypsies who had been talking to her backstage. As her tambourine locked in with Jordi's drums, the rhythm fell into place. 'Suddenly I had the crowd behind me. It was the best audience we'd ever had.'

By now all the prisoners were up front. After an encore

of the steamily sultry 'Fever', Frances passed the mike to Toni Rigo who belted out *El Rock de la Carcel* and his own rocker, *Pienso en Ti*, which he dedicated to his brother-in-law in the audience. Dave came back on stage and yelled 'Take out the papers and the trash . . .' as he launched into 'Yakety Yak (Don't Talk Back)', featuring Paul doing his yakety-sax solo. One of the older inmates caught Frances as she came offstage and asked her to dance. She immediately disappeared into the sea of crushed Coke cans and crushed lives, followed by Carmen and Kerstin. The jailbirds were on their best behaviour, waiting their turn for a whirl with the girls. Dave told us to skip all the medium-tempo numbers and keep the joint rocking; by now all the cliques had dissolved into a communal stomp. When we finally finished with 'Twist and Shout', in which the girls usually join us to sing backups, they brought their dance partners onstage with them, and half the yard joined in with the ascending harmonies, Dave stoking the last dominant G chord for as long as he dared before Jordi brought us crashing into the buffers of the final C sixth, amid cheers and stomping of Coke cans.

As we packed up the instruments after the show, several of the inmates came over. The verdict was in: we (or at least the girls) were a lot better than Sara Montiel. Jordi was chatting to someone who had once worked on his fishing boat and Dave to an Englishman who had asked to be transferred to Carabanchel, Spain's toughest prison, in Madrid. 'It's just that the quality of the drugs there is so much better than the stuff we can get in here.' A group of serious heavies were asking Juan for his spare electric guitar strings: 'I wonder if you have any light-gauge top E's, say a 0.9 or 0.8 . . .' Hearing this I had a macabre vision of a headline in the *Majorca Daily Bulletin*: 'Prisoners riot, garrotte warders with guitar strings, Deià musicians held for questioning . . .', but the demand was actually for use as tattooing needles.

A particularly hollow-eyed gypsy came over to me and asked to have a look at the Spanish guitar I had been playing on the acoustic numbers. It was a flamenco model I'd had since I was ten and it had matured beautifully. The wood had seasoned and dried out until it was light as a feather, and although it had been repaired several times the sound was rich yet biting. Juan Flores, *El Juanes* – a distant relative of the famous Lola Flores, he claimed – held it, weighed it, and tapped the soundboard, which on a good flamenco guitar should be thin and resonant since the thumbnail strikes it to punctuate the rhythm. He look approvingly at the luthier's label beneath the decorated sound-hole, began to tune it up a couple of semitones to get a sharper sound, told the technician to turn the equipment back on and launched into a classic *fandanguillo de Huelva*. He was good. Immediately a group of his friends gathered round and began to accompany him with the cross-rhythm of their handclaps; Juan began to sing one of his own lyrics:

> If you see a prisoner asleep, never wake him up
> Because he might be dreaming of being free.

The siren went off and the mike went dead. *El Juanes* turned to me and began the usual gypsy pitch: '*Oye, payo*, make me a gift of this guitar . . . I can't practise, I can't play, I'm dying in here without being able to play my music, I need a guitar . . .'

I recognized the typical sing-song lament used by gypsy

beggars in the Barcelona metro, the voice dropping down two tones and then gradually picking up a semitone, very much like a dog's whine. It is a vocal technique aimed at making the *payos*, the non-gypsy Spaniards, feel somehow responsible for the social plight of the whole gypsy population. I replied in the same beseeching tone:

'How can I give you my guitar? It's like a brother to me, I've had it since I was a child . . .'. But as a musician I was really touched at this state of injustice, finding myself in the presence of such talent unable to express itself, so I relented: 'Look, I promise to look for a second-hand guitar for you to practise on.' I had no reason to know at the time that he had a perfectly good guitar in his cell.

After the gig Toni's brother-in-law invited us up to Radio Centro, in a tiny room overlooking the main gallery, to be interviewed. The signal can be picked up in a radius of a couple of miles, so there are plenty of messages and requests between prisoners and their families. As we left, Pablo presented us with a Radio Centro T-shirt each, printed at the silkscreen workshop. Leaving jail was almost easier than getting in, even though two ETA prisoners had sawn through the bars of their cells six months earlier, getting as far as the parking lot; and only a week earlier, in Carabanchel Prison, some inmates had escaped in two speaker cabinets after a rock concert. Nobody searched my van.

Early the following Saturday Carmen and I went to the Palma flea market known as the *rastro* – the word means a trail or track, implying sniffing something out. While she checked out the second-hand clothes, I went off in search of a guitar for *El Juanes*. At the *rastro* you can find anything from a hot car radio to a (live) cold turkey, exquisitely restored antiques and assorted articles fallen off the backs of lorries, but nobody had a guitar to sell. At the far end of the market, past an old man selling rusty door locks, stood a particularly ferocious-looking long-haired gypsy with a very rough tattoo on his arm. A distorted *rumba* was blasting out of his boom-box and a dirty blanket was strewn with used cassettes of Las Grecas, Chiquetete, and Camarón de la Isla.

'A flamenco guitar?' he repeated, eyeing me up and down. 'And what would someone like you be wanting a flamenco guitar for?'

'Well, it's not really for me, it's for a gypsy in the Centro, who needs a guitar to practise on, and I said I'd find him one . . .'

'A gypsy? What's his name?'

'Juan Flores Fernandez.'

'My brother Juan! So you know *El Juanes* then?'

I felt like Arlo Guthrie in the army draft scene from *Alice's Restaurant* where he's put on the Group W Bench with the mother-rapers and father-stabbers, and is accepted as one of them. No, Sebastián didn't have a guitar (it later turned out that Juan wasn't his full brother either) but if I came the following Monday to his shack – the last one beyond the abandoned windmill in El Molinar – he'd take me to a radiator repair shop in Son Gotleu where the owner might have one for sale.

Carmen had always felt an affinity for gypsies and a fascination with their way of life and their music, but she was naturally wary of my venturing into their territory; after all, I had been mugged twice in Barcelona. 'Why don't you ask Gary to accompany you? He lives in La Calatrava and knows how to deal with gypsies.' But Gary, a streetwise *yanqui* who came up to Deià on weekends to sell the high quality *chocolate* he got straight from his gypsy neighbours, was out of town. I managed to set Carmen at ease and drove off.

El Molinar had been a fisherman's settlement a mile from the edge of Palma, on the old road to El Arenal, and after a lot of searching I found the gypsy camp. I was pointed past an abandoned sports ground, down an empty, wide paved street that petered out at the motorway embankment. Sebastián's *chabola* stood, rather shakily, on a piece of waste ground next to a closed fish processing plant. Luckily the National Police garage was within screaming distance.

Sebastián's family dwelling was put together from the usual detritus of an industrial estate, and built around a broken-down Transit van that obviously served as the master bedroom. A woman in her early twenties, about eight months pregnant, approached from the direction of the mains tap, with a bucket of water on one arm counterbalanced by a little boy under the other. 'Sebastián won't be long. Here, sit down.' She offered me a broken chair and we sat talking on the pavement of a wide street to nowhere, soaking up the late September sun that was sinking over the Serra de Tramuntana, silhouetting Palma's Cathedral and Bellver Castle, and illuminating her green eyes. Little Joaquín played in the gutter. 'When he was a baby he got into the newspaper because he was attacked by a rat in his crib. That was when they closed the fish plant and all the rats came into our homes. Look, there goes one now.' A cat-sized shape scurried over the plastic sacks of the roof. 'That's why we sleep in the *fragoneta*.' I smiled at this typically gypsy mispronunciation of *furgoneta*, the Spanish word for a van. This is the most common vehicle among gypsies and, true to their metalworking tradition, they have adapted the word to sound like a diminutive of *fragua*, a forge.

I felt surprisingly relaxed talking to Araceli – an unlikely Basque name for a gypsy – and somehow completely at home in these forlorn surroundings. It didn't seem to matter to her that her husband was an hour late; I didn't realize then that nobody in the family had a watch, and that only their primary-school daughters could read and write. A cock crowed from inside the *chabola*. 'That's Sebastián's prize fighter.' Then, 'You don't look like the rest of the *payos*. Where are you from?'

'My family is *extranjero* but we live on the other side of those mountains.'

'I've always wondered what's on the other side.'

Over the next few years, as Sebastián and I became musical companions and our two families close friends, she would have plenty of opportunities to take a look. A glimpse of the other side, not only of the mountains but of the many barriers that had been set up around her people since they arrived in Spain five hundred years ago.

# 11

# El Ventilador

The Evangelical Church of Philadelphia in El Molinar, commonly known as El Culto, is a funky little breeze-block shack, whitewashed inside and out, no larger than Sebastián's *chabola* across the wide empty street. A homely touch is provided by a hanging indoor plant and the white nylon curtains softening the sunlight that sears through the four small windows. A few rows of tightly packed rickety benches face a raised platform at one end, flanked by two shoddy PA speakers. Today the new-born Antoñita is being presented to the congregation. 'Later on we'll have her baptized in the sea,' says Sebastián. He loves to walk his dog on the nearby beach, and, unlike most *gitanos* – Spanish gypsies – he feels at home surrounded by salt water. But his blood is nomadic and a nomad on an island is, to quote the local expression, like an octopus in a garage.

Juanes had been transferred to a jail in Cuenca, from where he wrote to me that he had also 'embraced the Lord'. Sebastián found out that Juanes had a guitar all along, so we gave up our search. In the meantime we had discovered our musical affinities and began playing rumbas together in the *chabola*. Over the next couple of months we became close friends; Carmen immediately hit it off with Araceli, helping her to prepare baby clothes, while our two-year-old Rocío played on the dirt floor with Joaquín. Sebastián had suggested we become Antoñita's godparents – it's useful for a *gitano* (pronounced he-tahno) to have a *payo* (pie-oh) protector – but family pressures forced him to backtrack, so today we're at the Culto simply as guests.

About fifty *gitanos* are crammed into the tiny, airless space. We share a bench with Sebastián's grandmother, a wizened old lady in a black shawl that barely conceals her blue-spotted dress. In spite of being blind, she doesn't miss a thing. The local pastor, a *gitano* in his early twenties with a neatly trimmed beard, is wearing a dark suit like his superior, who visits from Barcelona once a week to keep an eye on things and add some extra fire and brimstone to the meetings. Hollering and haranguing in true Southern Baptist style, their voices – echoed by shouts of 'Aleluya!' – could fill a cathedral. In this confined space, however, they need a microphone to be heard above the din of the Honda generator outside the door, whose only function seems to be that of powering a PA system capable of drowning out the noise of the generator. In Spain, for *gitanos* as for *payos*, noise is joy, and while the Roman Catholic Christ suffers in silence nailed to a cross, the Evangelist's Jesus is radiant, preaching from the clouds surrounded by doves. This Gypsy Pentecostalism, like its equivalent in the US Bible Belt and inner-city ghettos, has brought a religious message home to an oppressed people by using their own musical language. As the call and response in the Culto rises in tone, reaching James Brown intensity, the congregation bursts into song. This is no Southern Gospel music but rumba-pop led by the younger gypsy women; Sebastián is strumming the guitar and a good-looking half-gypsy teenager in a hooded Eminem-style tracksuit is slapping a wooden box, a *cajón*, in time. Everybody joins in the handclaps, and I think I'm showing my understanding of flamenco by clapping on the offbeat until I realize that I'm on my own; when singing for the Lord, nobody shows off. Firing up this kind of enthusiasm, it's not surprising that Evangelism has established itself in all the *gitano* settlements in Spain over the last few years; it is much closer to the gypsy temperament than the solemn rituals of the Catholic Church.

Although the *gitanos* have provided Spain with a great part of its tourist image abroad, they account for less than 2 per cent of the total population. Over the centuries, when forced to settle down, most gypsies chose Andalucía, where the Arab legacy was still evident in the local culture and gene pool, allowing them to blend in more easily. Today, most Andalusian gypsies have been absorbed into the middle class, while maintaining their traditions and choosing professions compatible with their temperament and mobility: cattle- or horse-breeding, running market stalls and funfair shows, and, of course, the music business. But further north, nearly all the *gitanos* live in shantytowns on the industrial belts of the big cities, living off the rag trade.

In the Catholic Church in Andalucía, the gypsy soul has, over the centuries, found its own means of religious expression, especially during the Holy Week processions, when the purest flamenco voices can be heard singing to the Saviour and the Virgin Mary. There are strong gypsy cults following the various Virgins of Andalucía: La Macarena and especially La Virgen del Rocío, the Virgin of the

Morning Dew, after whom Carmen and I named our daughter Rocío.

The Catholic Church is committed to a sacred sense of place and this appeals to the Andalusian gypsy's love of *romerías*, festive pilgrimages to holy shrines. But when it's the mountain's turn to come to Muhammad, if you'll pardon the choice of metaphor, the cumbersome Catholic Church is too slow in following the mobile gypsy communities to their new settlements on the edge of the city limits. The Evangelists are quick to set up a Culto in any shop front or shanty-town *chabola* and attract a congregation at once, having now over eighty thousand gypsy adepts. In a recent episcopal document the Catholic Church admits to having 'not been good Samaritans with the Spanish gypsies ... [who] ... historically suffered the affliction of being rejected, outcast and, often, persecuted' and that although 90 per cent are baptized, few practise the Catholic faith.

I was surprised to discover that I knew more about the Romany people than any of those I met in El Molinar. 'My father speaks *caló*, but I only know a few words,' admitted Sebastián. Nor had he any idea of the history of his people, other than that 'we come from Egypt, that's where our name comes from, and that's the reason why Lola Flores is known as La Faraona', the Pharaoh Queen. The Evangelists take advantage of this popular misconception to convince the gypsies that they are one of the Lost Tribes of Judea, which is why Old Testament names are now in vogue – Araceli's next baby was named Isaí, Isaiah.

Two hundred years ago it was shown linguistically – and, more recently, proved genetically – that the Romany people originated in the Punjab, most likely among the Rajput caste. Probably escaping from the Islamic invaders, they gathered together artisans, musicians, cattle herders, and astrologers to form self-sufficient groups to travel westwards through Persia. Upon reaching Armenia, some followed the southern routes to Egypt and across North Africa, while others entered Europe through the Balkans.

The key to understanding this essentially nomadic people with no written history, nor ties to the soil, is to recognize the importance of the moment. The gypsies live the here and now more intensely than the rest of us, seldom looking further ahead than the next wedding or further back than the last period of mourning. Family history, that which defines the clan, only stretches back four or five generations, three of which may be living under one corrugated-tin roof. The families in El Molinar are aware that there are also gypsies in France (thanks to the Gypsy Kings 'who sing in Spanish but can't speak it'), but they find it hard to believe that Romany communities can also be found in Ireland, Sweden, Poland, and even Latin America. When I introduced Sebastián to Mark McShane, a thriller-writer living on the island, as *un gitano Australiano*, Sebastián's jaw dropped in disbelief.

Although the Culto and other more political gypsy organizations are trying to build up a consciousness of a shared identity, most *gitanos* only feel allegiance to their own clans. The main force controlling their politics is a fear of feuds and retaliations, and the best way to avoid these is to have the least possible contact with other clans. As in postcolonial Africa, where European-drawn frontiers often left two antagonistic tribes sharing an artificial nation, so the forced relocation of *gitano* families due to municipal planning have placed feuding clans in the same housing projects. This is one reason why Sebastián moved his family out of the Son Banya ghetto next to Palma airport and built this *chabola* near his father's. If Sebastián and Araceli answered our questions evasively or misleadingly it was because *gitanos* think us *payos* incapable of understanding the complexities of their social relationships.

In most minority cultures, one's identity is tied to a common homeland, history, and culture. The Rom have always have survived as a people by adapting to their surroundings, to local languages and even music. It is one's individual behaviour and morality (within the gypsy law), more than one's racial features or pedigree, that defines one's gypsiness, or gypsiness in general. Individual status is based first upon one's age and sex – a girl will often have to answer to her younger brothers – and then upon the social respect that one has gained, not upon power or wealth. The figure of greatest respect will become the 'Uncle' or patriarch of the clan, his position symbolized by his walking stick, the equivalent of a sceptre. He will meet with the other patriarchs to solve feuds and mark out each clan's sphere of influence. Body language is important; as the dancer Antonio Canales points out, when a *gitano* of status walks into a room, 'his shoes enter first and his body follows'.

A gypsy's allegiance is first to his immediate family, then to his clan, and only to other *gitanos* if threatened by *payos*. The first gypsies to arrive in Spain, known as the Rom or Roma people, came in groups of fifty to a hundred – a manageable number for travelling, yet strong enough to defend themselves – under the leadership of a 'Count' or 'Duke'. In five hundred years of tremendous changes, the basic social unit, the clan, has remained more or less the same size.

Around 1420 the first band of Romanies crossed the Pyrenees; others, who had taken the southern Mediterranean route, began to arrive via Gibraltar, while another group, escaping from the Turks, arrived by boat from 'Little Egypt'. This gave them the name gypsies, *egypcies*; in Spanish, *gitanos* from *egipcianos*. In Eastern Europe they are known as *zingaros* from the Greek word for 'untouchable'.

In the fifteenth century, the north of Spain was used to welcoming people from all over Europe who flocked along the pilgrim route to the Cathedral at Santiago de Compostela, in Galicia. The city was founded by James the Apostle near Cape Finisterre (the World's End), on the westernmost point of the European continent. The Rom clans, always careful to carry letters of introduction from their previous hosts, would present themselves as pilgrims and were received graciously. Not only did they bring useful skills, they also delighted the rich with their music, fortune-telling, and fairground antics. But now they had reached the end of the road – *finis terrae* – and as soon as their novelty wore off, the problems began. They had arrived at a crucial moment in Spanish history. In the last few years of the fifteenth century, the marriage of Isabel and Fernando had unified the kingdoms of Castille and Aragon; the Moorish king Boabdil had surrendered Granada, capital of Al Andalus where, over four centuries, the Muslims had established a flourishing culture symbolized by the Alhambra palace. The Christian *reconquista* of the Spanish peninsula inexorably forced the Muslims, like toothpaste out of a tube, back to North Africa. Meanwhile, Columbus had claimed the New World for Spain and the same year, 1492, a royal decree gave all Jews a few months to leave the country. Anybody with Moorish blood – and after ten generations of peaceful occupation, that accounted for much of the population – was forcibly converted to Christianity.

This ascetic, self-righteous, xenophobic Catholic fervour, as radical then as today's Taliban, set the country back by depriving it of its most learned and cultured citizens, the Muslims and the Jews. Even the bath houses were destroyed as symbols of infidel decadence; instead of washing themselves, the Christians resorted to burning incense in church to obliterate body odour. In 1499 it was the newly arrived *egipcianos*' turn to be given two months to abandon their language and dress, to settle down and find employment with a Christian master, or face expulsion. But in their travels they had mastered the art of bowing before the wind, adapting superficially to local customs without losing their own, and they managed to ride out the storm, while the Crown now turned its attention to expelling even the converted Moors. This was another royal blunder that drained the country of a good part of its economy and population, so the *gitanos* suddenly found themselves required to help repopulate the southern region of Andalucía.

All the gold from the New World couldn't replace what Spain had lost in art, learning, medicine, and commerce; besides which, most of that gold was being spent on conquering the rest of Europe, neglecting the heartland. The Spanish soul may have basked in the glory of God, but it was the *gitanos* who gladdened its cold heart with music, joy, and liberty. Living always on the edge of society, between persecutions and pardons, their communities became havens for all sorts of social outcasts: highwaymen and beggars, nuns and monks from religious orders that had fallen into disfavour, but mainly Moriscos who could pass themselves off more easily as *gitanos*. These 'converted' Muslims introduced Moorish traditions and music into the Rom culture, producing a rich mixture later to be known as *música flamenca*, literally 'Flemish music' – what a misnomer!

The Spanish Crown had close ties with Flanders, and the epitome of beauty in the Spanish Court was a blonde, rosy-cheeked *flamenca*. The word soon came to mean flirtatious, provocative charm; in a word, sexiness. The word is still used in this sense, even (and especially) when talking about a dark beauty: 'She's very *flamenca*.' The English word 'flamingo', a blushing pink bird, has the same root.

Their nomadic nature seemed to cut the *gitanos* out for temporary farm work, following the harvests around Andalucía: the olives, the wheat, the soft fruit, the grapes. They weren't considered Spanish citizens until the eighteenth century, and only then on condition that they had a fixed abode and didn't speak their language in public. In fact, it wasn't until after Franco's death that their full rights were recognized, and although the anti-*gitano* articles were retired from the Guardia Civil regulations in 1978, I can say from experience that when any *gitano* steps outside his normal circuits, he'll be frisked and questioned. Johnny Ram, an East London guitarist of Indian descent who lived and worked in Palma, can confirm this; he was repeatedly pulled in for questioning (not speaking a word of Spanish, they thought he was bluffing) until the local police began to recognize him as *el gitano inglés* and left him alone.

At Bedales, to my eternal disgrace, I was never able to play flamenco guitar as was expected of a Spaniard; my contemporaries had only ever heard of Manitas de Plata who, I never tired of telling them, was from the Camargue anyway. Flamenco, relying heavily on the thumbnail as a plectrum, was completely different from the classical guitar technique

I had been taught. As a teenager, however, I had learned the basic slap 'n' strum technique known as the *ventilador*, which lies at the heart of the rumba. As Gato Pérez sings:

> The secret of this machine lies in the *ventilador*
> Which hawkers and sailors brought back
> From the Caribbean and Ecuador . . .
> I'm sure it has even stumped James Bond,
> The Warsaw Pact, Nato and the Pentagon . . .
> The *ventilador*, gentlemen, what a machine!

In the same way an English child will play air guitar imitating his rock heroes, any little *gitanillo* will learn this right-hand movement on a stick or imaginary guitar before he gets to touch a real instrument.

- Stand with your right hand flat on your stomach.
- Bring your hand up towards your chin, the fingers flicking your belly.
- Bring the four fingers down as if to brush crumbs off your shirtfront.
- Flick your thumb back up towards your chin, thumbnail scraping your chest.
- Slap your belly, begin again: *a-chika-bom, a-chicka-bom*.

The guitarist is simply imitating a Cuban rhythm section: *a-chicka* is the *güiro* while the *bom* marks the downbeat, which is usually carried by the cowbell. Once you have mastered this, practise on an old broken stringless guitar for a year or two, adding percussive frills with your thumb and fingernails. The left-hand fingering comes later, when you can afford strings. A *gitano* will quickly pick up on any rhythm: if a bus jolts over a railway line or backfires twice, it will set any gypsies on board clapping in time.

Araceli assumed the *gitana*'s responsibility of somehow getting the food on the table. She would beg, do odd jobs, look after the kids, and then walk three miles to the market at closing time where the stallholders would give her any unsold perishables. Sebastián would walk the dog, look after his fighting cocks, repair the shack, and hang about with the other men. For years he had been having dizzy spells and was trying to get a medical certificate to allow him a disability pension. I couldn't understand how someone who sang and played as well as he did, living a couple of miles from El Arenal, couldn't make a good living playing at the hotels there.

'I was offered a gig at a hotel, but since I never learned to read I couldn't find the place. I couldn't ask anybody on the street because they were all foreigners, so I went home. And since I missed the first night, how could I go back? But if you and I played together, I'm sure we'd find plenty of work. Isn't there a music bar in your village?' I never need to be asked twice when it comes to a new musical adventure, so I organized a gig at a Deià bar, El Zángano ('The Lay-about'), billing us as Los Rumberos de la Noche, 'the Rumberos of the Night'. I played the bass while Phil Sheperd, a tall, amiable Deià painter with Ian Dury's voice, joined us on congas. Much as I had come to enjoy playing rock 'n' roll bass, it felt wonderful to loosen up and let the Latin side of my brain take the reins of the rumba. No longer was I bouncing on the saddle of a galloping horse; I was now perched on the back of a swaying camel, simply dropping a few well-placed notes here and there. Phil fell into a trance, getting so carried away that he'd overshoot the end of every song. Although the sound was a bit sparse, it brought a lot of people to their feet; the more people dance, the more they drink and now that the till was ringing, we were offered a regular monthly rumba night.

I took *rumba* to be another African word like tango, bongo, or conga, but I discovered its origin is Greek. In English it is often spelled rhumba, which makes etymological sense because it derives from the rhombus or diamond shape. The diamond shape is what you get when you divide the compass into eight segments, pointing to the principal winds that underlie the Mediterranean agricultural and seafaring traditions. This magical diamond sign, which appears on poker cards along with the heart, the clover leaf, and the spade, has other connotations to the Spanish: Franco's TV censors would place two *rombos* on the top-right corner of the screen if the programme wasn't suitable for the under-eighteens – perhaps it featured a kiss on the lips, or a woman in a bikini.

The masculine variant of the word, *rumbo,* came to mean a direction or course, while someone with *rumba* had a special charm, or prestige. By extension, especially in the dockside world of hookers and their pimps in Cuba, it came to define a provocative style of dancing and partying in general. By the 1930s, the Cuban rumba had been unleashed upon a world already seduced by the tango.

I've always been confused by these musical terms. An Argentine tango bears no relation to a tango from Andalucía; in a *bolero Mallorquín* the dancers leap about, whereas a typical Latin bolero like *Besame Mucho* is smooched to. When the Cuban rumba spread internationally in its various forms (boogaloo, cha-cha-cha, mambo) it was renamed Latin Jazz or Afro-Cuban music, then salsa. The word *rumba* in Cuba has reverted to its magical connotations, referring now only to the *batá* drums and voices that accompany the religious rituals of West African origin. In Spain, however, a *rumba* is a slick, upbeat, urban gypsy music. It is to classic flamenco what rhythm and blues is to the delta blues, what Algerian *rai* is to traditional Arabic music: a mongrel who still knows how to howl but prefers to snap at your heels. The original spirit is there, but now everybody can dance to it. It's been described as the bastard son of the late-night affairs between Spanish dockside gypsy music and the Afro-Cuban rhythms played by the sailors. The usual maritime route from the Caribbean passed first through the Canary Islands, then Cádiz, and finally Barcelona, where ships would spend time taking on supplies for the return trip. The Cuban rumba, as it first arrived on this side of the Atlantic, persists in its purest form in the Canary Islands, where there were no *gitanos*, and perhaps from there it returned to West Africa, where it evolved into high-life music.

The end of the Cuban war in 1899 brought many musicians to Spain to act in variety shows. In the port of Cádiz, they shared the bill with flamenco artists, many of whom adopted and adapted the style and called it *rumba flamenca*. The purist flamencologists consider it dance music 'with little artistic merit or Andalusian flavour'. Even less respect is granted to the commercial, pop-oriented *rumba catalana* whose melodies have a happier, more Caribbean lilt. If I compared the *rumba flamenca* to rhythm and blues, the *rumba catalana* would be rock 'n' roll. This style was born in Barcelona port, where the gypsy rag-and-bone merchants, with less respect for the classic Andalusian flamenco, would hang around the docks trading with the crews, adapting the Cuban right-hand technique, but disdaining the Moorish-rooted flamenco style.

In the 1960s, the *rumba catalana* hit a peak in the magical hands of Peret, who created rumba-pop, complete with twitching hips and spectacular *ventilador* technique, often spinning the guitar along the axis of the fretboard without losing a beat. Peret is a good example of the *gitano*'s gift for getting extra mileage out of something that others have discarded; he took a Puerto Rican song, *El Negro Bembón* ('The Big-lipped Black'), about a racist assassination in Panama, and reworked it as *El Gitano Antón*, about a racist assassination in Spain. In the 1980s, Peret did 'a Little Richard' and disappeared from the scene, becoming a pastor for the Evangelical Church and only singing for God, until he made a big comeback by closing the 1992 Olympic Games with his *Barcelona tiene el poder* . . . ('Barcelona has the power'), bringing the whole stadium to its feet.

If you want to take a country's true musical pulse, check out the cut-price cassette racks at the truck-stops and greasy-spoon cafés. In Spain they are evenly divided between the crooners and the *rumberos*. Or head for the funfair, where the People's Top Ten is blasted out through disco speakers over the noise of the dodgems and the tombola barkers. In this country, at least half the fairground repertoire is rumba-pop, and not only because the *gitanos* run the funfairs; they play the music that attracts the punters, music that makes people want to spend money. Sauntering around a funfair to the rumba rhythm makes everybody feel that little bit more alive, sharp, and daring.

Commercial rumba has never flagged, and is periodically given a push in a new direction by new talent. In the Seventies, Manzanita, a chubby Catalan gypsy in gold chains, added strings and horns to the mix, appealing to middle-class mums and the *Saturday Night Fever* crowd. The progressive rock audience were won over by Gato Pérez, an Argentine who had arrived in Barcelona as a child and added biting intellectual and social lyrics to the danceable beat. He had tried to apply his typically Argentine mastery of words to the rock idiom, but found that the rhythm of the Spanish language doesn't marry as happily with a four/four beat as it does with the rumba, which at that time was as unfashionable as beehive hairstyles. El Gato introduced the rock audience to the *rumba catalana*, the *guaracha*, and the cha-cha-cha. Over the next years the rhumba was periodically updated. In the early Nineties Kiko Veneno – a Catalan brought up in Seville – took up Gato's lyrical baton after his untimely death, then Ketama (three brothers from the flamenco dynasty of the Carmonas) fused it with African and Brazilian rhythms, until the street-punks Estopa gave it a rebellious snarl meriting a parental guidance warning. Estopa's singer refused to tone down his lyrics, explaining that 'today's Spain is *South Park*. The kids aren't stupid.'

Whatever was in vogue commercially, Sebastián preferred the classic *rumba flamenca*, with its lyrics of passion, transgressions of gypsy law, treachery: 'Give me poison, I want to die . . .' Emotional stuff. By our third Deià gig, the word had got around and people began to come from the neighbouring villages to dance. It was an eye-opener to watch this music work its sensuous magic on even the most standoffish Majorcans, stripping away their inhibitions in a way not even rock 'n' roll could. The rumba brings out the Flash Harry in every Spanish male and a brassy provocative charm in every female, even the hardest-nosed Basque or Catalan nationalist.

The *payos* – the Spanish in general – have a love-hate relationship with the *gitanos*, for they represent the dual nature of the national character. They are honourable among their own but feel free to stretch the truth before others; they have respect for their elders but not for public institutions; they have strong family ties but are very independent; in short, they represent the nonconformist, passionate, macho, musical, partygoing, tax-evading, procrastinating side of the Spanish character. Many *payos* would love to live a gypsy life, were it not for the deprivations and ostracism they'd have to suffer.

In the negative image of the gypsy as lawbreaker, capable of vendettas and crimes of passion, the *payo* recognizes the threat of the dark side of his own character. It's not so much racism as a schizophrenic interior struggle. I've seen *payos* exhibit tremendous sympathy for *gitanos* to their face but then show misgivings about allowing them into their house or attending the same school as their children. I can personally say that after having had dozens of gypsy visitors in our home over the years, many of which I had never met before, not a teaspoon has gone missing.

Not all payos like flamenco music, especially the *cante jondo*; I've heard a Majorcan liken it to 'the sound of a field hospital full of wounded Arabs', but this aversion is also felt towards non-gypsy singers like El Cabrero or El Lebrijano. By now Carmen and I were familiar figures around the shanty town, our white van often seen driving Sebastián back at five in the morning after a gig. Araceli laughingly told us that some of the *gitanos* from another clan thought we were junkies coming to score: with my hay-fever inflamed eyes, I was obviously a coke addict and Carmen, unnaturally thin for her age by *gitano* standards, must be into heroin. 'Better that they think you junkies than police informers.'

One day we dropped by to find that the *chabola* had been taken down to make room for blocks of flats; Sebastián had reconstructed it against the abandoned sports ground on the relatively ratless side of the street. Part of the old grandstand served as a first storey communal bedroom; the Transit van was reserved for the fighting cocks. In the old changing rooms lived another family of the same clan, whose grandfather was still a *canastero*, a basket weaver. I'd bring loads of the canes that were overrunning my orchard, tied to the roof rack, for him to make split-cane trellises to provide shade, which earned him good money.

We had been invited to eat a paella, Araceli's speciality, by the sea. We were to provide the expensive seafood, she would provide the rice, a logical division of responsibilities. As we packed all the food, pans, Antoñita's pram, and eight people into our battered white van, Araceli informed us that she'd invited a cousin, El Gorila, to come as well, and we'd have to drop by Son Banya to pick him up. Luckily his size didn't match his name; a meagre, dignified, elderly man in a pinstripe suit was waiting for us at the entrance to the ghetto, and he was offered the front seat.

Carmen and I could hardly understand a word of what El Gorila said in his gruff voice, except for occasional exclamations of '*Azukiki!*' But he had the rest of the carload in fits of laughter all the way to the picnic spot, which turned out to be as much of a dump as the place we had just left. At least some pine trees gave a bit of shade and a sea breeze fanned the campfire. The kids went off to play with a punctured football, El Gorila rocked Antoñita's pram, conferring a royal dignity upon the broken beach chair he had found to sit on, while Araceli and Carmen were preparing the paella. All the national mystique concerning the correct way to make this dish was overruled as Araceli set to work, ignoring Carmen's worried comments: 'Shouldn't you measure out the water first? . . . Don't you chop up the garlic with the parsley?' The final result was sloppy but delicious, and the leftovers were dumped unceremoniously on the ground with the picnic plates and the watermelon rinds. The general *gitano* attitude to rubbish seems to be that everything can be recycled or reused unless they themselves have finished with it, in which case it's past redemption and unceremoniously booted out.

As the kids collapsed in the heat for a nap, lulled by the loud droning of the cicadas, Sebastián picked up the guitar and launched into a pure flamenco style known as *bulerías*. In the same way that blues pianists simulate the 'blue note', unreachable in European tuning, by striking the two notes either side of it at once, so the flamenco guitarist will play a dissonant chord to insinuate the notes missing from the original Indian 22-note scale.

El Gorila, sitting bolt upright, followed the guitar phrasing with some sparse, well-timed handclaps, and began to croak. His voice had almost no range but it emerged from some mysterious, tortured cavity between the adenoids and the sinuses that must be unique to mature gypsy flamenco singers. It was a voice reeking of black tobacco and strong *cazalla* eau de vie, the spine-chilling lament of the *quejío* or complaint, a furious ranting against injustice that the gypsy is only allowed to express to his own people. There are moments when music breaks free of its container, and the voice that emerged from El Gorila's meagre frame sounded like the voice of his whole tribe, his ancestors, all the way back to the Punjab. Then he leaped to his feet, barked '*Azukiki!*' and the spell was broken.

After a lot of cajoling, El Gorila agreed to join us for the next gig at the Deià bar. The whole family came along, in spite of the misgivings about those mountain bends, just to witness the event. My brother Juan and Francés invited us all to supper beforehand under their grape arbour, beside the village torrent. El Gorila, who was well set in his ways, looked aghast at his plate of delicious spaghetti with fresh pesto sauce. 'What are you supposed to do with this?'

'Try it. Look, everyone else is wolfing it down.'

'I can't eat it, it's *payo* food.' And with absolutely no respect for the hostess, he dumped it directly into the torrent.

The gig was a bit of a letdown. El Gorila was stiff and nervous, nobody but his family understood his humour; he would only sing the first verse of a song before leaving Sebastián to finish it off. The audience was encouraging him, but he obviously felt daunted and out of place. On the drive back to Palma, as the mountain was beginning to be outlined by the approaching dawn, with El Gorila, Araceli, and the kids asleep in the back, Sebastián stayed awake to avoid getting car sick.

'I've been asked to play at my cousin's wedding in two weeks. I can't ask for any money, but I'd like you and Phil to play with me, and you can bring Carmen along.'

'Phil has to present himself personally in England before the end of the month to collect his dole money . . .'

Sebastián tilted his head to one side: '*Vaya*' – 'Say no more.'

'But there must be other percussionists who'd be willing to play at the wedding.'

'None that I would have confidence in.' This meant, not in my clan.

'What about that half-gypsy kid that played the *cajón* at Antoñita's christening?'

'Yes,' said Sebastián, 'Juanchi's good, but he only plays for the Lord. The Culto says that if you consecrate your music to the Lord, you can't also play for a living. So we'll have to do the wedding on our own. But don't worry, the *palmas* will be all the percussion we need. Oh, and bring your microphones and PA, it's a large hall.'

By now I was used to Sebastián's assumption that, as a *payo*, I had some sort of historical debt with him as a *gitano*. I usually tried to draw the line at being taken advantage of – he tried to talk me into keeping his fighting cocks in my garden – but an invitation to a gypsy wedding was worth being exploited for.

The wedding party was to be held in the huge dining room of a hotel in the tourist area of El Arenal at 8 p.m. Part of the clan had come over from Barcelona and all the guests were milling about the closed door. Nobody complained to the manager when he turned up with the keys at 8.30 to let us all in. Nor did anybody offer to help me and Sebastián haul in the mike stands and speakers; they might have stained their party clothes. The men were dressed to the nines; the favourite macho colour was black, from the raven-black curly locks glossy with brilliantine down to the polished patent leather shoes. The only splashes of white were the satin shirts with complicated ruffles down the front, and appliqué work worthy of a rhinestone cowboy. The women added the splashes of brilliant, almost phosphorescent colour in tight-fitting satin dresses, elaborate hairdos, and showy earrings. Sebastián and I, as musicians, were the only ones not obliged to dress elegantly – he was in a flowery shirt and checked trousers – but at least we had both shaved for the occasion.

Red velvet curtains surrounded the hall but, to my surprise, the tables were only laid with paper tablecloths. We set up the equipment while the groom plugged in a ghetto blaster to create some ambience by playing some ghastly techno-flamenco. Once the guests were seated the bride's family, who had footed the bill, began to pass between the tables handing out paper plates and Coke cups, cans of soft drinks, packets of crisps and ham sandwiches wrapped up in paper napkins.

About an hour later, the second course came round: pieces of chicken on a plastic plate. Carmen and I were the only *payos* in the hall, but nobody took the slightest bit of notice. Soon I was alone as Araceli dragged Carmen off to the ladies' room to smoke cigarettes with the other women, out of sight of the men. After another hour, the wedding cake was brought out. Sebastián was nervous; he would have been checking his watch had he known how to read one. As we took to the stage, he said, 'You don't know this first song, just wing it.' Miguelí, a vivacious, handsome motor-mouth of a man who had just come out of jail in time for the party, took the microphone and led the chorus of the ritual wedding song in *caló*, a descendant of the original Rom language: *Ay yeili, yeili*. Sebastián arched his eyebrows at me – the international musicians' code for 'Watch my fingers and I'll see you through.' I was swept along in the powerful surge of the slow camel-gait rhythm whose every third beat seemed to provoke a masculine pelvic twitch and an almost imperceptible hitching-up of female skirts. The bride and groom were hoisted up onto shoulders and carried around the room, showered with handfuls of *peladillas*, white sugared almonds.

Everybody will understand if a *gitano* family can't afford good food at a wedding feast, but no expense must be spared with the sugared almonds, which symbolize fertility. In this function they are obviously more effective than the *payo* equivalent, rice or confetti, judging by the size of a typical gypsy family. A wedding party will get through a couple of 20-kilo sacks of these almonds coated in a thick shell of gobstopper-grade sugar, heavy enough to crack a guitar or a skull if thrown with enthusiasm. At first, the children dash between adults' legs to grab them, but after a continual hail, bulging cheeks can hold no more and beneath the dancing feet they are soon ground down to a sticky paste. Brooms are brought out and the gluey gunge is pushed aside; Sebastián strums the opening chords of *Nos Vamos pa' Barcelona*, leading the dancers' feet onto the floor, my bass line governing the hips. By now we're sharing the stage with an ad hoc group of all ages and sizes, playing the *palmas* – synchronized handclaps – like a well-oiled machine. The *palmas* is a communal rhythm instrument. Someone lays down the on-beat, another the off-beat, then various rhythmic figures are interspersed over this structure to produce a staccato that seems to slap the dancers' faces first to one side then the other, causing arms to swirl and fingers to remember the subtle, symbolic movements of classic Hindu dances.

After an hour of rumbas, the whole process starts again, bride and groom held aloft as everybody dances around them singing *Ay yeili, yeili, yeili* and pelting them with yet more sweet projectiles. By midnight, most of the old folk had gone home, taking the sleeping children with them, and the party really got under way. Sebastián's father brought out his best home-grown marijuana and began to roll some potent spliffs in the corner with the other elders, most of whom had kept their hats on during the entire proceedings. Then the bottles of spirits were brought out, all cheap local imitations of famous brands. The gypsy favourite is the sickly-sweet imitation of Baileys, *Bailén*.

While the single women and girls took to the dance floor with the men, the married women made off to the ladies' room with all the bottles of *Bailén* and the contraband Marlboro Lights. None of the husbands seemed to notice: all their eyes were on Miguelí's sister, stamping and shimmying in her tight-fitting blue satin dress, challenging all-comers. Dancing the rumba, the woman becomes the bullfighter and the man the bull; she will provoke him and then sidestep his advance with a graceful curve of her body and a haughty look over her shoulder. In the context of relationships, the verb *torear*, to bullfight, means to tease, confuse, or keep someone guessing.

By now I'd got to know Sebastián's way of playing and singing well enough to anticipate the sudden breaks, the surprise endings, without having to take my eyes off Miguelí's sister either. Then one of Sebastián's cousins, a butch girl in her early twenties, was pushed on stage by her friends. She took the microphone and launched into a rumba with a tremendous voice and strong guitar style.

'Why don't you invite her to play with us? She's a knockout!'

'Her parents wouldn't allow it. She's from the pavement opposite' – a euphemism for homosexuality – 'and they've gated her until she finds a husband. They only let her sing at the Culto and for the family.'

*El Ventilador*

In the gypsy world, everything is clearly divided by gender. Sexual roles are clearly marked out, with no ambiguities, no Bowies or Boy Georges. This polarization is inflamed by the Evangelists, thus increasing their gypsy appeal even at the cost of alienating some of the more educated *gitanos*. Long hair like Sebastián's is considered macho, but short hair on a woman is suspect. Everything is unequivocally male or female; some of the older men even frown on their wives washing their privates too often because they want their woman 'to smell of woman'. This sexism even extends, with comic results, into language. Many modern Spanish words, as in English, have been shortened with use: *una radio-receptora* is now *una radio*; *una motocicleta* has become *una moto*, and *una fotografía* is *una foto*. A female noun ending in -o clashes with the *gitano* mentality, so they remedy this by carrying part of the article over to the beginning of the word, coming up with *un arradio*, *un amoto*, or *un afoto*. This is reminiscent of the way 'a norange' became 'an orange' in English.

Juanchi, now sixteen and a promising footballer, had tired of El Culto and was ready to move into the adult world. He was willing to play percussion with us, especially if there was a chance of pulling some girls. But first he had to make a *cajón*; his old one had fallen to pieces.

This instrument originated in the black neighbourhoods of Lima, Perú. Few Europeans have even heard of black Peruvians, let alone their particular Afro-Cuban rhythms. Until recently, neither had I. Perhaps the lack of African drums led to the invention of the *cajón*, originally an old tea chest or packing case. But then, with one of those brilliantly simple ideas that emerge, like the skateboard, from the scrapyard, someone discovered that replacing the back of an old speaker cabinet with a piece of thin plywood gave a deeper, fuller sound like a bass drum when thumped in the centre by all four fingertips at once. A slap on the flapping top edge, which is not nailed down, gives you a snare-drum sound.

Behind Sebastián's shack, in the sports centre's old swimming pool, now filled with rubble, we found a battered speaker cabinet the right size. A *cajón* has to be chair-height so you can straddle it and play between your splayed legs. To give the slap an extra sharpness, Juanchi nailed a thin strip of aluminium from a fridge shelf under the flapping edge of the plywood. The whole thing took ten minutes to make, and as soon as he straddled it and laid down a rumba beat, we knew it was going to pull everyone onto the dance floor.

The *cajón* was popularized on this side of the Atlantic by the guitarist Paco de Lucía and it rapidly caught on in the barrios, being effective, cheap, and easy to make. It is used mainly in flamenco or rumba, but as an unplugged, portable drum kit its possibilities are endless. Los Mártires del Compás ('Martyrs of the Beat') play funk, reggae, or even Argentine tangos on a *cajón*. A contemporary flamenco ballet features a dozen male dancers playing the instrument, creating a tremendous rhythm while stamping their feet on the stage.

With Juanchi on the *cajón*, the group began to cook; soon we were joined by Antonio, a wonderful guitarist and singer who was always impeccably dressed and of excellent disposition. Miguelí, when he was out of jail, would join the group, singing and playing *palmas*. Whenever there was a ten-second lull in the vocals, Juanchi would step in with some salsa lyrics; between the three of them they brought a festive flavour to the repertoire. Changing the group's name to Mimbre (the word for wicker, in honour of the *canastero* tradition), this fuller sound began to get us many more gigs, although the money had to be shared out between five. I had a lot more work as a roadie because, of course, nobody else had a vehicle or sound equipment. Several gypsy weddings came up, which, although great fun, I came to dread because it meant spending hours afterwards cleaning all the sugary almond paste off each cable with a wet rag. Besides, every bride was related to somebody in the group, so a big discount would have to be applied.

Our moment of public recognition was, significantly for the founder member, at Palma's huge *Festes de Sant Sebastià*. We played on a large stage in the square of Sant Francesc, close to the old gypsy barrio and red-light district. The stage backs onto the church of the same name, which houses the tomb of the thirteenth-century philosopher and alchemist Ramón Llull (Raymond Lully); behind are the cloisters where the Majorcan missionary Fray Juniper Serra studied before founding the California missions. The city of San Francisco owes its name to this church.

Having a couple of thousand watts amplify the work of your fingers for the first time is a heady feeling for any musician, especially if you can see over the heads of a thousand people dancing to your music. We did our job of warming up the crowd for the big flamenco acts that followed with a short, energetic set that earned us a good write-up in the press ('the full moon reflecting in their guitars . . .'). While classic flamenco guitarists always play sitting down, accompanying a *cantaor* – a solo singer – *rumberos* usually play and sing standing up. They carry the guitar on a very short leash, against the chest. As Carmen pointed out, a *rumbero* wears his guitar next to the heart; a heavy metal guitarist wears his next to the groin.

Playing in bars, at weddings, and at the occasional big fiesta was very good practice for the band, yet what we earned was hardly worth the effort of trying to organize four people with no transport, telephone, or sense of time, let alone of direction. But a lucrative new vein for Mimbre appeared by accident. The sculptor Ben Jakober, an old friend of Mati, is perhaps the island resident best connected to the high realms of the international art world. He telephoned me in an emergency, looking for music for a VIP party. Pa Amb Oli's singer was away, so I suggested Mimbre. First we could play some 'light' flamenco during the hors d'oeuvres, then lay down some rumbas until dawn, all for the considerable fee that Ben had been allotted by the hostess.

Many flamenco artists have had to survive by 'animating' fiestas held by the *señoritos*, as the rich landowners are contemptuously known. On the one hand it is humiliating to supply music and joy to those who have downtrodden your people and now have to buy back their own happiness; but on the other, it is a heady feeling to be able to control the arms and legs of those a thousand times more powerful than oneself. In this case, however, at least the fortune that footed the bill was not built on the toil of the Andalusian *gitanos* and peasants but upon a lucrative national chain of 24-hour drugstore-restaurants.

Some of the most beautiful country mansions in the Mediterranean are to be found hidden in the cool, lush folds of the Serra de Tramuntana foothills, many of which were originally Moorish palaces built near a natural spring. In the thirteenth century, the conquering King James of Aragon divided up these properties, still known as *possessions*, among his barons, which provided great wealth to twenty generations of local aristocracy; but by the 1950s, they were no longer economically viable and were sold off or gambled away. Now nearly all these possessions are either very exclusive small hotels or wonderful tax losses for the ultra-rich, with their orange groves, cypress trees, grape arbours, and vast stone water reservoirs turned into swimming pools.

At the end of a long dirt road near Puigpunyent, we drove into the cool evening shadow of the mountain and were confronted by a stunning mansion with a lily-covered pool reaching the foot of the main façade; to one side, an enormous esplanade, shaded by the traditional giant hackberry tree, overlooked the private valley filled with fruit trees, and perfumed by the smell of orange blossom. The valet directed my van to the service entrance, out of sight of the Mercedes, Range Rovers, and Porsches. Even Juanchi was turned out in his nattiest gypsy-chic wear. I never have anything formal in my wardrobe but I put together a loose, white, *Our Man in Havana* outfit.

The drugstore fortune notwithstanding, and although the hostess was from a powerful financial family, this was her coming-out party into the local high society. Besides the who's who of the local aristocracy, hoteliers, and political class, there were some guests who were on the island en passant – I caught a glimpse of the Mexican writer Carlos Fuentes and the dancer Nacho Duato, director of the National Ballet. As we serenaded the guests with some unobtrusive instrumental flamenco (my Cuban *tres* adding a Caribbean touch), passing among the tables on the huge terrace overlooking the valley, I was within inches of several people I had known well years earlier, each now important in one field or another. I was enjoying myself immensely because I could watch them safe in the knowledge that none would recognize me; not only was I out of context, but I was wearing the cloak of invisibility afforded to restaurant musicians, whose eyes diners always make an effort to avoid.

When the hostess announced the first course we retired to kill time until it was time to pump up the rumba. The band all stifled their laughter as the army of waiters brought out the minimalist nouvelle-cuisine starters. Then I remembered we hadn't negotiated our supper. 'If we have to eat the leftovers, we'll starve,' said Juanchi, well known for his footballer's appetite. 'Those look like leftovers to begin with!'

Just then, the head of the hostess's security team marched over to Juanchi; he and the other three gypsy faces immediately looked guilty.

'You're Paco's son, aren't you? The footballer? Your father and I worked together in a hotel. You all look hungry. I'll take you to the kitchen.'

The guests' food had been organized by a catering service; the real food was in the enormous Majorcan kitchen. The security guard introduced us to the *amo*, the *madona*, and their large family, the gardeners, bodyguards, chauffeur, valets – about twelve people, all Majorcans, who were sitting at the long kitchen table. In the centre of the *llar*, the Majorcan hearth – a whitewashed room within a room – a huge earthenware pot of *sopes mallorquines* was simmering over the embers. We were immediately made to feel at home as five extra places were laid at the table, a handful of thin slivers of dried farmhouse bread dropped into each empty soup bowl. 'The good thing about *sopes* is that you can always stretch it out with a bit more bread,' said the matronly *madona* ladling out the fragrant vegetable broth over the dry slices. Within arm's reach of every bowl was a plate of raw vegetables to accompany the *sopes*: giant radish, strips of light-green capsicum peppers, and spring onions. Then came the giant earthenware *greixonera de frit* – chopped offal, potatoes, and green peppers fried slowly with a lot of fresh fennel. This was followed by lamb chops marinated in rosemary, garlic, and lemon juice and grilled over the embers. After coffee, dessert, and a *coñac*, we made our way through the austere but beautifully furnished salons and out to the small stage that had been set up for us. The guests were being served a dessert consisting of 90 per cent aesthetics and 10 per cent substance. 'I don't understand why they starve the guests, while the servants get the real food,' said Juanchi, sticking a microphone into the hole in the back of the *cajón* to get a good bass-drum-like thump out of it. As soon as the champagne was served, he ripped into a rumba beat, Antonio and Sebastián's guitars letting loose a torrent of rhythm, my bass bouncing over (or under) it, as the guests began to flock to the dance floor.

By 3 a.m. we were exhausted, but the hostess wanted to keep the party going until dawn, which was only to be expected of someone who had pioneered the all-night drugstore concept in Spain; but the security man interceded on our behalf and got us an overtime bonus. We kicked off again with *El Tra-Tra-Tra*: 'Tonight I'm not going to bed, I've just come in off a drinking spree'. Three hours later we drove off into the rising sun with pockets bulging and the satisfaction of having discovered a rich vein waiting to be tapped.

On the strength of that party many more private gigs came up, but my rock 'n' roll duties came first, so I suggested they find another bass player and chauffeur – I didn't want to be depended upon as manager and roadie as well as musician. We were also having 'musical differences' over their idea of introducing an electronic rhythm box to replace the *cajón*, leaving Juanchi free to play the *timbales*, a pair of metal drums played standing up, also known as *pailas* or frying pans. Although I did try to engage with the rhythm box, it always carried on relentlessly, stubborn as a mule, with no respect for the dynamics of the music. More than once, we'd completely lose the beat. The other drawback was that somebody had to be ready to turn the damned thing off when the song ended, in true rumba style, with a flourish and a jolt.

I've always found it disheartening to see how *gitanos*, like many Africans, are seduced by shoddy, soulless gadgets, and was unable to convince Mimbre that their strength lay in their authenticity, not in the empty rush provided by electronics. I had hoped the rhythm box wouldn't last longer than its first set of batteries, but they were delighted with it. I told them that I had done my bit in helping to get the group off the ground, and that they could go a lot further without me.

The band found a keyboard player to fatten out the sound and fill in the bass notes. Sebastián's child allowance had been spent on a brand-new PA system, and Araceli's brother-in-law the mechanic acted as driver; but somehow the wind seemed to have dropped out of the band's sails. Whenever we passed by El Molinar to visit, there seemed to be some impediment to the band's progress; one or other weren't on speaking terms, a three-week mourning period had to be honoured with silence, Miguelí had been sent to jail, Juanchi had found a regular job with little free time, a recording contract had fallen through . . . but the real reason was that things had changed in El Molinar. Araceli had been jailed on a charge that she thought had been shelved four years earlier, so María's older sister Rosario dropped out of school to look after the younger kids and never went back to her studies. Within six months she had aged six years and gave up the idea of studying law.

It is the *gitano* women who are least content with their lot, who do the most to steer their families into the mainstream; the more the rest of society advances, the more they feel trapped in a backwater. Their roles are still dictated by traditional gypsy law. While the rest of Spanish women have been liberated, they still have to live as they used to fifty years ago, hauling buckets of water from the municipal tap; washing the kids, themselves, and the laundry in tin tubs; heating water and cooking over a flame; making do with no refrigerator or heating; at best, a 12-volt battery will power some bulbs and a car radio. The communal lavatory was a space between some bushes behind a wall. Araceli had begun to get a taste of how *payo* women live, not only through her contact with us but by getting a part-time job as cleaning lady. She dictated to Carmen a letter to the Queen, asking for more dignified living conditions for her family – electricity and running water, four solid walls and a roof – which was sent via a royal cousin who had bought a house in Deià.

After years of protests and negotiations, the rest of the *chabolas* had been razed to the ground to make room for more council flats. Perhaps as a result of the royal letter, the council was offering to pay reasonable rent on any flats in the area to relocate the *gitano* families temporarily until the blocks were finished.

We went to visit Sebastián and Araceli the night before they had to move out of their *chabola*, the last one left standing. A giant excavator had been chewing away at the sports ground, leaving only one last morsel uneaten, the part that formed their bedroom. El Juanes was there, looking so emaciated that I hardly recognized him. 'Whenever he comes out of jail, he gets back on smack,' said Sebastián, 'so he has to commit another crime to get back inside and clean himself out.'

'That's the truth, 'Bastián,' agreed Juanes. 'Tomás, which is your car?'

'That white van across the street. Why?'

'So I can make a mental note of it. I don't want to rob it by mistake.'

Outside, the *gitanos* were gathered around a bonfire of pallets, broken furniture, and fence posts that reeked of burning varnish and creosote; but instead of jokes and gossip, the men were silent. Their families had all been relocated nearby, but they had no idea how to live cooped up in a building, so they gathered in their usual place to watch the sparks rise into the night air and illuminate the great yellow jaw of the frozen mechanical dinosaur, looming over the scene.

The illusion of nomadic life could be maintained in an earth-floor *chabola*, but bricks and mortar gave an air of finality that the men obviously found oppressively jail-like. Loli, the social worker, had found Sebastián a flat nearby on which the council agreed to pay the rent, and Araceli was bubbling with enthusiasm about the fully equipped kitchen, the bathroom with running water, and separate master bedroom. The kids were wild with joy; they had been playing with the intercom and buzzing the street door open. But Sebastián was despondent, not only about having to find a home for his dog and his fighting cocks, but also because he sensed that there was no going back; no more drifting in and out of his clan's *chabolas*, dragging a chair out onto the street in summer to take the fresh evening air with them, or gathering around a bonfire in winter. From now on his life would revolve around the immediate family, not the clan; there would now be a separation between the home and the world. For a *gitano*, this was a prison in which he was his own jailer, obliged to carry jangling keys. He had to tell the kids to keep their voices down, smile at neighbours on the stairs, decide where to go or what to do, instead of letting the moment decide for him. And no longer would there always be someone around to keep an eye on the kids or tell him where they were.

More than once, when a clan of *gitanos* from the mainland had come over to 'spend August' on the island, Sebastián asked us to take his adolescent daughter María home with us until the heat died down. He was afraid that she might 'run away' with one of them, perhaps never to be seen again, like the song I remembered from my childhood about the 'Raggle-taggle gypsies-O'. María was a wonderful dancer and very *salada*, vivacious and charming, unlike her more serious sister Rosario. María stayed with us for a fortnight, attending our village school, where she was well received, until she discovered the list of parents' home numbers and had a little fun by impersonating the headmistress over the phone, informing distraught mothers that their children were to be expelled for bad behaviour. We had to take her back before worse befell.

Sebastián wasn't being paranoid about María's possible abduction. He and Araceli had run away together themselves, when he had finished his military service and she was just fourteen. 'Running away' and spending a night together under the roof of a member of the boy's clan is recognized under gypsy law as a valid union, even without parental consent, although the couple who take this step must get married the next day. If the boy brings the girl to his own home, the union is still valid, but the couple will not receive the same social respect as if they had taken refuge in an uncle or cousin's house. The most respectable procedure, of course, is to ask the girl's family for her hand and then celebrate a proper marriage with proof of virginity – the 'rose' as it is known – which is what, surprisingly, happened with María.

The father-in-law wasn't a mainlander but a local *gitano*, a one-legged knife grinder appropriately known as El Chispas ('Sparks'). He had lost his limb as a child playing on the railway line but had adapted so well to one-leggedness that the rehabilitation doctors often called upon him to show recent amputees how he played football, rode a bicycle, and climbed over walls. But the clincher to encourage any amputee would have been to watch him play the host at the *petición de mano*, the party that the groom's family traditionally gives after asking for the bride's hand. As cheerful as his teenage son was morose, El Chispas was the soul of the party. He seemed to be everywhere at once, serving food and pouring drinks, slapping backs. Sebastián admitted to me that he was in two minds about granting his daughter's hand; the boy seemed less interested in María's happiness than in showing off how he could switch TV channels from his digital wristwatch. Sebastián had also secretly hoped that María would become a professional dancer – she was taking classes at a flamenco dance academy – but, as a married woman, she would never be allowed to.

A few weeks later, the wedding took place. To pay for it, Sebastián pawned the PA system and got a loan from the bank against his disability pension for 'dizzy spells'. For, although the Molinar community had dispersed physically, the clan was still important, and Sebastián had to live up to his new status as father-in-law, only one step away from becoming an elder. A *gitano*'s individual prestige has to be won within the clan; his power has to be legitimized by the respect he earns for correct behaviour, and his honour as a man; part of this prestige comes from a show of disdain for accumulating wealth and possessions. Whereas a non-gypsy would be deemed irresponsible for spending more than he earns, a *gitano* is applauded for spending all he has (and much of what he hasn't) on a lavish wedding: wealth means nothing unless accompanied by generosity and extravagance.

By no means the least of a father's wedding expenses is the ceremony of the rose, the virginity test, which of course he isn't allowed to attend. Carmen, as a woman and as honorary auntie, was invited into the bedroom, while we men were shooed out of the house. She had first seen María as a skinny nine-year-old street urchin and had organized her first ever hot bath, with her sister and our daughter; now María had blossomed into a gorgeous sixteen-year-old gypsy woman. For this wedding-morning ceremony she had been to the hairdresser, manicurist, and had been made up and dressed in white in a new embroidered gown, robe and slippers, all tinsel and lace. She was laid on the dining room table, which was covered in the finest linen, and showered with sugared almonds. The older women sang the ritual *alboreás*, some of which have been traced back to the Sephardic Jewish tradition, although the ritual has also been attributed to the Andalusian Muslim influence: the shouts of ¡*olé!* were originally directed to Allah.

A respectable sum had been spent on hiring an expert in this ritual, an old *gitana*, sometimes known as *torera* or *matadora* for her task of drawing blood. Her wage varies according to her reputation, not only for doing the job painlessly, but for producing the most spectacular or beautiful rose. A very experienced woman can, for a large fee, even produce one in cases where it should be naturally impossible.

I might be going too far in suggesting that this ceremony was the origin of the tie-dye technique, but the principle is similar. An embroidered piece of snow-white silk or cotton is folded and twisted into a point with which the midwife breaks the hymen; the blood dyes the cloth, which, when smoothed out again, reveals a flower-like pattern, made up of three or more 'roses' or bloodstains. All kinds of auguries for the future marriage can be read into the number and beauty of the roses, which are then displayed to all: the bride has earned the right to be crowned with a tiara. I had somehow envisaged something a lot more spectacular than the little stains on the handkerchief that was eventually passed round among us men for our approval.

The feast was held in an open-air restaurant near the airport, one of the many converted farmhouses that cater for 'the BBC circuit' (*bodas, bautizos y comuniones* – weddings, christenings, and first communions). Mimbre, having disbanded a year earlier, re-formed for the event, which was promising to be a big one; cousins were coming from all parts of the mainland.

In the years I had played with Sebastián, including four gypsy weddings, I had heard the phrase *partirse la camisa* ('to rip one's shirt') in a lot of flamenco songs, but I had never seen it happen until María got married. By the end of the evening at least ten shirts – at about £150 each – were left in tatters. This is how the clan expresses its pride and joy in handing over the bride 'intact'. It's increasingly rare to see shirts rent asunder because today's *gitanas* no longer get married as soon as they are nubile, like their mothers' generation did; they have more contact with a permissive society and more time to take the opportunities it offers. Nor will an older, more independent gypsy bride submit so willingly to a rite that, although a source of pride for the clan, she considers a humiliation.

The party is the wedding, under gypsy law; the formalities carried out later at the registry hold no significance other than to legalize the marriage in the eyes of the *payo* establishment. María's wedding was by no means as elegant as the others I had played at, but tonight I was a guest, not a musician. The atmosphere was electric, right from the moment the couple arrived, already hoisted upon their respective families' shoulders. Paper chains and lanterns hung from the corrugated-tin roof, which rattled every time it was hit by flying sugared almonds; the stage, however, was high enough to stay clear of the sticky paste on the floor. After a year without playing, the band was full of energy and gave it everything they had. Juanchi was going like a locomotive on his new *cajón*, Miguelí and Antonio grinning from ear to ear and ducking stray almonds as they sang *Te Lo Dice el Camarón*, Luís playing muddy but solid bass lines, and Sebastián watching proudly as his daughter, one of the most beautiful gypsy brides anybody could remember, danced in the centre of the circle: her haughty, provocative, flashing eyes challenging any man to dare dance with her – their last chance – her presence filling every inch of the here and now, which for the *gitanos* is the forever and ever.

# 12

# North Coast Kaboogie

Spain has lost all its colonies but it still keeps two feet in North Africa. Ceuta and Melilla are the only cities in the European Community (until Turkey joins) to be found on a different continent, and both are as coveted by Morocco as Gibraltar is coveted by the Spanish. But there is a third city on that coast, within sight of the Iberian peninsula, that also lives and breathes and sighs in Spanish: Tánger, Tanjah, Tangier.

The Mother of Cities has been ruled successively by Phoenicians, Carthaginians, Romans, Arabs, Berbers, Portuguese, Spanish, and British. When the French and Spanish established their protectorates in Morocco, Tangier was granted self-rule. In 1923 it became an International Zone governed by the USA and seven European countries including Spain, becoming a very permissive and exciting place to live, inspiring the film *Casablanca*, and attracting many liberal and creative foreigners like Paul Bowles, William Burroughs, Matisse, and Rimsky-Korsakov. Its recent history has been closely linked to Spain's and at one point half the city's population was Spanish, with its own newspapers and radio. It has only become part of Morocco since the country's independence in 1956, but still maintains its international character.

From the top of the Pensión Marrakesh you can see over the populated rooftops of the tight medina – families cooking, musicians practising for a wedding – beyond the harbour and across the Straits to Tarifa on the southernmost tip of continental Europe; so near if you have a ticket and visa, so far if you don't.

Young people from all over North and West Africa, having been told that in Europe anybody on the street can summon banknotes from a TV screen in the wall, have converged upon this gateway to Eden, carrying their family's blessings in their hearts and life savings in their pockets. Whatever money is left will be handed over to a mafioso who will pack fifty or more of these illegal immigrants into a jumbo-sized inflatable speedboat, dodge the tanker traffic and patrol boats and, on the other side, push them overboard within swimming distance of a Spanish beach before speeding back into the safety of international waters. Of course swimming, for desert people, usually means drowning. Most of those who do gain the shore are caught (and some who don't, rescued) by the Guardia Civil, in their new role as Euro-Sentinels. The detainees are sent back on the ferry, the latest of countless waves of exiles that have, over the centuries, arrived in Tangier having been expelled from Spain's garden of paradise: before them it was the defeated Moors in the fifteenth century sighing for Al Andalus, followed by the Jews sighing for their Sepharad, and then the defeated Spanish Republican refugees in 1939 sighing for their land of liberty.

Any immigrant who can't afford a second attempt by speedboat will then try to stow away on a Europe-bound trailer in Tangier port, often resulting in an even less pleasant death than drowning. But however they attempt the crossing, they must first learn rudimentary Spanish to see them through the first leg of the journey, and in Tangier they can pick it up on the streets or by watching Televisión Española, which beams in sharp and clear.

In 1986, before Spain had joined the EU and become the tradesman's entrance to Europe, Carmen and I saw few black faces in Tangier. Cheap hotels like the Pensión Marrakesh attended to a summer trade of Moroccans seeking the cool sea breeze; in winter, Ahmed, the deskboy, could smoke kif and sleep on the couch all day without any interruption. Newly arrived backpackers, clutching their wallets and cameras, would try and get on the first train out of Tangier and down to the 'real' Morocco – Fez, Marrakesh, Essaouira. Even in spring, trade was slow enough for our friends Ralph and Mitsuko to be able to choose the best room in the *pensión* – a terrace overlooking the harbour, a window overlooking the market – at a giveaway price. We accepted their offer of spending Easter with them.

When we arrived on the midnight ferry from Algeciras, they led us through the sleeping medina, along silent Lover's Street with its tiny goldsmiths' shops specializing in wedding jewellery, to the narrow door of the *pensión*. The only person we crossed was a huge old security guard in a djelaba who delighted in telling visiting Spaniards how many of their countrymen's throats he had slit, a feat that earned him a place in Franco's personal Moorish Guard. The Nationalists had won the Spanish Civil War thanks in part to these Spanish-trained Moroccan mercenaries who had served as shock troops, the equivalent of the British Army's Nepalese Ghurkas. General Franco had later picked the bravest of these as his private guard. Having seventy thousand Muslim foreigners take the brunt of the fighting in the name of the Holy Church and the Fatherland didn't seem contradictory to the General. He probably never read a book from cover to cover, and his own ideology was little more than an anti-communist and anti-Freemason porridge of military–religious principles he had picked up as one of 'Death's Bridegrooms' in the Foreign Legion. He had promised the valiant Moors a golden sceptre if they defeated the Republicans, but the old man in the djelaba only carried a big wooden stick. He was one of the five thousand Moroccan veterans who at that time still received a laughably small Spanish military pension. Franco himself had placed his *moros* at the bottom of the pension scale.

The next morning over *café con leche* in the Café Gibraltar ('We milk our own cows') I complained that I'd been woken before dawn by a phantom biker. 'Some idiot woke me by revving up a motorbike and keeping the throttle open for ten minutes.' Ralph burst out laughing: 'That weren't no motorcycle, that was the loudspeaker of the minaret – the muezzin calling the faithful to prayer!'

Ralph, one of the world's most dyslectic poets, is from a Californian railroad family and was born a hobo. He had come to Spain to study art in Barcelona, later did graduate work in anthropology in Pamplona, and eventually drifted over to Deià and moved into some empty rooms above Carmen's bookshop. He was sitting the shop in her absence one morning when Mitsuko, a Japanese graduate student at Madrid University, wearing a rabbit-fur coat and high-heels, stepped off the bus and began looking through the poetry books. She had come to Majorca fascinated by the character of the thirteenth-century philosopher Ramón Llull, who had lived and taught two miles away. When Carmen returned to the shop an hour later they disappeared upstairs and have been together ever since; for Ralph and Mitsuko, Spanish is the loving tongue.

In Tangier they introduced us to the friends they had made there during their many visits. Dr Robert Shea, a grandiloquent man who had run away with the circus as a child, was now the head of the Old American Legation, which occupied a palace in the medina. This was the United States' first property abroad, a gift from the Kingdom of Morocco, the first power to recognize the rebel colony's independence from Britain. The palace boasted a museum and fine library that Ralph had almost to himself. Dr Robert led us to a small upstairs room; behind a reversible book-shelf we were shown into the secret cubbyhole where the Allied spies, operating a ham radio, collated information for the Normandy landings and the African campaign.

Then we left the holy medina to visit Paul Bowles in the bland 'new town', where we were almost bowled over by a headless chicken careering down the dirt street, splattering blood everywhere. We passed a new minaret and a walled-in modern bungalow, whose guard dog's barking had almost driven Paul mad. He told us how, having been unable to resolve the problem with the owners, he had first tossed some scraps of meat mixed with tranquillizers over the wall; the next batch was mixed with amphetamines. To poison the dog directly, for which Paul would be the prime suspect, would cause it undue suffering; this way the owner would assume it to have gone mad and shoot it humanely. As a strategy it had a certain circuitous Mediterranean logic to it with which, having grown up in Majorca, I was quite familiar.

'People who come to see me assume that, living in a Muslim country, I'd be thrilled with a bottle of *coñac* or Scotch, but I prefer to smoke the local kif. However, I don't want to seem ungrateful, so I accept it and then invite Ralph and Mitsuko over to help me get rid of it.' One of the recent gift-bearing visitors, Bernardo Bertolucci, was planning a film adaptation of *The Sheltering Sky*, a project Paul didn't seem too keen about. 'I'll get nothing out of it,' he said. 'I sold the film rights centuries ago for $100.' Nor was he particularly interested in the fact that Sting had turned a scene from the same novel into 'Tea in the Sahara', which The Police had released three years earlier. He seemed generally aloof from the competitive outside world, only interested in his own: writing and music. But this wasn't the 'don't bother me' attitude of a 76-year-old man, this was his true self speaking. He reminisced about his visit to Majorca thirty years earlier, pulling out an album of snapshots from the trip and pointing out the beach where he had almost been arrested by the Guardia Civil for swimming 'topless'.

I felt very comfortable in Paul's company: his story seemed to parallel my father's. He first moved here in 1931, shortly after Robert moved to Majorca, and, like him, was obliged to return to his homeland after seven years of living 'in paradise', Robert by the impending Spanish Civil War, Paul due to bad health. They both returned to their respective Mediterranean homes in the late 1940s, each with a wife, to settle there – free thinkers living under authoritarian regimes – until their deaths, Paul at 89, Robert at 90, having never met. Both had attracted literary friends to visit them, many of whom bought property nearby. Both had become the centre of media attention in their old age thanks to a screen version of a book whose rights they had sold decades earlier. Curiously enough, in 1929 they had also both been to France where they had visited Gertrude Stein, who had lived in both Tangier and Palma.

I don't know whether Stein recommended Morocco to Paul (as she had Majorca to Robert), but she did suggest to him that he give up poetry. He took her words to heart, and they tipped the scales in favour of a musical career. Having turned down Prokofiev as a music teacher in Paris, he studied with Aaron Copland, with whom he shared a house in Tangier in 1931.

Over the next ten years, Paul made a name for himself as a composer – he wrote well over a hundred pieces for piano and orchestra as well as some of the most successful musical scores in the history of the American theatre. He returned to Tangier in the late 1940s with his wife Jane, who had recently achieved literary success with her first novel. This inspired Paul to return to writing, which earned him even greater international recognition than as a composer, although he laconically attributed the change to the fact that it was impossible to keep his piano in tune in damp Tangier (he now used an electric keyboard to compose on). He pulled out some dusty old sheet music: 'It seems that people are now beginning to discover my piano scores after all these years. Who knows, one day perhaps someone will record them!' Meanwhile, his musical talent was only being tapped by the local American School for their annual play.

Paul's name was familiar to me as a child, not only from the beatniks and hippies who had passed through Morocco

– 'Like, you know, Paul Bowles was there, Bill Burroughs, even Brian Jones, man' – but from a record that had been knocking around the house since I was five. It was the MGM Chamber Orchestra's recording of Paul's *zarzuela* (a Spanish form of light opera) based on a play by Lorca. The Australian composer Peggy Glanville-Hicks had sent us the LP, which included some of Paul's texts that she had set to music. At that time she was working with my father on an opera based on his novel *Homer's Daughter*, which was performed at Delphi in Greece as *Nausicaa*. Connections, connections: the Mediterranean seems to draw threads from all over the world, but any communication between Morocco, Majorca, and Greece must pass via New York, Paris, or London.

Paul invited us and another friend, the photographer Cherie Nutting, to accompany him the next evening to a birthday party at his friend Mrabet's house, whose son was coming of age. We all piled into the old two-tone Ford Mustang, a car I'd only heard about in blues songs, which his aide and chauffeur Abdulwahid – another ex-Franco guard – steered, creaking and bouncing, around the puddles and pot holes to Mrabet's house.

Mohammed Mrabet was a storyteller in the Arabic oral tradition. Paul had become his transcriber and literary editor; together they formed one of the most unlikely yet fruitful teams in modern literature. Having left our shoes at the door, we men (foreign women were included in this category) were all shown upstairs into a dining room strewn with cushions and carpets. Sweet mint tea was served on low circular tables as we slouched or knelt – Paul sat cross-legged in the Arabic style – smoking kif and listening to our host while the women and small children prepared the feast downstairs. From the gales of laughter and snatches of song coming up the stairs, the real party was going on in the kitchen, as it so often does. Although Mrabet was an excellent raconteur, switching from English to Spanish and French, I would have much preferred to peek into the kitchen, but it was as much out of bounds to us as the dining room was to the women. The sound of partying, the songs now accompanied by tambourines and handclaps, grew to such an intensity that Mrabet, despite his magnetic personality, realized he was no longer the centre of attention. Carmen announced that she was going to join the ladies, taking Mitsuko and Cherie with her. Mrabet decided to pre-empt this breach of protocol with one of his own and – to the amazement of Paul, who admitted that this was the first time he had witnessed such an event in Morocco – the paterfamilias sent for the women and children to bring the music into the dining room. They took this transgression as a victory and set up a tremendous rhythm with handclaps, tambourines, and taut-skinned clay darbuka drums. There weren't enough instruments to go around, so the girls would snatch them from one another at each break in the music, punctuating the elation of the moment with wild ululations. The shy birthday boy with his wild eye also began to shimmy to the music. It was pure, wild joy, and finally even Mrabet joined in.

Although this was a new experience for me, I was familiar with the North African music that had hogged the long-wave radio band of my childhood. The sense of familiarity was increased by hearing it pour from these Moroccans whose faces reminded me so much of my Majorcan neighbours. The moment was short-lived; Mrabet's wife announced supper was ready. The girls ran out with the drums

and tambourines and returned with bowls of olives of vari-
eties unknown to me, brass plates of couscous, lamb and
prune *tajin* – did I imagine the pigeon pie? – followed by
the cake and candles, beside which Mrabet posed for the
camera holding a knife, as if he were the birthday boy.

The following evening we were having supper in Richard
Netherlin's flat deep in the medina, after a session in the
dingy steam baths nearby. Richard walks, talks, and trims
his beard in the Moroccan way: although North American,
he's impossible to pick out in the crowd at the Gran Zoco.
We had procured some wine in the New Town, but we had
it to ourselves: Richard drank no alcohol, nor did the other
guests, two handsome Muslim students from his school, the
American Language Center. I was surprised to see they had
brought along a steel-string guitar: among many other scare
stories, I had heard that the Moroccan Customs confiscated
Western instruments that might corrupt local youth.

Richard had not yet converted to Islam, but had been
here long enough to cook up an excellent couscous. After
supper the two Tangerines launched into some Algerian pop
songs that we immediately recognized, having heard a tape
of Magneu Dajmet blasting out from the underwear stall
opposite our table at the Café Gibraltar every morning. (The
vendor's half-wit son would toss bras and panties in the air
in time to this rai music as if winnowing wheat, chanting
'*Mrekelah, Mrekelah!*')

It's embarrassing to be identified as a musician in a foreign
land, handed a guitar and asked to 'sing something from
your country', especially if you're not quite sure which
country or culture is yours. This has happened more times
than I care to remember: in a Stolichnaya-soaked Moscow
apartment on New Year's eve or passing *Flor de Caña* rum

around a campfire on a moonlit Nicaraguan beach. But the most embarrassing moment had been a few years earlier on the Hungarian plain, where Carmen and I were studying bookbinding at the Kner Printing House, a huge establishment that printed anything from leather-bound bibles to the *Basil Brush Annual*. At the best restaurant in Békésczaba, our palinka-drunk comrades insisted we join the gypsy violinists onstage to play some flamenco. This was a predictable fiasco: the only common ground we musicians could find was that old lifesaver, *Besame Mucho*. However, the rounds of super-benzin (high octane) palinka made up for the musical disaster, glasses raised to 'Federico Gaaarcia Lorrrca! Salvadorrr Allende! Che Guevaaara!' The next day, not even the head of the department came in to work.

In Tangier, there was no alcohol to smooth out the creases in my repertoire, but Ralph came to the rescue and launched us into 'Window Shoppin'', which I remembered from my childhood – my father had inexplicably brought a Hank Williams record back from a lecture tour of the USA. Ralph was well into the second verse before I hit upon the key he was singing in, E flat. By this time he had grabbed Mitsuko by the waist and was jitterbugging with her in the scant square metre of floorspace, leaving me with my fingertips still tender after the steam bath to take a solo in an impossible key on a heavily-strung guitar probably built in a Soviet tractor plant. Luckily all eyes were on the dancers. Picking up courage, I launched into my favourite country blues song, 'Annie's Lover', who was

   . . . a big old man, he was an African man
   He never spent much time
   Worryin' bout de peoples in de big, big, big cities

All he did care 'bout was de cows and de chickens
And de sheeps and de goats and de ducks dat fly-y-y . . .

'You should all perform at my school!' said Richard. 'The
kids would love it!'

'You're on!' we replied.

Next day was spent on the roof of the *pensión*, drawing
up a list of all the American popular songs we knew, separat-
ing them into categories to make the show more educational:
spirituals ('Travellin' Shoes'), work songs ('Linin' Track'),
country blues (Ralph and Mitsuko playing pat-a-cake to
'Pick a Bale o' Cotton'), urban blues ('Nobody Knows You
When You're Down and Out'), vaudeville ('Diddy Wah
Diddy'), bluegrass ('In the Pines'), cowboy songs ('Ol'
Paint'), Dust Bowl ballads ('So long, Been Good to Know
Ya'), and ending with Country and Western and contempor-
ary folk (Dylan et al.).

It was one of the most enjoyable jobs we'd ever been paid
for. It went down a storm, especially the pat-a-cake routine,
which Moroccan street kids play lightning fast. As a finale,
the whole school joined in a singalong 'Goodnight Irene'.
We were immediately offered a tour of the other four American Language Centers in Morocco, but time only allowed
us to visit Fez. Even this made us feel like superstars, with
our train fare and accommodation paid for, the Fez show
was another resounding success as most students had never
heard the English language set to music.

The medieval medina in Fez was impenetrable to traffic
and so labyrinthine that any visitor who refuses a guide
inevitably gets lost. However, Ralph, who had rented
rooms here years earlier, brushed off the boys who buzzed
around vying for our patronage in English, Spanish, and

even Japanese, and led us confidently through the narrow alleys to pay a call on his old landlord Hassan. Groping our way through a narrow, unlit passage we found ourselves in a cool, dark house opening onto a small courtyard. The family was overjoyed to see Ralph. A child was sent off with a tray of leavening bread to the communal oven around the corner. While the bread was baking, the elder brother Hassan, a leatherworker, took us to his minuscule attic workshop and showed Carmen how to pare leather for bookbinding. On a corner we stopped to listen to an old blind man in a dishevelled djelabah sing *Habibi, habibi* . . . The Arabic 'h' is a rush of air that students of the language have to practise in front of a mirror until they manage to fog it up; this sound survives in Castilian Spanish as the letter 'j'. To impersonate an Arab, a Spaniard will reel off a phrase full of 'j's and drawn-out 'm's: *Jaime, bájame la jaula del jamón!* ('James, lower the ham cage for me'), or *La paja de Mahoma me moja* ('Muhammad's [expletive] is wetting me'). And whenever I heard the tone of Arabic conversation rise in the marketplace, I was reminded of Toni Morlà's side-splitting impression of a high-pitched Algerian radio football commentary.

The atmosphere in the medina of Fez was not so much medieval as biblical, evoking the streets of Nazareth I had visited with my parents at the age of five. The sounds and smells also brought back the Majorca of my childhood: the same sickly whiff of snails cooking, the sight of raw mutton attracting flies at the butchers', the same magenta-and-green dyed palm fronds woven into the basketwork, the same heavily laden donkeys, the same Arabic intonation in the worksongs, the same macho men leering at foreign girls. But these *moros* hadn't cottoned on to the change that had come over Spanish women since Franco had died. As we were stocking up with mineral water in a shop, a smarmy Moroccan tried to feel Mitsuko's bottom; Carmen caught him in the act and reacted by sloshing water all over him from behind. He fled into a café, his clothes soaked, trying to laugh this humiliation off before his scornful cronies.

We had time to polish up the repertoire on the roof of the *pensión*, while the proprietor's daughter showed Carmen – a natural redhead – and Mitsuko how to apply henna to their hair and let it dry in the sun; Carmen's soon shone like a stop-light. The concert in Fez went even better than in Tangier and we promised ourselves we'd get some more mileage out of our hours of rehearsals when we all returned to Majorca.

The sweetness of the Moroccans we had come to know had been soured by a few unscrupulous individuals bent on ripping us off, so we weren't too upset about leaving. Back in Deià, the old village inn or *fonda* was reopening after several years, this time as a bar with a magnificent terrace. Ralph talked Tomeu into hiring us for the opening of Sa Fonda. Perhaps inspired by the blind singer in Fez, he put up some posters announcing 'Country Blues with Blind Leroy and Sleepy Tom' (that was me – I'm always yawning). The 'blind bluesman' trick wasn't new; John Fahey had used it to get double billing and double pay by coming onstage after the interval as Blind Joe Death. (Other precedents were Blind Leroy Garnett and Blind Lemon Jefferson; then there's Sleepy John Estes and the rockabilly Sleepy La Beef, but the only Sleepy Tom I've heard of was a racehorse from Ohio who set a world record in 1879.)

For Ralph the dark glasses and walking stick was not so

much a disguise as a way of avoiding having to confront an audience of familiar faces. 'I ain't really blind,' he'd announce, 'I just cain't see.' The first half went so well that Leroy celebrated the interval with a few whiskies, condemning the second half to a shambles.

Before Ralph and Mitsuko headed off on their biennial migration to Japan we recorded our repertoire, including some of Ralph's own songs, on a four-track cassette machine. In their absence I added bass, drums, and electric guitar, Carmen's voice and tambourine and sent a copy to Radio Nacional de España, where it was aired on a 'weird demo tape' programme. Of course it was an unregistered pirate recording, sold only around the village – hence the name, Moonshine. Having one's own printing press is useful for things like running off cassette covers. The blurb ran like this:

> Leroy had sung in the streets of Kyoto and the avenues of Paree; Sleepy had busked from Piccadilly to the Ramblas. They teamed up in Tanjah and so began their career, which hit rock bottom in Deià. Leroy was run out of town, leaving only his voice on tape, and is lying low in the Orient; Sleepy, having smuggled a four-track into his cell, put together this cassette and is selling it to pay his bail.

It sold almost a hundred copies, becoming a hit among the village children, who especially loved 'Big Fat Mama', later adapted by Mitsuko to an even more erotic 'Big Fat Papa':

> Daddy, daddy, remember me
> I'm the little girl who climbed your tree . . .

But my own favourite was Ralph's rewrite of the 'Hesitation Blues', in which he lambasted the exploitation of Deià's bohemian image by the promoter of La Residencia:

> Hatchet Ball, he built a great hall
> Gonna make us waiters one and all . . .

So, can a white boy like Ralph, whose railroad family banned 'nigger music' at home, grow up to sing the blues? The blues form is so simple that it has become the pidgin English of musicians the world over: anybody can imitate it, but the truth of the blues, like the truth of flamenco, is in the feeling, not the form. This may explain why so many of the young musicians from Andalucía, both *gitanos* and *payos*, have such a natural affinity for the blues; the essence is the same, and even the word *soleá* (*soledad*, 'loneliness') comes to mean the same thing. However, in the rich and varied world of flamenco it's probably the *fandangos de Huelva* that come closest to the blues worksongs.

The Rio Tinto in Huelva, so called because its waters are tinted a wine colour by the iron sulphate in the mountains, is, according to Spanish scientists, the one river on earth that most resembles the ancient rivers on Mars. This was confirmed when the Mars Rover found jarosite, a mineral only formed in acid water conditions and named after the Jarosa Gorge in Almería where it was first discovered. The minerals in the mountains of Huelva have been mined since Roman times, but since the nineteenth century they were exploited by the British – hence Rio Tinto Zinc. Although the British engineers will be remembered for having introduced football to Spain, they obliged the local miners to work in terrible conditions that gave rise to some of the most heartfelt *cante jondo*, 'singing from the depths'. The women who packed the powder into the sticks of dynamite also had reason to wail; they spent their full working day unable to change position, their chairs strapped tightly to the work table to 'avoid accidents'. So it was logical that when flamenco met the blues, years later, it did so first in this part of Andalucía, almost on the frontier with Portugal. The turning point was *Blues de la Frontera*, a record by Pata Negra, a group of dope-smoking *gitanos* led by the Amador brothers in the early Eighties. Raimundo Amador now leads the flamenco-blues movement; he and B. B. King guest on each other's albums and although they share no common language, B. B.'s old Gibson, Lucille, and Raimundo's flamenco guitar, Gerundina, converse in the blues.

When I consider Neil Innes's immortal question, 'Can Blue Men Sing the Whites?', the image that comes to my mind is the game of pass the parcel: the more layers of wrapping paper on the outside, the harder it is to guess what's inside. Strip off the cultural padding and you'll uncover the same raw nerve screaming when it hurts. Take Mitsuko. In the blues idiom she'd be called 'a skinny yeller gal', but having lived a hobo's life for twenty years she has torn enough of her wrapping off for anybody to glimpse the big fat blues mama inside her tiny frame. In her stage persona, Lucy Chipango, she performs a real show stopper from the 1930s, a blues song in the Basin Street style called 'Shanghai Lil', which she sings in Japanese with all the smoky sultriness of a sleazy opium den hostess.

In Deià, Ralph discovered another closet blues enthusiast, a Welshman whose adolescence, like mine, had been marked by John Mayall and Peter Green and who had married into a Majorcan family. So with Dai 'Furry' Griffiths on slide guitar and mandolin we landed a gig in a new bar in Palma called Bluesville, around the corner from the old Guitar Centre, which only needed fifty people to pack it out. It's in an alley called Carrer de sa Ma d'es Moro, so named because centuries ago a Moorish servant was caught stealing and his severed hand was hung out of the window as a warning. Bluesville had opened the night before with a performance by a local band, Pep Banyo and the Blues Devils, and the smell of paint was still stronger than the smell of beer.

We were surprised to find an enthusiastic audience familiar not only with B. B. King and John Lee Hooker but also with our more rural heroes Sleepy John Estes and Taj Mahal. In case the local punters didn't pick up on the lyrics, Ralph had painted a whole series of giant full-colour cue cards illustrating the longer ballads, 'Casey Jones' and 'Frankie 'n' Albert', which he later sold to an art collector to pay for a trip to Japan.

Today there is a healthy Majorcan blues scene headed by Pep and by Victor Uris, a wheelchair-bound harmonica player, who founded L'Harmonica Coixa ('The Lame Harmonica'), one of Spain's most respected blues bands. If any Majorcan can feel the blues, it's Victor, who will sing of the woes of trying to drink away your cares while stuck in a wheelchair. One lyric goes 'By the time you've found a place to get off the pavement and cross the street, and negotiated the dog turds, the bar's closed down.' When Bluesville opened, it was a rather risky venture in the quiet backstreets of La Lonja, but it has survived ten years to become *the* live music bar in an area that is today the new Gomila, featuring night-life of every nature and bars serving *pa amb oli* until the early hours – to the continuing protests of the neighbours.

One day, Sor Victoriana, an elderly nun from Segovia

who taught bookbinding in Palma jail, brought a group of ten young offenders to visit Carmen's bindery. Afterwards, Ralph and Mitsuko came in with some wine, bread, and *sobrassada* to hand around; Carmen picked up her tambourine, I my guitar, and we all sang them some songs. Of course we were invited to play for the next *Festes de la Mercè*, and ended up playing three more gigs in the jail, two of them in the Women's Pavilion. Since Araceli was there, we managed to also get Sebastián and Mimbre on the bill. Whenever Ralph took off his Casey Jones cap and showed his bald head to the ladies, they all went wild. Most of them were gypsies or prostitutes, the only foreigner being a miserable young English girl who had given birth prematurely in her hotel; she hadn't dared tell her parents, and, in a panic, had stuffed the stillborn baby into a dustbin, where it was later found. Her wretchedness was only deepened by the presence of several toddlers who were allowed to stay with their mothers until the age of three.

It was Ralph who baptized my brother Juan and me as 'Johnny and Tommy Tombs, the Famous Texas Tombs Brothers' back in the early Eighties. He was surviving by writing for the island's English-language tabloid, the *Majorca Daily Bulletin*, at $6 a full-page article, four times a week; the scant royalties from a textbook translation of the Mayan classic *Popol Vuh* didn't even cover the cost of wine. The *Daily Bull\*\*\*\**, as it's known locally, has a hard time filling the 'Local News' pages with anything of interest to ex-pats; it gets most of its national news from its sister-paper, the tabloid *Última Hora*. Today, Deià's rich and famous could support a full-time pair of paparazzi, but twenty years ago if you wanted that kind of news you had to invent it, like the café gossips did.

Ralph decided to begin by beating Jorge Luís Borges at his own game. As a young man, Borges had written literary criticism for cash by reviewing books that had never been published; the reviews were so recherché that nobody checked them out. Ralph began his career in journalism with a review of a non-existent book by Borges, and carried on from there, inventing fabulous stories and biographies of his friends and neighbours inspired by any photograph he could get hold of. The Texas Tombs Brothers featured regularly in Ralph's regular 'North Coast News' section, which, after his meeting 'the Ineffably Beautiful Omitsu', was renamed North Coast Kaboogie as a tribute to both Japanese and American culture.

The Deià area had such notoriety for harbouring bizarre characters that few Majorcan residents questioned the truth of his stories. The editor, Andy Valente, took the ambivalent attitude of being aware but not knowing. Any village character would feature in Ralph's articles, including the dogs: Oofie the Tibetan circus dog, Rocky the town rake, Kinski the trained potato-digger. A photo of Dave Templeton with his eyes half-closed begot the character Blind David the Painter, who used his ten-year-old son Joe as his eyes, painting whatever Joe described. A snapshot of Carmen's flatmate Ana in a grass skirt inspired a new CV as a Hawaiian princess, whose drunken father had invented Planter's Punch. One reader drove up from Palma every day for a week in search of the 'Hawaiian princess', with whose image he had obviously fallen in love. But the star of Ralph's articles was Carmen because by repeating her full name (María del Carmen Mercedes del Milagro García-Gutierrez Gómez) several times he could fill half a page. He then invented a title for her: President of the National Siesta Club of Spain. This news item was picked up as a human-interest story by a visiting TV reporter and was mentioned on the national three o'clock news, to the amazement of Carmen's large family around the country. Televisión Española phoned up the Deià Town Hall wishing to interview the President of the Siesta Club, but the Municipal Secretary, without missing a beat, replied 'I'm sorry, she'd be asleep at this hour.' Ralph would seldom check with the subject of his 'fantasy journalism' before sending the article off to the *Bulletin* offices, which often earned him a cuffed ear in the bar or a reprimand in the letters column when he went too far.

Tommy Tombs stuck as my stage name with the Pa Amb Oli Band, but when playing with Blind Leroy I remained Sleepy Tom. (With the gypsies I was El Tomate.) I'd always insisted upon the Spanish spelling of my name, objecting to Thomas, Tommy, or Tom, but this was a convenient way of keeping tabs on my multiple persona. Lucia and Juan, although born in England, were also registered with Spanish spellings, but were never reduced to Lucy or Johnny, nor did William ever accept Bill. Like my forefathers (and probably fore-aunts) who preceded me, at school I was inevitably known as Gravy; only later did I reconcile myself with the name when I realized it's the English for salsa. I was also happy to discover that *tumbas* – 'graves' in Spanish – is the short form of *tumbadoras*, the bass conga drums.

The root of the name Mitsuko – and the more formal Omitsu – is the Japanese word for light; this suggested the Western equivalent 'Lucy' as a stage name. Every four years, Blind Leroy and Lucy Chipango (the ancient name for Japan) stick out their thumbs by any roadside or port facing east and set off to visit her family. They spend a year in the

Orient, a year in Spain, and the rest of the time on the road, often earning their transatlantic passage cooking on yachts. Having no money doesn't stop them planning their travels years in advance. Since our Moroccan adventure, there's been no stopping Lucy 'n' Leroy. Although they prefer a musical backing, they find it much easier to sing unconstrained by keys and beats to the bar, just the two of them out on the street, from Gibraltar's Landport Tunnel to Guatemala City, or being the first performers to entertain the prisoners at Essaouira jail.

When they perform in Spain I'm their guitarist; when in Japan, it's Hikihara (a.k.a. Hikiguitar), who has the same love of country blues as I do. Both Hiki and I have to adapt to their keys and rhythms; we are the grass, they are the tree. Although we've never met, it's nice to know I have a Japanese doppelgänger – or maybe I'm his, since Tomás means 'twin'. He also keeps me on my toes; Ralph will sometimes challenge me with 'Well, Hiki plays a sort of diddly-diddly-bong riff here. Could you do that?'

Since busking is forbidden in many places, the pair have another ace up their sleeve. 'In any city, a phone book will list the local secondary schools and language academies where we can offer a performance as the California Travelling Troupe. We put on a play in basic English, using a plot and the very stylized gestures of Chinese opera; this helps get the message across.' They have performed 'The Price of Wine' and 'The Treasure Map' in thirty-two countries, including the Philippines, Sri Lanka, Panama, and Turkey, occasionally also giving poetry readings and cooking classes. True bohemians with few possessions other than a stack of books and some kitchen knives (confided to us while travelling), they survive on a shoestring and the support of an international network of friends ready to offer them a city apartment or olive-picker's hut to house-sit. They treat either extreme as a luxury.

Majorca, and especially Deià, used to abound with these 'birds of passage', as they were described by Santiago Rusinyol in the early 1900s. Known variously as bohemians, beatniks, hippies and dharma bums, the question was freedom of movement with no ties or possessions, like lay dervishes or sadhus, beholden to no master but the occasional MasterCard in the case of the better-off hippies. Over the last twenty years this species all but disappeared due to the closure of the overland route to India, the tightening of border controls, the general encroachment of the modern state upon personal liberties, and the dearth of cheap accommodation. Foreign property-owners in Majorca used to look for someone to house-sit and keep the building aired and dry over the winter; now they prefer to leave the dehumidifier plugged in and pop over one weekend a month on EasyJet.

Today's free spirits usually have to slave half the year to finance the other half travelling; not Ralph and Mitsuko, who have seldom taken on a job that they didn't enjoy. How about Ralph's regular employment in Kyoto, sitting naked in a room with half a dozen Japanese girls? Art schools in Japan are attended mainly by female students and seem to have difficulty finding male life-class models, so the pay is good. Mitsuko penned several dozen calligraphic Christmas cards in Japanese for the owner of a freight airline in exchange for two seats to Tokyo. Any activity that seemed like real work would be self-aborted; in one lucrative job translating an ad for a German charter airline into English, Ralph rendered 'our modern aircraft' as 'our latest contraptions'. By the time the client cottoned on, Ralph had taken the money and run. Similarly, he'd avoid any kind of notoriety and the slightest indication of having made a name for himself would provoke a change of identity: Nelson alias Cardwell, Card, Ha'f Al-son, Blind Leroy, Leroy Pooh or Rats Brow.

When Brian Patten was asked in an interview which poet he would liked to have been had he not been Brian Patten, he named the unknown Ralph Nelson. By being so stubbornly true to themselves, Ralph and Mitsuko have become gypsies, an example of the life we'd all love to lead if we only dared cast off our moorings. They are equally true to their friends (their only capital), making sure we all keep in touch when they're away: 'Please pass this letter on to Paco and Antonia when you've read it', 'Don't forget it's Carl's birthday soon', etc.

They once invited us to lunch at Can La, a beautiful stone house in which they were squatting, within shouting distance of ours. The owner, Juanjo the Basque music promoter, had mortgaged it in order to finance Prince's tour of Spain, a disaster that left Can La in the hands of the bank. But he had kept a spare set of keys, which he passed on to Ralph and Mitsuko. When we arrived for lunch, the front door was wide open and the table laid for twelve people, the food and wine prepared in the kitchen, but there was no sign of the hosts; as other guests began to arrive, we all had to introduce ourselves. After an hour getting to know each other, it became obvious that this was a set-up. Then we found the note: '*Bon profit!* We'll do the washing up tomorrow.'

> Goin' down to Sóller
> Goin' to the Red Cross Store . . .

During a poetry reading to benefit the Red Cross Station in Sóller, Ralph and Mitsuko discovered a store-room full of EU-sponsored food for the needy. 'We have to send most of it back,' said María, the director, 'because hardly anybody in Sóller or Deià will admit to being poor; it's a question of pride.'

'Well, we're not too proud, and who's poorer than a wandering poet?' Paying no rent and having the staples free – biscuits, pasta, milk, lentils, salami, processed cheese, cans of beef stew – money can be saved for the real necessities: bread, wine, paper and typewriter ribbons.

The Ca n'Alluny theatre has witnessed some excellent performance poetry, including Adrian Mitchell, Roger McGough, and Brian Patten hot from their UK tour, but one of the most enjoyable was a reading of Ralph's poems illustrated by sound effects. The idea came from Miguel Bibiloni, a heavy-set stonemason from Sóller who could imitate any birdcall. Fourteen of Ralph's poems featured birds; Miguel sat perched in the carob tree above the audience awaiting his cues. Behind the backdrop curtain sat the sound effects team following the script, our shadows projected on the white sheet by the setting sun. Carmen 'walking' two upturned cups – bloop bloop – across a bucket of water, then beating eggs on a plate while the pianist and composer Carl Manker hit gongs, triangles, and shakers. Wally Fraza, Batabanó's Dutch percussionist, brought along his complete battery of professional percussion. For me, who had spent a childhood experimenting with sounds and always being told to shut up, this was a heaven-sent opportunity to imitate a ship's horn by didgery-doing down a length of hosepipe, tapping a large frying pan while swilling water around it (*woinggg boinggg*), using my mouth as a resonating chamber to alter the pitch of two pebbles struck together (*tiptip taptap top tuptip*) or blowing a double-reeded tooter made from a rolled-up carob leaf into a tall glass and giving it a wah-wah effect with my hands.

Mitsuko often slips traditional Japanese *senryu* (humorous haikus) into her readings, which beg sound effects:

> The summer relay races,
> When the mosquito hands over
> The baton to the fly.

> Ripping off a great fart –
> It's not so hilarious
> When you live alone.

Ralph and I have also tried our hand at blues *senryus*:

> Feelin' so blue, feelin' so beat
> Caught jetlag off the plane's shit-hole seat.

> Cat got my tongue, devil got my pants
> Feelin' mistreated by circumstance.

Ralph is an indefatigable letter-writer and door-knocker, always circumventing the usual channels and using the surprise factor to find work on his own terms when the wine money runs out. This doesn't always work: his offer to pay for a hospital operation in Palma by reciting poetry in the operating theatre was turned down. But surely the new, almost empty University of the Balearics wouldn't begrudge a small fee for a reading of 'Tough Minded Poetry' (Catullus, Villon, etc.) with musical accompaniment?

Any student from the Balearics had always had to go to the mainland to further his education, so there was no university tradition on the islands. For this, the first batch of local undergraduates, the new university was simply a continuation of secondary school, a degree factory. In the mid 1980s, although it had been open for three years, the new Universitat de les Illes Balears still lacked any atmosphere. No concerts or debating societies, not even flat-share or car-pool notices on the bulletin boards. Most students drove their own cars bumper-to-bumper to the campus and ten minutes after the last class, the car park was once again deserted. The Dean was willing to try anything to motivate the student body, even resorting to such outlandish offerings as Ralph's. The reading had been amply advertised, but at the door of the lecture hall only five poker-faced students stood waiting, clutching their books.

One of the professors had tried to scuttle the act by hiding the key to the lecture hall, so Ralph led his musicians and token audience to a corner of the empty, cavernous student's cafeteria. Ralph luxuriated in reading Catullus' most explicit lines to a disconcerted audience of four – one girl had already fled in embarrassment – while Fiddler Ed and I punctuated the juicy bits with trills, arpeggios, and slides. I empathized with these poor flustered rural Majorcans, whose only crime had been to want to study for a degree. They had no idea what to make of Ed, a lanky concert violinist who had been a street busker in Ibiza, sporting a white beard and gap-toothed grin; and as for Ralph, a burly escaped lunatic with a shaved head declaiming ancient pornography ... He ordered a round of beers for all and things began to loosen up. After a while more students joined our table as we diverged into a country hoe-down. So this was what university should be about!

Over the years I've found myself providing the musical accompaniment to all kinds of poetry, like Lady June's wacky couplets that she delivers at her exhibition openings:

The trouble with being open minded [flowing
    arpeggios]
Is that your brains fall out . . . [descending chords,
    random plinks and plonks]

A different case was a very stark, emotional reading at a Palma secondary school during the Sarajevo crisis, in which Toni Rigo (the diesel mechanic, published poet and would-be rock star) and Carmen read his war poems over my guitar improvisations, to an earnest adolescent audience.

My father once claimed that his novels were his show dogs, which he bred in order to pay for the milk for his cat, poetry; any money that came in from his poems was spent not on electricity bills but on antiques and beautiful objects. Carmen and I discovered for ourselves, after twelve years hand-printing and binding slim volumes of verse, that you can't live off poetry, although I'd add the qualifier 'unless you're from Liverpool'. Only once have I been paid for providing a sonic cushion for poetry – a recitation by Margarita Fuster of classic Majorcan poets in Palma's Municipal Theatre – but it took the Town Hall a year to cough up. Margarita, the daughter of a well-known literary columnist, grew up hearing the Majorcan post-war poets reading in her sitting room. With the same theatrical passion, she was able to enthuse a theatre full of ladies in mink stoles by declaiming some of the best-known, albeit slightly rancid, poems by Alcover, Llompart, and others, whose names are familiar to any Majorcan if only because they have streets or schools named after them. (My father also has a Palma street named after him: ironically, it's where all the best-known foreign bars were, just off Plaza Gomila.)

Ralph and Mitsuko, although they centre their existence around poetry, have never made a penny out of it either, but they have managed to be treated to slap-up meals at two of Deià's most expensive restaurants in exchange for poems extolling the chefs' genius.

# 13

# The Big One

The Kingdom of Spain, like the United Kingdom, is an amalgam of various cultures and languages, and although we have no Commonwealth as such, a similar relationship exists with its ex-colonies. Just as there are Irish communities in New York and Welsh in Patagonia, so you will find Majorcan and Catalan surnames in Venezuela and Cuba, and Galicians almost anywhere you look. Franco defined this historical transatlantic bond in typically Fascist terms as 'The Spanish Race' under the patronage of *La Virgen del Pilar*, Our Lady of the Pillar, whose effigy in Saragossa Cathedral is venerated in many a *jota*. As *The Child's Practical Encyclopaedia* of my Spanish schooldays explained, 'One [of Columbus's ships] was named the *Santa María*, and America was discovered on the Day of Our Lady of the Pillar. Does this coincidence not prove that God rewarded Spain thanks to the prayers of His grateful Holy Mother?' In fact the ships (probably acquired from the Knights Templar from their huge fleet, and still sporting Maltese crosses on their sails) were named after three dockside whores – *La Pinta*

('The Good-for-Nothing'), *La Niña* ('The Little Girl'), and *La Gallega* ('The Galician'). This last ship, a cumbersome cargo vessel captained by Columbus himself, was renamed *Santa María* to give more respectability to his venture, although his sailors still called her *La Gallega*.

The *Dia de la Raza* ('Day of the Spanish Race') was celebrated in the 1970s with a Hispanic version of the Eurovision song contest, even cheesier than the original. In political terms, Spain's commitment to the Race meant that Franco would support any Spanish-speaking military regime or dictatorship, however corrupt; if he refused to condemn Fidel Castro's, it wasn't out of a respect for the revolution but probably because Fidel was a Galician and a soldier like himself. He helped Castro sidestep Kennedy's embargo by importing Cuban cigars, allowing *yanqui* tourists to stock up with Montecristos at any Spanish airport.

October 12th is no longer the *Dia de la Raza* but a more politically correct *Dia de la Hispanidad*, celebrated in the USA as Columbus Day. King Juan Carlos, having presided over the peaceful transition to democracy in Spain, has done a great deal on his transatlantic goodwill trips to imbue this Hispanic identity with a respect for democracy, and has given the Spanish-speaking world a collective Head of State. To most Spaniards today the former empire was the Americas; other ex-colonies like the Philippines, Western Sahara, and Equatorial (Spanish) Guinea don't really count. Guineans visiting Spain, having been brought up in a totally Spanish-oriented culture, are shocked to find themselves treated like any other black Africans; likewise, a Spanish-speaking *saharaui* is still considered a Moor. Any *filipina* is taken to be a nanny or cook, unless she happens to be Isabel

Preysler, ex-wife of Julio Iglesias, mother of Enrique and paragon of beauty, style, and elegance.

To most native English-speakers except Canadians, 'America' is synonymous with 'the United States of . . .'. To a Spanish speaker the term usually comprises North, South, and Central America and the Caribbean. The strong cultural and trade links between the Iberian peninsula and the Americas, at least to the south of the Rio Grande, is perhaps seen by some as neo-colonialism. But although Spain is still considered *la Madre Patria* – literally, the Mother Father-land – her American ex-colonies have lost their inferiority complex towards us, just as we have overcome our own towards Europe.

Neither Spain nor Portugal has any possessions left in the Americas, while France maintains Guadeloupe and Mar-tinique, the Dutch still have Aruba, the Danes have Green-land, and the British possess the non-US half of the Virgin Islands, Anguila, Montserrat, the Caymans, Bermudas, Turks, Falklands, etc. Most of Latin America's economy is answerable to the USA. So if Spain and Portugal are still per-ceived as colonial powers, it's thanks to the Columbus cult.

The year 1992 was the Big One for Spain. The Olympics were to be held in Barcelona and the 500th anniversary of Columbus's 'voyage of discovery' was the central theme of Expo 92, the World's Fair in Seville. To complete the hat trick, Madrid was designated Cultural Capital of Europe. The new Spanish bullet train linked Seville with Madrid, to the greater glory of the Socialist premier, Felipe Gonzalez, an Andalusian himself. It was Spain's coming-out party after a difficult puberty, a hormonal change from dictatorship to democracy that served as an example to other countries about to undergo the same changes. Only one doubt marred the celebrations: should one really celebrate the anniversary of the conquest and subsequent massacre and slavery of the native Americans? Many of their descendants and sympathizers thought not. Throughout Latin America, indigenous villages, religious communities, trade unions, and political parties joined forces to counter-celebrate '500 Years of Indigenous Resistance'. The Native Americans had, after all, discovered the place and settled there a few millennia before the Europeans.

Most Latin American governments, including eventually Fidel Castro's, decided to back the official celebrations. President Balaguer of the Dominican Republic, site of Columbus's first landfall, sank his bankrupt country further into debt by commissioning a monumental lighthouse for the occasion to project a huge cross upon the night sky. The year 1992 was a chance for Spain to wrestle some of Columbus's prestige back from the Italians; the controversy about his origin flared up again, including a well-documented theory that the Admiral was in fact a Majorcan from Felanitx. Many Hispanics still link Colón – the Spanish spelling – with the word 'colony'; the fact that it actually comes from the Latin *colonia*, a landed estate, doesn't mitigate this popular association.

As the *Quinto Centenario* year 1992 dawned, official ceremonies were being planned to glorify Spain's links with Latin America, but at a grass roots level other events were being prepared to protest against the historical injustices initiated by the Conquistadors. It was pointed out that the whole Latin American debt plus interest could have been paid back with the gold that was mined and appropriated by the Europeans. The Majorcan Committee of Solidarity with Latin America was to coordinate the counter-celebrations on the island and needed someone to organize a concert. They approached me, not only for my sympathy with the cause, but for my musical contacts and my experience organizing benefit concerts in Deià and Sóller. Since my first gig as a bass player with the Offbeats in a concert to defend the island of Dragonera from the speculators, I've played for free:

*For* the victims of the Hurricane Juana in Bluefields (Nicaragua) and of the war in Rwanda; the Blood Donors of Majorca; the legalization of a deported Senegalese musician; a child's hospital in Managua; a cataract operation for Max (a popular Deià mongrel); the Vicente Ferrer Foundation in India; the International Childcare Trust orphanage in Kenya; Amnesty International; the Palma Animal Shelter; the annual barbecue for the Young Offenders at Palma jail; and two independent radio stations, among other causes.

*Against* the Gulf War and the war in Iraq; the beachside apartment project at Cala Galliota, and a yacht harbour at s'Estanyol.

Few associations in Spain ever get together unless there's food and drink laid on, so the preparations for the Anti-500 celebrations took place over a bread-and-oil feast for thirty. Since my trip to Nicaragua, I'd been in touch with the Solidarity Committee, although I often found them more dogmatic and less pragmatic than the people they were trying to help. Most of the members were well-intentioned leftists and religious workers, but I had kept my distance after they wanted to 'check the ideological message' of my audio-visual exhibition on the Nicaraguan revolution.

It was always the same soloists and groups who played for benefit concerts. We'd need a surprise name to top the bill, someone who'd be willing to play only for expenses and a token fee. My first thought was to approach Robert

'Wheelchairman' Wyatt, who was now living in Barcelona. Since leaving the Soft Machine he'd been a very outspoken and honest defender of the radical left and very sensitive to the situation in Latin America, but his condition didn't allow him to perform onstage anymore. He put me in touch with a couple of his more radical Spanish musical contacts, but I drew a blank. Then I got a call from Carlos Goyarrola, one of the Basque music promoters who had first brought the groups from the *movida Madrileña* to the island. 'Santiago Auserón is here with me and wants to buy a house on the north coast . . . could you show him around? He's also crazy about Cuban music. I'll bring him over to meet you.' Santiago had been the leader of Radio Futura, one of the top bands in Spain, with whom Ollie had toured.

Fourteen years earlier, after witnessing the last Canet Rock Festival featuring Nico, Blondie, and Daevid Allen's Gong, Santiago and his brother Luís had written the famous manifesto in favour of an autochthonous Spanish pop music. True to their principles, their band Radio Futura had given a new direction to the national rock scene by drawing from the pool of popular Spanish and Latin American culture, laying the foundations for what is now known as rock latino. Although the band split up amicably in 1990 while on the crest of the wave, today it is still a point of reference for any Spanish or Latin American rock musician. Carlos Santana had pioneered a rock-salsa fusion, but Radio Futura introduced the Spanish way of saying and playing into the rock mainstream. The naturally syncopated rhythm of the Spanish language – the stress falls usually on the second-to-last syllable – has always been at odds with the straight-ahead rock beat and has had to be either constrained or puffed out with 'oh yeahs' to make the words fit. Radio

Futura and their successors managed to adapt rock to the Spanish language and the Spanish imagination.

Carmen and I felt at ease with Santiago and his French wife Cathy. Although they were both highbrow intellectuals – he had studied philosophy at the Sorbonne, she was researching Mongolian culture – they were very down to earth. In fact they had met in a disco in Torremolinos. When the band became successful, Santiago, after suffering an initial contradiction between pop and philosophy, had managed to come to terms with his status as the Spanish 'thinking-man's rock star'; with his dimpled chin and good looks he was both teenage heart-throb and articulate spokesman for the rock scene. Since his band dispersed, he had been compiling a series of albums of traditional Cuban *son* with the aim of reintroducing this fundamental musical legacy to a new generation of listeners. Months spent sifting through the Cuban radio archives, documenting and obtaining permissions, bore fruit in the form of a five-CD set released in Spain, *Semilla del Son*. He had also produced a record for the veteran Cuban musician Compay Segundo, which anticipated Ry Cooder and David Byrne's ventures into Cuban music by several years.

One evening after supper on our terrace we brought out our instruments and discovered that he knew most of Batabanó's repertoire. We decided to take the guitar and *tres* across the street to the bar; I phoned Mati to bring his congas. It was the first time Santiago had sung in public since the band broke up, and we alternated classic *son* with Radio Futura material, which of course everybody in the bar sang along with. Stripped down to these musical basics, it became clear that many of band's mega-hits were constructed around the basic *son* structure, both musically and lyrically.

After we'd played together at the bar, I felt I could now broach the subject of the Anti-500 concert. 'I'd love to help you out,' said Santiago, 'but I don't have a band at the moment and I'm not ready to perform solo. I'll write to my friend Caetano; he'd be perfect.'

Caetano Veloso is one of Brazil's greatest singers. He had run foul of his country's dictatorship in the late 1960s and had lived in exile in London. On the last Radio Futura album, Santiago had sung his own Spanish translation of *Terra*, Caetano's haunting love song to the planet earth:

> I found myself in a prison cell
> When I saw you for the first time
> In a full frontal photograph
> Yet you were not completely naked
> But swathed in clouds . . .

The next time I saw Santiago was at Ollie Halsall's funeral in Deià. 'Caetano's in the depths of a depression and he's not performing. He's not even returning any calls.' Santiago was pretty dispirited himself: he had become a good friend of Ollie, who had stood in for Radio Futura's lead guitarist on their farewell tour. It was on this tour that Ollie had picked up the drug habit that took him to the grave. But a few weeks later Santiago was a lot brighter, having finally found an affordable house in the centre of the island; Deià was getting to be too expensive even for a rock star.

'Here's an idea for the concert. You know I produced Kiko Veneno's album in London? It'll be coming out in the autumn. I'll try to get him to come over, and we can see how the new songs go down with the audience.' Kiko Veneno – 'Frankie Poison' – was the stage name of José Maria López, a cult figure in the progressive flamenco scene, a man who had always gone against the grain. His family had moved from his native Catalonia to Seville, while most people went in the other direction. Like most Andalusians he had a way with words and had fallen in with gypsy musicians from the housing project known as *Las Tres Mil Viviendas* –the Three Thousand Council Flats. He joined the gypsies Raimundo and Diego Amador to form the first flamenco-blues group, Veneno; when it became Pata Negra, Kiko left taking the name with him. He was best known as the author of *Volando Voy*, the most popular song by the great Camarón de la Isla, who was to flamenco what Bob Marley was to reggae.

While the Amador brothers stretched the boundaries of flamenco with their *Blues de la Frontera*, Kiko had remained a cult figure, emerging sporadically with an occasional batch of idiosyncratic new songs. The time was ripe for him to shed his outsider image and move into the mainstream with a well-produced album full of strong material. Santiago had got him a proper record deal and produced the new album with Jo Dworniak in London. Kiko was enthusiastic about playing his new songs in Deià, but there was a hitch. He still held a daytime job as a Civil Servant in Diputación Provincial de Sevilla and had used up his year's holidays on the recording session.

Santiago negotiated a solution with Kiko's superior. 'If we pay for his boss to come along too, then it can be justified as a protocol trip. There's plenty of room in my house to put them up.' Things were beginning to take shape, and the key was the *son*. Santiago agreed that if I put together an acoustic group of local musicians for the occasion, then he could participate with Kiko. Between these two songwriters' material and some classic *son* we could put together a full evening's show. We'd all rehearse at Santiago's new house, which even had a pool.

Toni Morlà was an obvious choice for the band, since he still remembered all the Batabanó repertoire and could sing some of his own Cuban-inspired songs. The other key element was the brilliant guitarist and showman Joan Bibiloni, who, since touring with Daevid and Kevin, had become a successful producer and could put together the best rhythm section on the island. We also needed some backups – Carmeta from Batabanó and Lucia and Ramón's daughters Natalia and Laia.

Santiago had diligently recorded cassettes of all his and Kiko's songs for the musicians, so everybody came to the rehearsals well prepared. I'd never worked with such professional musicians before, and in two afternoons we learned about three hours' worth of new material. The name of this one-off band was the pun *Fora Son* – Majorcan for 'out, sleep' or 'wake up' – and even though the musicians' names took a discreet second place on the poster, word of the gig spread like wildfire across the island. The venue was Deià's Municipal Park, a larger version of the Ca n'Alluny theatre, which could seat three hundred and hold over a thousand in all. The village's reputation for creating a magical atmosphere added to the attraction of Santiago's fame, Kiko's legendary status, and the treat of seeing Toni and Joan share a stage.

After the left-wing nationalist band Coanegra had warmed up the crowd with an hour of Majorcan folk-rock, Fora Son took the stage. We'd all had supper in the baker's house, which backed onto the Park and served as our dressing room. The gate had sold 1,200 tickets but more people had slipped over a neighbour's wall and were even perched in the olive trees. The Solidarity Committee had never congregated more than a couple of hundred people for the cause and were overwhelmed at the turnout. Their original reticence at my budget disappeared; a hot September night can generate a lot of thirst and the bar had covered all the expenses by itself; the rest was profit.

We made our way through the crowd, dressed in loose, Caribbean white, Santiago wearing a jaunty spotted handkerchief. He had proposed we begin with Caetano's *Terra*, from Radio Futura's posthumous album, a song he had never sung in public. 'It's the antithesis of a typical opening number. It's a strange and intimate song, the melody starts on a dissonant note ... I'm sure it will grab the audience's attention and create the right atmosphere for the rest of the night.' The sound engineer was faced with the nightmare of equalizing four acoustic guitars, a double bass, an Argentine bongo player, a Brazilian on congas and my *tres*, which had a tendency to howl in feedback if I got too close to the microphone.

Onstage, I experienced the same sort of feeling as the Mermaid Theatre show with Robert, Spike, and Isla: rejoicing in the knowledge that anything could happen and that the performers had no more of an idea than the audience of how the evening would develop. A loose group of heterogeneous yet like-minded individuals generating a complicity between themselves and the parkful of people. The rehearsals had been no more than a first handshake; now we were all getting to know one another onstage. Kiko, with his Andalusian gift of the gab, immediately established a rapport with the audience, not just the *alternativos* who knew his songs from way back; the general reaction to his new material, with the audience immediately picking up on the refrains, gave us all a foretaste of the stir that his comeback record was going to make.

Santiago acted as master of ceremonies while Joan Bibi-loni and Toni counterbalanced the mainlanders with funny Majorcan asides. Toni and I played the most Cuban-flavoured of his songs in Catalan, with the rhythm section following us faultlessly. Suddenly a drunk wandered up to a microphone – I hadn't even considered stage security – but Santiago dealt with him amiably: 'I'm sorry, sir, you have to pay extra if you wish to watch from this area.'

A voice from the audience yellled 'Speak in Catalan! We're not in Spain here!'

'Well, nobody asked for my passport!' retorted Santiago. 'I saw no frontier. There are no such things as frontiers. There is only water, the earth, the clouds . . .'. The audience cheered and the heckler shut up.

When we reached the end of the song list, we'd been on stage for three hours and finally left the audience singing the refrain of *Semilla Negra* into the night. There had been no trouble and the only damage had been caused by some gatecrashers trampling a neighbour's flower bed. The con-cert had made a large profit, which was sent to Guatemala to fund an indigenous-language radio station there.

Ten years later, people still talk about that magical evening, and the local TV broadcasts some rather shaky video footage of the concert every few months. As a musical experiment it inspired Santiago and Kiko to embark on a national tour with Kiko's old band mate from Veneno, the gypsy bluesman Raimundo Amador, accompanying each other's songs. When the tour reached Barcelona to play at the prestigious Palau de la Musica, I was invited over to join the line-up with my *tres*. I've seldom enjoyed myself musically as much as swapping Cuban riffs with Raimundo Amador in the hotel lobby. Raimundo is only fractionally taller than Joan Bibiloni, with a broad, wicked grin and thin moustache that gives him the air of a seedy pimp or a pusher. One of the most versatile guitarists in Spain, he's equally at home playing blistering blues licks or *bulerías* on his custom-built flamenco guitar. After their tour, Kiko, Raimundo, and Santiago – now known as Juan Perro – each began a successful solo career, redefining contemporary Spanish music in terms of *mestizaje*, cross-breeding.

Any long-time foreign resident or visitor to Deià will be able to recall the moment in which he realized that the village was no longer the one that had captivated him. I remember a young English couple in 1969 complaining: 'Now they're selling coloured postcards in the village shop. That's it, that's the end.' About the same time, my brother William felt that the Deià of his childhood had disappeared along with the agricultural way of life. Many Majorcans now referred to the village as the 'elephants' graveyard'.

For some, Deià 'died' along with my father in 1985; for others, Kevin's departure in the 1990s or Lady June's death was the final nail in the coffin. When Mati died in 2002, after many years as patriarch of the artists and master DJ of the village parties – he was always up on the latest dance music from all over the world – his funeral took the form of a Yoruba ceremony with Senegalese drummers and Cuban *santero* dancers. At this party the sangría was spiked not with LSD but with a pinch of the painter's ashes.

There is always something to mark the end of an era. In ten years time, these will be 'the good old days' to the people who are at present buying or building houses here. Faces from Deià's past will continue to reappear at the bar when least expected. But whatever the exact date of Deià's demise,

I'll always remember the Counter-Centenary concert as the grand sending-off party for the crazy, irresponsible, inspiring place where the impossible happened, where reality could be magical.

It was in the late 1980s that Deià II, as Carmen defines it, began to emerge, alongside the four-star Hotel La Residencia. (The fifth star was only withheld for lack of lifts to the upstairs rooms.) The mayor at this time, the grandson of the mason who built Ca n'Alluny, had been a classmate of Jordi and had also left school at the first opportunity. But he realized that the *artistas* were the village's greatest asset. The previous mayor had seen the protection order on the village's heritage (won by the lobbying of my father and other influential foreigners) as an obstacle to growth, but his successor realized the upmarket potential of a well-preserved beauty spot. If all houses were to be built of local stone as the conservationists demanded and not just faced with crazy-paving slabs, this would provide well-paid work to stonemasons. Anybody wishing to live in this bohemian paradise would have to pay through the nose for the privilege. A few isolated mansions built in the style of Majorcan manor houses would bring in much more revenue than cheap apartment blocks. Their owners would also have large lumps of cash to sink unobtrusively into further expensive renovations and landscape gardening. The super-rich employ gardeners and cleaners, spend money in local restaurants, and cause fewer problems than the bohemian troublemakers. Higher rents would get rid of the unproductive layabouts, leaving only those hard-working artists who sold well.

By the late 1990s, the foreign homeowners were polarized into two groups that barely overlapped socially: the old *artistas* who had settled here while property was cheap, and the invisible New Rich – corporate lawyers, company chairmen, arms dealers – who never set foot in the bars and could sell their mansions to one another for fabulous sums with nobody but the gardener even noticing.

A first-class job of taxidermy was beginning to turn Deià into a stuffed reproduction of itself, as had happened in other Mediterranean 'bohemian hang-outs' – Cadaqués on the Costa Brava, St Paul de Vence on the Cote d'Azur, and Portofino in Italy. But only true bohemians could put up with Deià housing conditions – old smelly cesspools and no running water – so a new water grid and sewage system was laid. After laying the pipes, the ancient cobblestone mule steps running past our house were repaved with new stones and now look like a set of false teeth, too regular to be real; they have lost the natural cadence and rhythm of the original, which had been designed to match a mule's gait.

The opening of the Hotel La Residencia was a decisive moment in Deià's history. Axel and Kristen had promised the village its own Chelsea Hotel that would serve as an extension of the bohemian atmosphere of the foreign community and stimulate the arts by attracting potential art buyers. The couple decorated it impeccably and recruited the hotel staff from local families, a risky gamble that paid off by earning the hotel the full loyalty and cooperation of the village authorities, and gave it carte blanche for future developments.

During the running-in period the hotel housed some colourful characters like the terminally ill American who budgeted his generous expenditure to the exact week he'd been given to live, dying right on schedule. Despite the prices, the Deià crowd would often drop by the hotel for a drink at the bar until one evening when Mati, with Axel's permission, organized a party for his village friends by the hotel pool. It was a low-key affair; Narcís Serra, a regular summer visitor for years and at the time the Minister of Defence of the Socialist Government of Spain, was happily tinkling away on my Nicaraguan marimba while Mati played his congas. Some hotel clients complained about the noise to Reception, who asked us all to leave. Axel was unavailable by phone to intercede, so Mati started up a *guaguancó* rhythm on his congas and began a provocative rhythmic chant: *Fascistas fuera, viva ETA*. At the mention of ETA, the Minister's bodyguards bustled him, protesting, out of possible danger, while several of Mati's guests jumped fully dressed into the pool to add to the mayhem. The Deià crowd were obviously too unruly to mix with the hotel guests.

La Residencia was too expensive for most of the foreign community's friends or hangers-on and had to depend on less arty clients to pull through. The original idea of providing studios for artists-in-residence was shelved and the 'arts club' appeal of the hotel was played down in favour of its fitness centre, pool, private beach, and conference facilities. (The Pa Amb Oli Band, with Ollie, was once hired to play there for a roomful of chartered accountants from Milton Keynes, who, after ten minutes of hostile stares and mutual incomprehension, turned out to be one of our most appreciative audiences.) The only interface that remains between the hotel and the local foreign community is the art gallery, although when the noisy, flamboyant Deià crowd turn up for an exhibition opening, the hotel clients tended to shy away.

When one of the hotel's original investors found their assets frozen, Kristen offered her ex-ex, Richard Branson, the opportunity of buying into the operation. For the next decade La Residencia became a Virgin Hotel and Axel and Kristen soon moved on to apply their magic touch to other Mediterranean island projects. Virgin Headquarters imposed conservative regulations for decorum (shirts to be worn outside the pool area) and kept the village loonies at arm's length. After the 11 September attacks, Branson divested himself of La Residencia, which now belongs to Orient Express Hotels and has been refurbished to even greater heights of luxury.

The Residencia school of design developed by Axel and Kristen – impeccable stonework, reproductions of Majorcan furniture, modern art decorating whitewashed walls, elegant white shutters, old Arabic roof tiles used as outdoor wall-lamps – marked a trend in rural renovations and neo-Majorcan stone villas. In the 1990s, the island was moving upmarket and becoming the California of Europe. Cheap summer beach apartments were out; the new mobility afforded by air shuttles and the possibility of working via the Internet allowed well-off Northern Europeans to spend a good part of the year on the island and was turning every Majorcan village into another Deià II.

The Majorcans say that if you stand in your doorway long enough, the whole world will go past. Nobody needs to stand in their doorway for long; La Residencia has put up many celebrities, from Princess Diana and the Emperor of Japan to Tom Hanks and Pierce Brosnan. The village now rivals Ibiza as a name-dropper's heaven. The glam-rock duo Erasure restored a large *finca* overlooking the valley; Andrew Lloyd-Webber bought two houses nearby; Caroline Corr got married in the village church, with Bono, The Edge, and her famous siblings on hand. Bob Geldof and Annie Lennox can have a drink at the bar without anybody paying them any heed; the Majorcan attitude is, 'Just because you're famous, don't think I'm going to take any notice of you.' One evening in the mid 1980s Mike Oldfield, who had come to visit his old chum Kevin, jammed with the band in the bar Las Palmeras. As the clock struck midnight, the owner unceremoniously pulled the plug on us, right in the middle of a soaring Oldfield guitar solo. 'Sorry,' explained Kevin to the bewildered superstar. 'Town Hall regulations. The bar can't afford the fine.' Perhaps the Majorcan speciality *par excellence* is humble pie.

It's often said that people come to Deià to find themselves, but many don't like what they find. In any case, everybody sooner or later returns for a second look, if not at themselves, then at what's left of the place that affected them so. Many return cautiously, the worse for wear and incognito; others, like Kevin, who drops by occasionally, look a lot better than when they left. Dia Luker, who belonged to my generation of Deià brats before leaving for the USA, returned a decade later to the scene of her ugly-duckling adolescence as the swan-like Diandra Douglas on the arm of her husband Michael. Having created a Majorcan-style home in California, the couple tried to buy Miramar where Diandra had lived as a teenager with her mother, the first house that the Austrian Archduke bought in Majorca a hundred years earlier and the site of the missionary school founded in the thirteenth century by Ramón Llull. But Miramar wasn't for sale at any price, so they settled for s'Estaca, a whitewashed Sicilian-style palace with a North African vaulted roof, built by the Archduke for his Majorcan lover, Catalina Homar.

S'Estaca stands surrounded by palm trees and stone-terraced vineyards barely a hundred feet above the open sea. To the right lies La Foradada, a rocky outcrop with a huge hole in it, in whose lee the Archduke would moor his yacht. The house itself shimmers like an otherworldly apparition hovering between the rocky coastline and the sheer cliffs that tower above it. This slightly eerie quality led Tony Richardson to choose it to shoot his 1970 film *Laughter in the Dark*, based on Nabokov's novel of obsession, starring Nicol Williamson and Sian Phillips. Since the Douglases moved in with their teenage son, the place has shed its ghostliness. After Diandra and Michael remarried neither wished to give it up so they have a time-share arrangement. The Pa Amb Oli Band has been hired to play there for both parties, once enjoying the luxury of having Catherine Zeta-Jones and my niece Natalia singing backups to 'Mustang Sally' and 'Dancing in the Street'. On another occasion when arriving with the band equipment, I approached a balding man in dark glasses who appeared to be overseeing the catering arrangements. 'Where should we set up?' I asked. 'How the hell should I know!' retorted Jack Nicholson.

I've tried to keep the central theme of this book to a grass-level view of Hispanic culture through the ears of popular music; of course there is also plenty of highbrow musical activity that would fill another book, although I'm not the one to write it. At the last count there were over twenty pianos in the village and two professional concert pianists who have been here since the 1960s, Suzanne Bradbury and the composer Carl Mansker. In certain quarters, the village is best known for classical music since the Deià International Festival was founded in 1978 by Pat Meadows and Stephanie Shepard. They now manage to bring musicians as prestigious as the Brodsky Quartet to their spectacular sunset concerts at the Archduke's cliff-top residence at Son Marroig.

Valldemossa also hosts some of the world's top musical names at the Costa Nord (North Coast) Cultural Centre. This venture was set up by Michael Douglas to show his appreciation of the local culture and landscape and, en passant, to appease the Valldemossa Town Council for having overstepped some building regulations while renovating s'Estaca. Costa Nord's intimate open-air auditorium has seen musicians like Van Morrison, Pat Metheny, and Compay Segundo playing there for a select audience.

Deià is no longer the 'Indian reservation' of the Sixties and Seventies. There are still tribal full-moon parties at the Cala, but instead of dope-smoking hippies playing congas there's a DJ with a huge sound system powered by a generator and groups of *alternativos* playing didgeridoos, darbukas, and djembés. Visitors who drive down to the beach in the daytime now have to feed the parking meters every couple of hours. The Deià *verbena* is no longer celebrated in the Park for fear of keeping the hotel guests awake and is now held on an open-air basketball court. The village can now boast two banks, five bars, sixteen restaurants, and seven hotels – ample for a population of seven hundred. This is now the tonic in any Majorcan village, where one can find rural hotels with mentions in the Michelin Guide, but few cheap *pensións*.

The 1990s saw Majorca shed its 'charladies' island' image among the Germans and become the stylish place to buy and reconvert a farmhouse, especially among those of pre-retirement age. This 'German invasion' generated a lot of friction in the agricultural hinterland as new homeowners fenced off rights of way and tried to impose their urban habits upon peasant neighbours. This situation prompted me to write a handbook for these new rural homeowners explaining how the traditional Majorcan architecture, diet, society, and agriculture function. My aim was to convince them to adapt to the island before they adapted the island to themselves. The upward spiral of prices seems to have peaked in 2001, by which time much of the dirty money in Europe had been put through the Spanish real-estate laundry before the Euro could show up the stains.

Today there's a lot more contact between the foreign and Majorcan kids than when I was a teenager. Catalan is the official language in most village schools and in Deià English has also been introduced at kindergarten level. The musical ambience in the village has given rise to three or four predominantly Majorcan bands. On Millennium Eve, while the Town Hall organized a big bash in a huge marquee, twenty-five Deià musicians organized an 'anti-millennium hype' party, playing for free in La Fábrica, the seediest bar in town. (We had decided to donate our fee to charity but we never got paid.)

Apart from the veteran Pa Amb Oli musicians, Frances, Carmen, Dito, Ralph, and Mitsuko, the up and coming generation showed that we were free to retire whenever we wished. Xingo, the son of a Guardia Civil, had been taught guitar by Ollie Halsall and was now producing electronic music; his brother Alfredo played bass with the local *agro-pop* (peasant-pop) group. Jiva, of the Deià youths who had learned some basic chords from Juan, now headed his own power-blues trio. Juan's son Llewelyn and his band of teens amazed us all in their first public appearance by launching into a bilingual hip-hop number whose refrain 'My asshole hurts' was chorused with gusto by all the schoolchildren. Llewelyn, now a chef, records his own drum 'n' bass grooves, one of them featuring a loop of his grandfather Robert's voice singing the Indian regimental song *Hai! Hai! Kuchh parwah nei . . .*

The Pa Amb Oli Band has been lucky enough to count upon several excellent lead guitarists over the last few years – the New York jazz player Michael Sheffrin; Guillermo Pérez de Diego, who was part of the *movida Madrileña*; a Nashville cat called Zack; our resident Welsh bluesman Dai Griffiths; and Frances's son Brendan, who has a university degree in music. We still only play when we feel the need and act as the village house band, often backing some of the singers who wash up on our shores: Eric Burdon, Sarah Jane Morris, 'Little Charles' Walker of the Sidewinders, and the divine Curtis Jones. Our regular guests include three of Simon Gough's children, Samuel, Tamasin, and Dickon, all professional singers. Pa Amb Oli, in different permutations, has also spawned many one-night bands: a country combo fronted by Frances, Kid Xisca y Los Coyotes; jazz-funk, Los Rambos del Ritmo; power-blues, Theoboldo Power; and Dylan, Three Bob Night, to name a few.

Ralph and Mitsuko decided to put an end to their acting career after performing in thirty-two countries, but are learning new songs to perform when they return from Japan. Toni Morlà, after working as PR man for a Cuban music club in Palma now has a regular gig playing in a piano bar. He recently published a local bestseller, his memoirs of the night-club scene in the 1960s and 1970s, *Memories d'Un Brusquer* (the local expression for a rowdy teenager). In Barcelona, Teresa Rebull has also published her autobiography. The *nova cançó* movement is no longer the voice of protest but of consent; it has become the *cançó oficialista*, which, along with *rock Català*, is now largely subsidized and supported by the Catalan regional government. A few rebels like Pau Riba manage to survive outside the official circuit.

The Canterbury musical web continues to grow. Daevid Allen's latest project is called the University of Errors and featured Kevin Ayers as guest on their last US tour. Robert Wyatt is still composing and releases a new record every few years to critical acclaim. Twenty years after her *Linguistic Leprosy* LP, Lady June brought out her second album, *Hit and Myth*, which included three songs I had recorded with her in my printshop on my four-track cassette. She died in 1999, two days before she and Frances were to open their joint art exhibition at La Residencia. The show went ahead as planned, with June's sculpture of a skeleton riding a rusty bicycle dominating the centre of the hall. Her funeral was held at the Ca n'Alluny theatre; little cellophane bags of her ashes were sellotaped to helium-filled balloons on which everybody wrote their farewell message.

Marcelino visited us when his group of *joteros* from Teruel was invited to the Sóller Folk Festival. Sitting on our front terrace drinking wine, he sang us a couple of *jotas* a cappella, his tremendous voice resounding around the natural amphitheatre of the Deià valley and bringing our startled neighbours to their rattling windows.

Sebastián was obliged to take a part-time job as gardener for the Palma Town Council, where he met Abdul, a Senegalese drummer, singer, and dancer from the disbanded Wonkhaï Palma. Together we set up an Afro-flamenco band that only performed twice before disintegrating: Abdul is even more disorganized than the *gitanos*. Sebastián continues with Mimbre, which has begun a new lease of life with Antonio's son, a brilliant percussionist. The flashy new sound system that Sebastián bought with his disability pension went up in smoke and he's gone back to scrounging the Pa Amb Oli equipment off us.

Majorca now receives a large number of 'sub-Saharan' immigrants, most of whom have risked their lives crossing the Straits of Gibraltar illegally. I love playing with West African musicians, whether it's the bass with Abdul's own band or playing high-life music on my guitar with Aguinaldo from Guinea-Bissau or with Donald Dore from Sierra Leone. The laid-back sweetness of this music makes it a joy to play, especially on warm summer nights.

The Palma live music scene continues to grow, although since the Guitar Centre closed down twenty years ago nothing has taken its place as a venue for completely acoustic music. Ramón sold the Indigo in the 1970s but it continues to operate under the same name as a piano bar as it approaches its fortieth year. Ramón directs the National Jazz Orchestra, which features Natalia as vocalist, and writes music for TV.

The big bash of 1992 certainly helped Spain take its rightful place in Europe and the world and bury its recent past, although many of the top posts in the Partido Popular, who governed the country from 1996 to 2004, were occupied by the offspring of members of the old Movimiento Nacional. Of Franco's ministers, only Manuel Fraga Iribarne, founder of the PP, is still in politics as President of the Galician Autonomous Government. In the 1960s, when he was Franco's Minister of Information and Tourism, Fraga asked my father to give a lecture on tourism in Madrid. Robert replied that he'd be honoured to do so, but until Deià was connected to the electrical grid, his working day was too short to take on extra work. Power lines appeared almost overnight and brought 220-volt electricity to the village in record time. Being able to pull strings was one of the few advantages of a dictatorship; under democracy, Deià has been waiting five years for a broadband Internet connection.

The only thing that sets Spain apart from the rest of the EC countries today is the excellent relationship it has maintained with Latin America, with the Arab world (a relationship rather strained after President Aznar's full support of the Iraq invasion), and even with the Israelis, all of whom have sentimental ties to the Iberian peninsula. Despite Isabel and Fernando joining their kingdoms in the fifteenth century to drive out the Muslims, to banish the Jews, and brutally colonize the Americas, Spain is still referred to as *Al-Andalus* by the Arabs. To the Sephardic Jews in the Southern and Eastern Mediterranean, many of whom still speak *Ladino*, a medieval Spanish, it is still *Sepharad*, whilst to the Latin Americans Spain will always be *la madre patria*. All this gives us an important role in world affairs as mediator between these peoples and as a bridge between them and Europe. Spain has over the years lost many of its signs of identity – few people have time to sleep a siesta – but it's still a raucous, lively culture that is not afraid to express its feelings, even if it keeps the neighbours awake.

The Hispanic character can be summed up in an elegant phrase which, had I found an equally elegant translation, would have been the title to this book: *¡Que nos quiten lo bailado!* – roughly, 'They can stop the music, but let them try and take away the hours we've danced!'

P.S.

Ideas,
interviews
& features ...

## About the author

## About the book

## Read on

# A Craftsman by Trade
*Louise Tucker talks to Tomás Graves*

**What did you want to be when you grew up?**
I decided to write my first book at the age of eight; my aunt Clarissa had had a book published at that age. I got no further than the title (*The Three Fights*) and decided it was too much work. Later I went through a phase where I wanted to design boats. My mother would have liked me to be a plumber. Had I taken her advice, I'd have made a fortune! As it is, I'm a craftsman printer by trade.

**What or who inspired you to write this book?**
It was asking to be written and I happened to be listening.

**You usually refer to your father as Robert, not my dad or father. Is that because he was, as you mention, more of a grandfatherly figure and distanced from you by his age?**
We all called him Father, never Dad, but in the book it looked awkward; in my mind he was the epitome of Robertness (Robertitude?) so it was natural to call him by name.

**When writing this book did you ever feel that you were in your father's shadow or was his legacy positive and enabling?**
Had I begun to write at an early age, perhaps his shadow would have been too overpowering; however, he was always very supportive of anything I wrote for the school magazine and he enjoyed my letters.

2

I took heed of his advice: 'Only write when you have something to say and you know what you're talking about.' Had I tried my hand at poetry, that would have been a different matter. But writing prose is fairly commonplace in the Graves family; among my published relatives I can think of my grandfather Alfred Percival, aunts Clarissa and Roz; uncle Philip; my sisters Jenny (Reuters correspondent in Rome), Catherine and Lucia; my brother William, my cousins Paul Cooper, Roger Cooper and Richard Percival Graves, and some of the next generation seem set to go . . . My brother David, who was killed in action in Burma before I was born, was also a very good poet, albeit unpublished. My mother's family, although lawyers, have also produced a couple of authors.

I only began to write and translate books when I had had my fill of printing them. Robert also printed books by hand, but I proved myself a better craftsman, so we're quits!

**How do you think it affected you to grow up surrounded by so many artists, musicians and writers? Were there advantages and disadvantages to this?**
One advantage of growing up in a flock of black sheep is that you learn to accept difficult people, those who ask the hard questions that make humanity progress.

**Amongst all the famous people that you have met, from Amis and Borges to Mike ▶**

‷ One advantage of growing up in a flock of black sheep is that you learn to accept difficult people, those who ask the hard questions that make humanity progress. ″

3

# A Craftsman by Trade *(continued)*

◄ Oldfield and Robert Wyatt, who has made the biggest impression on you and why?

Probably Krishnamurti for liberating us from our fears. He came to talk at Bedales, accompanied by Dorothy Simmonds who ran the Krishnamurti School nearby at Brockwood Park. She hadn't seen my parents in 20 years but picked me out among 500 long-haired kids: 'You must be Beryl's son.' I visited them at Brockwood several times and was amazed how Krishnamurti, instead of answering questions, asked them, prompting everybody to come up with their own answers.

**One of the clearest impressions in your book is that Majorca, as known to the main British tourist trade, bears little relationship to Mallorca, the Catalan-speaking part of the island. Was this one of your intentions, to enlighten your readers about the real Mallorca, and are you at all concerned that the book, like *Driving Over Lemons* and *A Year in Provence*, may create a whole other tourist trade?**

I think what distinguishes my three books from the *Expats-renovate-a-Mediterranean-farmhouse* genre is that I write from the inside looking out. (It was my niece Manuela, incidentally, who gave the title to *Driving Over Lemons* when helping the author buy his farm in the Alpujarras.) I wrote my last book, *Bread and Oil*, in Catalan with local readers in mind; on translating it into English I kept the same tone, making few concessions to a different readership. The fact that it was well received by the British and US press encouraged me to maintain that Mediterranean perspective in *Tuning Up at Dawn*. People seem to feel comfortable reading about food and music, so I felt I could slip in some historical, social and political background without being too pedantic. (Writing directly in English, I had to check myself every so often to keep from falling into a British mindset.) Although I see *Tuning Up* as a book about Spain as a whole, much of the action takes place on Majorca and that's what the publishers wanted to focus on. From the feedback I've received, I feel that the book will strengthen ties that readers already have with the Mediterranean rather than open any new markets. I just met a guitarist who had been conceived in Deià but had never visited the island because of its package tour image – until someone gave him my book.

**One of your bands referred to itself as Fam, Fam i Gana (Hungry, Hungry and Starving), a name inspired by the small fee you received. You frequently mention how poor the fees are: is it possible to survive financially as a jobbing musician on Majorca or is the money a bonus rather than a necessity?**
The standard pub or hotel gig, which may or may not be compatible with a daytime job, pays about £30 per musician in a band, and Majorca's cost of living is one of the highest in Spain. A lot of musicians play two gigs a night, often with different bands, especially in the summer or at weekends; live music ▶

❛ In the last 20 years cultural boundaries have disappeared to a great extent, and there are now millions who don't know which country is theirs. This stereoscopic view seems to provide a rich vein for music and literature. ❜

## A Craftsman by Trade *(continued)*

◀ in bars usually begins after midnight, which allows you to get in a hotel gig beforehand. But the local authorities have been clamping down on small venues, banning live music at places like Palma's Bluesville. Is it possible to survive? My friend the harpist Jay Ansill, who has played with British and American folk musicians and worked with Maria del Mar Bonet, passed on the following definition: 'A semi-pro musician is one who keeps a daytime job to support him. A professional musician is one whose spouse keeps a daytime job to support him.'

**6 I took heed of my father's advice: "Only write when you have something to say and you know what you're talking about." 9**

**Your father described novels as show-dogs, the bread and butter work that paid for his cat, poetry. Do you have a show-dog and cat and what are they?**
With me it seems to be all cats. One non-profit activity subsidizes another.

**It is often said that people come to Deià to find themselves, but many don't like what they find. What have you found and do you like it?**
I found Carmen and she helped me find myself. Introspection is not my forte and if I'm happy with the way I am, it's because I'm too busy enjoying life to do much soul-searching. If and when I need to take a good long look inside myself and face the music, I'd probably go somewhere else to do it, like the story of Nasruddin looking for his house key at midnight under a street lamp. A passer-by offers to help, but after a while asks, 'Are you sure you lost it here?'

'No', replies Nasruddin, 'I dropped it on the other side of the street, outside my door, but there's more light here.'

**'It's embarrassing to be identified as a musician in a foreign land and asked to "sing something from your country", especially if you're not quite sure which country or culture is yours.' That refers to your experience in North Africa in 1986: 20 years later, do you know which country is yours?**
No, but I no longer feel any need to know. In those 20 years cultural boundaries have disappeared to a great extent, and there are now millions who don't know which country is theirs yet lose no sleep over it! However, this stereoscopic view seems to provide a rich vein for music and literature.

**Is there a difference between your British and your Mallorquí personalities?**
I'd say I have one personality which has to deal with or question my British, Spanish or Mallorquí brain cells accordingly. One's perspective is often built into the language at hand. In English I can simply say 'I am'; but in Spanish or Catalan I have to think more specifically: 'my essence is' (*ser* or *ésser*) or 'my condition is' (*estar* in both languages). This allows you to answer the question 'Is Michael Jackson black or white?' very clearly: '*Es negre, i està blanc.*'

**Are there any books that you wish you had written?**
No. Perhaps a few I'm glad I didn't. ▶

6 People seem to feel comfortable reading about food and music, so I felt I could slip in some historical, social and political background without being too pedantic. 9

## A Craftsman by Trade *(continued)*

◄ **Who are your main influences, both in writing and in music?**

Whoever my literary influences are (and I'm sure someone will point a few out), I'm not conscious of them. I try to bear in mind some of the precepts of clear writing outlined in *The Reader Over Your Shoulder* by my father and my mother's first husband, Alan Hodge. My training as a typographer taught me that any design which interferes with getting the message from the author to the reader is bad typography; the same often goes for literary style, the written equivalent of design.

In music, I prefer to be warmed or moved than impressed. I listen to Taj Mahal, Leon Redbone, John Martyn, Lowell George, Toots Hibbert, SE Rogie, Cayetano Veloso, Gal Costa, Jonathan Richman, Tom Waits, Robert Wyatt, Ry Cooder, Billy Bragg, Nina Simone, Sandy Denny, Compay Segundo, Nelly Furtado, Pascale Comelade ... ■

# Life at a Glance

Author photo © Pere Colom

**27 January 1953**  Born in Palma de Mallorca, the eighth child of an eighth child.

**1964**  Begins boarding school in England.

**1972**  Studies Typographic Design at the London College of Printing.

**1975**  Moves back to Spain, working as designer, photographer and musician.

**1979**  Travels to Nicaragua to document the Sandinista revolution.

**1980**  Joins Pa Amb Oli Band, meets future wife Carmen.

**1983**  With Carmen as binder, sets up The New Seizin Press in Deià to produce books entirely by hand until 2000.

**1987**  A daughter, Rocío, is born.

**1993**  Visits US, gives talks on the Seizin Press at Brown, Harvard and Dartmouth.

**1996**  Marries Carmen, translates *Beloved Majorcans* into English and begins writing and translating his own books: *Un Hogar en Mallorca* (in Spanish), translated as *A Home in Majorca*; *Volem Pa Amb Oli* (in Catalan, published by JJ de Olañeta), translated as *Bread and Oil* (published by Prospect Books, UK, and University of Wisconsin Press, US; also published in Holland as *Brood en Olie*).

**2004**  Publishes his first book in English, *Tuning Up at Dawn*. Also contributes to *Time Out Guide to Mallorca & Menorca* and *Rough Guide to the Balearics*.

# A Writing Life

**When do you write?**
Early morning and late afternoon. A
10-minute siesta is important.

**Where do you write?**
In the only free corner of my print shop,
surrounded by ancient cast-iron presses
and typecases.

**Why do you write?**
To share with others some of what I have
been lucky enough to absorb.

**Pen or computer?**
An old Apple Mac Powerbook.

**Silence or music?**
Relative silence.

**What started you writing?**
Certainly not having an author as father. I
offered to translate a book I thought needed
translating, and that led to a book proposal –
at the age of 45. Besides, I found it easier to
write books than to print them.

**How do you start a book?**
With the chapter headings. Then I just fill in
the blanks.

**And finish?**
Having trained as a compositor and printer, I
enjoy the fine-tuning as much as the writing
itself, although a second pair of eyes would
point out that I'd never make a living as a
copy-editor. So it's really the deadline that
tells me when enough is enough.

**Do you have any writing rituals or superstitions?**
None of my many rituals or superstitions are related to writing.

**Which living writer do you most admire?**
Probably José Saramago.

**What or who inspires you?**
Finding the missing piece to a jigsaw – discovering parallels and contrasts between languages and cultures.

**If you weren't a writer what job would you do?**
I write, but I'm not a writer. I've always got several pots on the boil: designing, editing a magazine, playing music, working with my hands.

**What's your guilty reading pleasure or favourite trashy read?**
As a child, the *Beano*, *Mad* magazine and cereal packets. Now I get a lot of laughs out of badly translated subtitles.

# Singing through the Barricades

*Tomás Graves on the music of protest that lies behind* Tuning Up at Dawn

MY MOTHER'S GENERATION used to put an upturned eggcup in the centre of a steak-and-kidney pie to keep the crust from collapsing; it would be removed as the pie was served. The eggcup around which this book was baked was a chapter documenting my six-month trip to Nicaragua shortly after the Sandinista insurrection had ousted the last in the dictatorial dynasty of the Somozas.

Here I discovered a music that was not just a reflection of the national character, not even a vehicle for change: it was the motor itself. Protest songs had helped to bring about political changes in many countries from Spain and Chile to the US, but in illiterate Nicaragua popular music evaded the dictator's grasp to become the backbone of the revolution. It was a music that didn't kill anyone but could get you shot. Musicians have often been in the front line, but in Central America it ceased to be a metaphor. Christian Liberation Theory, national history, how to handle weapons or prepare explosives – it was all in the songs broadcast over clandestine radio, on cassettes copied from copies on double-deck boom-boxes, performed surreptitiously in factories or rural church meetings, learned word-for-word in school playgrounds. The old Spanish saying '*la letra con sangre no entra*' ('you can't beat the lesson into a schoolchild') was proved just as true under Somoza's regime as under Franco's. With the help of a simple melody on guitar or accordion, the word can cut through the government barriers to all ages and levels of society far more effectively than speeches or leaflets.

Looking back on my Nicaraguan experience 20 years later, I realized it not only gave a jolt to my social conscience, it also reflected my own dual nature; the Spanish-speaking Pacific side of the country was separated from the English-speaking Atlantic side by mountains and jungle. And beneath both languages, there were the traces of older, autochthonous cultures. This was the central theme to my book. Once on paper, however, this belligerent central chapter sat uncomfortably, poking out through the otherwise uniform crust of *Tuning Up at Dawn* until it was pulled out, awaiting its turn to be expanded into a book of its own.

Since *Tuning Up* was published in hardback, I have received a lot of gratifying feedback (to use a hackneyed musical term) and a few alternative views of the events and anecdotes which I write about. But this new edition could only accommodate spelling corrections and minor changes (no mention is made of the political upheavals here since the 2004 Madrid bombings), so you can find these comments at **www.deia.info/ tomasgraves** – and post your own. You will also find more images of the characters in the book on this website and on pages 14–16, as well as some audio files. ▶

Pa Amb Oli Band 1986: Tomás, Dave, Ollie, Juan, Carmen and Frances

Juanchi, Sebastián and Tomás

Mati Klarwein, self-portrait circa 1958

Sleepy Tom and Blind Leroy

Tomás, Lucia and Robert outside Ca n'Alluny, 1970s

Toni Morlà

# Have You Read?

### *A Home in Majorca*
His first book, published in Spain, is a
practical guide for those who have chosen
to live in rural Majorca, covering all aspects
of Mediterranean life from traditional
architecture to rights of way, water
management, flora and fauna and even
village politics.

..................................................................

### *Bread and Oil*
Food, social history and cultural
commentary are the main ingredients in this,
Tomás Graves' second book, a collection of
recipes and insights centred on *pa amb oli*,
the bread and oil that were the main staple of
the Majorcan diet for generations.

..................................................................

### *Time Out Guide to Mallorca & Menorca*
### *Rough Guide to the Balearics*
Tomás Graves contributes to both of these
guidebooks to the islands.

# If You Loved This,
## You Might Like...

*Snowball Oranges: One Mallorcan Winter,*
*Viva Mallorca!: One Mallorcan Autumn* and
*Mañana Mañana: One Mallorcan Summer*
Peter Kerr
The author and his wife swapped their
Scottish farm for a home in Mallorca. Kerr
tells the story of a new life in a different,
warmer and more laidback country.

......................................................

*Wild Olives*
William Graves
Tomás Graves' older brother also grew up
mostly in Majorca and this is the story of his
childhood, his relationship with his father
and how he manages to forge his own
identity separate from that of his father.

......................................................

*A Woman Unknown*
Lucia Graves
Lucia Graves' memoir focuses on her
childhood on Majorca but also tells the story
of the dramatic changes in Spanish history in
her lifetime and their effects on the lives of
women. Graves' perspective is filtered
through her biculturalism and bilingualism.

......................................................

*Goodbye to All That*
Robert Graves
Writing, especially autobiographical writing,
is very much a Graves family occupation, as
Tomás Graves points out, and it seems apt to
recommend Robert Graves' own famed
autobiography of his time at public school
and his experiences in the First World War.

# Find Out More

**MAJORCA SITES**

**www.illesbalears.es**
**http://mallorcaweb.com/eng/**
Tourist sites with certain pages dedicated to
Deià.

**http://deia.info/**
A site completely dedicated to Deià.

**http://sollernet.com**
Information and forums about the
Deià–Sóller area.

**ROBERT GRAVES SITES**

**www.robertgraves.org**
The Robert Graves Trust, Society and
Journal are based at St John's College,
Oxford, and the website provides lots of
information including research resources,
bibliographies, audio clips and details
of events.

**MUSIC SITES**

**www.dalecruse.com/Big Bottom**
An attractive and easy to navigate site
dedicated to music, particularly bass
guitarists, which includes an interview
with Tomás at **www.dalecruse.com/
weblogarchives/2005/02/
interview_in_tu.html**

**www.planetgong.co.uk/**
History and mysteries of Daevid Allen, Gilli
Smyth, Didier Malherbe and others of the
Gong family. ▶

## Find Out More *(continued)*

◄ **www.rarevinyl.net/canterbury.htm**
Links to all offshoots of the Canterbury
scene.

**www.olliehalsall.co.uk**
Site dedicated to the life of Ollie Halsall
including clips of him playing with Kevin
Ayers, Tempest and The Sex Beatles!

**www.kevinayers.info/**
The official Kevin Ayers site.

**www.strongcomet.com/wyatt/**
Information about Robert Wyatt.

### MATI KLARWEIN

**http://visionaryrevue.com/webtext3/
klarwein1.html
www.mati-klarwein.com/zeitdok/
seite1.html**
Two sites dedicated to the painter Mati
Klarwein.

### FLAMENCO

**www.esflamenco.com/enindex.html**
English page on Flamenco, Rumba . . . you
can even buy flamenco dancer's shoes here. ■